D1600761

DONOSO CORTÉS

UTOPIAN ROMANTICISTIC AND POLITICAL REALIST

DONOSO CORTÉS

UTOPIAN ROMANTICIST AND POLITICAL REALIST

John T. Graham

UNIVERSITY OF MISSOURI PRESS

Columbia 1974

ISBN 0-8262-0155-5

University of Missouri Press, Columbia, Missouri 65201
Library of Congress Catalog Number 73-85460
Printed and bound in the United States of America

I would like to acknowledge the assistance of the University of Missouri–Kansas City, which furnished the research grant in 1968 that allowed me to begin this project. I would also like to thank the late Thomas P. Neill, as my original mentor on Donoso; my wife Alsy Izurieta Graham, for helping me with loving patience as interpreter, assistant, and stenographer; and Dón Manuel and Señorita Pilar Donoso Cortés, for their help, courtesy, and friendship.

J.T.G.
January 26, 1974

CONTENTS

LIFE AND THOUGHT OF DONOSO CORTÉS

(1848)

Prophet of that vast cataclysm
But terrified to behold its abyss . . .

*

I am the revolution, socialism,
almost all that ends in ism . . .

(1851)

Madame Revolution dead of consumption
Madame Reaction playing symphonies.

***

Revolution and war and captivity

*

I feel Europe dying. From her ruin
Another Europe, another world is to arise.
Toward its setting moves the sun . . .

*

And still Europe listens in fright
Thundering, thundering o'er the boundless steppes
The swift gallop of new Attila.

*

Come down again to the world,
Come down again, O Messiah!

Gabriel García y Tassara, *Poesías* . . .
(1852–1872)

Donoso Cortés, while he was a diplomat in Paris
late in his life.

DONOSO CORTÉS

INTRODUCTION

A century ago Juan Donoso Cortés was hailed by Gabriel García y Tassara, his poet expositor, as a "colossal talent, errant genius," for his "Christian philosophy" and "his gift of prophecy."[1] Today he is unknown, literally or figuratively, to many who admire Ortega y Gasset or Unamuno, yet he too was a Spanish thinker of truly European outlook and stature—a more prophetic philosopher of history than the one and an unorthodox religious philosopher like the other. But Donoso courted oblivion when he deserted the liberal tradition to become the leading conservative intellectual of the European reaction to the revolutions of 1848, which was a spent force by around 1860. Peter Viereck states, however, "In some ways he remains the subtlest intellect in the entire history of conservatism."[2] Certainly, despite a varied influence even to the present, he remains one of the most neglected and ill-understood of modern thinkers. Although too disorganized or too advanced and prophetic to be properly understood even by his contemporaries, he was actually a representative and significant thinker with a mind that was bold and original as a whole. In fact, he was perhaps the first Christian positivist, with a 'positive politics' of 'crisis, transition, and normalcy,' but was the obverse of Comte; he became a renegade against bourgeois power, wealth, and mores but was opposite to Marx; he was a new social and democratic conservative midway be-

[1] Gabriel García y Tassara, "Un diablo más," in *Poesías de Gabriel García y Tassara*, pp. 357, 365. For his lines on the frontispiece page, see pp. 199, 362, 364, 388, 394, 403, 409, 453, and 462, all from "Un diablo más" and "Messiah."

[2] Peter Viereck, *Conservatism From John Adams to Churchill*, p. 63.

tween Metternich and Bismarck, but had protofascist nuances like Louis Napoleon and Carlyle; he deserted the idea of progress for the conception of the cycle and prophesied a decline of the West and apocalyptic doom for modern civilization long before Spengler or Toynbee, yet, like Marx and the romantic utopians, he also dreamed of a future perfect society—but truly a "City of God on earth." He was a romantic idealist, but with a streak of cold realism, a thinker bent on action, an ascetic moralist embroiled in *Realpolitik* who, although he preferred voluntary moral and religious revival, wanted to save society and civilization against its will through dictatorship. In short, he was a living paradox, a modern Quixote, a man of sharp contrasts in life and thought whom no one has ever been able to comprehend as a whole and whom most have either scorned or never known. In a spirit of detachment, this biographical, political, and history-of-ideas study is an analytic and synthetic effort to see Donoso and his thought in the context of their age and "climate of opinion."

Donoso's remark that his whole life had been quite ordinary and Louis Veuillot's observation, "The short life of Donoso Cortés contains few incidents and is in some ways only the history of his thought,"[3] are both grossly oversimplified. To be sure, a biography of a professional intellectual such as Donoso must concentrate on his ideological formation and development from liberal to conservative, from progressivist to cyclicist, from man of the world to ascetic Christian. But his personal history of ideas also includes his deep involvement in the intellectual side of the conservative reaction after 1848 (a topic which has been neglected by historians) and in the related counterrevolutionary politics and diplomacy surrounding Louis Napoleon's coup d'état of 1851. Although Donoso was an intellectual, he was not just a disengaged political theorist. He always played an active political role, which was the practi-

[3] Louis Veuillot, *Oeuvres de Donoso Cortès . . .*, I, ix; Donoso, quoted by Bois-le-Comte, paper in the archives of the Donoso Cortés family, Don Benito, Spain.

cal affirmation and often the source of his ideas. This biography also relates his life and politics to his philosophical, historical, social, and religious thought; it presents him as a social scientist comparable to Comte and Spencer, who was, however, tormented with pessimistic visions inspired by Vico's cycle and Saint Augustine's dualism. In fact, his position as a whole was a cyclic, Christian positivism or affirmativism, and his historical world view transcended a descent into a hellish barbarism of world wars and world revolution to the rise of a universal "City of God," an apocalypse and radical dualism that Tassara versified in "Lucifer" and "Messiah."

DONOSO'S CONSERVATIVE REACTION TO 1848

Donoso Cortés was to the European revolutions of 1848 what Edmund Burke and Joseph de Maistre were to the French Revolution of 1789: a critical and prophetic voice of tradition that called for reaction and reconstruction and which warned that anarchy, tyranny, and ruin were the fruits of revolution. For him revolutions were the lighthouses of history and Providence, pointing out the perils and course ahead, and the revolutions of 1848 were only the threat of a greater scourge to come, of more radical and more universal demagogic and socialist revolutions, both communistic and anarchistic.[4]

Compared to his predecessors, however, Donoso was the first of a new breed of social-democratic conservatives. Parallel to Comte, he became the first positivist conservative, long before Maurras and Brunetière,[5] in the Christian and monarchist traditions. Romantic in inspiration but a cyclic realist in application, he was not too timid to grapple boldly with the future, to try to shape and guide it, rather than to stand pat on a tran-

[4] Juan Juretschke, ed., *Obras completas de don Juan Donoso Cortés*, II, 210, 214, 269.

[5] See W. M. Simon, *European Positivism in the Nineteenth Century* (Ithaca, N.Y., 1963), pp. 159–61. Simon confirms that Comte became an "ultra-conservative in politics" (pp. 153–54). No studies of Comte mention Donoso, of course.

sient status quo or retreat into a vanished past of eighteenth century or middle ages. He was thus much more open to change and reform than were Burke, de Maistre, or Metternich, and he was neither aristocratic nor absolutist but, like Comte, a former bourgeois become elitist. What he encountered in the revolutions of 1848 was not just a carryover from the Enlightenment, French Revolution, and liberal middle-class rebellion; it was the beginning of our world of democratic, nationalistic, and socialist ideologies, of discontented and impatient masses, of the threat by the bureaucratic state to become omnipotent, and of scientific-technological revolutions afoot in industry, transport, and communications. Although he was contemporary of Disraeli and Bismarck at the beginning of their careers, he was a visionary and was well ahead of them in trying to resolve these acute modern problems and needs. His answer was not merely a negative political reaction but a program of positive reform—a calling of the traditional monarchic states of Europe back to a renewal of Christian life and purpose and an adoption of a democratic basis in manhood suffrage and social-economic reforms. In this way he hoped to forestall future socialist revolution and totalitarianism centered in Russia and Germany, from whose ambitions he expected world war and world revolution to develop.

DONOSO'S INFLUENCE AFTER 1848

This "prophet" of conservatism has had considerable, sometimes baneful, influence on two eras of history: after the European revolutions of 1848 and since the Russian revolution of 1917. Before his death he had become the leading theorist of the reaction that dominated the Continent from 1849 into the 1860s. Unable to foresee the still unknown dangers of fascism in his own solutions, he called for dictatorship or firm authoritarian government, and suppression of revolutionary movements, as well as restoration of a conservative Concert of Europe. He condemned the bourgeois eclectic liberalism of pre-1848 as necessarily a transitional stage to socialism in dialectic, economics, and politics.[6] At the same time, he was one of the first penetrating, farseeing critics of the new socialism, both the anarchism of Proudhon and the communism of Marx, Saint-Simon, and the utopians. On the positive side, however, like the Prussian Radowitz and more than the Austrian Bach, he recommended democracy, although under authoritarian or Caesarian forms, which Napoleon III and Bismarck were to use. Like de Maistre and Comte, he also called for a great spiritual and moral renewal and revival, for a freedom of action and inspiration of religion in society,[7] a demand that was as much beyond the capacity of the Christianity of his time to achieve as it was beyond Comte's pantheistic cult of Humanity and Science.[8] In contrast, his program for political and social reconstruction would have required an initial show of force, the characteristic method of the incipient new age of realism that he sanctioned.

While the aged Metternich hailed Donoso as the foremost conservative intellectual, political theorist, and parliamentary orator of that era, most liberals scorned him as a medieval bugbear and traitor to their cause. Alexander Herzen, the brilliant Russian social anarchist, however, wavered between admiration and, like Proudhon, contempt. Louis Napoleon, Pius IX, and Spain's queens received Donoso's counsel. The queens were beyond saving; the pope evidently took his advice on a *Syllabus of Errors* but not on social-economic teaching, and Louis Napoleon, glad for Donoso's support for a coup d'état, so disappointed him as social reformer and reviver of a counterrevolutionary Concert of Europe that he predicted his downfall in a second Waterloo. Frederick William IV of Prussia and the later William I and Bismarck, Nicholas I and Nesselrode of Russia, and many other German, Russian, Austrian, and French conservatives knew of his speeches or writings. In-

[6] Juretschke, II, 149, 303, 449, 639.

[7] Juretschke, II, 198–201, 636.

[8] See L. Levy Bruhl, *The Philosophy of Auguste Comte* (New York, 1903), pp. 23–26. Auguste Comte, *The Positive Philosophy* . . ., trans. Harriet Martineau (Chicago, N.Y., n.d.), pp. 429, 433, 438.

termediate to Leo XIII and the social encyclicals, French and German social thinkers developed his ideas of solidarity and corporatism. He was also a friend and confidant to both Montalembert and Veuillot as they were emerging as the respective leaders of liberal and conservative Catholics in France in a fight leading up to Vatican I and renewed with Vatican II. Guizot, Ranke, Schelling, and Comte were among the historians and philosophers who agreed with certain of Donoso's unusual and pessimistic ideas on history and civilization.

Although Donoso's ideas of political reaction and historical pessimism exerted an influence in increasingly narrow circles well beyond the 1860s, neither his politics, nor his philosophy of history, nor even his social ideas were very well understood until long after his death, in many ways not to the very present. His most praiseworthy earlier influence was in the field of social thought and reform; the most regrettable later effect of his writings was to abet fascism.

DONOSO'S INFLUENCE SINCE 1917

After decades of neglect, Donoso's influence began to revive shortly after the Russian revolution and World War I, when it was remembered that he had predicted just such catastrophes. Now some of the frightened, disillusioned, and ambitious again read his words as a living commentary on their own times. Ironically, in so far as his authoritarian concepts of dictatorship and plebiscitary democracy anticipated twentieth-century fascism, he contributed to the very totalitarianism he had foreseen and abhorred, notably through Professor Carl Schmitt in Germany.[9] Fascists, conservative monarchists, and

[9] As socialist Luis de Araquistain observed, the "resurrection" of the thought of "the great professor of counter-revolutionary dictatorship" was soon followed by dictatorship, which Carl Schmitt openly advocated for Weimar Germany. See Araquistain's "Donoso Cortés y su resonancia en Europe," *Cuadernos* (Paris: September–December, 1953), 3–11. On Schmitt, see Viereck, *Conservatism*, pp. 67–68; also Andreas Dorpalen, *Hindenburg and the Weimar Republic* (Princeton, N.J., 1964), pp. 93, 124, 167–70; Christian Graf von Krockow, *Die Entscheidung* (Stuttgart, 1958), pp. 62, 65; and (disputing Schmitt's interpretation of Donoso's

clericals then siezed upon him as a prophet amid the great crises because his justification of dictatorship, force, and drastic solution and his criticism of liberalism, parliamentarism, and communism all seemed so timely.[10] Since the second world war, however, he has largely outlived the protofascist label and fascist distortions, so his social thought and doctrine of corporative monarchy (Christian, hereditary, limited, social, and democratic) have made him the darling of conservative monarchists in Franco's Spain,[11] where the restoration by 1967 was becoming rather Donosian.[12]

---

theory of dictatorship) Diego Sevilla Andrés, "Donoso Cortés y la Dictadura," *Arbor*, 24 (January, 1953), 62ff. Schmitt truly misrepresented Donoso on dictatorship, either intentionally or because he did not understand him, in both his *Dictatorship* (1921) and *The Necessity of Politics* (London, 1931), p. 57. For Schmitt's works specifically on Donoso, see the Bibliography; also for the various newspaper articles on Donoso by other German writers influenced by Schmitt or by Hans Abel's new translations of Donoso's speeches and letters (1920), especially as relating to Oswald Spengler's theme of *Decline of the West*. On the "Nazi" Schmitt, see: A. D. Greenwood, *The German Revolution* (London, 1934), pp. 151, 242, 314ff, and Jacques Maritain, *The Twilight of Civilization* (New York, 1943), p. 35.

[10] On the interest in Donoso in postwar (Dolfuss's) Austria, see: Bela Menczer, "A Prophet of Europe's Disaster," *The Month*, 183 (May, 1947), 270. In Spain, Falangist Eugenio D'Ors and Ramiro de Maetzu's quasi-Fascist *Acción Española* were among the many who saw Donoso as a prophet of the troublous 1930s; see Bibliography for articles and also the following works describing Donoso's revival: Santiago Galindo Herrero's *Donoso Cortés y su theoría política*, pp. 168f; and Luis María Anson, *Acción Española* (Zaragoza, 1960), Ch. 8 and pp. 37, 78ff, 89, 128, 179.

[11] On the reinterpretation of Donoso in the postwar era since 1945, especially in Spain, see Rafaél Calvo Serer, "Europa en 1949," *Arbor*, 12 (March, 1949), 348–49—in regard to "a politics of reconstruction and justice," wherein Donoso is seen as advocating dictatorship only as a means to reestablish "social and political order," terminating in hereditary monarchy with power above the dictates of mass democracy. Also, for Spanish attitudes not always monarchic toward Donoso since 1950, see Calvo Serer's *Nuevas formas de democracia y libertad* (Madrid, 1960), pp. 34ff, 354ff; Francis G. Wilson, "The New Conservatives in Spain," *Modern Age*, 5:2 (Spring, 1961), 150–56; their interest in Donoso was primarily social.

[12] Franco's *ley orgánica* of 1967, which made future provision for restoring monarchy, states in Title I, Art. 2 that "unity of power" (which

Gradually, since the 1920s Donoso has been reappraised by critical, sometimes nonpartisan, scholars. They have seen him in an ever more positive light as an incisive philosopher of history in a pessimistic, prophetic line stretching from Saint Augustine through Vico to Spengler and Toynbee; as a conservative political theorist of lasting strength in the traditions of Burke, de Maistre, and Metternich and foreshadowing Franco and de Gaulle; and finally as a pioneer Christian social thinker who anticipated later sociologists and papal encyclicals.[13] His cyclical outlook on history also carried over into his politics and social thought, more than once giving them a prophetic, dynamic, recurrent, and contemporary effect in eras of crisis. But neither his historical, political, nor social thought have ever been adequately understood, for besides being cyclical, they were also a species of Christian positivism relating closely to Saint-Simonism and Comte. His ideas are deceptively lucid, but very subtle, complex, and interwoven and so unfamiliar and scattered that they are difficult to synthesize; therefore they continue to mislead even careful scholars. Donoso died too soon to summarize the whole body of his thought, define its affiliations, demonstrate its remarkable unity and breadth, or elaborate many of its implications.

INTERNATIONAL SCHOLARSHIP ON DONOSO

During the revival of interest in Donoso's works in the twentieth century, serious scholarship, as distinct from literary, journalistic, and political impressions, has continued to become broader in scope as well as attract international attention through the celebration of the centennial of his death in 1953.

---

was Donoso's chief constitutional principle) will be one of the two main principles (with a form of corporatism) of the monarchic state: *Referendum 1966, Nueva Constitución* (Madrid, 1966), pp. 71, 72–73, 172–73; Brian Crozier, *Franco* (Boston, 1967), pp. 286–493; Diego Sevilla Andrés, *Historia constitucional de España, 1800–1966* (Valencia, 1966).

[13] See the Bibliography and the following section and footnotes on international scholarship, especially in regard to Spain, for example, note 25, on philosophy of history.

A biographical and analytical basis has now been laid for an adequate understanding and synthesis of his life, thought, and influence. Germany and Austria led in scholarship between the world wars, but scholars in Spain assumed the leadership in research and interpretation in the late 1940s and 1950s. With the rise of the United States and the decline of Britain amid world wars and revolutions, scholars in these countries have at least shown some interest, but France, Donoso's adoptive intellectual homeland, has been laggard, despite the authoritarian Gaullist movement. An international exchange of ideas, which began in the 1930s between German and Spanish writers on Donoso, developed into an important dialogue and disputation that reached a climax during the centennial of the 1950s in Madrid, where Spanish, German, Austrian, Hungarian, and English-speaking scholars participated in conferences at the Ateneo.

Although the upsurge of interest in Donoso in Germany and Austria in the 1920s and 1930s in large part inspired only superficial and partisan pieces, which like Schmitt's, were only pertinent to the current crisis, a few valuable books appeared. In 1935 Edmund Schramm provided the first real biography of Donoso, the reading of which is a prerequisite to any breadth of perspective and understanding of Donoso.[14] His study of this antiliberal thinker was researched in Spain before the civil war. It contains very useful information concerning "young Donoso," a period of his life that had been neglected, but is weak on "the great Donoso" after 1848. As a whole, it is defective in interpreting its subject's mental and political evolution and character. Admiring Donoso's penetrating critique of Western ideology and civilization, Austrian Alois Dempf (1937) contrasted Donoso as a political philosopher specializing in moral theology with Vitoria and Mariana as

[14] Edmund Schramm, *Donoso Cortés, Leben und Werk eines Spanishchen Antiliberalen*; with only one more exception (noted), the Spanish translation by Ramón de la Serna is frequently cited in this study: *Donoso Cortés, su vida y su pensamiento.*

moral theologians specializing in political philosophy.[15] One of Schramm's students, the Franciscan Westemeyer, made a very scholarly study (1941) of Donoso's lay theology, "theology of history," and "political theology,"[16] narrow topics that some clerical scholars have deemed paramount.

After 1945 scholarly interest in Donoso waned in German lands, largely in reaction to Carl Schmitt's view of him as a prophet of fascist dictatorship, so since that time little original work concerning him has appeared. In 1949 Schmitt compiled his earlier articles into a book and added a worthwhile chapter vaguely comparing Donoso with Tocqueville, Comte, and Marx, although Spain's Suárez Verdeguer still preferred to see Donoso as essentially a medieval thinker.[17] Schmitt, however, had already, perhaps irreparably, injured the Germans' image of Donoso. Before he became chancellor of West Germany, for example, Kurt Kiesinger stated that he was as much repelled by Donoso's grim pessimism as attracted to Tocqueville's moderation.[18]

In Spain the revival of study of Donoso culminated in the observances of the centennial of his death, which stimulated a great outpouring of studies, commemoratives, and anthologies for years before and after 1953. At the Ateneo various papers on Donoso were read, several of which were published in the pamphlet series—"Crece O Muere."[19] A number of

[15] Alois Dempf, *Christliche Staatsphilosophie in Spanien.*

[16] P. Dietmar Westemeyer, *Donoso Cortés, Staatsmann und Theologe.*

[17] Carl Schmitt, *Donoso Cortés in gesamteuropaïsche Interpretation*; Federico Suárez Verdeguer, *Donoso Cortés en el pensamiento Europeo del siglo XIX.*

[18] Kurt Kiesinger, "The Rule of Titans–The Work and Warnings of Alexis de Tocqueville," *Universitas,* 4:2 (1961), 125; also see *Der Grosse Brockhaus,* 3 (Wiesbaden, 1953), 319, which sees Donoso in terms of historical pessimism and dictatorship. German publications on Donoso virtually ceased after the early 1950s.

[19] For a useful account and listing of Spanish writing and addresses on the occasion of Donoso's centennial, especially in Madrid in newspapers and at the Ateneo, see Santiago Galindo Herrero, "Introduction," in P. Dietmar Westemeyer, *Donoso Cortés, hombre de estado y teólogo,* pp.

articles appeared in learned journals, especially in *Arbor* and *Revista de estudios políticos*, and in centennial editions of the newspapers *ABC*, *Informaciones*, and *Hoy*, and the Institute of Spain and the Institute of African Studies sponsored centennial addresses and pamphlets. After an original, very incomplete, five-volume compilation of Donoso's works by Tejado, Juretschke's B.A.C. edition (1946) in two compact volumes, although not as complete as claimed, became the standard reference. In 1970, however, Valverde brought out two new volumes with many more documents, a comprehensive new bibliography, and lengthy introduction.[20]

Serious monographic studies, doctoral dissertations, and books began to appear in Spain with Díez del Corral's chapter on Donoso as Spain's leading doctrinaire liberal (1945). Two of these works were prize-winning centennial books by Galindo Herrero (1957) and Monsegú (1958) on Donoso's political and historical thought.[21] A slim introductory volume by Suárez Verdeguer was published in 1964, and Saiz Barberá devoted a volume to Donoso's Christian historical thought that was published in 1968.[22] Besides identifying doctrinaire liberalism as a major stage of Donoso's political evolution, Díez del Corral was the first to stress the continuity and unity of his ideas, a characteristic that Fernández Carvajal has demonstrated better than anyone to date.[23] Galindo Herrero and Suárez Verde-

---

25–28; Schramm's pamphlet is *Donoso Cortés. Ejemplo del pensamiento de la tradición*.

[20] Carlos Valverde, ed., *Obras completas de Juan Donoso Cortés*.

[21] Galindo Herrero, *Theoría política*; Bernardo Monsegú, *Clave teológica de la historia según Donoso Cortés*.

[22] Federico Suárez Verdeguer, *Introducción a Donoso Cortés*; Juan Saiz Barberá, *Pensamiento histórico christiano*, I.

[23] Luis Díez del Corral, "Donoso Cortés doctrinario . . . ," in *El liberalismo doctrinario*, 495–96; Rodrigo Fernández Carvajal, "Las Constantes de Donoso Cortés," *Revista de Estudios Políticos*, 95 (1957), 75–107. Only generalizing about "the unity of the figure and the thought of Donoso," the former affirms that a "fine red thread" runs unbroken through all of his periods and crises; the latter identifies elements and lines of "continuity," but they are not the ones emphasized in this study.

guer, however, continued to emphasize his conversion of 1847 for its disjunctive effect on his life and thought,[24] a viewpoint that is still advanced although it is too extreme. The first half of Galindo Herrero's book was an improved biography with some new documents out of the family archives, but the second half was mainly an uncritical anthology of Donoso's monarchist writings. Investigating Donoso's Augustinian theology of history, Monsegú unfortunately ignored the more basic Vicchian philosophy of history. Javier de Silió in a doctoral thesis examined Vico's influence on Donoso in relation to his later pessimistic outlook on western civilization.[25] After having previously demonstrated that Donoso's earliest position (1830–1836) was liberal–conservative instead of radical,[26] Suárez Ver-

[24] Santiago Galindo Herrero, "Donoso Cortés en la última etapa de su vida," *Arbor*, 25:89 (May, 1953), 1–17.

[25] Francisco Javier de Silió, "Vico y Donoso Cortés" (diss., the Angelicum, Rome, 1949). In "Donoso Cortés, en su tiempo y en el nuestro," *Arbor*, 17 (September–October, 1950), 58 and 63, Javier de Silió claims that Donoso's "historical vision" is "the foundation of all his work." Thomas P. Neill made a similar statement in "Juan Donoso Cortés: History and 'Prophecy,'" *The Catholic Historical Review*, 40 (January, 1955), 398. A better study of Donoso's "theology of history" than Monsegú's is that of Jules Chaix-Ruy, *Donoso Cortès, théologien de l'histoire et prophète*. Ch. 3 is on Donoso's interpretation of Vico in 1838, but the emphasis thereafter is not on philosophy of history but on *le mystique* (Ch. 5) and on eschatology in reference to the *Essay* of 1851 (Ch. 6). In that work he sees Vico's influence (p. 147), but not in regard to philosophy of history, because for him as for Monsegú, Donoso's later preference for Saint Augustine's dualism and moralism over Vico's cycle in the structure of history (Juretschke, II, 209) was the last word. Ramón Ceñal also considered Vico before the *Essay*; see "La Filosofía de la historia de Donoso Cortés," *Revista de Filosofía*, 40 (January–March, 1952), 92–98. Possibly someone has published a genuine demonstration of Vico's continuing great influence in Donoso's later thought, in works I have not yet seen, such as: Alberto Caturelli, *Donoso Cortés: Ensayo sobre su filosofía de la historia* (Córdoba, Arg., 1958); R. Ceñal, "J. B. Vico y Donoso Cortés," *Pensamiento*, 24 (1968), 351–74; Hans Barth, "Juan Donoso Cortés und Giambattista Vico," in *Hortulus Amicorum*; or Johannes Maria Höcht, *Donoso Cortés, Untergang oder Wiedergeburt des Abendlandes?* (Wiesbaden, 1953).

[26] Frederico Suárez Verdeguer, "La primera posición política de Donoso Cortés," *Arbor*, 16 (July–August, 1946), 73–98.

deguer contributed little that was new in his *Introduction.* Although Saiz Barberá's study contains some good insights, it is as a whole disappointing, despite its bulk; where Monsegú contrasted Donoso with Toynbee, this author compares him with Danilevsky. Most provocative since Díez del Corral are Fernández Carvajal, who discovered that Donoso had positivist connections, and Calvo Serer, who took Donoso's final politics for a Christian social and popular monarchy of a corporative and plebiscitary type.[27]

Since 1945 scholars in the English-speaking world, where Donoso has always been nearly unknown, have finally begun serious investigation of his life and thought. Long after Orestes Brownson tried and failed, Germans such as Joseph Bernhart, Goetz Brief, and Heinrich Rommen at last awakened some sustained interest in Donoso in Britain and the United States since the 1930s and 1940s.[28] In the 1950s Peter Viereck, Thomas Neill, Bela Menczer, and J. P. Mayer wrote articles and chapters on him, but there have been no studies of book length, except for unpublished doctoral dissertations of his political and social thought by John Kennedy, Raymond Copeland, and myself.[29] Peter Viereck's chapter on Donoso in *Conservatism* (1957) is still perhaps the best short exposition of his politics in any language, although Donoso was not a reactionary 'ottantottist' (one who wanted to go back to 1788 to the old regime), but a cyclic thinker. Both Neill and Menczer employed the "prophet" theme. Where the former wrote a short biography and a lucid article on his historical thought, the latter translated the famous "Speech on Dictatorship" and explored his conservative political thought in relation to Metternich.[30] J. P. Mayer, like Ludwig Fischer twenty years

[27] Fernández Carvajal, "Las Constantes," 84, 87–88.

[28] Consult the Bibliography for these lesser works on Donoso.

[29] John T. Graham, "Donoso Cortés on Liberalism"; Raymond F. Copeland, "Donoso Cortés and His Social Thought." Professor Thomas Neill directed both dissertations.

[30] See especially Menczer's "A Prophet," and Thomas P. Neill's "Juan

earlier in Germany, reassessed the *Essay on Catholicism, Liberalism and Socialism* (1851) in 1953 as a City of God.[31]

Recently Donoso's name appears in more and more works, and his speeches or *Essay* are included or excerpted increasingly in new studies and texts on general history, intellectual history, politics, and philosophy of history. In Manfred P. Fleischer's *The Decline of the West?* (1970), he is the only nineteenth-century political theorist prior to Nietzsche who is included as an important predecessor of Spengler and Toynbee; however, his "Speech on Dictatorship" (1849) had previously appeared in an earlier students' manual by Eugene N. Anderson (*Europe in the Nineteenth Century*, Vol. I, 1961). William L. Langer's massive *Political and Social Upheaval, 1832–1852* (1969) devotes one half of a page to Donoso. *The Conservative Tradition in European Thought* (1970) by Robert L. Schuettinger contains a section of Donoso's *Essay*. None of these newest presentations, unfortunately, really shows any valid understanding of Donoso's life or of his political or historical thought.

THE PRESENT NEED FOR THIS SYNTHESIS

What is still missing in Donosian scholarship everywhere is an adequate synthesis of either his life or thought, or, since he was an intellectual in politics, of his life *and* thought. All the partial studies suffer for lack of a comprehensive synthesis. Besides utilizing basically independent research in Donoso's published and unpublished writings, I attempt in this volume to assess and bring together almost all that is valid and significant from special research, viewpoints, and insights on this extraordinarily complex man and thinker, so as to present not just "the young Donoso" or "the great Donoso" but "the whole Donoso." As the first really comprehensive study of him at-

---

Donoso Cortés, Prophet of Our Time," *Catholic World*, 170 (November, 1949), 121–27. Other works by these authors are in the Bibliography.

[31] J. P. Mayer, "Donoso Cortés' De Civitate Dei," *Dublin Review*, 225 (Spring, 1951), 76–88. Ludwig Fischer, *Der Staat Gottes*.

tempted in English or any other language, this book differs from all previous investigations not just in scope, detail, and complexity but in interpretation of the subject in general and in specifics. It is an effort to depict Donoso not only as politician, intellectual, writer, orator, courtier, statesman, diplomat, and, finally, prophet but also as a Spanish thinker of European stature in philosophy, religion, and the social-science fields of politics, sociology, and history. In short, it is a consideration of Donoso as a many-sided man of thought and of action who displayed a great deal of intuition or foresight and exercised important influence on men and affairs in his time.

Much more than any previous study, this biography is an attempt to reveal Donoso's private life and personality, not merely his impersonal thought and rather few public actions. Reticent and chary of intimate details, he refused to furnish Veuillot with any personal biographical information to publish with his *Essay*, because he regarded the common habit of boasting in public with confessions, interviews, autobiographies, and the like as ridiculous for anyone of so humble a state as himself. "After God, my life belongs to my relatives and friends, but the public has nothing to do with me nor I with it."[32] He left us, therefore, no autobiography, but he kept some private diaries for a few years, which record his personal relationship with the Spanish court, the queens, and leading politicians.[33] Moreover, a poet friend, Tassara, has left us a versified satire–ode concerning the high points of his life and the stark visions of his cyclic historical outlook in "Un diablo más," which this study examines for the first time.[34] Memories of friends and acquaintances—Pastor Díaz, Veuillot, Montalembert, and Tejado (his first brief biographers), and Hübner, Raczynski, Meyendorff, Bois-le-Comte, Mazade, and others from the diplomatic and literary worlds—reveal how his con-

[32] Juretschke, II, 556.

[33] See Valverde, II, for "diaries" covering parts of 1844–1846.

[34] García y Tassara, "Un diablo más." Schramm mentioned Tassara but did not use him (pp. 329–30).

temporaries reacted to him. His own letters and diplomatic reports, his two accounts of his conversion, and bits and pieces from his other writings also give us much useful evidence of his mind, character, and personality. Finally, the family archives preserved by Don Manuel Donoso Cortés at Don Benito is a rich lode of personal data that has still not been wholly exhausted after use by Tejado, Schramm, Galindo Herrero, Valverde, and by myself. The letters, books, papers, and notes there are very helpful to pierce the veil that Donoso drew around his family and private life. They reveal information concerning his tastes, habits of reading, study, and prayer, his many close friendships with people both great and humble, and his fatal illness. Especially after his "conversion" of 1847, he appears a tortured spirit, torn between moderation and excess, Europe and Spain, politics and religion, reason and faith, the flesh and the spirit, the City of the World and the City of God. Nevertheless, above the sharp contrasts a unity of personality and of thought slowly and painfully emerge for the patient researcher.

One volume cannot examine all the disputes and problems involved in Donoso's political and intellectual development nor demonstrate all of the unity and richness of his thought. Nevertheless, there was a pattern and a unity to Donoso's life, thought, and action in all its dimensions (historical, philosophical, political, social, cultural, and religious), but it was a unity of development that was cyclic and purposive. No one crucial year of radical change divides his thought, but 1828, 1838, 1847, and 1849 are milestones that mark its evolution in three or perhaps four interconnected eras.

Following are some related conclusions that one may draw from this book, generalizations which challenge most previous interpretations. First, no one can understand "the great Donoso" without knowing "the young Donoso," the later conservative without the earlier liberal, because his thought as a whole and in all its parts grew and evolved over his entire lifetime, preserving its unity, continuity, and coherence even through his conversion of 1847 and the revolutions of 1848. Second, his cyclic philosophy of history—a synthesis of Vico, Saint Augustine, Saint-Simon, and Hegel—is the one factor most basic for understanding his mature thought on philosophy, politics, society, culture, and religion. Third, Donoso developed a system of thought which, as a whole, was a kind of Christian and monarchic positivism, or 'affirmativism', often very similar to Comte yet perhaps owing nothing to him directly but rather to Saint-Simon and the Saint-Simonians.[35] Arising only from careful research and reflection, this belated conclusion fits the accumulated evidence and the prior reconstruction of his thought as a suitable name and probable relationship. A search of Donoso's depleted library and the family archives turned up no additional evidence of the influence of either Comte on the Saint-Simonians on him. Just to read Comte's *Social Physics* after having studied Donoso thoroughly, however, is to discover identical phrases and ideas, startling parallels, and possible sources not only for much of the latter's mature view of European history but first of all for his politics of crisis, transition, and normalcy and even his social thought, yet there are also crucial inversions. If he actually used Comte, it was not for the purely scientistic positivism of Littré and of the later nineteenth century but for Ortega's spiritual Comte.[36] This neglected Comte was the romantic preacher of social regeneration under the aegis of a positive religion and ethics, whose famous theological–metaphysical–scientific triad was given a cyclic turn by Donoso, as in *The Doctrine of Saint-Simon* (*Exposition de la doctrine de St. Simon*) to end up in

[35] For Saint-Simon's "positive" ideas, which anticipated the later Comte, see Frank E. Manuel, *The New World of Henri Saint-Simon* (Cambridge, Mass., 1956), pp. 130, 135ff; and G. D. H. Cole, "Preface," *The Doctrine of Saint-Simon. An Exposition. First Year, 1828–1829*, trans. Georg. G. Iggers (Boston, 1958), p. viii; and Iggers, *The Cult of Authority. The Political Philosophy of the Saint-Simonians* (The Hague, 1958), pp. 189–90. For Donoso's link to Saint-Simonism in editor Andrés Borego, see Fernández Carvajal, "Las Constantes," pp. 84, 87–88.

[36] José Ortega y Gasset, *History As a System* (New York, 1962), p. 79.

a new theological mentality and epoch,[37] comparable in Donoso's mind to Vico's divine age and Saint Augustine's City of God.[38]

These three conclusions together result in a substantial reevaluation and revision in the interpretation of Donoso.

[37] *The Doctrine* (Iggers) pp. xxii and 222–25. Manuel (*New World*, p. 147) also points out that Saint-Simon used the cyclic principle in his later works on the philosophy of history.

[38] See Leszek Kolakowski, *The Alienation of Reason, A History of Positivist Thought*, trans. Norbert Guterman (Garden City, N.Y., 1968). He finds persistent romantic, utopian, religious, and messianic interests in the forgotten Comte, the utopian visionary.

Chapter I

ROMANTIC, REBELLIOUS YOUTH

Juan Donoso Cortés was born into a tumult of war and revolution, just a year after the Spaniards' *Dos de Mayo* uprising of 1808 against Napoleon, which grew into a bloody guerrilla war of national liberation led by juntas of reactionary nobles and clergy. The effort of enlightened bourgeois leaders in 1811–1812 to establish a liberal regime that reflected the French revolutionary constitution of 1791 was soon set aside by the restoration and reaction under despotic Ferdinand VII. This conflict between classes and ideals which represented the old national traditions and the newer forces from France and Europe divided Donoso's generation almost as deeply as the later Hispanizers and Europeanizers of the Generation of 1898. After growing up as a romantic bourgeois rebel, Donoso spent his life trying to reconcile the liberal and traditionalist heritages but at the end sadly waited for world war and socialist world revolution to overthrow both monarchs and liberals in Spain and Europe.

FAMILY AND SOCIAL BACKGROUND

Juan was born on May 6, 1809, at Valle de la Serena, in the arid western province of Extremadura, while his parents were fleeing from the path of French troops after a disastrous battle at Medellín.[1] Don Pedro Donoso Cortés was a successful lawyer, a well-to-do provincial bourgeois who was then mayor of the town of Don Benito. A descendant of conquistador Her-

[1] On the Battle of Medellín, see Gabriel H. Lovett, *Napoleon and the Birth of Modern Spain* (New York, 1965), I, 329.

nán Cortés,[2] he and his wife (doña Elena Fernández de Canedo) boasted of *hidalgo* ancestry and, although they held no titles at that time, lived nobly in a one-story townhouse with courtyard and stables (the present No. 6 Calle Donoso Cortés), with lands and herds of cattle and sheep at Valdegamas some sixteen miles northeast across the Río Guadiana.[3] Juan was the oldest of their seven children and had great affection for the two brothers nearest him in age, Pedro and Francisco (Paco). Years later he wrote that, granting freedom, "a man is what the family into which he is born and the society in which he lives and breathes are."[4] Fondly recalling his early life, he remembered the tenderness and love of family intimacy and the splendor and magnificence of the Extremaduran countryside, blooming bright in spring but in summer sere and stark, with harsh contrasts that perhaps subtly disposed him toward extremes.[5] The social, economic, and religious background of his parents was a much more significant factor, however; he grew up under the influence of bourgeois wealth and ambition, a French style of liberalism, and stubborn conservative loyalty to monarchy and the Church, as well as of strong provincial roots.

[2] Gabino Tejado, ed., *Obras de don Juan Donoso Cortés . . .*, I, ix. Tejado's biographical introduction was the first, and it is the most basic for this chapter for he utilized and organized Donoso's papers in the family archives at Don Benito. For more facts on Donoso's origins, also see Santiago Galindo Herrero, *Donoso Cortés y su theoría política*, pp. 38–39; and Edmund Schramm, *Donoso Cortés, su vida y su pensamiento*, p. 12. All later references to Schramm are to this Spanish edition instead of to the German original.

[3] Señor don Manuel Donoso Cortés, descendant of Juan Donoso Cortés and custodian of the family archives at No. 6, Calle Donoso Cortés, Don Benito, most graciously informed me and my wife Alsy on many details of family background and relationships. His niece, Señorita Pilar Donoso Cortés not only showed us portraits and various other mementos of her ancestor but also very kindly drove us to see the area of Valdegamas and her own *finca* nearby.

[4] Juan Juretschke, ed., *Obras Completas*, II, 489.

[5] Juretschke, I, 46; II, 317f. This is the thesis of Francisco Elías de Tejado, *Para una interpretación extremeña de Donoso Cortés*, pp. 79, 89, 100–102.

The rural sector of the French and Spanish middle classes to which Donoso Cortés family belonged craved the economic security and social prestige of land and, if possible, title, but they resented aristocratic and clerical privilege and predominance.[6] They desired the absolute monarchy to become constitutional and parliamentary, preferably by reform instead of revolution. They opposed Jacobin democracy, however, particularly social revolution for economic equality, a viewpoint Juan boldly addressed to Ferdinand VII in 1830.[7] Following his father in the profession of law, most of his career he would be a courtier–politician in service to a constitutional authoritarian monarchy, which was middle class in basis. Although his mother was a pious Spanish Catholic, his father was only perfunctory in rearing the children in the ancestral faith, since his belief had been somewhat eroded by the French Enlightenment and liberalism.[8] Early in his life, Juan was also indifferent to religion, but he gradually underwent a conversion, to become, after 1847, both spiritually and intellectually a committed Christian. Only then did he actively promote democratic and social reforms under Christian and monarchic auspices. After receiving part of Valdegamas in 1829 and eventually the title of marquis, Juan became an absentee capitalist landlord who was interested in agricultural societies and new technology for irrigation but did not express concern for the welfare of peasant tenants until many years later. When he had studied commerce and the industrial revolution in England, France, and Prussia, he came to fear the possibility of social revolution in the cities; even in his traditional world of peasants and *patronos*, he ultimately was dismayed by social upheaval that resulted from the liberals' seizure and exploitation of Church lands from the 1830s.[9]

[6] Edmund Schramm, *Donoso Cortés, ejemplo del pensamiento de la tradición*, p. 16. Also see Leonore O'Boyle, "The Middle Class in Western Europe," *American Historical Review*, 71 (April, 1966), 827ff.

[7] Juretschke, I, 53, 62.

[8] Schramm, *Vida y pensamiento*, pp. 13–15.

[9] Juretschke, I, 582; II, 337, 340.

REVOLUTION AND THE UNIVERSITY

A bright and precocious child, Juan studied at home under a tutor from Madrid, Antonio Beltrán, from whom he learned some Latin, French, and the basic subjects he would need at the university. Already an avid reader, especially in history, he often laid aside his books only when his mother snuffed the candle late at night.[10] By 1820, at the age of eleven, he had set off for the University of Salamanca to prepare to study law, which Pedro and Manuel also took up later.

Salamanca's faculty was already committed to the ideas of the Enlightenment, which had entered Spain during the reign of the enlightened despot Charles III. Like other European universities of the Restoration era, old Salamanca was a hotbed of new liberal and revolutionary sentiments, especially during the Spanish revolution of 1820 when Ferdinand VII once more was forced to accept the Constitution of 1812. Juan responded ebulliently to his professors' enthusiasm, eagerly tasting the exciting ideas in writings of Voltaire, Rousseau, Diderot, Benjamin Constant, and perhaps Destutt de Tracy and Bentham. The next year Don Pedro transferred him closer to home to a newly reopened Royal College at Cáceres where he could live with his friend, José García Carrasco, whose sons were then ardent liberals. Initially, the political situation there was less disturbed than at Salamanca, but a year later, when the college became a provincial university, it too adopted liberal views and was therefore closed with the reaction of 1823. By then Juan had completed most of his prerequisites, especially moral philosophy, and was ready to go on to the University of Seville to matriculate in 1824 and to graduate in 1828 with a law degree.[11]

[10] Tejado, I, ix; Schramm, *Vida y pensamiento*, p. 17. Comte Charles de Montalembert, *Oeuvres de M. le Comte de Montalembert*, XV: *Oeuvres polémiques et diversés*, II, 191.

[11] Tejado, I, xi; Schramm, *Vida y pensamiento*, p. 25. Miguel Muñoz de San Pedro, "La Esposa de Donoso Cortés," *Revista de Estudios Extremeños*, IX (1953), pp. 401–3. Schramm, *Vida y pensamiento*, p. 29.

The liberal three years (1820–1823) came to an inglorious end when the once-fierce Spanish masses passively watched a French royalist army march in to overthrow the constitutional regime which irritated Metternich's reactionary Concert of Europe. Feeling like young José Carrasco, Juan "loved liberty as a judge loves justice, as a poet loves beauty." The revolution had been a magic idea promising to rejuvenate Spain and Europe in the "brighter dawn" of a "golden age," whereas the white terror that followed was a shameful effort to imprison Spain in a "stupid immobility" of "theocratic and feudal institutions." In his frustrated idealism, he wrote a poem, "The Revolution of March 10 in Cádiz," expressing his "longing to die for liberty at the blast of the battle trumpet," cursing the "bloody hands" of the "ferocious tyrant."[12]

To make revolution was glorious, but to study law was not very exciting. At Seville Juan found that he much preferred the more liberal avocations of poetry, philosophy, and history. With other youths from the provinces—several of whom became his lifelong friends and also later had prominent careers in journalism and politics, such as J. F. Pacheco, Juan Bravo Murillo, and Gallardo—he joined a circle of talents who called themselves Sons of Apollo. They dedicated poetry to "Sacred Clío," discussed the reigning empirical philosophy from Locke to Bentham, and dreamed of founding a new academy, rather like the earlier group led by Lista y Aragón.[13] They crafted verses on love, politics, and religion, sometimes in the official classicist form, sometimes in the new style of romanticism. Impartially celebrating the "Birth of Venus" and the "Birth of Christ," Juan also composed odes to Nature, the rebel Padilla, the poet Meléndez, and dedicated one to beer! Although he failed to finish his "Memories" ("Los Recuerdos"), his stu-

[12] Juretschke, I, 52, 67, 142. Paper in Donoso Cortés family archives, Legajo 15.

[13] Paper in Donoso Cortés family archives, Legajo 15. Nicomedes Pastor Díaz, "Don Donoso Cortés," in *Galería de españoles célebres contemporáneos*, VI, 234.

dent pleasures at Seville probably resembled those of his later good friend, the poet Tassara, who recalled climbing the famed Giralda tower to see the city, walking along the Guadalquivir near the Torre de Oro, enjoying a secret tryst with the Gypsy girl, or "Venus," under the happy sky and marvelous sun of Andalusía![14] One of his student papers, "On Taste" ("Sobre el Gusto"), echoed a refined hedonism out of Horace and Condillac, equated perfection with sensation and study, and acknowledged only that which had its foundation in nature as beautiful.[15] He also found time to construct an epitome of universal history and progress, which foreshadowed his later efforts to compress history into general principles, laws, and forces.[16] Least impressive was his project concerning law, a "Treatise on Universal Legislation," which he abandoned after projecting two parts: "on Nature in General" and "On Nature here on Earth."[17]

During summer vacations Juan studied privately with his father's friend, don Manuel José Quintana, a famous poet, professor, and hapless liberal politician of 1812 and 1820 who was then confined in rural exile at the hamlet of Cabeza de Buey east of Don Benito.[18] Mainly neoclassicist emphasizing form, he directed Donoso in an extensive course of readings and discussions and writings of the eighteenth-century Enlightenment.[19] This Socratic tutoring undoubtedly benefited the youth, who ever afterward respected Quintana, even when they competed to be tutor to the queen after 1840, but the literary, philosophical, and political views of the older generation could not long satisfy the young romantic.[20]

[14] Gabriel García y Tassara, *Poesías*, pp. 54–55.
[15] Papers in Donoso Cortés family archives, *Legajo* 15.
[16] Tejado, I, p. xii. This composition is apparently lost.
[17] Paper in Donoso Cortés family archives, Legajo 15.
[18] Tejado, I, xiiif.
[19] E. Allison Peers, *A Short History of the Romantic Movement in Spain* (Liverpool, 1949), pp. 6–7.
[20] Letter to Durán in Schramm, *Vida y pensamiento*, p. 40. Juretschke, I, 23; Carlos Valverde, ed., *Obras completas*, I, 758–60.

GROWING UP AND SELF-EDUCATION

Donoso was not anxious to practice law after his graduation from the University of Seville in 1828. Thirsting for personal and intellectual freedom and independence, he decided to join the cosmopolitan literary and cultural circles and social life of the nation's capital, Madrid. Calling him "the son of my prayers, friend of complete confidence," Quintana gave him a letter of introduction to the poet Durán, which praised his predilection for poetry, literature, and philosophy.[21] Whether or not he stayed with Durán or with Beltrán or the Carrascos, he came to know all the leading poets of Madrid within a few years.[22] He was so pretentious that he barely condescended to explain for a friend that the way a poet differs from the mere versificator is in his knowing how to communicate with delicacy and enthusiasm the sentiments of the heart and "the voluptuousness and poison of love."[23] When the cost of his high life and pleasures got him into trouble with his creditors and with his father, Juan answered don Pedro insolently, dismissing his counsels as a joke and demanding money enough to pay his debts and to live with decorum and honor in respectable company; he claimed that his "40 or 50 reales a month!" would only buy candy for a child or support a dull provincial life.[24] Determined to stay in Madrid and to live as well as possible, the prodigal son demanded a big advance out of his future dowry, even if it meant selling lands. "On money matters I do not intend to argue with anyone, because nothing interests me less." Beltrán had to explain to the angry don Pedro that the behavior of Juanito at Madrid was not bad nor vicious; he was simply too proud and too rash in reply to the reprimands of his father. On the whole, "I have found him full of virtue and

[21] See Schramm, *Vida y pensamiento*, p. 40.

[22] Pedro Gómez Aparicio, *Historia del periodismo español* (Madrid, 1967), I, 225–26.

[23] Juretschke, I, 41.

[24] Galindo Herrero, *Theoría política*, p. 28; Valverde, I, 169–70.

knowledge," which promise that he "will give honor to our nation and to his house."[25]

Within a year (July 1829) Juan had returned to Don Benito, where, instead of joining his father to practice law, he claimed to be busy with serious studies, from which he did not wish to be diverted by any kind of obligations.[26] His notebooks reveal that he was still studying history, philosophy, and literature, including the works of Montesquieu, Voltaire, and Rousseau, but he was now strongly interested in romantic writers such as Mme. de Staël, Chateaubriand, Sir Walter Scott, and Schiller.[27] He also drew his first reflections on dictatorship in times of social crisis from Ferguson's *History of the Roman Republic*. Reeducating himself for a more contemporary need and viewpoint, he was about to reject the eighteenth-century ideas of the universities and of Quintana and to proclaim his intellectual independence as a romantic.

When members of his circle at Seville, who were still dreaming of forming a new academy, wanted to discuss the empirical philosophy of Destutt de Tracy by letter that summer, Donoso proclaimed that reason and philosophy were independent and, for that reason, he did not want to discuss "Tracy" except within the whole historical context of philosophy and metaphysics from Plato to Kant and Hegel.[28] In the name of beauti-

[25] Galindo Herrero, *Theoría política*, p. 49.

[26] Juretschke, I, 17, 19f: Donoso mentions receiving several earlier letters. He later performed legal work for his father from Cáceres by mail, according to don Pedro in a letter February 8, 1833, in the Donoso Cortés family archives, Legajo 57.

[27] Schramm, *Vida y pensamiento*, pp. 43–45, also lists the specific works from which Donoso extracted. See Galindo Herrero, *Theoría política*, pp. 71–74, for a fuller listing. Although I missed the student notes to which these two referred, I found a copy of Schiller's "The Diver" in his student notes and a paper listing eight of Scott's novels—*Ivanhoe*, *Waverley*, *Guy Mannering*, *Rob Roy*, etc. I do not think Quintana suggested these new studies, but see the opinion of Frederico Suárez Verdeguer, "La primera posición política de Donoso Cortés," *Arbor*, 16 (July–August, 1946), 79.

[28] Juretschke, I, 13–17.

ful youth, however, he was eager to join in virtuous battle against the "weak and silly" older generation, who "pervert the heart" and rend "Humanity" with their "monstrous systems." The empiricism of the ideologues was perhaps a "retrograde step" and "fatal epoch" in the march of "the human spirit." Even more vehement against that corrupting and materialistic philosophy, Pacheco, one member of the group, accused not only Cívico, Claros, and Gallardo but also Donoso—"*Sí, Señor, a tí!*"—of atheism.[29] Declaring that his own religious faith had survived the allurements of modern philosophy at Seville, he preferred the traditionalist Bonald, or Kant and the transcendentalists. Having already good naturedly chided Pacheco about his revolution in ideas and having pointed out the sophisms in that "rascal Bonald"—with whom materialistic Cívico should go "suck his fingers"—Donoso considered the accusation unfair, because he was no longer happy with the philosophy of the Enlightenment. To the others he explained that, since no philosopher's logic is without error, one sacrificed independence of reason and looked at the world through a pinhole by adhering to only one philosopher or one system instead of studying all of them. Only a narrow spirit could be satisfied with "Tracy" alone, whose vaunted analytic method was no more adequate than the invariable definitions of mathematics to grasp the vague but unified composite that man really is, in all the dimensions of his being and nature. That fixed system, the acme of empiricism, he therefore called a prideful but puerile philosophy.[30] Donoso's own modest skepticism was actually the initial statement of his new philosophical eclecticism, which apparently echoed a new *History of Philosophy* (*Cours de Philosophie*, 1828) by the French eclec-

[29] Schramm, *Vida y pensamiento*, pp. 35–39. This letter (August 1, 1829) is still in the archives at Don Benito, and the quotations are from it; from "Elija" (pen name), it ends with "J" and "P" [?], and names all of the group except Claro, whose views were decidedly opposite; only Pacheco's ideas were of this kind.

[30] Valverde, I, 171–73.

tic, Victor Cousin. As a sane alternative to both traditionalism and empiricism, eclecticism served him in thought and politics for the next twenty years.

PROFESSOR AND POET

During that same summer of 1829, on Quintana's recommendation, the College of Cáceres offered young Donoso a professorship of humanities (aesthetics, literature, and history).[31] To appear reluctant, he imposed strict and haughty reservations on what duties he would perform. He could not waste his time with basic courses in rhetoric and composition, and while history interested him as the philosophical story of human progress, the library was too inadequate, but he was willing to teach literature, elucidating the text with the higher principles of the humanities, because that would fit in with his current interests and reading.[32] Despite his impertinence, he was hired for the term of 1828–1829.

Obliged by his position to give an opening-day address at Cáceres, Donoso delivered a pretentious liberal–romantic manifesto in the form of an historical outline of the development of European poetry and literature in relation to the progress of the human spirit in philosophy. Claiming to speak less from erudition than from the natural simplicity of the heart, he defined the difference between the ancient and modern civilizations as the key to the difference in their literatures.[33] In contrast to ancient paganism, he presented the idea (from Turgot, Chateaubriand, Cousin, and Guizot) that medieval Christianity had so elevated European sentiments that it had effected a moral revolution, which was clearly reflected in literature.

[31] Schramm, *Vida y pensamiento*, p. 46.

[32] Juretschke, I, 19–21.

[33] Juretschke, I, 23–46 passim, especially 34–35 and 39ff. Schramm, *Vida y pensamiento*, p. 50 points out the similarity to Chateaubriand. Three copies of discourse are preserved in the Donoso Cortés family archives as well as the scrap referred to in this paragraph. Some of his notes in tomes and on Cousin and Guizot relate directly to the themes of this discourse.

Since he regarded the classicism of eighteenth century as an aesthetic and philosophical regression in the spirit of pagan antiquity, it was the nineteenth-century romanticism, especially of Mme. de Staël, Byron, and Durán, to which he looked for true progress and enlightenment in harmony with the older Christian traditions of Europe. He developed the conception of this basic distinction between Christian and pagan (or rationalistic) civilizations for the rest of his life, not only in the realm of culture but also of politics. Nevertheless, a stray note shows that his intent then was actually more conciliatory and eclectic: Both "classicism and romanticism . . . are equally" parts of human nature.

Pedagogically Donoso's lectures on literature at Cáceres were a dismal failure. His indecision about his future in teaching was resolved by almost total lack of student interest in his course. Since his lectures were outside the required curriculum, only two students enrolled, and only one persevered—Gabino Tejado, who recalled none of his instructor's most fecund principles of literature when he later became his loyal disciple and biographer.[34] How Donoso's ego must have suffered from such a rebuff!

Because he was unsuccessful as a teacher, for several years Juan considered becoming a professional poet. His surviving works were meager for anyone aspiring to the laurel, however. Besides a lyric political work written in 1829 to hail "The Coming of Cristina" as Spain's hoped-for liberal queen, he had composed only an elegy on the death of the Duchess of Frias, spouse of a great poet, and a poem to celebrate the wedding of a friend in Madrid.[35] After 1830 political interests intervened, and he wrote nothing until the Spanish Academy sponsored a competition in 1832 on a theme of medieval chivalry and heroism: "El Cid Campeador and the Siege of Zamora." When he

[34] Tejado, I, p. xvi.

[35] See Juretschke, I, 9–12 and 49–50, for these poems as well as "The Siege of Zamora," I, 76–96, especially 79; the wedding poem (Madrid, January of 1829) is in Legajo 15 of the Donoso Cortés family archives.

learned that these official classicists did not like most entries, he published his openly romantic epic on the Cid at his own cost in 1833, defiantly proclaiming himself a son of the nineteenth century, who denied that poetry must always be subject to certain fixed and invariable rules that did not allow for changing social sentiments. As a consolation he won an honorary membership in Seville's Academy of Belles-lettres in May, but he henceforth forsook poetry for politics, and Spain may have lost a potentially great poet.[36]

A BOURGEOIS MARRIAGE AND TRAGEDY

In January of 1830 while still at Cáceres, Juan Donoso Cortés married Teresa García-Carrasco when he was twenty-one and she nineteen. He had known her since he had stayed with her family from 1821 to 1823, and, although her appearance was plain, the match was a good one by bourgeois standards: profession and land joined to commerce and land. If don Pedro was moderately wealthy, don José had become truly rich. Both fathers had recently sported confirmed titles of *hidalguía*,[37] and both eldest sons, Juan and Juan José, were to become respectively Marquis of Valdegamas and Count of Santa Ollalla in the 1840s. The business of José Carrasco e Hijos in Madrid was the basis for the administration of very profitable operations in wool and hides at Cáceres and in the provinces.[38] Teresa got a dowry of *fincas* (farms) and money; Juan's was worth about 100,000 reales and included half of Valdegamas.[39]

In their several years of marriage Juan developed a deep,

[36] See the judgment of P. Francisco Blanco García, *La literatura española en el siglo XIX*, I (Madrid, 1899), 172. This critic regarded Donoso's early poetry—especially "The Siege of Zamora," for its "oriental extravagance" and "Gongoristic opulence"—as indicative of a career full of promise, prematurely terminated.

[37] Unpublished documents, Donoso Cortés family archives, October 20 and November 20, 1818. Miguel Muñoz de San Pedro, "La Esposa de Donoso Cortés," *Revista de Estudios Extremeños*, 4 (1953), 397, 407.

[38] Juretschke, I, 52.

[39] Information from Don Manuel Donoso Cortés of Don Benito, July of 1971. Also see letter from Juan Donoso Cortés to don Pedro Donoso Cortés (August 18, 1828) in Valverde, I, 169.

tender, and enduring love for his little "angel," Teresa. She was described as intelligent, discreet, and self-denying, pious and agreeable, and notable for her exquisite femininity and innate goodness, but she did not emerge into public prominence nor exercise any definable influence on her husband's thought and career. We know little of their marriage except the tragedies.[40] First their only child, María, died at two years of age in 1832. Then around April of 1835, after Juan had been sick with a fever, Teresa contracted a grave illness of some kind and died early in June while convalescing in Cáceres.[41] To lose his "adored wife" was a terrible blow to Donoso. "Never did a purer soul dwell on earth: everybody called her angel." "Happiness is at an end for me," he wept; "in my heart only sadness dwells."[42] "Her blessed memory shall never leave me," he promised her mother, and several years later he praised Christian woman (as compared to the pagan) as "an angel of peace" who drives away a man's gloom and sorrow as a beloved companion.[43] A spirit of melancholy, a romantic "gift of tears," perhaps a sense of remorse and responsibility henceforth dogged him, and he did not remarry. Except for his loyal service to queens Isabel and María Cristina and his later affectionate connection with Empress Eugénie, women no longer played any visible part in his life. His increasing dedication to his political career may have reflected this tragedy and grief.

INTO POLITICS AND GOVERNMENT

The July Revolution in France and the birth of Isabel II in Spain made 1830 a propicious year for young Donoso to enter

[40] Muñoz de San Pedro, "La Esposa," 401f, 407–10, 417.

[41] Donoso's request for a leave of two months to take his ailing wife to Cáceres is in the Donoso Cortés family archives, among decrees of appointment to the Ministry of Grace and Justice. The letter in which Juan wrote that he was bedridden several days with a fever, also in the archives, is dated March 27, 1835.

[42] Letters from Donoso to his mother-in-law (Madrid, 16 and 19 June 1835) and to Andrés Máximo (same dates) in Donoso Cortés family archives.

[43] Juretschke, I, 404–5.

politics. With grave fears from the first event but with immense hopes from the latter, he understood prophetically what must come to pass:[44] the establishment of a new bourgeois and constitutional monarchy, also in Spain under Isabel, who had been declared successor to the throne by decree of pragmatic sanction. Hopefully, this change would be instituted without either revolution or a bloody reaction by the pretender, her uncle Don Carlos.

Sensing the opportunity for a career in service to his country, Donoso plunged into forbidden political activities in Cáceres, Extremadura, and Madrid alongside his brothers-in-law to organize *Cristinos* in support of María Cristina, Isabel, and a constitution. They soon ran afoul of police and government. Suspicious of the liberal faction, Ferdinand VII had authorized arbitrary banishment by 1832, and local police magistrates ordered Juan José Carrasco and very possibly Donoso into rural exile. Of two appeals that Donoso then drafted, one, an intellectual and conservative profession of his political faith, is much more appropriate to his situation than that of the young merchant.[45] Along with some generals and governors, Donoso's father was apparently among some counsellors of the crown who had joined their cause apparently, but his brother Pedro opted for Don Carlos.[46]

By October of 1832 Donoso was at San Ildefonso, northwest of Madrid, to present a political petition for the *Cristinos*. Just after the Carlists had attempted a palace revolution, he addressed "to the king" (actually to María Cristina) a bold liberal manifesto on behalf of Isabel's succession, her supporters, and constitutional government. At last he put his legal and historical studies to use in this *Memoria*, to uphold the pragmatic sanction as true to Spain's ancient law of female succession under which Isabella I had ruled, as against Philip V's

[44] Juretschke, I, 817–18.

[45] Juretschke, I, 51ff, 67, 839; 57ff.

[46] Schramm, *Vida y pensamiento*, p. 12, mentions this title. Juretschke, I, 860, 890.

French Salic law on which Don Carlos rested his claim. Speaking openly now as a doctrinaire eclectic who abhorred both anarchy and despotism, he called for a new system of government, new in its middle-class basis and cabinet system but traditional in its Cortes and magistracy.[47] Perhaps it was only coincidence that the course of action that he recommended was the one María Cristina began to take immediately after this crisis; she let the exiles return, restored the magistracy, convoked the Cortes for June, and permitted the *Cristinos* (and through them the middle class) to emerge as a legal political force. Less than a year later she granted the *Estatuto Real*, a conservative constitution. In November she also authorized the separate publication of five hundred copies of Donoso's *Memoria* over the objection of the state censorship.[48]

Through María Cristina, Donoso made a most auspicious debut into the Court and civil government. If he did not accompany the gorgeous procession in which the royal family returned to the Oriente Palace in October, he had established Madrid as his permanent residence by February, 1833.[49] Then, with a royal decree of appointment, he entered the civil bureaucracy in the Ministry of Grace and Justice, where (again

[47] Juretschke, I, 67f, 70f.

[48] Schramm, *Vida y pensamiento*, p. 29. Papers in the Donoso Cortés family archives reveal Donoso's problem with the censorship and the queen's support. Also see Valverde, I, 224–25, for two of the letters, although my notes indicate that the first letter (November 16) was to María Christina (among "Varias cartas a V.M.M.C.") rather than to Ferdinand and that she wrote to the Ministry of Grace and Justice ordering the return of the confiscated documents and pamphlets.

[49] Juretschke, I, 870f. See Schramm, *Vida y pensamiento*, p. 43, and Galindo Herrero, *Theoría política*, p. 52. This and other decrees of his appointments are preserved in the Donoso Cortés family archives. He started in the "Indies" section, was transferred by order of María Christina to the "España" section on September 30, 1834, and was appointed chief of his section on September 18, 1836, and chief of the section of the Secretaría del Despacho of the Ministry of Grace and Justice on January 13, 1840, to replace Manuel García Gallardo. Also see Pastor Díaz, *Galería*, VI, 249, whose claim is confirmed by a letter of appointment from María Christina in the Donoso Cortés family archives: "Mi secretario con ejercicio de decretos."

with royal favor) he advanced from fifth clerk to head of his section in just three years and by 1834 was one of María Christina's secretaries in charge of decrees. Supported by this position and income, he relied on his talents as a thinker and writer to open a career in party and parliamentary politics.

Chapter II

POLÍTICO
'POSITIVE POLITICS', MODERATISM, NATIONALISM

Reflecting on the era of transition between the July Revolution of 1830 and the European revolutions of 1848, Donoso remarked that to refer to it as an era of liberty was like calling someone free who walked between two policemen. The system of 'positive politics' which he worked out during those years was equally restrictive; only police, soldiers, and dictators would have been able to establish it, since neither nationalism nor monarchic authority would have been strong enough to override popular resistance. Still, his admittedly absolutist politics of 'crisis' was not the finished system of despotism that J. S. Mill saw in Auguste Comte's *politique positive*, for Donoso really wanted liberty to balance order in his subsequent politics of normalcy, which included social reforms and a kind of democracy.[1]

Although young Donoso's opposition to the Spanish reactionaries of the 1830s gave him a reputation for radicalism, he seems to have become a moderate, or liberal–conservative soon after 1830, and when deep crisis actually arrived, he found himself (like Guizot) more in support of order than of liberty.[2] Until 1836 his political creed was largely derived from French theoreticians: It included a doctrinaire liberalism of Guizot's

[1] Juan Juretschke, ed., *Obras completas*, II, 643. John Stuart Mill, *Auguste Comte and Positivism* (Philadelphia, 1866), pp. 98, 122.

[2] Peter Viereck, *Conservatism from John Adams to Churchill.* (New York, 1956), pp. 64–67. Federico Suárez Verdeguer, "La primera posición política de Donoso Cortés," *Arbor*, 16 (July–August, 1946), 87. Juretschke, I, 420.

type, eclectic *juste-milieu* principles from Cousin, and a system of representative government like Constant's—all joined, however, to a dogmatic realism either from Saint-Simon and the Saint-Simonians or from his own devise, which disposed him gradually to advocate dictatorship as a way out of worsening crisis into reconstruction and normalcy. Apparently the general dynamics of Donoso's politics, if not its forms, was either conceived directly from Saint-Simon or from his disciple Comte—both of whom developed a system of what they called a 'positive politics'—whose terminology of three stages of 'crisis', 'transition', and 'normalcy' repeatedly crops up in Donoso's political writing of these years.[3] This similarity, however, was for the first and only time half recognized in 1834. Donoso the young doctrinaire moderate was in part a crypto-Saint-Simonian. Later, as a self-styled absolutist and advocate of dictatorship, he surpassed Comte as a positivist conservative, becoming distinctively Christian and monarchic and also social-democratic in a sense.

CRISIS: DOCTRINAIRE LIBERALISM OR DICTATORSHIP?

During 1833 both Carlists and liberals organized and armed in anticipation of Ferdinand VII's death. At the Carrasco's house in Madrid and at cafés Donoso attended meetings of liberals and heard their proposals to stir up mobs in the streets to seize power, even while they sought the good will of palace and government through his connections. Whether he conspired with them is uncertain, but he was probably among those whom he said were misled in contributing to revolution in hope of advancing progress, liberty, and civilization. Before long he felt deceived and disillusioned by liberal groups like the *Cristinos*, presumptuous men who wanted to pull down "the structure of our secular institutions" and "to raise up an-

[3] Juretschke, II, 60, for Donoso's mature statement of this positive politics of crisis, transition, and normalcy.

other of their own devise."[4] By April 1834 at latest he spoke out publicly for the *Estatuto Real*, monarchy, and moderation, along with his young friends Pacheco and Bravo Murillo on *La Abeja*. By August he had disavowed all political parties.[5] The Carrascos did not follow Donoso's example. Rufino, at least, was still a radical, and Juan José was an influential member of the Chamber of Commerce, whose merchants and *Bulletin* Donoso later identified with the Spanish revolution.[6] Although he suspected his relatives of revolutionary activity as late as the Mutiny of La Granja in 1836, he strove to get along with them and praised Juan José as devoted to María Cristina in 1841. After 1843, however, he regarded him as a mediocrity with neither morals nor political principles.[7]

After adhering to *La Abeja*'s program for romanticism, moderation, and constitutional monarchy, Donoso's first bid for stature as a political writer was *Reflections on Diplomacy* (1834) a pamphlet on European foreign policy as it related to internal politics. Apparently a takeoff in part from Saint-Simon's *Reorganization of the European Community* (*Réorganization de la société européenne*, 1814), it too attacked the old balance-of-power system as obsolete and called for cooperation by the liberal powers of France and Britain in a new Quadruple Alliance of 1834 to establish constitutional governments in Europe. He especially wanted to preserve Spain and Portugal from intervention by Metternich's reactionary Concert of Europe for Don Carlos and Dom Pedro. The triumph in Europe of bourgeois states similar to the July Monarchy by

[4] Manuel Muñoz de San Pedro, "La esposa de Donoso Cortés," *Revista de Estudios Extremeños*, 4 (1935), 414. Juretschke, I, 860ff, 872; 808–9, 864–69, 890ff.

[5] Pedro Gómez Aparicio, *Historia del periodismo español* (Madrid, 1967), I, 201–12. Juretschke, I, 118, 149–50.

[6] Muñoz de San Pedro, "La Esposa," pp. 416–18; Santiago Galindo Herrero, *Donoso Cortés y su theoría política*, p. 52 and note; and Suárez Verdeguer, "La primera posición política," p. 86. Juretschke, I, 51, 879.

[7] See Carlos Valverde, ed., *Obras completas*, II, 128. Muñoz de San Pedro, "La esposa," pp. 420–24; Valverde, I, 751, 760, 744; II, 44, 59.

means of aid from liberal nations, especially from France, was the only existing international policy of intelligence and reason, claimed Donoso, but it was far short of Saint-Simon's European parliament and union. For domestic politics he believed the conservative *Estatuto Real* potentially ideal if representative government would be added, but Spain should not adopt a policy as democratic as Louis Philippe's Charter of 1830, which took too much power from the king and gave too much to the people. In footnotes he criticized the liberals of 1812 and 1820 as too antimonarchic and democratic for the ordinary course of things after the passing circumstance of the popular war of liberation. Perhaps regretting *La Abeja*'s campaign against Jesuits, inquisition, and clerical property, now that a terrible massacre of regular clergy had occurred in Madrid, he called upon the government to uphold law and order before a social revolution broke out.[8]

A radical reviewer for the ultraliberal, Anglophile *Mensajero de las Cortes* ridiculed his *Reflections* as Frenchified, Francophile, and plagiarized—especially from Buchez, actually a Saint-Simonian, but not identified as such.[9] Despite Donoso's mortified and vehement protest that he knew of no such person, the reviewer was not far wrong, since the work was indeed a patchwork of unassimilated ideas, even if from as many unnamed thinkers as Donoso claimed. Critics could more easily detect the bourgeois *juste milieu* of Guizot and Cousin, however, or flashes of Chateaubriand's style, than Saint-Simonian ideas in it. Pacheco defended it as expressing the new romantic spirit, whereas Pastor Díaz excused it as premature and too theoretical.[10] If synthesis was still beyond Donoso's powers, he at least forecast his thought for years to come: He advocated a system of bourgeois doctrinaire–liberalism, eclecticism, and

[8] Juretschke, I, 103, 134ff; 134–44; 60ff, 119, 134f, 148–49; 120f; 97–98.

[9] Juretschke, I, 155 (note)–57.

[10] Nicomedes Pastor Díaz, "Don Donoso Cortes," in *Galería de españoles célebres contemporáneos*, VI, 242–49.

crisis politics and predicted Russian expansion that would provoke great wars between East and West.

Despite the unconditional support that Donoso and his friends had pledged to the *Estatuto,* it could not work effectively with a deepening crisis of civil war on the Carlist right and near-revolution on the liberal left in 1835. Although professing himself a friend of force, Donoso nevertheless warned María Cristina on January 1, 1835, that to replace moderate Martínez de la Rosa with a reactionary cabinet would so violate the principles of representative government as to constitute a coup d'état. Under these circumstances the only alternative to revolutionary anarchy would have been military dictatorship, which her "sergeants" lacked power to impose.[11] Like Guizot, he reminded her of Charles X's fate from "jumping out of the Charter." Eight months later, deciding that neither queen nor cabinet could cope with the dreadful crisis, where he saw the Inquisition on one side of the battlefield and assassins on the other and nowhere an effective social power, he called upon the Cortes to cease discussing and to act to assume temporarily absolute and constituent power to save the throne and nation.[12] Only then, in such moments of crisis, could the popular house assume the supreme power. Instead, the radicals took charge under Prime Minister Mendizábal late in 1835. As a loyal government employee, Donoso preferred him to either anarchy or military dictatorship. At this time he did not object to Mendizábal's anticlericalism and seizure of Church properties, so he helped him in Extremadura to win over the revolutionary juntas, which he viewed as "Committees of Public Safety" or as inquisitions worthy of "blessed Robespierre and venerable Torquemada" and as usurpers of the authority of State, Church, and Army.[13] Donoso was rewarded the fre-

[11] Juretschke, I, 160–62.

[12] Juretschke, I, 179–81.

[13] Donoso's commission, dated September 22, 1835, is in the Donoso Cortés family archives; also an unpublished letter to Don Juan Alvarez y Mende (27 March 1836).

quently bestowed Cross of Charles III for this service and even assisted as secretary of Mendizábal's cabinet in May, 1836, just before it resigned in a dispute with the queen over control of the army.[14]

When invited by Mendizábal, the Cortes had exercised a constituent power only in devising a new system of voting and elections. In a pamphlet Donoso urged a bold but narrow bourgeois–elitist viewpoint: Instead of popular sovereignty and the direct, democratic system of 1812, implement the policy of the July Monarchy and invest voting and control of office almost exclusively in the educated and propertied middle class as a new legitimate aristocracy ruling by right of 'sovereignty of intelligence.' In this way the more able and intelligent would govern not as delegates controlled by constituencies but as independent representatives.[15] Although his proposal clearly echoes Guizot's and Royer-Collard's principle of 'sovereignty of reason' as a justification for restricting suffrage and political power to the bourgeoisie on the basis of wealth and education, it also resembled Saint-Simon's intellectual elitism.[16] Power to the bourgeoisie as a new ruling class was his current solution for the crisis and 'exceptional state' which Spain still suffered. If 'one alone' were strong and intelligent enough to save and to reconstruct Spain, he would be the legitimate ruler, but because only the middle class possessed the qualities of a new ruling class, then legitimize it and free it for 'action', not only 'in the present crisis' but thenceforth, for 'the normal state of society.' A popular sovereignty of the whole people was possible only in a 'state of crisis and excep-

[14] Gabino Tejado, ed., *Obras de don Juan Donoso Cortés*, I, xxvii; Galindo Herrero, *Theoría Política*, p. 60; Pastor Díaz, "Donoso Cortés," pp. 249–50. Donoso retained copies of the meetings of the Council of Ministers for May 12 and 13, which state the issue; in Donoso Cortés family archives.

[15] Juretschke, I, 191ff.

[16] Luis Díez del Corral, *El liberalismo doctrinario*, pp. 502–3. Also compare with Saint-Simon's elitism in *Selected Writings*, ed. and trans. by F. M. H. Markham (Oxford, 1952), pp. 1–16.

tion', and then only when the population was united in national war, as it had been against Napoleon, not when it was divided as in the present civil war in Spain. As an intellectual Donoso, of course, expected to be a member of the class that governed. Indeed, one can detect some of the selfish personal and class interest he later discerned behind the doctrinaires' sovereignty of reason. In the whole liberal era of restricted suffrage there was scarcely a more sophisticated rationalization for the upper bourgeoisie to block the poor from the troughs of power. For relative contribution to the civil war, he came perilously close to placing a greater value on bourgeois riches than on the life's blood of the Spanish masses. Pastor Díaz claimed that Donoso influenced the Cortes by his eloquence and logic to enact the restrictive system of voting and representation, under which he first entered parliament.[17]

Before a new bourgeois and moderate government could become established, new crisis intervened. The Mutiny of La Granja (August 10, 1836), a radical revolution, turned Antonio Alcalá Galiano and his moderates out of office, prevented the Cortes in which Donoso had won a seat (representing Badajoz) from meeting, and forced María Cristina to replace the *Estatuto* with the old Constitution of 1812. Protesting and despising this revolt vehemently in a letter, Donoso soon got a chance to attack the democratic dogma of the radicals in public at the Ateneo.

In the 1820s and when it reopened in 1835 the Ateneo (Atheneum) of Madrid had served more as a center for liberal political propaganda than for study and investigation. Now largely under the control of moderates, it offered Donoso its very prestigious chair of Constitutional Political Law in October of 1836 in place of exiled Alcalá Galiano.[18] Already some-

[17] Juretschke, I, 120f, 187, 197–99; 421; 201; Pastor Díaz, Galería, vi, 250.

[18] Edmund Schramm, *Donoso Cortés, su vida y su pensamiento*, p. 83ff. Ramón de Mesonero Romanos says that the Progressives almost closed the Ateneo in 1836 as politically opposed to them: *Memorias de*

thing of an expert in constitutional law, Donoso accepted the challenge eagerly. Only recently he had promised a synthesis of the principles of constitutional law, mainly of the French doctrinaire–liberal and eclectic type, which he, Pacheco, Bravo Murillo, and other young Spaniards had been assimilating and promoting as a moderate alternative to both Carlism and the revolutionary liberalism of the eighteenth century to which the older generation of radicals still adhered.[19] In a series of evening lectures in the Ateneo's great hall, he concentrated on sovereignty as the most basic question of political theory and government. After explaining that the purpose of government is both foresight and resistance, he presented his principle of sovereignty of intelligence as a universal fact and an absolute dogma. He defended it as a *juste milieu* between the equally despotic doctrines of Bonald's divine right of kings and Rousseau's popular sovereignty; it alone was able to reconcile liberty and order. With an impressive display of erudition, he required not only the doctrinaires Guizot and Cousin but also philosophers from Plato to Vico, Hegel, Saint-Simon and the Saint-Simonians to affirm that the most intelligent have the right to rule, since the principle of intelligence, acting as a divine and social force in history, had justly bestowed sovereignty on the middle class as Europe's new ruling class.[20]

The magnum opus of Donoso's liberal years, these lectures at the Ateneo comprised a very influential theoretical synthesis, or system, of doctrinaire liberalism, or political eclecticism.[21] His exposition of doctrinairism was more coherent than

---

un setentón, Natural y vecino de Madrid, I (Madrid, 1881), 160–66. The Donoso Cortés family archives contain the letter of appointment (October 2, 1836) and another (November 19) authorizing him to begin his public lectures at 6 P.M. on November 22, as well as his later appointments in March, 1837.

[19] Juretschke, I, 192. Marcelino Menéndez y Pelayo, *Historia de España, seleccionada en las obras del maestro por Jorge Vigón*, 6th ed. (Madrid, 1950), pp. 306–7.

[20] Juretschke, I, 219, 270, 303; see especially Lecture 9, pp. 303–18, 301–2.

[21] Tejado, I, xliv.

in the French masters themselves, but also more dogmatic and rigid.[22] The Ateneo then appointed him president of the section of moral and political sciences as a sign of how highly it regarded his lectures. Indeed, for many years they left a persistent mark on Spanish political thought, especially on moderatism.[23] Primarily because of these lectures, a recent historian of doctrinairism, Díez del Corral, rates Donoso as Spain's leading doctrinaire liberal.[24] Among Moderates, Pastor Díaz credited them as the first historical and philosophical investigation of sovereignty in Spain; the later premier, Antonio Cánovas del Castillo, judged them the best at the Ateneo for another decade, and legal and political scholar Joaquín Costa evaluated them in 1884 as the most important political speculation in Spain since Francisco Suárez in the sixteenth century.[25]

After having promoted doctrinairism, Donoso abruptly switched to a theory of dictatorship to answer radicals such as Gallardo, who was furiously attacking him as a *Guizotin*. Affronted by this bold new theme, however, either the Ateneo or Jose María Calatrava's government cancelled the rest of the lectures.[26] Combining the ideas of classical dictator and romantic hero from Vico and the Saint-Simonians, Donoso now suggested dictatorship as a way out of Spain's crisis. He ridiculed the radicals as too stupid to know how to rescue society from dire crisis and then to move it on into a normal state except by the panacea of reform and new constitutions. Consequently, as he had previously looked to the absolute power of parliament and the middle class as a solution, he now openly

[22] Díez del Corral, *El liberalismo doctrinario*, pp. 493–94, 503–5. Ch. 24, "Donoso Cortés doctrinario . . .," is the best available critical analysis of the Ateneo lectures, although a lucid précis was made in 1845 by Pastor Díaz, p. 147ff.

[23] Schramm, *Vida y pensamiento*, p. 88.

[24] Díez del Corral, *El liberalismo doctrinario*, p. 493, calls Donoso "the most eminent of them all."

[25] Pastor Díaz, *Galería*, VI, 257. Antonio Cánovas del Castillo, *Collección de escritores castellanos*, Vol. 18: *Problemas contemporáneos*, II, 145–47 passim. Schramm, *Vida y pensamiento*, pp. 68, 90.

[26] Schramm, *Vida y pensamiento*, p. 95; 98–99. Tejado, I, XXX.

proposed a dictator, a strong man of superior intelligence and will, perhaps a new Napoleon or modern Caesar, as an alternate way to save society.[27] He feared that Spain was suffering less from political revolution than from a social revolution of corrupted minds and mores, which only very strong government and laws could remedy; the only alternative was death for the society.

TRANSITION: LIBERALISM OR ABSOLUTISM?

Between romanticism and reaction in the Restoration and realism, positivism, and *Realpolitik*, which triumphed in Europe after 1848, came the eclectic bourgeois–liberal era of the July Monarchy. Donoso believed that an eclectic outlook—tolerant, middling, and indecisive—characterized the middle classes and liberalism in Europe as a whole, not only in France, through Guizot's doctrinairism and Cousin's eclecticism, but also through Benthamism in Victorian Britain and through Hegelianism in Germany.[28] As Spain's "hammer of eclecticism,"[29] he long continued to apply the eclectic method of *le juste milieu* in politics and thought to strike a balance or compromise between conflicting ideas, values, and parties of right and left as appropriate for such an era of transition between revolutionary crisis and hoped-for normalcy, or stability. With recurring revolutionary crises (1836, 1840, 1847, 1848), he returned to the expediency of dictatorship or absolutism, but always he yearned for and planned for normalcy, until finally he concluded that eclectic liberalism was essentially weak and

[27] Juretschke, I, 274ff, 281, 302, 325ff, 331. Compare Vico's "strong man" (I, 568) with the same figure (I, 275–76) or function (I, 328) in the Ateneo lectures.

[28] Juretschke, II, 222, 234, 620–21. On French and Italian eclecticism and liberalism, see Guido de Ruggiero, *The History of European Liberalism*, trans. R. C. Collingwood (Oxford, 1921; Boston, 1961), pp. 160, 169, 303, 307. For Spanish doctrinaire liberalism and eclecticism, see Díez del Corral, *El liberalismo doctrinario*, 475ff. On the prevalence of the *juste-milieu* frame of mind even in Britain before 1848, see V. Starzinger, *Middlingness* (University of Virginia Press, 1966).

[29] Menéndez y Pelayo, *Historia de España*, p. 309.

transitional, so only absolute power could settle the lingering crisis and usher in normalcy.

When he proposed dictatorship at the Ateneo in 1837, Donoso provoked suspicions that he was abandoning the doctrinaire–liberal ideology and becoming "Isabel's absolutist."[30] Every investigator has detected in him a new authoritarianism, and Donoso admitted to Guizot in 1843 that indeed he was an absolutist. Nevertheless, he was at pains in 1837 to show the continuity of his politics, to demonstrate that he had never been a *Guizotin* on the essential point of separation of powers, and thereafter we hear no more of his principle of intelligence. If not a doctrinaire purist, however, he was still an eclectic until at least 1845. Formerly he opposed absolutism with liberalism. Now, he deemed absolutism dead. Radicalism, however, was still a very lively threat;[31] he henceforth opposed it with a conservative and monarchic authoritarianism that reflected Bonald and de Maistre more than Guizot. Throughout, his politics also remained positive in adapting form and tactic to situations of crisis, transition, or normalcy and with more flexibility than Comte. Liberalism was acceptable if it would work; if it would not, then one should resort to an elitist dictatorship or an absolutism that was neither aristocratic nor divine right.

Although the Progressives' Constitution of 1837 was a surprisingly moderate compromise between the documents of 1812 and 1834, Donoso wrote a pamphlet to express his opposition to its spirit of parliamentarism because its principles seemed unsuitable for a normal state of society. Fearing that a doctrinaire threefold division of power favoring the Cortes would end in governmental anarchy, he followed Bonald by calling for an authoritarian 'unity of Power' under the Crown, but he accepted the usual bourgeois guarantees of free press, responsible government, and concession of power in voting and

[30] Federico Suárez Verdeguer, *Introducción a Donoso Cortés*, p. 66.

[31] Valverde, II, 38. Juretschke, I, 335–37; 334, 342–45, 352; 365. Schramm, *Vida y pensamiento*, p. 104.

public office to the middle class as a new ruling class. He conceded bourgeois sovereignty of intelligence only as the supremacy of a service class in Bonald's sense, definitely not as an institutional supremacy, which he wanted vested not in parliament but in the Crown, to defend Isabel's throne against "bloody democracy" in the future. Of course, he could not persuade either the Cortes or other moderates to accept his main principle of 'unity of Power', and nobody grasped the subtlety of his distinction between crisis and normalcy or between institutional and class sovereignty. Not until this constitution broke down over an unworkable separation of powers in 1840 did he appear vindicated. In the meantime, trusting that the political revolution was now over, and hoping for reconstruction, but still fearing that social revolution might follow, he prepared to live with parliamentary sovereignty during the era of transition.[32]

In the first general elections under the new constitution, two new political parties competed: the Progressives (*Progresistas*), which included the old radicals (*exaltados y doceañistas*), and the Moderates (*Moderados*), in which old and new moderates joined with conservative Isabellines as Constitutional Monarchists. The Mutiny of La Granja had completed a split among liberals that had been growing ever since 1834–1835. Adhering to the Moderates, Donoso described it as a "mesocratic" (middle-class) constitutional party, situated between reactionary Carlists and democratic radicals, and Pastor Díaz defined it as a liberal–conservative party, intent on ending the revolution and beginning reconstruction. The two new parties compare best not to British Whig–Liberals and Tory–Conservatives but to Guizot's so-called party of resistance (or order) and Thiers's party of movement, with the Carlists akin to the ultras. Agreeing on basic liberal rights and freedoms, they nevertheless found it difficult to cooperate in a party system of government because of different philosophies and objectives.

[32] Juretschke, I, 338ff; 352ff; 365, 367; 370, 377. Donoso in *El porvenir*, quoted by Gómez Aparicio, *Historia*, I, 238.

Inheriting the old empirical outlook, the Progressives inclined more to democracy and to revolution and were more parliamentarian, anticlerical, and Anglophile than the Moderates, whose doctrinairism and eclecticism made them more antirevolutionary and more bourgeois, clerical, and Francophile. Where Progressives preferred Thiers's English-style monarch who reigns but does not rule, Moderates allowed the queen a little more power, as in the July Monarchy. Exaggerating these differences, Donoso charged that the Progressives were friends of permanent revolution, obliged to realize in practice all the evils of their radical doctrines.[33] Not really trusting the opposition as loyal, both parties were too ready to resort to *pronunciamientos* and coups, rebellions and juntas, military force and dictatorship instead of parliamentary debates and votes to settle their differences. After a few years, coup followed coup, General Narváez after General Espartero, moderate dictator after radical dictator.

Setting up a newspaper, *El Porvenir* (*The Future*), to attack the Progressives and to propagandize his views as those of the Moderates, Donoso ran as candidate for parliament again in 1837 and won. In "Humbling Comparisons" he linked the progressive doctrinaire–liberal ideas of the Moderates to the magnificent July Revolution and the old antidemocratic dogmas of the Progressives with the wretched Mutiny of La Granja. With the slogan "Religion, Liberty, and Intelligence," he proposed for his party a social program for reconstruction, peace, and harmony: "Our Program or death."[34] When the Moderates were victorious, he triumphantly compared himself on the front page to a matador taking a bow after dispatching a dangerous bull,[35] the Progressive cabinet and government, and took his seat from Cádiz in the Cortes alongside his friends Pacheco and Bravo Murillo.

[33] Juretschke, II, 236; I, 73, 370f, 378, 663. Pastor Díaz, *A la corte y a los partidos* (Madrid, 1846), pp. 42, 45.

[34] Juretschke, I, 370f; 375ff.

[35] Pastor Díaz, *Galería*, VI, 253. Gómez Aparicio, *Historia*, I, 247–38, on *El Porvenir*; his helpers were Bravo Murillo and Zorilla.

Like his friends, Donoso eventually led his own small parliamentary faction, but in 1837–1838 he was too young, conceited, ambitious, and inexperienced to fill a very significant role. His acutely embarrassing maiden speech flopped so very much like Disraeli's. Oh, to shine like Demosthenes, Cicero, or Mirabeau, to be worshipped as a genius in parliament for the divine power, magic, and eloquence of his purpled words.[36] After warming up earlier with a few words on dictatorship in times of lawless crisis, he tried to deliver his first speech on March 31, 1838. Although the business of the day was commonplace economics, he began pompously to cite from Mirabeau and stridently to invoke Providence on behalf of the government.[37] As Cánovas del Castillo recalled it, his straining for grand effects, his violent attitudes, the disharmony of his voice, the very originality of his paradoxical and exalted ideas fitted so ill with the situation that the whole chamber joined to drown out his voice in laughter and clapping.[38] It was not until he had practiced for almost a decade, found a more appropriate time and topic, and learned to modulate his voice and abandon theatricals that he became a great speaker.

If he could not yet be a notable orator and statesman in parliament, Donoso decided, he would continue to play the positive political, historical, and social philosopher or publicist of his party in the Moderate press. Most notable was his work on *Correo Nacional* for Andrés Borrego, who was promoting a social program, apparently based on Saint-Simonism, that challenged both Moderates and Progressives.[39] By its terminology, ideas, and positions, "Critical Opinion on the Doctrinaires"

[36] Juretschke, II, 645–46.

[37] Schramm, *Vida y pensamiento*, pp. 120–21. Tejado, I, xli, xliii.

[38] Cánovas del Castillo, *Problemas contemporáneos*, II, 175–77.

[39] See Rodrigo Fernández Carvajal, "Las Constantes de Donoso Cortés," *Revista de Estudios Políticos*, 95 (1957), 84, 87–88, on Borrego as a Saint-Simonian. Although Gómez Aparicio (I, 216), does not ascribe a Saint-Simonian character to *Correo Nacional*, he does say that under Borrego it stood for a religious, political, and social "reformism," especially for Catholicism, monarchy, and improvement of the lot of the working classes and peasants.

(1838) was the most clearly Saint-Simonian or positivist of all Donoso's political writings. It anticipates almost identical views on the doctrinaires expressed by Comte in *Social Physics* in 1842, and it forecasts his own objectives up to 1848.[40] Eclectic methods of critical analysis and tolerant compromise, he admitted, were admirably suited for an unsettled era of transition, such as existed in France from 1830 to 1836 or even yet in Spain, but, he insisted, they become impotent for a normal era of stability and progress, when social reorganization requires a more 'dogmatic', 'complete', and 'synthetic' philosophy and politics.[41] If he did not yet break with the eclectic ideas of Guizot and Cousin, it was only because Spain's crisis had given way to a transitional era, but already he had begun to prepare for normalcy.

In articles on "The Absolute Monarchy" and "Spain Since 1835," Donoso elaborated a positive program or formula of regeneration, which he believed his country would need in order to get through the era of transition and into future normalcy: a dogmatic and nationalistic symbol of 'monarchy, Church, and people', combined with the newer European liberalism.[42] Carlists and Progressives therefore were not as wrong as they were incomplete in their monarchic–absolutist and democratic principles, which went back to the very origins of Spain. Historically the monarchy had always been the one institution that best embodied all of these essential elements of Spanish society, monarchism, religion, and democracy, and the consti-

40 Compare with Auguste Comte, *The Positive Philosophy . . .*, trans. Harriet Martineau (New York and Chicago, n.d.), pp. 42, 408–10, 416–20, especially pp. 418–20, 426, 437 on the "Stationary School," that is, eclectic doctrinairism. On Cousin and Comte, see Jean La Croix, *La Sociologie d'Auguste Comte*, 2d ed. (Paris, 1961), pp. 3–5; W.M. Simon, "Two Cultures in Nineteenth-Century France: Victor Cousin and Auguste Comte," *Journal of the History of Ideas*, 24 (January–March, 1965), 45–58, on notable "spiritualistic" similarities.

41 Juretschke, I, 415ff.

42 Juretschke, I, 502, 526ff. See Richard Herr, *The Eighteenth-Century Revolution in Spain* (Princeton and New York, 1958), p. 443, for a similar slogan of 1808–1812: "Religion, King and Country."

tutional monarchy must also satisfy all of these indestructible interests if it were going to capture the popular mind and survive as a permanent form of government.[43] This formula of Spanish nationalism aroused little interest among Moderates, however, until he restated it seven years later; they accepted neither a unitary idea of monarchy nor democracy.

The grave weakness of the constitutional monarchy in the face of civil war with the Carlists and threatened revolt by the radicals, made Donoso look abroad for allies once more in 1838–1839 in a review of "Diplomatic Relations between Spain and France" and "The Eastern Question." Recognizing that the Quadruple Alliance of 1834 had remained a dead letter because of the triumph of material and territorial interests over ideological and political principles in European diplomacy, he again called on France as the historic, political, cultural, and religious leader of Latin Europe to assist Spain now in the name of unselfish idealism. In gratitude Spain would line up behind France's bourgeois–liberal and Roman Catholic system against Russia's absolutist and Orthodox system, if it should come to an armed contest for world domination, a war that might regenerate both East and West, in whose age-old struggle he saw an ineluctable movement toward world unity. Soon despairing of the prudent July Monarchy, however, he thought that commercial and industrial Britain might challenge Russia's bid for world mastery, as her star rose above the sinking crescent of Islam.[44]

As the Spanish Civil War died away during 1838 with neither foreign intervention nor world war, a new internal crisis arose from the revolutionary spirit of radicals in the provinces, Madrid, and the army through 1838 and 1840. Appointed in February of 1838 to a committee to draft a law on the "state of siege," Donoso argued for local military dictatorship to defend

[43] Juretschke, I, 320, 473; 481ff. On the meaning of *formula* as *dogma*, see I, 469, 472, and 478, and compare with Comte, *Positive Philosophy*, pp. 42, 408–10.

[44] Juretschke, I, 429–66 passim; 441–61; 605–13.

the security of state and society against rebellion, regardless of rights of individual liberty.[45] Next, a crisis arose in the central government over the conflicting checks and balances of Crown and Cortes over budget, taxes, and right to prorogue. Charging that radical parliamentarians were turning a weapon of last resort into a common means of obstruction in order to seize power, he insisted in the press that ministerial responsibility and general elections would check any abuse of royal prerogative.[46] Then Baldomero Espartero, captain general of Aragon, involved the army in politics with a proclamation against the Crown's decision to dissolve the Cortes for new elections. As a counsellor to María Cristina, Donoso wrote to the general in July, 1840, to urge his neutrality in politics and to ask that he disavow his vile flatterers and cooperate loyally in support of the elections, the new Cortes, the Crown, and the constitution to consolidate peace, liberty, and order.[47] Otherwise, he warned, his illegal intervention would force the cabinet to resign and drastically set back "the pacification of this unfortunate nation." Elections were held, and Donoso returned to the Cortes as well as to the Ministry of Justice, but only briefly.[48] "The mutiny of July in Barcelona," he said, "was turned into the revolution of September in Madrid."[49] Sensing revolution, he left for France, ostensibly for reasons of health, before the outbreak.[50]

Espartero and the September Revolution. The September revolution of 1840 was a *pronunciamiento* in Madrid, which brought General Espartero and the Progressives to power after

[45] Paper in Donoso Cortés family archives. Juretschke, I, 627ff.

[46] Juretschke, I, 649ff, 662f.

[47] A copy of an unpublished letter (undated and unsigned) is in the Donoso Cortés family archives; it was on July 1 that Pérez de Castro dissolved the Cortes and called for the new elections.

[48] Santiago Galindo Herrero, *Donoso Cortés y su theoría política*, pp. 77, 86.

[49] Juretschke, I, 691.

[50] Tejado, I, liv. Gabriel García y Tassara explains Donoso's absence from Spain as being a "victim of a political ostracism," *Poesías*, p. 364.

the Moderate government had sought to revoke the Basque *fueros* and to take control of local authorities by a new municipal law. Moderate leaders went into exile, followed by María Cristina who resigned as Regent in October and left Isabel behind. Sensing outrage to the Crown, Donoso joined María Cristina to serve her loyally and to oppose Espartero's regime throughout its three years. He edited her manifesto of November, to which the new government replied by rejecting the queen's guardianship council of which Donoso was a member.[51] In May, 1841, he returned to Madrid as her accredited agent to treat with Espartero, but no agreement was reached because she refused to resign the disputed guardianship.[52] After the general resolved upon an open debate of that issue in the Cortes, Donoso schemed and manoeuvred in vain to block it, then to hoodwink the queen mother's many bitter enemies such as González Bravo, and to rally support among Moderates such as Carrasco. Carrying out his special charge to defend her in the Moderate press,[53] he claimed to uphold "the almost deserted standard of monarchic and conservative principles," as he called upon the Cortes to halt before "the last traces of a dwindling monarchy entirely vanish."[54] His mission to Madrid failed. He returned to Paris just in time to avoid becoming involved in a bloody military attempt to abduct Isabel and her sister.[55] A different plot that he joined in Paris, a secret military cabal to overthrow Espartero, was also abortive.[56]

59 See Juretschke, I, 700f.

52 For the story of his personal activities as María Cristina's agent, see Valverde, I, 743–94—a correspondence never before published.

53 Tejado, I, lvi; Juretschke, I, 691 (note). Valverde has doubts about what Donoso actually wrote and published in *Correo Nacional* (I, 795, note), but (if not in the same form as in Juretschke, I, 665–90) compare this with Donoso's statements: Valverde, I, 752, 761, 792, and 822.

54 Juretschke, I, 671ff.

55 Schramm, *Vida y pensamiento*, p. 129; Tejado, I, lvii.

56 Papers relating to a secret military order (1840–1843), with oath, ceremony, and minutes are in the Donoso Cortés family archives. The nature of the documents suggests that Donoso was indeed a member, contrary to Schramm.

As a last resort to preserve the power of the monarchy and to end his exile, Donoso turned to private diplomacy. In negotiations with Guizot in November of 1842 to arrange a marriage for Isabel, Donoso included a proposal that the great powers intervene to terminate Espartero's regency and to declare Isabel of age to rule in a strong consultative monarchy with a liberal charter and a new concordat. A year later in another interview, Guizot asked him to promise to keep representative government in Spain. In a disconcertingly direct answer, Donoso declared that he was an absolutist because he was persuaded that representative government was a calamity for Spain, that it was at best a necessary evil.[57] Nevertheless, neither he nor the liberal Moderates would try to overthrow those institutions. Guizot was satisfied but initiated no action against Espartero.

Very depressed over the future of his country, Donoso decided in 1843 to write a historical vindication of the queen mother and his party, a *History of the Regency of María Cristina*, which was a very partisan indictment of both Carlists and radicals. The triumph of darkness, error, and anarchy in Spain, he said, had almost destroyed his faith in progress, but he still hoped that truth would finally win out.[58] Before he had finished the introductory chapters, however, Espartero had fallen in a coup by Generals Prim and Narváez in August, 1843, after many of his Progressives had become disaffected.

Returning to Spain and to the parliament, Donoso advocated on November 7 that the Cortes simply declare Isabella II of legal age to rule. This solution was the one most likely to soothe the divided nation, since the queen was a symbol of national unity. "She is a child of 13 years, yes; but she is something else besides; she is an institution 14 centuries old." His justification for dispensing with the constitution was that restoring order to society was more important than maintaining existing laws. Laws, he said, were made for society, not society

[57] Valverde, I, 930–31; II, 38.
[58] Juretschke, I, 810–11.

for laws. After he had advised the deputies to follow the tradition and custom of their forefathers, they did in fact suspend the law to let Isabel begin her reign. Some accused Donoso of casuistry and inconsistency, however, for having earlier insisted on adhering to the letter of the law in María Cristina's case.[59] Actually, Isabel was too young and too inexperienced to govern, and Donoso knew very well that María Cristina or Narváez would actually rule while Donoso would advise, all from "behind the curtain," as he put it.

The Rise of Narváez and Dictatorship. As an influential courtier, Donoso conferred often in María Cristina's behalf with rival political leaders in 1844 concerning the form and composition of the government and the program of reforms he had discussed with Guizot in 1843. He continued this function until premier Gonzáles Bravo had been eased out and General Narváez had risen to power and had committed himself to an authoritarian reform of the constitution and new concordat. Neither Donoso nor María Cristina had any reason to endorse or trust González Bravo, since the ex-radical had viciously attacked them in *El Guirigay* in 1839, but they were better able to control his actions and feared his desertion to the Progressives less than they dreaded Narváez "the tiger" as a potential new Espartero and dictator. Since general and premier disliked each other, they could play one against the other and exploit divisions in the weak coalition cabinet. As minister of finance (*ministro de hacienda*), Donoso's brother-in-law Juan Carrasco was a useful informer, but he refused their requests to regulate the *Bolsa* (stock exchange), where manipulations were enriching some politicians and damaging the Court's reputation, or to halt the very profitable sale of clerical properties for the sole purpose of getting a new concordat from Rome.[60]

[59] Juretschke, I, 909f; 911, 671.

[60] See Valverde, I, 748 and II, 41–73, especially 46–48, 50–51. Valverde is the only source (Donoso's diaries) for the events related below: II, 44–49, 50f, 57–58.

Instead, he reminded María Cristina what Charles X's sad fate had owed to clericalism.

Because of the unsettled conditions in Catalonia and other provinces, Donoso argued to the premier, the queen, and the French ambassador that the only way to avert anarchy was to continue to use martial law and dictatorship under state of exception in these localities, instead of immediately returning to the regular play of institutions. He warned María Christina that the revolution was "rising to a head," and that it had to be prevented "at all costs," because it would attack the throne and dynasty. A change of ministry, he thought, would not be as effective as reforming the Constitution of 1837, especially by abolishing the unruly local *milicias* of the National Guard.[61]

While a crisis developed at Madrid because of the weakness of the cabinet and the ambitions of Narváez, Donoso tried to put off the general, while urging González Bravo to undertake reforms. Knowing that Narváez's supporters were booming him, he advised María Cristina on April 19 that the crisis was such that they could not maintain the status quo any longer but that to change the ministry was also serious and dangerous. A purely Moderate cabinet would ruin the monarchy within a month by provoking either revolution or military coup, but a Narváez ministry, although it was the only one possible and even inevitable, should be avoided except as a last resort, as avoiding Scylla only to fall into Charybdis. Accordingly they agreed to urge González Bravo to abandon his current policies and to proceed with reforms of the *Bolsa*, the anticlerical laws, and the constitution. When Bravo asked if fear of Narváez had prompted this pressure, Donoso pretended to the premier that all of Narváez's power rested in his principles. Because it was only Narváez's person that was objectionable, why not implement the reforms and thus rob the general of his banner and principles? González Bravo then answered that he was ready to reform the constitution in the most monarchic sense and to do

[61] Valverde, II, 44, 46–47.

all that was wanted of him in regard to clergy and provinces but not to proclaim absolutism. Narváez, he warned, was moving toward dictatorship as commander of the garrison at Madrid, where his threats made it almost impossible to govern. Although ready to resign meekly the next day, he decided instead to reform his cabinet. Only then did Carrasco agree to regulate the *Bolsa* and to suspend sale of some church lands, but he warned María Cristina at a full cabinet meeting that with Narváez opposed, no ministry could survive.[62] This confession of impotence brought the crisis to a head and prepared the way for Narváez to take over as President of the Council of Ministers on May 3, 1844.

Even now Donoso did not support Narváez, neither his person nor his principles, for he would always doubt that he had any. When María Cristina had supposed that with Narváez they might get a cabinet of quality, made up of independent persons with opinions of their own, he had replied that Narváez would never endure any kind of opposition from his colleagues. But that might be an advantage because the general would be charged with "responsibility . . . as great as his power," and he could not blame others for failure. Bravo Murillo and Mon favored appointing Donoso to the Ministry of State, although he demurred and instead recommended Bravo Murillo for the Ministry of Justice.[63] Narváez wanted neither of them, however, and he met all feelers with a peculiar reluctance to take charge. Deciding that he would be far more dangerous as commander of the army about to escort the queens to Barcelona than in power as premier, Donoso pressed María Cristina to appoint him. "I told her majesty that things could not continue this way, . . . that the Ministry utterly lacked prestige and could neither govern nor sustain itself any longer."[64] Because a long, hot summer of revolutionary fevers lay

[62] Valverde, II, 51; 53–60 passim.

[63] Valverde, II, 52, 60, 62; 54, 66ff, Gómez Aparicio, *Historia*, I, 317, confuses Viluma with Donoso, but they were of similar mind and "system" (Valverde, II, 67).

[64] Valverde, II, 59; 57, 60.

ahead, "it was necessary to organize a determined ministry, and no one was determined except General Narváez." Reluctantly the queen agreed. Against his own inclination too, he helped to put into power the general who was to dominate Spanish politics off and on for the next decade as a notorious liberal dictator.

Thoroughly convinced of the necessity of authoritarian reforms of the constitution, Donoso now began to connive with María Cristina, Premier Narváez, and Viluma (at State) for a coup d'état to impose them from above by decree and force rather than try to proceed through a liberal parliament. Suspecting that Narváez had some scheme of absolutism in reserve, he learned from him at a dinner in Madrid that his system for reform was tantamount to a coup and that he would dispose of any revolutionary resistance by mass arrests and exiles. Whereas ministers Mon and Pidal wanted to reform the constitution only through the Cortes, Narváez preferred carrying it out alone and, if the Cortes disagreed, to proclaim the queen absolute. "I told him that that was my system," wrote Donoso, "and that he could count on me." María Cristina also liked this plan, provided that it did not compromise her with the Spanish liberals and with the French. Donoso therefore urged her to get out of the country but to stay beyond reach of Louis Philippe, who incidentally also told her to leave Spain. The queen mother also required that the cabinet unanimously agree to the coup and that she get all of the desired reforms, but Donoso, using Viluma to sound out his colleagues, could not produce the unanimity or the resignations, not even when the whole cabinet was called to join the Court at Barcelona, where he and Narváez could bring pressure on them. In vain Donoso tried to persuade Mon and Pidal to work with Narváez and Viluma for reforms by decree to avoid a dangerous crisis and thus to assure the salvation of the state from revolution. On the contrary, they charged that Viluma's scheme would lead to Carlism and Narváez's to his own dictatorship. Mayans warned that if Mon resigned the whole Moderate party would follow him, although it was uncertain that the Cortes would agree to Mon's scheme that it reform the constitution. When rumor of the coup then leaked out to a hostile Moderate press and Progressive leaders began consulting, María Cristina backed away from Narváez's system of firmness, which she could get only by openly committing herself before the whole cabinet. Consequently, Viluma resigned on June 2, but Narváez remained and convoked the Cortes for July 4. Since it was not constituent, it was left for Donoso to argue later that "the constituent power resides only in the constituted power"—in "the Cortes with the King"—as a traditional Spanish doctrine.[65]

When Narváez's government introduced the project of constitutional reform before the Cortes, Donoso emerged as the leading expert and secretary of the committee on reform. Contrary to his friends, the puritans Pacheco and Pastor Díaz who thought the plan inopportune, he called for a bold course of reform. Now, at this moment of repose after civil war and revolutionary anarchy, was the most opportune season and circumstance to remove from the constitution those anarchic maxims that contradicted the principles of social order, so as to establish the permanent tranquility of the state against future revolutions.[66] Historians have recognized him as the soul of the committee and the brain of the project, even as Jaime Balmes did then.[67] Casting the opinion in the now-familiar style of *juste-milieu* doctrinairism, he proposed changes which reflected his previous criticism of the Constitution of 1837; if the Cortes remained more or less supreme, the Senate was deprived of its outdated hereditary character and put under the ultimate control of the Crown; the bourgeois National Guard

[65] Valverde, II, 63–64, 65; 66, 67; 69–71, 72–73. Juretschke, II, 4.

[66] Galindo Herrero, *Theoría Política*, p. 86ff. Gómez Aparicio, *Historia*, I, 317, claims that Donoso wanted something closer to the *Estatuto Real*. Juretschke, II, 4–7, 32.

[67] Valverde, II, 76 (ed. note). Díez del Corral, *El liberalismo doctrinario*, p. 51; Jerónimo Becker, *La reforma constitucional en España* (Madrid, 1923), p. 105ff.

and the independence of municipalities were abolished as sources of revolutionary coups and juntas; and the press, deprived of the guarantee of jury trial, was left exposed to official controls in the future. Unable to persuade the committee to replace the weak doctrinaire division of power with his own concept of unity of power in the monarch, he had to be content with a consensus of powers in "the Cortes with the King."[68] Remarkably durable, Donoso's Constitution of 1845 was overthrown by *pronunciamiento* and revolution in 1854 and 1868, but it was restored after 1856 and revised after 1876; it lasted until 1931. Not until Franco's Organic Law of 1967, however, was Donoso's principle of unity of power explicitly adopted.

Besides reforming the constitution, Narváez's Moderates also wanted to modify the relationship of Church and State and to seek a new concordat. Dissatisfied with their bill of temporary endowment for 1845 as recompense for the earlier nationalization of Church property in 1836 and 1837, Donoso (in a speech on "Cult and Clergy") proposed that it was the opportune time for a definitive law of 'mutual independence' of the temporal and spiritual powers.[69] His proposal was an eclectic formula that fell between the old royalist and the new revolutionary solutions; it was comparable to the American doctrine of separation or to Montalembert's liberal–Catholic idea of free Church in a free State, but its terms were closer to Guizot's description of the historic relationship of the two powers and closest of all to Saint-Simon's and especially Comte's positive maxim that the spiritual power should be independent of the temporal, that each of them should be sovereign in its own department.[70] Although he condemned the radicals for their

[68] Juretschke, II, 12–17ff; 29–31. See Luis Sánchez Agesta, *Historia del constitucionalismo Español* (Madrid, 1955), pp. 252–54: the formula "Cortes con el Rey" was meant to deny constituent popular sovereignty for a "historical constitution" based on king and Cortes.

[69] Juretschke, II, 25f.

[70] See Comte, *Positive Philosophy*, pp. 600–605, and J. F. P. Guizot, *Meditations and Moral Sketches*, trans. John Butler (Dublin, 1855), pp. 84–92—from an article of 1838.

sequestrations, he accepted as permanent the alienation of Church land and the abolition of tithes and mortmain. In their place the State should guarantee an independent annual income for the clergy out of public funds derived from the growing liquid wealth of modern commerce and industry.[71] Such ideas were too advanced to incorporate in the resulting law, but, when Bravo Murillo would finally conclude a concordat in 1851, the State would offer the clergy permanent bonds based on the national debt. When the government now decided to return unsold Church properties to the clergy, Donoso supported it and rationalized his new position with a parade of facile logic and clever subtleties. The liberals were amused by his reversal, but it greatly irritated Catholics such as the priest–politician Balmes. Rejecting the absurdities and sophisms both of the radical anticlericals, who would give back nothing, and of the reactionary Carlists, who demanded all, he proposed that to return the lands *sans* mortmain was not an economic question but a matter of reparations and high politics—just, convenient, prudent common sense as well as an impartial liberal and Christian compromise between ultramontanes and regalists—that would uphold both powers as independent.[72] Thereafter he always supported mutual independence of Church and State as proper for normal and civilized times.

NORMALCY: CHRISTIAN SOCIAL-DEMOCRATIC MONARCHY

While the Moderate decade (1844–1854) was being institutionalized and as stability seemed to be returning, Donoso clearly felt that the revolutionary crisis was over, that the current eclectic era of transition also would soon end, and that the coming normal epoch would require a stronger government and a new positive political doctrine for Spain. Without

[71] Juretschke, II, 28–29. On the effect of Donoso's speech, see Angel Salcedo y Ruíz, *Historia de España* (Madrid, 1914), p. 696.

[72] This speech has been published for the first time in Valverde, II, 106–20; see especially 106–111.

a comprehensive nationalistic program to win the people and nation as a whole, not even Narváez's military power would be enough to sustain the Moderates long in office. To serve such a program, he offered his formula of 1838, expressed now as 'Catholicism, monarchy, democracy, and liberalism', and presented it as Spain's 'political trinity' and 'complete Spanish truth'. Much as Disraeli then advocated Tory democracy, Donoso was proposing by his formula a kind of social democracy but under the leadership of the bourgeoisie instead of the moribund aristocracy. Already he had slipped into the preliminary draft of the Constitution of 1845, a declaration contrary to the prevailing laissez-faire spirit: He asserted that the masses of the poor had an indisputable right to expect the middle-class government to relieve its sufferings and to extend a helping hand in the name of the brotherhood among Spaniards. He defined the term *democratic* as the government's obligation to give the working classes a moral, religious, and substantive education, to guarantee their right to "bread" and a fair share of all social benefits, and finally to grant them a complete participation in all local and material interests but not in national political power. If Jaime Balmes thought that Donoso's analysis of the component elements and principles of the Spanish nation was an excellent caricature, reactionaries deemed it revolutionary just to use the word *democracy*.[73] No one perceived that he was finally about to abandon eclecticism and doctrinairism for a dogmatic politics of normalcy which was basically Saint-Simonian or positivist or that he was now borrowing also from the liberal and social Catholicism of France.

In March of 1847 Donoso openly stated the dynamics of his positive politics of crisis, transition, and normalcy, when he predicted an epoch of normalcy and of domestic stability for Spain and a general war or diplomatic congress for Europe in the near future. His presentiment of a major denouement in

[73] Juretschke, II, 17–22, 30–31, 32–33; 11; 33. Jaime Balmes, *Obras completas*, ed. Casanovas, XXXVII, as cited by Juretschke, II, 22; also see II, 29–30.

national and international affairs caused him to shape his thought and activity to meet the expected changes. He said he deeply sensed that the postrevolutionary era of transition, the period when anarchy and order or governmental power and popular revolution were in a balance, was about to end in Spain and would be followed by a normal epoch. During this epoch a strong nationalistic government could carry a united society with it. As a European phenomenon, the era of transition since 1830 in which the reactionary system of Metternich and Nicholas I was balanced by liberalism and nationalism, or intervention by self-determination, also would soon terminate with either a general war or a diplomatic congress. Given his perspective of 1838 on eclectic doctrinairism, he meant that this policy of weak transitional liberalism no longer suited either the foreign or domestic affairs of the times. Neither Guizot's pacifism and international balance of powers nor by his parliamentarism with its constitutional balance and separation of powers was adequate. Donoso's own system of positive politics for normalcy, however, was not yet complete or ready. What content should he finally give his national symbol of 'Catholicism, monarchy, democracy and liberalism' to serve a synthetic and creative purpose in an era of normalcy? What turn should national self-determination take in diplomacy? In both its internal and external dimensions, nationalism was a large part of the policy of strength that he had been urging for two years past. A government could unify a divided society, and a party could attain truly national dimensions by adopting a symbol on which all minds could unite, one that comprised all of the elements constituting Spanish and European civilization. Leaving until later the full elaboration of his symbol into a new dogmatic political theory of Christian liberal and social-democratic monarchy, he addressed himself to Spanish nationalism, or *españolismo*, first, as one aspect of the democratic factor particularly in foreign policy.[74]

[74] Juretschke, II, 60; 76; 21f, 31.

Nationalism and the Spanish Marriages. Although Donoso was more nationalistic than either Saint-Simon or Comte, he was much more moderate than the later 'integral' nationalist and positivist, Charles Maurras; he never lost sight of the greater European society and order. *His españolismo* was still a restrained liberal nationalism, which admitted some international responsibility to balance the rights of nations. When González Bravo defined nationalism as an *unlimited* right of national will and inviolability, he denounced this as a "monstrous" confusion of "right and might." Having sympathized with the oppressed nationalities of the great European empires, with "green Ireland" and Poland, "that Ireland of the Slavic peoples," he promoted Spanish nationalism in the affair of "the Spanish marriages" in 1846–1847 and espoused the cause of Italian unity and freedom under papal leadership in 1847. He hoped that this nationalism would be a liberal–conservative and even Christian force, but he was wary of its revolutionary past and potential extremism, as in the French revolution when foreigner meant the same thing as enemy and when the French tried to enslave all other nations.[75] When the European revolutions broke out in 1848–1849, he was frightened by the demagogic revolutionary force of what he called Germanism and Mazzinian and Hungarian nationalism, in which he foresaw the renewed xenophobic nationalism that arose after 1870.

How a popular war could unite a people around their government was a historical phenomenon which Donoso understood well.[76] The Spanish marriages of 1846 also alerted him to the national solidarity, particularly in respect to Portugal and Africa, that could be aroused against the great powers of England and France in a smaller nation if it adopted an independent foreign policy of nationalistic self-assertion. If he had favored French hegemony in the era of crisis and weakness,

[75] Juretschke, I, 707; 753ff; II, 85, 100.
[76] Juretschke, II, 18.

now he wanted Spain to stand firmly on her own feet in preparation for an epoch of normalcy. As it turned out, however, the Spanish marriages won for Spain only the enmity of Britain, which more than offset the brief favor of a decrepit July Monarchy. The course of events also produced serious crises for the Spanish Court, cabinet, nation, and even for Donoso himself, who, in trying to place the interests of nation and monarchy above the personal passions of queen and queen mother, was forced to break with the monarchy temporarily.

Donoso's private diplomatic role in the Spanish marriages was much greater than either recent or contemporary accounts suggest. As María Cristina's principal agent—her "confidential intermediary" Guizot called him—with both France and England, he assumed roles with varying degrees of importance throughout the negotiations.[77] In Paris in 1842 he had started the whole affair by suggesting María Cristina's younger brother, Trapani, as consort for Isabel. Although later rejected as a wretched choice, was at first politically preferable over either Coburg or an Orleans both to the Moderates and to France and England at the Chateau d'Eu conference of 1843. After he had informed poor Isabel, he encountered the first snag. The interests of Spanish politics and European diplomacy clashed over María Cristina's desire to go back to Madrid; both Bulwer for England and Guizot for France feared that if she returned to Spain, she might proceed so hastily with the Trapani match as to upset their plans or their new *entente cordiale*. In December of 1843 Donoso argued with both Louis Philippe and Guizot that without her presence the Spanish revolutionaries would oust the conservatives. For prudence, the king lamely consented. Guizot, however, imposed three conditions: Trapani would be Isabel's con-

[77] The French ambassador, Bresson, described him so to Guizot: F. P. G. Guizot, *Mémoires pour servir á l'histoire de mon temps*, VIII (Paris, 1867), 320. Also see E. Jones Parry, *The Spanish Marriages, 1841–1846* (London, 1936), p. 231.

sort; there would be no European imbroglio; and representative government would be retained in Spain. With these stipulations, he was ready to give any aid short of breaking with all the rest of Europe. In Madrid Donoso encountered ever greater obstacles to Trapani, however. Premier González Bravo, who called it a French intrigue and another family compact, protested that Spaniards despised Neapolitans and that Trapani was a student of the detested Jesuits. During the crises within the cabinet of 1844, while neither Court nor ministers could decide whether to meet Trapani at Barcelona, Spanish public opinion turned so strongly against him that Donoso defended María Cristina's vacillation to Bresson and Carini, the French and Neapolitan envoys who wanted to conclude the match while Bulwer now opposed it.[78] She wanted a marriage that would be good both for her daughter and for the nation, which was then still so unsettled that Narváez regarded the Trapani proposal as madness.

A year later, in July of 1845, Donoso had returned to Paris to confer with Guizot and Louis Philippe on possible candidates. He agreed that the Carlist Montemolin was then as impossible as the return of the *ancien régime*, but Trapani, whom Guizot still wanted as an immediate solution, would be impossible at any time because nobody wanted him. Thereupon, Guizot conceded that Spain might select whomever were least unsuitable, so long as he were a Bourbon and did not set the great powers at odds. Surely Donoso knew how serious Anglo-French enmity would be for Spain. "*Vous faites de l'histoire, M. Guizot.*" Dining with Louis Philippe at Neuilly that night, Donoso thought an Orleanist was just what Spain needed. That family he found enchanting: "The queen seems a saint; the king, the best of fathers." Louis Philippe was very pleased when he proposed an immediate match between one of his sons and Isabel, but he demurred for fear that the French

[78] Juretschke, II, 37–38; Valverde, I, 920; II, 33–34; 31–38, 41, 50, 53, 58, 61, 64–65, cf. I, 931.

would accuse him of having unseemly personal and dynastic ambitions.[79]

Piqued that foreigners should dictate her own and Spain's affairs, María Cristina sent Donoso to Ambassador Bulwer at Madrid some time before November of 1845 to ask for Prince Leopold of Saxe-Coburg for Isabel. With the skill and "eloquence for which he was remarkable," Bulwer recalled, Donoso explained the unhappy position of Isabel and Spain and wanted Spain to break loose from French hegemony.[80] When he determined that the proposal was official, Bulwer eagerly proceeded in secrecy, until Aberdeen suddenly denounced the negotiations. The incident embarrassed Donoso and the Spanish Court and offended the French, who in return were disposed to break the Eu agreement, as Guizot now warned in a memorandum of February 27, 1846—although Aberdeen already deemed Britain free to follow her own interests.

Whenever María Cristina approached both the French and English courts for either an Orleanist or Coburg prince, they vetoed each other's candidate. When Aberdeen and Guizot, with Victoria and Louis Philippe, met the second time at the Chateau d'Eu in December of 1845, the same problems occurred as in 1843, except that now they limited poor Isabel's choices to either her uncle Trapani or one of two Spanish Borbón cousins, radical Enrique or effeminate Francisco—incestuous, impolitic, or repugnant alternatives. Although Guizot now wanted the Orleanist Duc de Montpensier to marry the Infanta Luisa Fernanda, he promised to wait until Isabel had an heir, so as to observe the Treaty of Utrecht's ban on dynastic union of France and Spain.[81]

With prospect of neither Coburg nor Orleans for Isabel,

[79] Valverde, II, 121–23, cf. II, 131–32.

[80] W. H. L. Earle Bulwer, *The Life of Henry John Temple, Viscount Palmerston*, III (London, 1870–1874), 220. Peter de Polnay, *Queen of Spain, Isabel II* (London, 1962), pp. 104–5. On time and circumstances, see Valverde, II, 123–25.

[81] Edmund B. d'Auvergne, *A Queen at Bay* (London, 1910), p. 264ff. See Valverde, II, 124–25.

María Cristina resolved once more on her younger brother. As Donoso now firmly opposed Trapani, he was finally obliged to break with her. "In fulfilling my duty, I had told the queen-mother that the projected marriage would probably cost her daughter her crown." Anticipating that he would express this opinion to Isabel, María Cristina forbad her to receive him as usual at the Oriente palace in January of 1846. Such an order seemed inconceivable to him, the most loyal and discreet of servants. Resolving forthwith to break with María Cristina but needing a good excuse to accuse her without compromising the young queen, he tried in vain to persuade Isabel actually to refuse to see him, but instead had to listen as she "complained for the hundredth time that her mama treated her badly" until it was too late to make the break with any graciousness. As the renewed Trapani candidature provoked an angry outburst of public opinion and a crisis of state, Donoso was unfortunately caught in the middle and, so he said, almost lost his mind trying to avert a monumental scandal.[82]

On January 18 Bravo Murillo and Gallardo asked if he would help them block that dismal marriage in the Cortes. Unable as a courtier to participate directly, he persuaded them to ask a majority of deputies quietly to sign a confidential resolution to the cabinet. Raging and cursing against the proposal in the corridors of the Cortes, Narváez actually provoked more deputies to sign. Suspicious of everybody, he grabbed Donoso to ask if he had "refused to sign only because of his relations with the palace." To Donoso's evasive response, the general then declared that he would defend the royal prerogative to the death, but not Trapani. After his cabinet had agreed to reject Trapani, Narváez promised at least to submit any such proposal to the Cortes.[83]

Finally Donoso broke with María Cristina when her husband, the Duke of Riánsares, Fernando Muñoz, crudely blustered that he was not fit to enter the palace unless he repudi-

[82] Valverde, II, 127; 128.
[83] Valverde, II, 125, 128.

ated the deputy petitioners as disloyal and dishonest. Fearing an unheard-of scandal, he replied that María Cristina had long been aware of his opposition to the match with Trapani, that the Cortes could legitimately intervene in a royal marriage, and that he hereby ended his relationship with the two of them.[84] When Donoso could have injured María Cristina by making public her impolitic love letters to Muñoz, he wrote instead a newspaper article in which he accepted blame for having initially suggested Trapani in 1842.[85] Although Trapani was, in fact, repugnant to Spaniards, he explained that there were grave difficulties with the other candidates too. Moreover, three important factors conflicted: the European balance of power, the sovereign interests of Spain, and Isabel's domestic happiness. Europe had a right to be heard, nothing more; the initiative was properly the queen's; but the nation through the Cortes rightly had an absolute veto over the final decision about a royal marriage. If this made the Crown "very heavy," a duty of self-sacrifice went with it. Through the French foreign minister, Lavergne, Donoso informed Guizot that the whole Spanish nation was so violently opposed to Trapani that it was ready to revolt.[86] While the Moderates "watch crossed-eyed," only "that great gambler," Narváez, supported a throne isolated between the fanatics of right and left. "And what is the sword of one man for the defense of a throne placed between a Restoration and a July Revolution?" Because of Trapani and the allegations about the queen's wastefulness and intrigues and her husband's deals at the *Bolsa*, María Cristina's great unpopularity was a *fait accompli*. Unable to abandon her by voting against Trapani in the Cortes or to destroy Isabel by voting for him, Donoso declared, "I abstain from all action and retire to my tent."

Six months later Donoso decisively reentered the negoti-

[84] Valverde, II, 128–29.

[85] A large bundle of these letters, signed *Baltasara*, are in the Donoso Cortés family archives. See Juretschke, II, 37–41, for the article.

[86] Valverde, II, 130–33.

ations after Britain's new foreign minister Palmerston provoked a scandalous crisis with a crude public assessment of the marriage problems. Dismissing the Moderates as advocates of arbitrary power and a reign of terror and calling for control of the Progressives, he put Coburg at the head of the list of suitors for Isabel, promoted Enrique while rejecting Francisco as neither manly nor princely, and dismissed Montpensier even for the Infanta as intolerable for English interests in Spain, Gibraltar, and North Africa, and for the *entente cordiale*. His rash insolence infuriated the Spaniards and freed Guizot to disregard the Eu accord. Nevertheless, María Cristina swallowed her pride and tried again for a compromise by seeking Coburg for Isabel and Montpensier for the Infanta Fernanda. Once more Donoso handled negotiations, but with the English alone, since Guizot was now working through Mon. Donoso was not very enthusiastic about María Cristina's attempt to bind both great powers in friendly dynastic ties with Spain, but he and Bulwer sent the new proposal to Palmerston in London. When no definite answer had come within a week (August 15), Donoso correctly determined that Palmerston was either rejecting the offer or refusing to change British policy, which Donoso distrusted as prorevolutionary.[87]

Weary of the whole business, Donoso now urged the Court to go in precisely the opposite direction: to forget England and line up with France alone. Since no combination of Coburg and Montpensier could please either or both powers, Spain must resolve to be a friend of one and an enemy of the other. He frankly advised María Cristina to decide for France, because "England will always more or less protect the revolutionary interests here" and in Portugal, whereas France naturally inclined "to uphold the conservative and monarchic interests here." With Montpensier to marry the Infanta, whom could Isabel marry?—either Trapani or Francisco. If she chose Trapani, let her call Narváez and play all her stakes, but Donoso

[87] Bulwer, *Palmerston*, III, 258–63, 266–67; 270–71, 278–81. Valverde, II, 140–42.

wanted a month's headstart to run away as far as Saint Petersburg. Better that she pick Francisco. The Cortes and the nation would accept him, and she could overcome the great repugnance of "the little queen." Professing to speak with heart in hand as a good Spaniard for the nation's interests, he urged her to delay no longer but to decide now for the French solution. During his next communications with Bulwer, he heard that Britain would "spare nothing to bring about a complete overthrow in Spain." Alarmed but angry, the Court and cabinet decided for France and ordered Donoso to break off all political relations with Bulwer at once.[88]

Palmerston and Bulwer did not give up easily. Learning on August 25 that the "absolute and absolutist fool" Francisco would marry Isabel, Palmerston ordered that Montpensier be blocked from marrying the Infanta. The Spanish marriages, Bulwer now argued to Donoso, were not a purely Spanish matter; for by involving France, the Orleans dynasty, and previous international agreements, they had become a very serious affair for all of Europe. Let him not count on any French alliance; at least counsel delay. When Spain officially announced on August 26 that the two weddings would be celebrated together in Madrid on October 10, Palmerston furiously repudiated the *entente cordiale*, declaimed against violation of the Treaty of Utrecht, and instructed Bulwer to "agitate, agitate, agitate" to get the Cortes to reject the marriages.[89] After the cabinet had persuaded the Cortes, however, Donoso rose to calm Pastor Díaz's fears of dangerous foreign complications, especially with mighty Britain. On September 17, he argued that Spain's independent action rested upon the new liberal nationalist principles of national inviolability and nonintervention, whereas the Treaty of Utrecht reflected the outworn balance-of-power diplomacy.[90] Palmerston soon had to accept

[88] Valverde, II, 140–44. Guizot, *Mémoires*, pp. 319–20.

[89] Bulwer, *Palmerston*, III, 282–84. Letter of Bulwer to Donoso (August 31, 1846) in the Donoso Cortés family archives.

[90] Juretschke, II, 43 (note); 47–53.

the marriages as *fait accompli,* but Donoso never forgot his truculence and threats.

In March of 1847 while Spain still seemed capable of taking initiative in foreign affairs, Donoso demanded special attention to the nation's permanent interests in the Iberian peninsula, in Africa, and in the recent marriages in opposition to both England and France. His dazzling nationalistic harangue appealing to Spanish pride and patriotism, evoked tempestuous bravos.[91] Let Spain have a genuine foreign policy, like Britain, Russia, and the United States—the only powers with such.[92] Spain must be concerned about Gibraltar, seek to end Britain's domination of Portugal, and try to forestall a French grab of all North Africa. His analysis of the French dilemma in Algeria later seemed prophetic, but his effort to show that Spain had better prospects arising from geographical, ethical, military, and religious continuity with Africa scarcely convinces.[93] If he anticipated later European imperialism, he also foresaw in part why colonialism finally collapsed. Highly civilized France, he said, represented such a cultural disparity and discontinuity with her conquered Moslems that she could not assimilate them as Russia was reputedly doing with her Asian aggregations. But to exterminate North African culture, which would barbarize the perpetrators without civilizing the victims, France would require at least fifty years of profound peace that she would not get, since any great danger in Europe would require her armies back on the Rhine. Even without renewal of British imperialism, he regarded England as more dangerous than was France, because, "if France is at our doors, England is in our house"—in Gibraltar and Portugal where she had

91 Schramm, *Vida y pensamiento,* pp. 154–55.

92 Juretschke, II, 61.

93 A pamphlet was published on Donoso and North Africa by the Instituto de Estudios Africanos in Madrid (1955): Diego Sevilla Andrés, "Donoso Cortés y la misión de España en Africa," and Manuel Fraga Iribarne, "Donoso Cortés ante la crisis de España: su visión ante el problema Africano," in *Africa en el pensamiento de Donoso Cortés.* Juretschke, II, 65–67.

broken Spain's political and moral unity. In a burst of patriotic fervor, he exclaimed, "The Spanish people . . . still keeps . . . enough manly dignity not to fall under perpetual tutelage like a Roman woman"![94] Finally, after skirting the delicate question of the queen's free consent in the question of the Spanish marriages, he denied that Palmerston or the Treaty of Utrecht could force the Infanta or the Cortes to renounce right of succession for her children. Above clamorous applause, he cried, "That will not be done . . . we shall not disinherit a daughter of our kings while there are gentlemen in the Cortes, Castilians in Castile, and Spaniards in Spain."[95] There was no heroic response to this powerful speech; the Moderate government was too weak, and Donoso knew it.

Scandal, New Crisis, and Dictatorship. International repercussions from the Spanish marriages were mild compared to the sordid domestic scandal and the crisis in the Spanish Court and government, which saddled the nation with a virtual dictator in General Narváez, just before the revolutions of 1848 plunged Europe into a general crisis of unheard-of proportions. Since poor "Paquita" (Francisco) could not satisfy Isabel's ardor, General Serrano soon emerged as her favorite and paramour. When María Cristina intervened and insulted Francisco, he angrily departed for the Pardo threatening not to return to the indifferent Isabel, unless the queen mother left Spain. She did and Donoso accompanied her to Paris. In letters from April to September of 1847 Riánsares sent Donoso spicy, caustic comments, wherein Isabel advanced from a pleasure-loving, irresponsible brat into a virago who would keep anyone under the bed.[96] Already in April the scandal was public knowledge and soon became acutely embarrassing and politically dangerous for Pacheco's Moderate government

[94] Juretschke, II, 68, 71–75.

[95] Juretschke, II, 73.

[96] These "secret" letters (perhaps 40 in packets) are in Legajo 14 in the Donoso Cortés family archives.

which had concluded and defended the unhappy marriage.

A directing junta of the Moderate party, of which Donoso was a member, tried to help Pacheco end the scandal and to reconcile the royal pair, with María Cristina as key and pawn. Selected to communicate its requests to her, he pursued his own objectives, at first by offering her private advice directly contrary to its unanimous view and later by preparing Narváez to take power again as a way to end the crisis and avert revolution. He did not want her to return without the queen's consent and thus risk embarrassment and banishment, until he could force Isabel to commit herself. Finally on July 25 he could report that when Isabel had concluded that her mother was indeed coming back, she had summoned her ministers in the middle of the night, angrily berated them, and commanded them to ban her from Spain. While the junta viewed as deplorable the mutual recriminations between mother and daughter, it admitted that the former had fulfilled both duty and decorum. Despite Donoso's fears, the summer Court at La Granja ended without catastrophe but with scandals in abundance, while his friend Pacheco faced the gravest of cabinet crises over the continued separation of Isabel and Francisco.[97]

Concluding that Pacheco could not reunite the royal couple, Donoso felt that revolution was probable unless an effective new cabinet were formed soon. Disliking the bad taste, mediocrity, or dishonesty of Mon, Carrasco, González Bravo, and Salamanca who were bidding for Pacheco's job, he decided that he preferred Narváez again to any such colorless ministry. His predictions to the general, as he steered him toward power, proved amazingly accurate, although he modestly granted that he might be half wrong on some small matter. One can only wonder at his methods, however, as he sought to make fools of them all at La Granja and the Pardo. Refusing to believe any promises given to Pacheco, he was convinced that nothing short of force would separate Serrano from Isabel, a task for

[97] Valverde, II, 182–84, 186, 188–89; 184–87; 188.

which only Narváez would serve.[98] "Serrano fears you like a nightmare," he told Narváez. He correctly advised the general that he would have to wait until after a weak transitional cabinet had come and gone (Salamanca's) before he could take over. "Power is coming to you, and it is coming straight and irresistibly, but not now." With frightful catastrophes and the unhinging of society looming, Donoso foresaw a test of force in which, he told Narváez, "You are the one in whom I place all my confidence." Later he informed María Cristina, "Narváez is getting ready" to resume power, "but he is using means of which I do not approve." Having told him to take anyone useful, even if he were hated, but never anyone despised, he now saw that Narváez was choosing colleagues who were really not decent and who would compromise him fatally and that he was assuming too fierce a manner too soon.[99] But, he reflected, a Moderate cabinet of mediocrities would soon be followed by Espartero and the Progressives, whom Isabel had already sounded out.

Almost exactly as Donoso predicted, Narváez took over again on October 4, 1847, so Spain was already ruled by a virtual dictator when the wave of revolutions struck Europe five to six months later. Donoso was not entirely surprised. He had recently feared revolution in Italy and the Austrian empire as well as in Spain, but he never anticipated so deep or general a crisis as that of 1848. There was no normalcy yet, if ever.

[98] Valverde, II, 188–89; 193. Valverde's opinion on this question (II, 195, note) appears sounder than that of Natalio Rivas, *Anecdotario histórico* (Madrid, 1960), p. 489, because he takes more account of Donoso's realism.

[99] Valverde, II, 194; 190–91.

Chapter III

INTELLECTUAL AND MAN OF THE WORLD

HEROIC YOUTH AND DANDY

The romantic era was an age of restless youth, alternately dominated by melancholy and alienation, or ambition, ostentation, and rebellion; it was also an age of youth movements, such as Mazzini's Young Italy, Heine's Young Germany, and Disraeli's Young England. Donoso and his young friends from the provinces strove to popularize both romanticism and moderation in *La Abeja* after 1834; without trying to initiate a Young Spain, they accepted the challenge of youth with enthusiasm. How appropriate for the Ateneo to turn to Donoso to seek "the new idea, the one which is bound to prevail, from a youthful brow"! He proclaimed the mission of the Spanish youth was no less than "to purge the earth of monsters," to free it from the ideas of the older generation of the eighteenth century.[1] Let society concede the brilliant role of prophets and martyrs in revolutionary times to its youth. As he neared thirty, Donoso grew more modest and wiser, however.

From a portrait at the Ateneo glares young Donoso at about the time when he had established himself as an intellectual of note at Madrid.[2] Hauteur and intelligence mark the proud face, high forehead, and bright eyes. In his twenties he possessed regular features and average good looks and effected the

[1] Juan Juretschke, ed., *Obras completas*, I, 211–12, 289.

[2] This portrait hangs in the Ateneo; also in the *Enciclopedia universal ilustrada*, Vol. 18 (Barcelona, 1884–1886) and *Diccionario enciclopédico U.T.E.H.A.*, Vol. IV (Mexico).

sartorial elegance of the dandies of the romantic era with fashionable black coat, immaculate linen, colorful cravat, and ringlets of hair, and by unmistakably superior air. Bulwer's "Pelham," that paragon of wit, good taste, and refinement, could have been his model, except that Donoso was more intellectual and more ambitious, like Disraeli's "Vivian Grey," ready to seize the world as his "oyster" and pry it open with brilliance and talent. As "a man whose character is the most unbending independence that ever was, the most absolute scorn of authority and example,"[3] he aspired to the genius genre of Byronic hero. Such arrogance bespoke a fierce pride of intellect and self-reliance, but also exaggeration. Certainly his style of life, dress, thought, and writing was not wildly romantic; for moderation's sake he became an eclectic in everything. Only toward the end of his life did he become a romantic extremist, but never in taste or dress. His dandyism was restrained, polished. He was as vain about his appearance as about his honors, decorations, and titles, the accounts of which are carefully recorded. He could afford to indulge his fancies with expensive items from Paris, such as the toupee to cover a bald spot after his mid-thirties, his fashionable walking stick of carved ivory, fine Spanish cigars, and Parisian sweets, not to mention the exquisite furnishings he later bought to refurbish the Spanish embassy in Paris. Bills from Paris tailors and good hotels suggest that he lived luxuriously when official missions took him to the French capital in the mid-1840s. A Parisian confectionery in July of 1845, for example, added up a week of daily purchases and noted at the bottom that Donoso sent his "maid" in a carriage every day to pick up his bonbons.[4]

An accomplished traveler and tourist, he became familiar with the most interesting spas, cities, and palaces. He knew the fashionable baths and beaches at Valencia, and apparently San

[3] Juretschke, I, 155f.

[4] Letters of Donoso to "Paco" (Paris, April 16, August 31, 1851). Many such bills survive in the Donoso Cortés family archives. Don Manuel Donoso Cortés and Señorita Pilar Donoso Cortés preserve the personal effects and some furnishings.

Sebastian and Biarritz, but he preferred the open surf. The quality of the water, he thought, was indifferent, compared to "the continuous pushing and pounding of the waves," for maximum relaxation and tonic.[5] As a courtier he became an habitué of Spain's numerous royal palaces, especially the Oriente, La Granja, and Aranjuez, but he also visited the Escorial and most of Spain's historic cities, not only Seville and Salamanca but Barcelona and Valencia at various times and Avila and Toledo, which he described as a gold mine for anyone artistically inclined. Burgos, Leon, and Seville, on the other hand, were musts for anyone who wanted to know Spain's grandeur and history.[6] Apparently he also visited Granada to judge from the colloquialisms which he collected from that area. Probably Donoso helped to set the fashion for all those pretentious and ambitious youths who posed as "directors" of newspapers and regularly attended the "*Hipodromo, teatro Español,* and *Drama*" often without pay, just for the sport or glory of it.[7] However, none of his critical reviews of theater, opera, or concert hall are identified, except his praise of Pacheco's melancholy Byronic hero, *Alfredo,* although he could thoroughly enjoy Shakespeare, or laugh heartily at Molière.[8] Only in his later somber moralism he could publicly oppose building Madrid's great opera house, *El Teatro de Oriente,* as a mere "monument . . . to material pleasures."

He was always a joiner, a frequenter of clubs, salons, theaters, and literary societies—even to the end when it had become a burden and a dubious pleasure. He graduated out of Quintana's literary circle at Madrid in the early 1830s to become not only a member of the Ateneo but also of the prestigious Parnasillo in the 1830s–1840s and the Liceo after 1837, with such poets and literati as Larra, Ventura de la Vega, Zorrilla, Hartzenbusch, Campoamor, and Tassara, and the art

[5] Letter of Donoso to Paco (1851).

[6] Letter of Donoso to Raczynski (June 9, 1849), in Juretschke, II, 779.

[7] Pedro Gómez Aparicio, *Historia del periodismo español* (Madrid, 1967), I, 371–72.

[8] Juretschke, I, 167ff, 753; II, 773; II, 336 (Oriente).

critic, Mesonero Romános. At social gatherings when he was not "on stage," Donoso was relaxed, very capable of the wit and raillery that is almost entirely absent from his formal writing. His friend Tassara vividly recalled in verse his playful moods on such occasions when "Donoso was argument itself:/ Champion of reason or of sophistry. . . [and] argued/ Just for the fun of it, like fools used to do."[9] In turn Tassara became virtually his poetic Boswell, casting into verse the great events and thoughts of his life, especially his prophetic historical vision. Although Donoso occasionally wrote verse for Tassara, it was not because he was a poet but because he was a special kind of critic that he was welcome in that company of poets and litterateurs. He seldom commented on individual works but on the general styles and values of the classic and the romantic schools, with a persuasive, irenic, eclectic purpose.

JOURNALIST AND PUBLICIST

Preeminently a professional intellectual after 1830, young Donoso relied on his brilliance to establish his worth, in an ambitious, restless quest for fame and position in service to crown, party, and country. He was never very interested in becoming prime minister, however, for he prized actual power less than honor and influence, particularly in matters intellectual and theoretical. Surprisingly versatile, he aspired to formulate new literary, historical, political, and social doctrines of an eclectic, then of a positive, type in press, lecture hall, and parliament. While proclaiming the nineteenth century in Spain as a new age which needed new ideas from young leaders, he belittled the older generation of radicals as shallow imitators who lacked genius, understanding, or competence. Pretending exact knowledge of history and of the evils suffered by society in its "fevered state" of crisis, he asserted that he was the only Spanish philosopher able to discover by reason, logic, and his-

[9] Gómez Aparicio, *Historia*, I, 225. Francisco Escobar García, "Semblanza de Donoso Cortés," *Revista de Estudios Extremeños*, IX (1953), 183. Gabriel García y Tassara, *Poesías*, p. 358.

tory the truths for which society cried out.[10] Critics often derided and ridiculed him for this blatant arrogance. In 1839 González Bravo, for example, parodied him without mercy as "Cock-a-doodle-do" in the satirical *El Guirigay*, and others had ridiculed him as a *Guizotin*, who plagiarized from the French doctrinaires, or in one case, from the Saint-Simonians.[11] He, on the contrary, insisted that he assimilated from many masters. At any rate, by 1845 he was the leading constitutional theorist of the Moderate party and a liberal–conservative supporter of middle class, monarchy, and Church who expressed a yet unappreciated interest in a kind of social democracy.

This young intellectual developed an extraordinary range of interests and talents. He aspired to be one of those universal men of liberal education like the great Renaissance humanists and artists, the geniuses of the seventeenth century, the philosophes of the Enlightenment, and the intelligentsia of his own era. Spaniards call his type a thinker (*pensador*): One who develops wide interests in philosophy, politics, history, and literature, but is not as a whole, very systematic—men such as Unamuno and Ortega.

In the nineteenth century it was almost customary to mix politics not only with law but also with journalism, literature, scholarship, or some other calling. Shortly after he finished his education, Donoso declared that man had been born only to put into action all of his faculties.[12] "Now the same man will be a philosopher in his study, a legislator at the head of government, a poet in communion with the muses, and an orator in the turmoil of passions." Such breadth of interest he saw in Quintana and also in Guizot and the French eclectics, all of whom had dealt with political theory, philosophy, literature, history, education, and active politics. He noted that an intellectual's stock in trade is ideas and that for a writer, a lecturer

[10] Juretschke, I, 211f, 289, 329, 330, 331, 471ff; 155, 157.

[11] Edmund Schramm, *Donoso Cortés, su vida y su pensamiento*, pp. 99–100.

[12] Carlos Valverde, ed., *Obras completas*, I, 173.

or professor, and a parliamentarian, there are three great vehicles by which they reach the world: the press, the chair, and the rostrum. Donoso used all of these instruments and played all of these roles. "Intellectual work," he remarked, "is so artificially divided in this great workshop of the world" that where some strove to discover first principles, others systematized them, while still others applied them to government and society. "To the first category belong the lawgivers of the nations; to the second, the publicists; to the last, the statesmen."[13] While he never pretended to find first principles like a Plato, Augustine, or Newton, he did criticize and draft constitutions, and by 1848 he had emerged as a statesman. First, however, he was a publicist of note, working to systematize the ideas of others in the press, at the Ateneo, and later in the Cortes.

After his unsuccessful debut in parliamentary politics, Donoso turned back to serious journalism from 1837 to 1843, his most intense and productive years, but thereafter he contributed only on rare occasions. Writing on literary, cultural, historical, philosophical, social, religious, and political themes, he became, said Pastor Díaz, more than a newspaperman—"a publicist in the broad and great sense of the word"—a pundit who took an elevated, learned approach to current issues. In his *Historia del Periodismo*, Gómez Aparicio rates Donoso as an effective young editor of *Porvenir* in 1837. Thereafter he was more a writer than a journalist; his "Letters from Paris" (1842), for example, would be more properly classified as philosophical–political interpretation of events than informative reporting.[14] Lacking, perhaps, the skillful journalist's capacity to recapitulate or to sum up briefly, he preferred to approach any subject in a scholarly and leisurely fashion, methodically examining it in several successive articles. Usually study and reflection, history and philosophy, graced his po-

[13] Juretschke, I, 81; 120, 735.

[14] Nicomedes Pastor Díaz, "Don Donoso Cortés," in *Galería de Españoles célebres contemporáneos*, VI, 252–53. Gómez Aparicio, *Historia*, I, 290, 287f, 375.

litical and literary work, and his solidity of treatment and range of interest were impressive. Society and events moved so rapidly in a revolutionary age, he complained, that a thinker's ideas would be outdated before he could expound them fully in a book, which is precisely what happened with his unfinished *History of the Regency* (1843). "Only the periodical press, never resting, follows society in her flight and keeps pace with her transformation."[15] All his life he followed this journalistic policy, never pausing to sum up his position as a whole or explain it in depth, not even in his one finished book, the *Essay on Catholicism, Liberalism and Socialism* (1851). Nevertheless, the growth, continuity, and culmination of a serious philosophical mind characterize his writing, not the day-to-day shifts of newspaper journalism.

After first working with Pacheco and Bravo Murillo on *La Abeja* in 1834–1835, he founded and edited *El Porvenir* in 1837. He also served as writer or editor for *Revista de Madrid* in 1838 and *El Piloto* in 1839, worked for Borrego on *El Correo Nacional* from 1838 to 1842, and for *El Heraldo* from 1842 to 1843. Then, after several years away from the profession, he returned to work fitfully with Pacheco on *La Patria* in 1850, and greatly influenced Bravo Murillo's *El Orden* in 1851.[16] Other writers and editors with whom he collaborated were Tassara, Pastor Díaz, Mesonero Romános, and Cánovas del Castillo. Continuing the staff and much of the program of *La Abeja, Correo Nacional* became virtually the official publication of the Moderate party; its successor, *El Heraldo,* finally became too ardent a supporter of Narváez and of eclecticism after 1849 for Donoso's taste.

Donoso's early journalistic style was less romantic than eclectic; rather turgid, only rarely did it evince luxuriant, vigorous, or beautiful passages which reminded Pastor Díaz of Chateaubriand. His very seriousness of intent hampered free and fluid expression. Unrelieved by lightness or humor, the prose he

[15] Juretschke, I, 205.

[16] Gómez Aparicio, *Historia,* I, 201, 226f, 237f, 244, 289f, 372–83f.

wrote until 1842 is heavy, artificial, tiresome, and repetitious, with contrived parallelisms and marathon sentences. Despite his vaunted eclectic compromise between romanticism and classicism, he united more of their vices than virtues. Contemporaries criticized his foggy obscurity and opinionated affectation, judging him either as too rhetorical or too emphatic.[17] As a whole, his eclectic style preserved the exaggerations of romanticism without its spontaneity and the order but little of the polished urbanity and grace of classicism. None of his early works would be read today either for beauty or for content; rather, his literary and intellectual reputation rests on the later works, which are sometimes unabashedly romantic, almost Gongoristic in excess.

One can detect in Donoso's style, in fact, a cyclic progression from the rebellious romanticism of his youth, to the eclecticism of his transitional middle period, to a genuinely positive style, a more natural or realistic expression foreshadowed in his "Letters from Paris" (1842), developed in his factual diaries of 1844–1846, and best seen in his diplomatic reports from Paris after 1851. However, for both normalcy and the revolutionary crisis of 1848–1851 he returned to an overripe, florid romanticism, full of exaggeration and paradox, as in the *Essay*. He believed that in either stage of the cycle, only such dogmatic utterance could appeal to the general public.

SCHOLAR AND CRITIC: ROMANTICISM VS. CLASSICISM

If Donoso's library finally numbered over a thousand volumes, which were not catalogued and mostly divided and lost,[18] we cannot know all works and authors he read over a

[17] Pastor Díaz, *Galería*, VI, 249.

[18] The present so-called catalogue of Donoso's library at Don Benito, first made in 1914, covers not the books of his library but the papers in the archives, some of which were bound into volumes (tomos) by Gabino Tejado in the 1850s, others in packets (legajos). Several tomos, legajos, and many books, which Schramm could examine, were permanently lost in 1938—notes and extracts in Tomes A and F on de Maistre, Bossuet,

lifetime. An omnivorous bibliophile, he was always reading and collecting, and like de Maistre often studiously taking notes,[19] many of which are preserved in bound tomes at Don Benito. "The wise maxim of Apelles, *Nulla dies sine linea*, could have been his motto," remarked Pastor Díaz, who attributed to this habit his later remarkable erudition and facility with ideas and expression.[20] Donoso was well read, with a surprising diversity of interest in literature, history, biography, politics, law, social studies, economics, and philosophy, and he even read a few works in science, or natural history, medicine,

---

Thomas Aquinas, Saint Augustine, and Machiavelli. Notes in the surviving tomes and bundles sometimes coincide with what little remains of the library. Schramm overlooked the "book lists," scraps of paper Donoso carried around to Paris publishers and bookshops from 1847 to 1853, with some entries marked "X" for importance and others with his comments. Bills cover some purchases after 1840. How much he actually bought of all he sought, one cannot know. In 1971 the library proper still contained works by about fifty authors and more than 130 volumes. Don Manuel Donoso Cortés, however, said that the original library was divided six ways in 1853 among brothers and sisters of Donoso and that, of the sixth part remaining at Don Benito, only one seventh was recovered from "the reds" after 1938. If the original division was more or less equal and if Don Manuel's recollections are correct, then Donoso's library would have comprised over 5,000 volumes when he died—a figure which seems excessive for that time, although he had the interest, wealth, and servants to find and purchase that number. Obviously, he did not read all he bought, but his lists of books in the Ateneo and Biblioteca Real indicate that he also borrowed freely. To judge by the book lists and library, he purchased most of his books (except the Spanish) in Paris on his several trips to the city and during his residence there in exile or as ambassador. Foreign books in his library generally fall into groups published from 1838 or 1839 to 1843, others from 1847 to 1849, and others from 1851 to 1853. By contents, dates, and handwriting, most of his surviving purchase lists seem to date from 1849, when he was on his way to and from Berlin; they contain not only many religious and theological works but also some German authors (Görres, Hegel, and Savigny) and German (and Hungarian) subjects. The personal library he built up at Paris—undoubtedly with some duplication of authors and works—between 1851 and 1853 was shipped to Don Benito by his brothers. What survives there now are largely later works of religious piety and theology along with ancient classical authors, but very few of the secular works he is known to have read.

[19] Juretschke, II, 318.

[20] Pastor Díaz, *Galería*, VI, 260–61.

and later much in religious history, hagiography, theology, mysticism, and Scripture. Able to read French as easily as Spanish, he bought more books in Paris than in Madrid after 1840, a number of which were in English, a few in Italian, and some with German authors in French translation. With a dictionary he could handle English, Italian, and Latin authors, but not German.

Sorting through papers, notes, and copy books from his schooldays until late in life, Donoso's earlier biographers (Tejado, Schramm, and Galindo Herrero) discovered a wide variety of authors and titles—some of which are now missing from the library at Don Benito—many of them well known and many more now forgotten.[21] The number of still-famous or notable authors, from the various periods in history and literary schools that are mentioned in his purchase lists, notebooks (Tomes), and surviving library is impressive: classics—Plato, Aristotle, Xenophon, Herodotus, Polybius, Demosthenes, Livy, Seneca, Tacitus, Sallust, Caesar, Cicero, Petronius, Quintilian; patrology—Chrysostom, Cyprian, Ambrose, Tertulian, Augustine, etc.; Scholastic and mystical—Aquinas, Suárez, Molina, Luis de Granada; Renaissance and seventeenth century—Machiavelli, Shakespeare, Leibniz, Bossuet, Fénélon; eighteenth-century Europe—Montesquieu, Rousseau, Hume,

[21] See Schramm, *Vida y pensamiento*, pp. 44 and 50 for authors and titles of his youthful reading in 1828 and 1829; also Santiago Galindo Herrero, *Donoso Cortés y su theoría política*, pp. 71–74, 151. Most of the works they list, incidentally, are not among those which Donoso cited in his published works (Juretschke's edition). Schramm (p. 44) mentions Rousseau's *Émile*, *La Nouvelle Héloise*, and *Confessions*. *Émile* appears in Donoso's *Obras* (Juretschke, I, 308; II, 360) as well as *Le Contrat social* (I, 308; II, 85, 348). Schramm also found notes on Voltaire's *Siècle de Louis XIV*, *Dictionnaire philosophique*, and *Essai sur les moeurs*, to which one can add at least his *Treatise on Toleration* (II, 348) and surely *Candide*, as well as other historical works (I, 794; II, 90). To the *Persian Letters* by Montesquieu (Schramm), add *The Spirit of the Laws* (II, 360), notes to which are in Tome C (Donoso Cortés family archives). Schramm also adds Helvetius' *De l'Esprit*. Donoso often referred to Hobbes's *Leviathan* (II, 84), and to Gibbon's *Decline and Fall of the Roman Empire* (I, 793), with notes in Tome B.

Gibbon, Burke; nineteenth-century France—de Maistre, Guizot, Thiers, Cousin, Lamartine, Mignet, Michelet, Proudhon, Buchez, Lamennais, Montalembert, Ozanam, Lacordaire, Remusat, Blanc de Saint-Bonnet, Falloux, Dupanloup, etc.; nineteenth-century Britain—Hallam, Grote, W. Scott, Newman, and Wiseman. Although he studied Vico, Voltaire, Bentham, Byron, Chateaubriand, Bonald, Mme. de Staël, and Constant and read more extensively than the list suggests in areas such as the Renaissance, seventeenth century, Enlightenment, liberalism, and socialism, one must allow for the great losses through partition of the library by Donoso's brothers and sisters in 1853, then to destruction by "the reds" in 1938. Schramm, however, compiled a more complete list before 1938, and Donoso's published writings are another source. Unfortunately, one cannot always decide what he read carefully, skimmed, or only wanted to read if he could find it and had leisure. Certainly he was serious and systematic about his reading, and one can often correlate undated notes with his current writing.

Until now, little emphasis has been placed on authors such as Hegel, Leibniz, Bossuet, Saint Augustine, and Thomas Aquinas, whose works he purchased before or after 1840.[22] They are, however, very significant for understanding his thought, especially the *Essay* and his philosophy of history. During the 1840s, long before he employed the dialectic in the *Essay*, he apparently knew of Hegel at closer hand and more reliably than through the interpretations of Cousin or Proudhon, since he apparently bought the *Aesthetics* (*Ästhetik*) in French translation in 1843 and was looking for Willme's four volumes as the "best" in German philosophy through Kant and Hegel in 1849. An unrecognized influence is Leibniz, in whose *Works* (*Oeuvres*) and *Thoughts* (*Pensées*) he studied

[22] For references to, or comments on the authors in Donoso's works, see Juretschke, I, 40, 311f, 540, 543, 800; II, 91, 222, 609. He appealed to Augustine and Aquinas equally in 1849, as against eclecticism (Juretschke, II, 222; cf. II, 609); they were in Tome A; Thomas in Legajo 14.

ideas of faith and reason, good and evil, space and time. He bought Saint Thomas' ten-volume *Summa Theologica,* more than one edition of Saint Augustine's *City of God* and of Bossuet's *Discourse on Universal History* (*Discours sur l'histoire universelle*) and *History of the Variations of Protestant Churches* (*Histoire des variations des églises protestantes*).

During the 1840s Donoso purchased many of the ancient classics and the Greek and Latin Fathers. He was probably engaged in serious study and historical reflection in that period because he also obtained several ancient histories (Grote's *History of Greece,* which he considered the best) and histories of ancient philosophy (Heinrich Ritter), religion, politics, commerce (A. H. Heeren), and slavery. He also bought a Latin grammar and anthologies and histories of Latin and Greek literature.

Educated primarily in the classical–humanist tradition from Renaissance to French Enlightenment, Donoso knew at first hand the major literary, philosophical, political, and historical works of the greater *philosophes.* He admired Montesquieu's genius, Voltaire's sparkling style, and the seductive powers of Rousseau; he knew the works of Diderot, Turgot, Condorcet, and leading empiricists from Condillac to Destutt de Tracy; and he was interested in such leading British thinkers as Bacon, Hobbes, Locke, Newton, Hume, Gibbon, and Bentham. The more skeptical and materialistic the outlook of the Enlightenment became, the more he disliked it. Above Gibbon's *Decline and Fall of the Roman Empire,* whose scholarship he admired, or even Montesquieu's *Spirit of the Laws* (*De l'Esprit des lois*), he came to rank the genius of Vico's *New Science* (*La Scienza Nuova,* 1725), whose cyclic philosophy of history he regarded as more profound and realistic than the idea of progress from Condorcet, Guizot, or Hegel. Among Renaissance writers, he admired Petrarch; he detested the principles of Machiavelli but was nevertheless fascinated by him, and he took copious notes from his works. He never cited Thomas More or Erasmus despite his great interest in utopias. Even as a romantic youth he developed an aversion to the basic critical and rationalistic spirit of the modern classical tradition as a whole, especially in the Enlightenment.[23]

From the first, Donoso's inclination was toward the romantic era and kindred ages of the medieval Gothic and the Baroque. Later accused of being an idolater of the Middle Ages, he also always admired the late sixteenth and seventeenth centuries of genius, especially Spain's golden age, for the idealistic figures and intellectual and aesthetic works that did not indicate the spirit of materialism and unbelief of the eighteenth century. He esteemed Shakespeare, Cervantes, Góngora, Calderón de la Barca, Lope de Vega, Milton, Molière, and Racine, and especially Pascal, Leibniz, and Bossuet, as the later but more magnificent fruit of a Christian civilization in decline, at least as much as the blooms of that civilization at its flourishing medieval apogee, such as Dante, Tasso, Aquinas, and Alfonso X. Among the Romantic writers whom he read, he placed Chateaubriand first for his *The Genius of Christianity* (*Le Génie du Christianisme*, 1802), but he also read Mme. de Staël, Byron, Scott, and later in Paris, Lamartine, whose works he purchased and criticized as the poetry of a pantheistic democracy.[24]

While Spaniards still fought a kind of "battle of the books" over rival literary styles, Donoso argued for compromise in "Classicism and Romanticism" (1838), for an eclectic *juste milieu* to combine the best and avoid the worst of each style.[25] He persuaded a large number of Spanish writers to adopt the eclectic approach instead of either romanticism or classicism, despite his own mediocre style.[26] Before he was thirty, he had

[23] Juretschke, I, 43, 309, 793, 943; 59, 156, 308f; 537ff, cf. 291, 315, 318, 810; 39, 301f, 404; (lost Tomo F contained most of Donoso's notes on Machiavelli, but some are preserved in Tomo B) 28ff, 33, 43.

[24] Juretschke, II, 632; I, 37ff, 40f, 91, 368f, 404, 410ff; II, 212, 368, 609; 44ff, 311f, 167, 761ff.

[25] Juretschke, I, 383, 408–9.

[26] E. Allison Peers, *A Short History of the Romantic Movement in Spain* (Liverpool, 1949), pp. 136–37, 155, especially Ch. 5, "The Rise

disavowed youthful romantic extremes of rebellion, frenzy, and disorder, the contempt for authority and restraint of any kind. Nevertheless he preferred the individual moral and spiritual freedom and spontaneity of romanticism to the dry, artificial, external spirit of the classical tradition, with its naturalistic and materialistic tendencies. It boiled down, he thought, not just to different perceptions of nature, or to opposing form to feeling, but to essential differences between the ancient and modern, pagan and Christian, civilizations. His consistent theme in literary criticism was that Christian civilization had made a greater contribution to literature than either ancient classical paganism or the new paganism of the Renaissance and Enlightenment. From Turgot and Chateaubriand he had advanced to an idea like de Maistre's, Saint-Simon's, and Comte's: The middle ages had effected a moral regeneration as the basis of later social, as well as cultural, progress.[27]

MENTAL PROFILE: LOGIC, PREDICTION, RELATIVISM, SYNTHESIS

"There are three sources of certitude for man," asserted Donoso at the Ateneo: reason, authority, and history, if they are in agreement.[28] The structure and methods of his own reason, of course, outweigh the successive philosophies, which he borrowed largely from others. Chief characteristics of his mind were logic, prophetic projection, and a historicist relativism which offset elements of determinism in his dogmatic exaggeration, laws, and principles. These qualities were complementary and were evident throughout his life. Synthesis was always the ultimate aim of his analyses. Although his conception

---

and Triumph of Eclecticism." E.A. Peers, *Historia del movimiento romántico español* (Madrid, 1954), II, 187–89. Donoso did not convince his friend Zorrilla; see Peers, *Historia*, II, 315, 427.

[27] Juretschke, I, 172, 406–7; 389–97, 401–6, 578f; II, 212; 171–73, 406f; II, 207ff. Auguste Comte, *The Positive Philosophy of Auguste Comte*, trans. Harriet Martineau (New York, Chicago, n.d.), p. 603ff, 627. Juretschke, I, 393ff, 398ff–including the cult of woman.

[28] Juretschke, I, 303; in the *Essay* of 1851; II, 526.

of the meaning of reason, authority, and history changed considerably, efforts to synthesize them were already visible in his youth and were emphatic in the end, as in the *Essay*.

Perhaps his study of law sharpened Donoso's mastery of logic. Quintana and Spaniards first, and later Montalembert and the French, were to admire above all his unusual talent in logic, debate, and demonstration.[29] Almost always he was better at critical analysis of radicalism, or socialism, however, than at summarizing his own systems, despite his resolve to move on to dogmatic synthesis, which he was never to attain formally for his thought as a whole. Toward the end of his life, it is true that he was "a transcendent synthesizer," but more in thought than on paper.[30]

Although he was familiar with the deductive method of Descartes, Donoso developed a dynamic style of logic that was more similar to Hegel's dialectic. He was too much a romantic to accept classical clarity and consistency as always necessary for truth in development. Most of all, his logic consisted in drawing all of the consequences out of ideas, either those of his foes as subjected to *reductio ad absurdum* or those of the French doctrinaires, Saint-Simonians, and traditionalists, which he wished to make more complete, forceful, coherent, and positive. Where he projected an ideological development, it was because he believed that this logical sequence must someday occur in the practical order unless men were to aban-

[29] Schramm, *Vida y pensamiento*, p. 40. Galinda Herrero, *Theoría política*, p. 49. García y Tassara, *Poesías*, p. 358.

[30] Jules Barbey D'Aurevilly, "Les Oeuvres et les hommes" (XIXe siècle) in *Philosophes et écrivains religieux* (Paris, 1912) pp. 35–36. Jean Antoine At, *Les Apologistes espagnols aux XIXe siècle: Donoso Cortès*. (Paris, ca., 1898), pp. 14–16. Marcelino Menéndez y Pelayo, "Principales Apologistas," in *Historia de los Heterodoxos españoles*, Vol. VII of *Obras completas*, 416. Even more than Menéndez y Pelayo, At saw Donoso as "a transcendent synthesizer" of the rank and type of Saint Augustine, Bossuet, and de Maistre; Montalembert criticized him for striving too hard to coin a good generalization, and Pacheco also noted his constant search for a "simple and absolute" *synthesis*. Charles Montalembert, *Oeuvres*, XV (II), 216. Pacheco, in Schramm, *Vida y pensamiento*, p. 19.

don the principle concerned. Human inconsequence, or merely pragmatic behavior, might hold back the full elaboration and application of an idea, but only temporarily. The law of progress, he said, is a fatal law that comprises "a series of logical and inflexible consequences which have to be realized and fulfilled."[31]

From his logic, therefore, always came his irrepressible urge to prognosticate, which he developed eventually into a remarkable power of logical and historical prophecy. Having first attributed the French Revolution to the critical ideas of the Enlightenment in the fashion of de Maistre and Saint-Simon, he came to fear a similar cause-effect relationship from such ideas well before the revolutions of 1848. At first he applied his method of divining the future from the logical progression of dominant ideas when he called Spanish radicals implicit democrats and republicans, and later he tried to project the logical outcome of liberalism and socialism.[32] Unlike Hegel or Guizot, he did not halt the progress of reason or dialectic with the present but extended it boldly into the future, like Comte.

Finally, from dialectical projections, more than from a romantic style, came that spirit of exaggeration for which he was always criticized. Looking to the future not only made him overemphasize principles and consequences in his foes but also forced him to assert his own ideas the more resolutely, because (like Comte) he believed that only a dogmatic philosophy and politics could carry over into a normal era[33] and that only dogmatic form and expression could capture the mass mind during crises by a popular symbol, formula, idea, or principle.

Such calculated dogmatism did not make Donoso regard any particular philosophical, literary, or political system as absolute, or forever true or useful. All were relative to time and circumstance, to the cyclic and progressive changes of society,

[31] Juretschke, I, 267; 202, 230f, 649, 685; II, 502f, 511ff; 480; II, 495; I, 168, 656f.

[32] Juretschke, I, 39, 43, 810; 323, 378f.

[33] Juretschke, I, 416f.

with its variable needs, sentiments, and mentality. Echoing Mme. de Staël, he observed very early that "there are certain analogies in the development of the different faculties of intelligence," all of which correspond roughly with a people's stage of social development.[34] His choice of style, philosophy, and politics therefore always followed his estimate of the times; all of his multifarious pursuits were interrelated to correspond to the condition of society. He could have developed his idea for such a social unity of human action from the Saint-Simonians, or Vico, all of whom linked political, linguistic, religious, and philosophical forms with social development.[35] Since Dilthey developed his thought on *Weltanschauungen*,[36] the interdependence of all of man's activities is something that literary, cultural, and social historians have continued to consider in reference to climates of opinion, world views, eras, and styles such as the Gothic, Renaissance, Baroque, Enlightenment, Romantic, Realistic. Donoso is among the many, including Herder, J. S. Mill, and Taine, who consciously anticipated the broad effects of such a *Zeitgeist*, or spirit of the age.

Although he believed that systems and styles are relative to the circumstances in society, Donoso (like Comte) held that there were a few basic maxims, principles, or laws which survived all social transformations, to remain perpetually valid as absolutes, or at least as constants. Some he called primitive and anterior to reason, but others he regarded as well established by reason and history. When (like Saint-Simon) he boasted ludicrously, "Archimedes looked for a lever to move the universe; give me a principle: I shall build societies," he was trying to demonstrate that his youthful principle of intelligence was such an absolute, as exemplified through reason

[34] Juretschke, I, 81, 416; 79f, 168.

[35] Juretschke, I, 416, 567–68. Giambattista Vico, *The New Science*, trans. T. G. Bergin and M. H. Fisch (New York, 1961), pp. 21, 33, 36, 64 and 283ff. Comte, pp. 459–61.

[36] Wilson H. Coates, *The Ordeal of Liberal Humanism*, Vol. II of *An Intellectual History of Western Europe* (New York, 1970) pp. 261–62.

and history. His cyclic principle was more durable, either as in Vico's three social epochs (divine, heroic, human) or in his positive politics (crisis, transition, normalcy), which he derived from Saint-Simon if not from Comte. When he could no longer accept the concept of progress, he embraced the cycles as comprehensive and realistic explanations of social and political change, which were merely continuity or evolution and which he thought could as easily be regression. To the cycle he added the basic principle of dualism in man, society, and history, which he derived from Cousin in 1836 and later found in a more radical form in Saint Augustine.[37]

Other principles that Donoso held as laws throughout his life were 'unity and diversity' and 'action and reaction', which he applied as forms of dualism constituting reality or as a dialectical and alternating mode of development in thought, politics, and history. Moreover he always held to a 'principle of identity', a metaphysical absolute that helped him avoid a fully historicist relativism in philosophy, history, and social thought. He found both identity and unity and diversity first in Cousin, who had taken them from Leibniz, before he himself studied Leibniz. Also in Cousin was an idea of social attraction and repulsion, a kind of social Newtonism or social dynamics, which Donoso likewise shared with Saint-Simon and Comte. Other more specifically political principles that he regarded as absolutes were such variations of unity and diversity as unity of power and hierarchic and corporative society to safeguard both order and freedom. He adopted these ideas especially from Bonald and de Maistre.[38] Such constants were his

[37] Juretschke, II, 637. Comte, in *The Positive Philosophy* (pp. 36, 429) identified these "fundamental maxims," or "social principles," as "general ideas," which serve as "a rallying point of social doctrine" for reconstructing a normal state of society. Juretschke, I, 61, 187; II, 221, 526, 608, 638–39; 135, 303; II, 122. Comte, *Positive Philosophy*, pp. 440, 540; Juretschke, I, 215f; II, 207ff, 460f.

[38] Juretschke, I, 164, 312, 322, 435, 473; II, 122, 189, 352, 438, 533, 543, 611. Comte, *Positive Philosophy*, pp. 37, 457, 819 (action and reaction). Juretschke, I, 164, 214, 542, 810; II, 145, 609; 340–41, 638–39.

consistent rules of thought, his absolutes, the structural and dynamic principles that unite his thought as a whole almost from first to last, as few have perceived.[39]

Because he was eclectic, Donoso did not claim that his particular ideas were original, but the syntheses he worked out were his own. Except for a rare genius, new discoveries of basic principles seemed to him impossible. One of his favorite maxims was from Ecclesiastes, "Nothing new under the sun." By this verse he meant that by arrangement or emphasis one could make only new combinations of already existing basic ideas to fit changing circumstances of society. He excelled at simplifying and systematizing the ideas of others: Victor Cousin's eclecticism; Guizot's doctrinaire liberalism; Turgot, Condorcet, Saint-Simon, Guizot, perhaps Hegel for a progressive theory of history, and Vico and the Saint-Simonians for a cyclical pattern of politics and of social, intellectual, and cultural history. Plainly, Donoso did not borrow from any one thinker or school; he assimilated from the whole spectrum. Insisting on his independence, he denied that he was the echo or disciple of anyone, if that meant accepting ideas without judging them. "But if you call disciple one who learns and master one who teaches, then no one admits more masters than I."[40] In fact, he read and borrowed widely, and because he was therefore original as a whole, he refused ever to acknowledge any one master—not Guizot, Cousin, Vico, or de Maistre, let alone Saint-Simon, Buchez, or Comte. He always rejected labels; he denied being either a *Guizotin* in the 1830s or an absolutist neo-Catholic follower of de Maistre in the 1850s, and no one tried to call him a Saint-Simonian or positivist after 1834, until now. He was in fact something of all three, and more. Of his presumed masters, he was most reluctant (in 1834) to ac-

[39] Although Luis Díez del Corral perceives connections between all periods of Donoso's thought, he does not identify them: *El liberalismo doctrinario*, p. 495. But see Rodrigo Fernández Carvajal, "Las constantes de Donoso Cortés," *Revista de Estudios Políticos*, No. 95 (1957); his "constants" are not the ones cited here, however.

[40] Juretschke, I, 156; II, 94, 750; I, 156.

knowledge the Saint-Simonians, and most open in discussing Guizot and the eclectics (after 1837 when he began to desert them), while only once did he advert to de Maistre—in gratitude for being described as his intellectual heir mainly in secondary considerations.[41]

PHILOSOPHY AND POLITICS: ECLECTICISM, POSITIVISM, TRADITIONALISM

Not only in philosophy, but in his doctrinaire politics, in literary norms, and even in history, Donoso was a convinced eclectic in the years 1828–1837. If he claimed to prefer the German idealists from Leibniz to Hegel over both the materialistic empiricists and the romantic traditionalists, his own first position was actually eclectic, not only in philosophy but in politics.[42] Plainly he depended on Victor Cousin's *History of Philosophy* (1828) for much of his initial knowledge of European philosophy, probably for his first introduction to Leibniz, Hegel, and Kant, as well as Vico.[43] Cousin's philosophical formulation of *le juste milieu,* as well as his abstract and impersonal principle of intelligence, were axioms that became the building blocks of his youthful theorizing.[44] Royer-

[41] For Donoso's critical opinion on the eclectics and doctrinaires, see Juretschke, I, 413ff, 790–800 (Guizot), and II, 222, 620; on the Saint-Simonians, I, 155, 315f, 469 and II, 453, 461f, 464, 511 (*Essay*); on de Maistre, II, 576.

[42] For Donoso as an eclectic, see Juretschke, I, 147, 172, 217ff, 310–15, and II, 19–21; for young Donoso on the "schools": I, 13ff, 39–40, 45, 316–18.

[43] See Victor Cousin, *Course of the History of Modern Philosophy,* 2 vols. (N.Y., 1852), especially Vol. II for the distinction between *idealism* and *sensualism* and much else that Donoso apparently used in the Ateneo lectures: for example, unity and diversity, duality, religion as "true philosophy," the description of the eclectic critical method, the role of ideas and of war in history, philosophy of history, etc. Juretschke, I, 291 (note) suggests Cousin for Donoso's first knowledge of Vico.

[44] See Juretschke, I, 796 (note); principle of *intelligence*— I, 129, 135, 215–16 (a "law" of society), 278f, 302 (in progress and history), 193ff, 302, 318–20 (in government and sovereignty); he used *le juste milieu* between extremes, mostly in political matters. I, 68f, 219, 277, 320, 330f.

Collard and Guizot gave him his idea of a sovereignty of reason vested in the middle classes.[45] From Guizot, most of whose works he read, he learned not only the politics of compromise, balance, and division of power or parliamentarism, which he rejected between 1837 and 1842, but also the impartiality, comprehension, and tolerance of eclectic historical and social analysis.[46]

For the needs of a modern society in crisis or transition, Donoso long found the most sensible and useful approach in the eclecticism of Cousin and Guizot, especially their method of analysis and compromise between opposing forces. Like Aristotle's golden mean, their *juste milieu*, or middle way in everything, impressed him for its fairness and breadth. By avoiding the fanaticism of both left and right, old and new, it reached a suitable balance, partaking of whatever were true in both extremes. Moderation and middle position seemed to him necessary in politics and ideally suited to the middle class. Since Europe had been torn by contradictory ideological and political systems ever since the revolutionary eighteenth century, he judged at the Ateneo in 1837 that the time was ripe for a compromise that utilized whatever might be permanent and necessary in absolutism and democracy, idealism and materialism, so as to reconstruct society on a basis of middle-class constitutional monarchy and eclecticism. Beginning his own eclectic game of dialectics, he tried to balance justly and without caprice between revolution and reaction, liberty and order, individual and society, in short, between all the conflicting forces within man, society, and history.[47]

Eclecticism left Donoso much room for adaptation in philosophy, politics, and history. He saw that Cousin was nearly as vague on method as on criteria for the truth he sifted from opposites. Must he therefore adopt a precise position between

[45] Juretschke, I, 191ff, 312ff; cf. II, 447, 623–24, 646.

[46] Juretschke, I, 786–89, 800ff. On a book list of 1852, Donoso still entered Guizot's *Histoire des origines du gouvernment representatif.*

[47] Juretschke, I, 312, 793; 150, 194–95, 320; also II, 236.

empiricism and idealism, matter and spirit, reason and faith, when every viable philosophy is relative to, must reflect, and serve contemporary society? There was no reason to accept all of Guizot's political theory or his historical analysis of social-political elements that had survived 1789 in France, since a workable constitution must adjust spontaneously to Spain's own more conservative social character and needs. Guizot derived "his politics from history, his history from philosophy, and his philosophy from common sense,"[48] a process he too could follow for the era of transition.

If eclecticism were socially useful and necessary for a transitional epoch, Donoso had decided by 1838 that it was philosophically, politically, socially, and historically incomplete and inadequate for a normal, stable epoch.[49] It lacked dogmatism and synthesis. By nature antidogmatic, rejecting the very possibility of either absolute truth or absolute error, its power for unifying generalization or synthesis and leadership was therefore very weak. Like Comte and the Saint-Simonians, he believed that for a socially effective synthesis one had to take a single exclusive principle and declare it dogmatically, because only thus could one hold the allegiance of the masses into a normal, organic epoch.[50] Already he had felt obliged to turn Cousin's intelligence into a dogma, around which he systematized doctrinairism and organized his earlier thought on history and diplomacy. Like Saint-Simon, he believed that "An idea is a principle of cohesion." Since he could not accept the synthetic dogmatism of either democrat Rousseau or absolutist

[48] He attributes a wide variety of activities to the eclectic school—philosophy, history, and political and social theory, on which he tried to improve; Juretschke, I, 216, 384, 416, 473, 794; 800; II, 222; I, 934; II, 148, 416, 481f.

[49] Juretschke, I, 415–18; also see 794, 800ff; cf. II, 60.

[50] This expectation of a new dogmatic intellectual–political–social synthesis is strikingly similar to that of the Saint-Simonians. See Georg. G. Iggers, *The Cult of Authority. The Political Philosophy of the Saint-Simonians* (The Hague, 1958), p. 6, and Comte, *Positive Philosophy*, pp. 42, 410.

Bonald, he offered Spaniards in 1838 and again in 1845 a kind of synthesis of Rousseau and Bonald (or de Maistre) in a dogmatic formula of authoritarian, democratic, and religious monarchy.[51]

Both Donoso and Comte were keenly anticipating a normal epoch by 1846–1847 and were preparing for it with social and political philosophies of history. Donoso was working on some new *Outlines of History*, and Comte was repeating himself with *A General View of Positivism* (*Discours sur l'ensemble de positivisme*). When eclectic translation ended not in stability but in a vast new revolutionary crisis, Donoso became as scornful of eclecticism as was Comte, who had ridiculed *le juste milieu* as a "bastard middle," or Jules Simon, who later called it a "bastard dialectic." If one were really free to choose between opposites, eclecticism was a silly game of chance, concluded Donoso; if not, it was an absolute system and hence not really eclecticism.[52]

From the mid-1830s Donoso gradually became a Saint-Simonian positivist, very similar in many ways to Comte. Both pretended like eclectics to combine the true and necessary elements of old and new to find an appropriate position somewhere between incomplete extremes, but both also tried to provide what they called a complete position, a dogmatic synthesis, in philosophy, politics, sociology, and history.[53] Nevertheless not once did Donoso mention Comte. Perhaps the only time Donoso saw Comte's name was in 1837 when he read *The Doctrine of Saint-Simon* (*Exposition de la doctrine de St. Simon*) in which Comte was criticized as a renegade.[54] If he ever knowingly read one of Comte's works, it was probably his *Social Physics* of 1842, because whatever he shared with

[51] Juretschke, I, 419; also 105, 189ff, 215, 277ff, 376ff; 135, 215; 519–20, 535; II, 20, 31.

[52] Comte, *The Positive Philosophy*, p. 418. Juretschke, II, 222. Jules Simon, *Victor Cousin* (Chicago, ca. 1888), p. 92.

[53] Comte, *Positive Philosophy*, pp. 401f, 431ff, 437, 448, 816; cf. Donoso's earlier criticism: Juretschke, I, 310–16, 416–17.

[54] Juretschke, I, 315–16.

him was already far developed before the *General View* of 1847, even the notion that Europe needed a new positive or affirmative philosophy and social sciences. Although the parallels between their political, social, and historical thought and method after 1835 finally became too numerous for accident, these similarities may have been due to what they had in common with Saint-Simon, the Saint-Simonians, and the traditionalists.[55] When he was at the Ateneo reading on the so-called social school, Donoso may have encountered Comte's initial ideas of the 1820s for a positive politics of crisis and normalcy under Saint-Simon's name, although he used this terminology before 1837.[56] They developed parallel themes in many areas: philosophy of history and prediction; a positive politics of crisis, transition, and normalcy; a sociology, or social statics, of hierarchy and unity of organization and structure under an elite of the more intelligent and capable; finally, even a theory of authoritarian dictatorship for times of crisis and for the reforms and reconstruction that must precede normalcy. As a positivist, however, Donoso gradually became the obverse of Comte—so often alike, yet contradictory on fundamentals. Both passed through a bourgeois and rationalistic phase, but Come had moved on to a republican and atheistic but scarcely socialist position, whereas Donoso stayed within the monarchist-Christian tradition, which he salted with socialism.

For some of his abstract and religious principles, Donoso had to turn to traditionalism instead of to the positivism of Saint-Simon or Comte, both of whom scorned metaphysics and theology equally. In 1837 he still rejected that divine idealism of de Maistre, Bonald, Chateaubriand, Lammenais, and

[55] See Iggers, *Cult of Authority*, pp. 42, 59, and 186, on Saint-Simonian borrowing from the traditionalists; also Iggers (ed., trans.), *The Doctrine of Saint-Simon: An Exposition* (Boston, 1958), pp. xv–xvi.

[56] Juretschke, I, 119f, 180f, 198f (*crisis* and *normalcy* terminology). On Comte's debt to the traditionalists, see Jean Lacroix, *La Sociologie d'Auguste Comte*, 2d ed. (Paris, 1961), pp. 20–21.

Ballanche as contrary to reason and liberty. Within a year, however, influenced by Guizot's optimism, Hegel's example and perhaps even by Saint-Simon's *New Christianity* (*Nouveau Christianisme*, 1825), he predicted that rationalism soon would resume a Christian outlook. After realizing his naïveté, he warned that, although reason needed faith for certainty, "philosophy is putting an end to faith." Since he has found eclecticism so incomplete, he had by 1842 begun to borrow heavily from the Christian and Catholic schools of philosophy of Saint Augustine, Bossuet, the traditionalists, and Leibniz.[57] Clearly, he could not thereafter adopt Comte's scientific type of positivism as a general philosophy, for it relegated the old theological philosophy to extinction. If he had not yet read Buchez as a religious Saint-Simonian in 1834, however, it appears that he did read him, notably his *Essai d'un traité complet du point de vue du Catholicisme*, by 1849 as perhaps France's first Christian socialist.[58]

Since Donoso's positivism was always more historical, political, and social than it was philosophical, he was able to remain a positivist in the social sciences while adopting theological first principles after 1847. Hence, he did not simply become a latter-day traditionalist but a positivist *sui generis*. Philosophically he thus remained an independent synthesizer. The acme of his Christian positivism would be the *Essay*, with its bold affirmations, theological sociology, and theology of history.

[57] Juretschke, I, 316–17; 573; 754, 779, 800. E. L. Woodward, *Three Studies in European Conservatism: Metternich, Guizot, and the Catholic Church in the 19th Century* (Hampden, Conn., 1929, 1963), p. 170.

[58] Iggers, *The Doctrine of Saint-Simon*, pp. xiv, xviii. Philosophically, Saint-Simonian positivism was much closer to Donoso's position than was Comte's. Compare Leszek Kolakowski, *The Alienation of Reason. A History of Positivist Thought*, trans. Norbert Guterman (Garden City, N.Y., 1968), p. 10, with Iggers, *Cult of Authority*, pp. 6, 186, 190. However, Comte too became religious, even millennialist in his later outlook; see Kolakowski on "the forgotten" romantic side of Comte, pp. 46–47, 65, 71–73.

PHILOSOPHY OF HISTORY, HISTORY, AND SOCIOLOGY

In his library Donoso had far more histories and biographies than anything else, and most of his reading, writing, and reflection in history was broadly philosophical in spirit.[59] In 1847 he offered a philosophical "definition" of history "in general" as "the biography of the human race," which "comprises all the events of interest to humanity and the exposition of their causes." Synthesizing all of these aspects was too big an undertaking for any mere historian; only a philosopher of history or a theologian of history ever had the temerity to try. Such daring speculators were the writers whom Donoso prized most. Earlier he had also defined philosophy of history as a "history of the human race," uniting all the particular histories of peoples with their revolutions and catastrophes, according not to simple chance but to inalterable laws that were providential and eternal. Of all those who made the effort to write such

[59] Although Donoso mentioned and quoted a wide variety of historians in his published works (Juretschke, I, 541, 792f, 933ff, 944; II, 90ff), his only published "book" review (in *Revista de Madrid*, 1843), was actually a lengthy comment on the lectures of F.G. Moron at the Ateneo (ca. 1841), published as a "*Curso de historia de la civilización de España*" in 6 volumes after 1871, according to Juretschke. Finding Moron's views conveniently similar to his own outlook on ancient and early European civilization (I, 932ff), he did not merely paraphrase him but set forth his own views of Herodotus, Thucydides, Xenophon, Livy, Sallust, Tacitus, Machiavelli, Bossuet, and others in political history or philosophy of history, including Saint Augustine, Vico, Montesquieu, Voltaire, Hume, Gibbon, Robertson, Chateaubriand, Schlegel, Hegel (Gans ed. 1837), Niebuhr, and Savigny. From other contexts (I, 290ff, 540–47) we know that he was already familiar with all, or almost all, of them. Donoso possessed Savigny's *Traité de la possession* (Roman law) when he visited him in Germany in 1849. Later he wanted to purchase the *Philosophie de la vie* of Frederick Schlegel, whose ideas on religion and world history he set forth at length (I, 935ff, cf. 188ff, 222, 248ff). Probably he first encountered Herder's ideas in Cousin, in the *Course of the History of Modern Philosophy* (I, pp. 222–25), and Hegel's in *Fragments philosophiques*. Hegel's name first appeared in his lectures at the Ateneo in 1837, the year when the famous *Lectures* was published, but Donoso probably did not read it until some years later, despite its similarity to his eclectic view of history (I, 281, 305).

history, only Vico, Bossuet, and Saint Augustine ever satisfied Donoso for long. "The man who achieved this undertaking," he said, "would be the true founder of the philosophy of history."[60] Until 1847 that man, for him, was Vico. Thereafter, in imitation of Saint Augustine, he began to construct his own philosophy of history, which one can discern in the "Letters to Montalembert" (1849) and the *Essay*. Nevertheless, for Donoso philosophical history was no end itself but only a means to measure one's place in time or in the stage of development of society, state, and civilization. Thus he drew his formula of Spanish nationalism and his cyclic politics of crisis, transition, and normalcy, which he adapted to Vico's cycle of civilization, largely out of history. At the same time he developed a kind of historical sociology, which paralleled both Comte and the Saint-Simonians.

The course of Donoso's self-education in history was broad and complex; it lasted his lifetime. His interest in history did not begin or end with philosophy of history. He also translated and wrote history and studied all kinds of it. Always fascinated with history, he did not prize mere narrative so much as general laws, forces, tendencies, and movements that he could abstract from the histories of nations, empires, civilizations, revolutions, laws, constitutions, diplomacy, and religions, from social and economic histories, general or universal histories, and finally philosophies of histories. From classical historians of his childhood such as Thucydides and Livy, Donoso had gone on to study historians of the Enlightenment: Montesquieu, Voltaire, Gibbon, and finally Hume. If he always regarded Hume as England's greatest historian, he came to see Voltaire, once "the prince of history," as actually a falsifier of history.[61] After 1830, in reaction to the defects and intolerance of eighteenth-century historians, he had turned to the romantic era. Among the scores of contemporary lesser historians whom he read, one finds greater names such as Hallam, Grote,

[60] Juretschke, II, 113; I, 541; 792, 944; 547.
[61] Juretschke, I, 291–92, 544, 793, 934.

Michelet, Mignet, Sismondi, Guizot, Lamartine, Thiers, Savigny, Niehbuhr, and Johannes von Müller.[62]

Gradually, Donoso began to try his own powers as a historian—first as translator, abridger or amender, and finally as a writer of history. Both to increase his usable historical knowledge and to improve his ability to translate English, he wrote extensive extracts and condensations. Considering Hallam's account of the two seventeenth-century revolutions especially interesting, he summarized his *Constitutional History of England* up to 1776 in twenty-six pages, and he reduced Hume's *History of England* up to 1215 to eighty pages.[63] After preparing with Lardner's *History of Spain and Portugal,* to the reign of Isabella, he was ready for Dunham's *History of Spain,* which he translated up through the Visigoths. Later he added "a review of the more noted Spanish historians" and collaborated with Alcalá Galiano in writing a translation and expansion of Dunham in seven volumes (Madrid, 1844–1846).[64] By then Donoso had actually written an incomplete *History of the Regency of María Cristina* (1843), for which he had accumulated a substantial documentation in original govern-

[62] Of nineteenth-century historians whom Donoso used, the more famous besides Hallam were: Michelet, *Principes de la philosophie de l'histoire* (1831) on Vico; William H. Prescott, *History of the Reign of Ferdinand and Isabella the Catholic,* 6th ed. (Boston, 1839), Guizot's *Histoire générale de la civilization en Europe* (1828); Mignet, *Histoire de la révolution française* (1824); Sismondi, *Historia de las repúblicas italianas* (1807), in Spanish; and Johannes von Müller, *Allgemeiner Geschichte,* 3 vols. (1811ff), in trans. as *Historia universal.* In his library or notebooks are numerous other histories in French, English, or Spanish translations, such as Camefigne's *La diplomacia entre Francia y España desde los Borbones* and *Diplomacia entre la Prussia, la Russia, y la Inglaterra.* See Galindo Herrero, *Theoría política,* pp. 71–74. The volumes in the Donoso Cortés family archives include notes from Prescott, Müller, and Camefigne.

[63] These works are excerpted and summarized in the volumes in the Donoso Cortés family archives: Tomos B, C, D, E, and G; Hume and Hallam are in B.

[64] Samuel Dunham's original was 5 vols. (London, 1833) and was a *History of Spain and Portugal.* Donoso got credit from Galiano only for "a review of the more noted Spanish historians," vol. 4 (1844).

mental and military source materials and book lists of histories and contemporary tracts of all kinds for the period from 1833 up into Espartero's era.[65] If it had been finished, his magnum opus as a historian would have been a valuable work, despite its polemics.

To read or write particular history did not attract Donoso so much as to ponder general and universal history, especially philosophy of history. He particularly admired Guizot's tolerant, balanced, eclectic view of progress in the *History of Civilization in Europe* (*Histoire de la civilisation en Europe*, 1828), which he praised as a work of erudition and genius. Guizot did not condemn Christianity nor view the Middle Ages as merely a dark parenthesis in history. Although he regarded Guizot as the greatest general European historian in an age of national history, he found his power of generalization and synthesis too weak for truly world history and not adequate to show the real unity and character even of European civilization. The scope of J. A. Müller's *Universal History* (*Allgemeine Geschichte*, in French translation) was more daring than Guizot's, but Donoso did not prize the work or the author so highly. To supply what Guizot lacked in breadth and vision he turned instead to the philosophers of history, yet not to Condorcet nor even mainly to Hegel, but to Vico, Bossuet, and Saint Augustine.[66]

Condorcet's idea of indefinite progress and perfectibility in his *Sketch* (1793) soon struck Donoso as a shallow and parochial view of history, even for modern Europe, much less for world history. Cousin's providential "Intelligence" formed the basis for his initial eclectic but quasi-Hegelian outlook on history. Gradually, however, he mixed and transformed this

[65] The Donoso Cortés family archives (Legajo 28) contains a large number of documents from 1833–1839, including diaries, memoirs, and copies or originals of official correspondence from María Cristina, ministers, and generals, and histories or summaries of military campaigns of the civil war.

[66] Juretschke, I, 292; 416f, 789; II, 394–96; I, 792–93. See Tomo G for J. A. Müller, also Legajos 5 and 17.

narrow world view, which terminated with the rise of Guizot's middle class, with elements from de Maistre, Saint-Simon, Vico, Herder, and finally Schlegel. In Hegel's *Lectures on the Philosophy of History* (*Vorlesungen über die philosophie* der *geschichte*, 1837), which Donoso apparently acquired in Gan's edition, history was explained as the progressive dialectical unfolding of a divine and social reason in history, moving from East to West. Apparently he studied Hegel too late to become truly a Hegelian, but, like Proudhon, he appropriated the concept of dialectic for his own cyclic philosophy of history. Besides being unable to accept Hegel's German and Prussian conclusions, he was bothered by a recurring, nagging doubt: What if the whole progressive West itself, and not just some one nation or empire, were in serious trouble and declining?[67]

Through Michelet or Cousin, Donoso found in Vico's *New Science* (1725) a cyclic theory built on Greco-Roman history that he believed was more logical than the idea of simple progress, whether indefinite, bourgeois, or Hegelian. By 1838, when he had reduced and systematized Vico's loose theory of three recurring epochs, he asserted that the current time corresponded to the civil or human era before renewed breakdown and barbarism.[68] Although he still believed that progress could occur, he now set the course of perfectibility within the limits of an inflexible circle. For a while he still believed in contemporary human progress within the limits of a cycle or

[67] Juretschke, I, 810; 103ff, 188f, 222ff, 237, 248ff, 278–302 passim, 583, 934f; 934; II, 113; I, 810; II, 149–50.

[68] Juretschke, I, 566. For earlier references to Vico, see Juretschke, I, 291, 318 (1837), and for probably even earlier use of his ideas, see I, 82, 98, 187. On Donoso's knowledge of Michelet, see I, 547. For a comparison between Donoso's and Michelet's expositions of Vico, see Ramón Ceñal, "Vico and Nineteenth-Century Spanish Thought," in *Giambattista Vico, an International Symposium*, ed. Giorgio Tagliacozzo (Baltimore, 1969). It is probable that Donoso discovered Vico's essential ideas first in Cousin before reading Michelet, that for this reason Vico's conceptions appear in his writing as early as 1835 or even 1833, but not Vico's name prior to 1836.

perhaps within a spiral, which could account for all vicissitudes by a repetitive social and political pattern. Since he had always preferred to combine intellectual and social interpretations of history, Vico also confirmed his view that ultimately ideas rule history, that social and universal history was essentially a history of ideas, of divine ideas less abstract than Hegel's. By 1845, however, he also recognized a material-economic basis for social-political change, succinct but remarkably like Marx's without being a materialistic interpretation of history.[69]

Ultimately Vico contributed most to his recurring doubts about the progressive character of the modern revolutionary movement in Europe. After the next act in the Spanish revolution (1840), he began to supplement his study of Vico with Saint Augustine's *City of God* and with Bossuet's *Universal History* (1681), to which he first adverted in 1838.[70] The residue in Vico of a moral and religious causation, which seemed to echo Augustine and Bossuet,[71] disturbed him when he applied it analogously to modern Spain and to Europe. Convinced now that religion was the only indestructible foundation of human societies, he thought that a society that followed its sophists and deserted its faith would soon abandon its mores and end up in an internecine revolutionary situation, in an anarchy from which (as Vico put it) only dictatorship, catastrophe, or death could deliver it, unless there were a re-

[69] Juretschke, I, 168, 569; 557f, 569; II, 28, 340. Giambattista Vico, *The New Science*, pp. 59, 61–62, 82–83.

[70] Juretschke, I, 543, 810f.

[71] Vico, p. 20 (par. VII–132, 133, VIII–136), p. 381 (par. 1106). J. B. Bossuet, *A Discourse on the History of the Whole World* (London, 1686), pp. 445–50, 483, 505, 548–57 (on Rome). Reflecting Saint Augustine, Bossuet made virtue (persistence, perseverance, patience, love of liberty and country), as the main causes, under Providence, for the rise of nations or empires and vice (as "corruption of manners" from pride, overweening ambition, material abundance and pleasures, luxury, effeminacy, and individual and class dissension). While Vico seems to attribute all of this ultimately to alterations in the social class structure and dominance, Donoso later decided that the ultimate determinator in history is moral, as in Bossuet and Augustine (Juretschke, II, 209; cf. I, 543, 648).

turn to religion.[72] If modern civilization were to avoid the fatal downturn of the cycle, he felt that it must again accept the inspiration of its historic religion, which no new pantheistic cults of mass humanity of Lamartine or Saint-Simon could supplant. Until the revolutions of 1848—except for a pessimistic interlude after 1840—he could hope that Spain and Europe were still progressing, that the cycle had not yet passed its zenith.

His quest for a convincing historical world view led Donoso into social analysis after 1836, a kind of rudimentary historical and comparative approach to political sociology, which reflected Condorcet, Guizot, and Vico, but most closely paralleled the Saint-Simonians and Comte.[73] Paraphrasing Condorcet much as Comte did, he detected in social history a "march in a constant direction toward a determined and fixed point," which reflected its intellectual and moral tendency. "Since the present is only the realization of past tendencies, one can calculate by them the destiny of man and the normal state of nations" and societies. Like Comte and the Saint-Simonians he initially rejected the old metaphysics and instead based his method of investigation on history, which "if less rigorous and exact," was nevertheless "strict in itself and bristling with difficulties and obstacles." From Condorcet and from Montesquieu, "who explains everything by history," he went on to study the social school of Saint-Simonians of which both Comte and Buchez had been a part. He observed that the "social and philosophical principles which they proclaim do not belong to them" but that they had borrowed their fecund ideas from others, including Condorcet and de Maistre, and had given them absurd or ridiculous applications. He decided to use the same principles in a more logical way. Vico

[72] Juretschke, I, 539, 582, 810; 573ff (cf. 98, 367ff), 568–69, 578ff, 597.

[73] See Comte, *Positive Philosophy*, pp. 481–83 on historical method in sociology and pp. 456–57 on the possibility of scientific prevision of social phenomenon by the comparative method.

then reinforced his interest in new social phenomena and the laws of social behavior and development.[74] Donoso abandoned the idea of simple progress for a repetitive cycle of social classes and political forms through divine, heroic, and human epochs in the rise and fall of civilization.

With an historical method and cyclic outlook, he analyzed Spain's past and present and contemporary Europe through its diplomatic problems, especially the Eastern Question. Like Saint-Simon and Comte, he found a still-disturbed condition of transition prevailing. Europe had to find a way out of the crisis brought on Europe by the Enlightenment, French Revolution, and the vast Napoleonic wars, and the threatening nationalist disintegration of the Ottoman and Austrian empires. Spain and the whole West were at a point in Vico's human epoch where they must decide whether they were going "up" into a new social-political era of stability and normalcy or "down" into chaos and ultimate anarchy. He found his country, European civilization, and the world, in great need of regeneration and reconstruction. He hoped the rejuvenation would be led by the French in the West and by the Russians in the East, perhaps culminating in a contest for world domination, world unity, and world civilization by force of arms and by other more fruitful competition. By such a regenerating leadership, he thought, could not be merely intellectual, cultural, political, or economic, it should also be religious; the result should be the triumph of liberal France and Catholicism or of absolutist Russia and Orthodoxy. To be truly progressive in nature, he intimated, the new world age would have to initiate a return to religion, to show some of the religious manifestations of Vico's divine epoch, in order to continue healthy even as a civil and human epoch. The

[74] Juretschke, I, 169, 479; 944; 315f, 469; 540, 547. Through Ballanche, Vico seems to have been a common link between Donoso's thought and that of the Saint-Simonians. See *The Doctrine of Saint-Simon*, ed. G. Iggers, pp. 223–24; Juretschke, I, 318; Iggers, *Cult of Authority*, pp. 28–29.

material unity of the world, he seems to have thought, would again become the basis for its moral and spiritual unity, as formerly under the Roman Caesars.[75]

The bold application that Donoso then made of Vico's ideas in regard to the modern world appears indirectly in Tassara's verses "To Don Juan Donoso Cortés" (1841). "I feel Europe dying,/ From her ruins another Europe,/ Another world is due to arise." Distilling the essence from Donoso's speculation of 1838 on Russia and the Eastern Question,[76] he announced that the future lay with the North and East, with the Russian people. As "new Attila," these "barbarians" would overcome moribund old Europe, which was so corrupt and atheistic, so degenerate in mind and heart, that she had no future unless she would be conquered and subjected to a bloody chastisement and expiation. Tassara and Donoso promised each other to fight the monster of human pride and corruption, sustained only by the desperation of hope, awaiting the new "sun of redemption," the return of the Messiah, after the terrible days of agony, after the "hecatombs and tears of blood."[77]

Later Tassara confessed that he did not understand what he had written. They were Donoso's ideas, reflections of a passing fit of black pessimism during exile, when he abandoned the contemporary belief in the guaranteed progress and indefinite perfectibility of man and society.[78] The miracle of steam power in industry and transportation, world freedom of trade, the increase and refinements of culture and material pleasures, together with the erosion of religion by rationalistic philosophy, were advances that had to lead to enervation and decline in patriotism, mores, morals, and civilization. Europe would degenerate to Vico's darkness of anarchy and barbarism before

[75] Juretschke, I, 429ff, 583ff; 82, 168, 326f; 377f, 461f; 591, 622ff, 782; 461, 810; cf. 131–32; 573ff, cf. 598; 576.

[76] Tassara, *Poesías*, pp. 197–201.

[77] These verses anticipated Tassara's "Un diablo más" (1851–1852).

[78] Tassara (pp. 364–65) attributed these ideas to Donoso.

happier times returned, when "truth, the daughter of God," should again reign as "queen of the world."[79]

Donoso evolved from the confident, arrogant rationalizer who had promised to solve society's problems at first by an absolute principle, then by dictatorship, to the agonized doubter who despaired at the merely human prospect. Henceforth Donoso had found Condorcet's limitless progress incompatible with Vico's cycle unless he could fuse them together in an Augustinian vision of a final City of God. Regarding blind faith in indefinite natural progress as naïve, he no longer accepted optimistic syntheses of progress and nonregressive cycle such as Hegel or Comte offered. For him, humanity "from the beginning until the end of time" was "subject to the same growths and declines; . . . it does not advance in one path except at the price of falling behind in another." His doubts surpassed those of the Saint-Simonians, who warned that progress was sometimes accompanied by great struggles and retrograde resistance, that mankind was perhaps still becoming sick through science instead of recovering its health through a return to religious faith.[80]

Obviously religion was Donoso's last and culminating intellectual interest. It was a concern that coincided with his growing social commitment and positive politics and that climaxed after his conversion in 1847.

[79] Juretschke, I, 809–11.

[80] Juretschke, I, 810. Iggers, *Doctrine of Saint-Simon*, p. 221.

Chapter IV

MAN AND CHRISTIAN: THE TWO CITIES

Man, in Donoso's view, is inharmonious and antithetical in his very nature, a permanent contradiction, even to the grave.[1] Contrasts in his own life and character were sometimes extreme: The spiritual exaltation of his conversion in 1847 clashes violently with the tragic physical disease that caused his unusually pious death in 1853. Something of dualism or dichotomy truly marked his personality, thought, and outlook. "Donoso *fogoso*," with the "words of fire," was also "Donoso *doloroso*," with the romantic "gift of tears."[2] Pacheco recalled that the boldness of his talent and great power of intellect were offset by a timidity of character, an almost feminine sensitivity, and a child-like heart.[3] Still, although Donoso too humbly admitted that there was no harmony between his maxims and his actions,[4] one should not actually sunder the unity of his character, thought, and action. Some interpretations consider what he did before his conversion or before the revolutions of 1848 as of little or no consequence to what he did afterward. They separate "the young Donoso" in Spain and "the great Donoso" of European fame after 1848 as if the newer religious side of his thought and life were so decisive as to render his worldly, political, and intellectual endeavors in-

[1] Juan Juretschke, ed., *Obras completas*, II, 24, 300.

[2] Spaniards still commonly use the first term for the second; see Joseph Bernhart, "Donoso Doloroso," *Living Age*, 342 (August, 1932), 544–50.

[3] Pacheco, quoted in Edmund Schramm, *Donoso Cortés, su vida y su pensamiento*, p. 19.

[4] Juretschke, II, 588.

significant unless reduced to a narrow theological framework.[5] On the other hand, because Donoso was still obviously engaged in the political world even after his conversion, it is too easy to agree with the fascist Eugenio D'Ors's description of him as "hot rhetorician, cold politician," as if he were all words and no action. Donoso told Guizot, however, that the world is not "saved by thought alone but also by action, since man thinks only with the intent of acting later in conformity with what he has thought."[6] Even though he feared to exercise political power himself, he tirelessly urged bolder leaders such as Narváez and Louis Napoleon to enforce his system and program for him. Yet these realistic political efforts in turn make exceedingly strange contrast with his private asceticism and charitable activities as a social Christian. Supposing that his conversion was like Saint Paul's putting on "the new man," the old natural man was still there. Donoso felt keenly and strove to overcome that inner conflict, weakness, and deficiency. His personality was as complex as his thought. His European restraint, humanity, and polish held in check certain one-sided Spanish traits that provided him force, drive, and intensity. Despite his later admiration for the saints over the secular heroes who have ruled this world, he found himself a citizen of both the City of God and the City of the World, faced with often contradictory claims that brough him anguish and indecision for which there was no eclectic solution.

By a remarkable accident, Donoso sensed in 1847 that an epoch of transition was giving place to an epoch of conclusions, not only in the European political world but also in his own personal life. This was the year of his "conversion," as he called it, an intensely personal spiritual and emotional experience that coincided with another "conversion" in his leading ideas, altered to fit the changing times and society. Neither con-

[5] This *manqué* interpretation is too characteristic of Spanish and clerical studies, for example, Suárez Verdeguer and Monsegú.

[6] Juretschke. II, 557.

version was very sudden, for, he later admitted, they had been "preparing" in his mind and spirit over some years past. Already in 1838 he had predicted his shift in thought to a more dogmatic and synthetic position to suit a normal era, and the intellectual foundations of his unforeseen religious conversion were almost as old.[7] After 1847, his year of decision, his new religious fervor advanced apace with his new thought in politics, philosophy, history, and sociology. He developed a system of positive Christianity or Christian positivism, which was a mixture largely of de Maistre's religious philosophy of traditionalism with social sciences comparable to Comte's. He seized upon the liberal reforms of Pius IX in 1847 as a convenient pretext to proclaim a new millennial epoch both for himself and for the whole Western world, ironically just before the Ateneo and Spanish Academy awarded him the nation's highest honors for his past thought and services as an eclectic and doctrinaire Moderate and just before the revolutions of 1848 broke out to mock all of his high hopes for the emergence of a great organic epoch of normalcy that might also become a City of God on earth. Religious and secular conversions and millennialism, incidentally abounded in that romantic era, from Chateaubriand and Mme. von Krüdener to Owen and Comte.[8]

Donoso was not the only one to be wrenched back to reality by the shocks and disappointments of 1848. Nevertheless, if he then preached force and dictatorship for Spain and Europe to cope with the new general revolutionary crisis and the threat of socialism, he did not abandon his ideal of Christian social-democratic monarchy. Despite his frustrations, he did not forsake politics and diplomacy, although he wanted nothing more than to withdraw from a world that seemed to him to

[7] Juretschke, II, 60; 210; I, 416f, 573ff.

[8] Both Comte and Bismarck experienced conversions in the 1840s, the former's centering on Clothilde de Vaux. On Owen's millennialism, see J. F. C. Harrison, *A Quest for the New Moral World: Robert Owen and the Owenites in Britain and America* (New York, 1969).

be going mad with materialism and destined to end in world war and world revolution. In the years after 1848, while he made deep personal impressions on individuals both as a man and as a Christian, he made extraordinary efforts as an intellectual, politician, and even diplomat to initiate a return to genuine Christianity that might change the inevitable and retrogressive course of events which he discerned in Western Civilization. However, he began with himself in his conversion and in his personal relations with others as a social Christian. His letters to such notable individuals as Montalembert (1849) and his *Essay on Catholicism, Liberalism and Socialism* (1851) set forth an influential apocalyptic and millennialist theology of history. In these writings, he imitated not only Saint Augustine's *City of God* by his radical dualism but also Chateaubriand, by stressing the beauty of Christianity, and Comte, by offering a sociology of order. The emphasis on logical necessity, however, was as before, peculiar to Donoso.

CONVERSION OF HEART AND MIND

In Mme. Swetchine's salon in Paris in 1853, Donoso said that the marked change in his character and personality after 1848 was due more to a conversion than to a mellowing from age and experience. With simple dignity he explained his conversion as a return to Christian ideas after having lost his convictions through too much reading in French and Latin authors.[9] However, he had confided to Blanche-Raffin, "I was always a believer in the depth of my soul" and would have died rather than abjure the faith, although it was not a faith of the heart but of the head, and therefore not strong, active, or pervasive.[10] Sensing a monstrous contradiction between his mind and his conduct, he conceded nothing to his talent or reason;

[9] The salon story is in Schramm, *Vida y pensamiento*, pp. 189–92, in Bois-le-Comte's secondhand version and also in a letter in the Donoso Cortés family archives.

[10] For Donoso's account of his conversion to Blanche-Raffin, see Juretschke, II, 224–27.

they were too weak and life was too short. The mystery of his conversion, he stressed, was one of tenderness of heart, which first led him to love his brother Pedro, later to love the poor as a brother, and finally to love God and religion. Still, "God had prepared me" with two instruments, first a friend and then a brother, the goodness of the one and the pious death of the other, between 1842 and 1847.[11]

The friend who influenced Donoso was a Spanish musician, Massarnau, whom he and Raffin knew at Paris around 1842.[12] Although Massarnau was not brilliant, he was nevertheless simple, upright, religious, and devoted to good works. Considering himself an *honnête homme*, Donoso could not understand why he should regard his friend's virtue, *honnêteté*, to be of a higher order than his own. Massarnau had answered, "Because I have remained a Christian while you no longer are." Donoso pondered this disconcerting reply "often" over several years until his dying brother explained that it was the difference between natural and supernatural, or worldy and Christian virtue.[13]

The culminating experience that promoted Donoso's conversion was the death of his favorite, always-pious brother Pedro in Madrid in June, 1847. Rushing home from Paris to witness Pedro's final days of suffering, Donoso was touched to the very heart; he wept at the sight and confessed that he would always weep at that memory. He had lived and died like an angel, Donoso recalled. "From then on I swore to love and

[11] Juretschke, II, 225.

[12] Carlos Valverde, ed., *Obras completas*, I, 52–54; II, 342, correctly identifies Massarnau, but I disagree with his new date (June, 1847) for Donoso's conversation with Massarnau. The close juxtaposition of it with Pedro's death in the salon story may be only poetic licence. What does thinking "often" and "middle of my life" mean to a man of forty-two, and was not Donoso in Paris with María Cristina both in 1840–1843 and 1847? Most significant is the fact that through Massarnau Donoso met Blanche-Raffin, who claimed to be his oldest friend in Paris and whose recollections were of Donoso's writings of 1842. Letters, Raffin to Donoso (July 15, 1849; May 2, 1850), in Donoso Cortés family archives.

[13] Schramm, *Vida y pensamiento*, pp. 190–91. Juretschke, II, 225.

adore, and I do love and adore . . . my brother's God . . . I did not love Him, but God willed that I love Him." In this way he explained the mystery of his conversion.[14]

Thereafter Donoso turned from a perfunctory Christian into a zealot whose conviction became invincible and whose intense faith ruled his whole life in thought, words, and actions. The change not only soon became visible in his glowing eyes, arresting speech, kindly and gracious manners, and in an extraordinary life of piety and good works, but also in the deep depressions, gloomy apocalyptic outlook, alienation from the world, and monkish desire for withdrawal and solitude that his poor health and occasional collapses reinforced and partly induced from 1849 onward. Intellectually his conversion to good principles (as he later described it to Montalembert)[15] moved him to change from an eclectic into a Christian positivist, a transformation that required considerable thought, time, and effort, despite the fact that he had already long been preparing for a normal epoch. The intensity of his intellectual commitment to Christianity thenceforth was undoubtedly caused by his religious conversion.

EUROPEAN SOCIAL CHRISTIAN AND SPANISH ASCETIC

In its intellectual and social roots Donoso's conversion began in Paris during his exile. He was especially inspired by the liberal and social Catholic movement of the 1840s with such leaders as Montalembert, Ozanam, and Lacordaire, the friends of Blanche-Raffin whom he had met through Massarnau around 1842.[16] Besides reading in "the Catholic school" of thought—not only Saint Augustine and de Maistre but very much of Lamennais and perhaps Lacordaire—Donoso had contact with political and literary circles which may well have included the *cercle Catholique*, a Christian center with library

[14] Juretschke, II, 224–25.

[15] Juretschke, II, 210.

[16] See footnote 12 and Juretschke, II, 225. "Blanche-Raffin," in *Dictionnaire de biographie française*, VI (Paris, 1754), 618.

and public lectures by Ozanam, Lacordaire, Montalembert, and Ravignan.[17] Exactly when he made lasting personal contact with that group is not certain, but by 1848 he was already on sufficiently friendly terms with Montalembert to send him two volumes by the mystic Luis de Granada and to receive in return an effusive letter dedicated to their friendship and bonds of sympathy in religious, political, and social faith.[18] Finding memories of former encounters too brief, Montalembert desired to know Donoso more fully in the future. His reply was dated January 4, 1849, the very day on which Donoso delivered the speech on dictatorship which, Montalembert observed later, suddenly made him famous in Europe. Only then did Louis Veuillot, pugnacious editor of *L'Univers*, and other French acquaintances pay much attention to a foreigner to whom they may have been introduced previously. Undoubtedly, however, they had influenced him to develop as a social Christian and to espouse causes at the Cortes in 1844–1845 such as mutual independence or freedom of Church and State, social responsibility for the bourgeoisie, and material rights and religious education for the masses.

There are several descriptions of Donoso in years after his conversion, some of which stress his Spanish asceticism while others see the more humane and affable European traits, but all were impressed by his genuine Christianity. On a scrap of paper, he once wrote, "The great patrician and the perfect Christian are formed by the same virtues." It was for these religious and humane virtues that his friends admired him.[19] One of his later portraits seemed to reflect the change that was coming over him: One can see there a truly humane and hum-

[17] See Juretschke, II, 778–83, 790, 800. Tome D in the Donoso Cortés family archives includes notes from his readings in Lacordaire and Falloux along with others from Saint Augustine, de Maistre, and Lamennais. Paul Schimberg, *The Great Friend: Frederick Ozanam* (Milwaukee, 1946), p. 162.

[18] Letter, Montalembert to Donoso (January 4, 1849), Donoso Cortés family archives.

[19] Paper preserved in Donso Cortés family archives.

ble man with a plain but relaxed and kindly visage, which was redeemed and dominated by gentle, luminous eyes, without a visible trace of the old pride and arrogance.[20] Count Hübner, the Austrian ambassador who thought that he had the temperament of a monkish ascetic, recalled that this "little Southerner" would have been quite ordinary, except for the noble fire in his eyes and his superb spirit.[21] In a beautiful tribute, Montalembert saw him as a man who tried to be all things to all men "what the Italians call an *uomo simpatico*." He was a genuinely, charming man, whose expansive and vivacious innocence made religion likeable and Christian virtue attractive, who despite his black pessimism stayed young of heart, playful of mood, always agreeable, always ready with a friendly smile, enjoying everything around him in an intelligent way, always ready to forgive and to encourage. "That is what made knowing him so easy and so sure, what gave his whole being something penetrating, endearing, and irresistible."[22] Veuillot also sensed in Donoso a delicacy and sincerity of heart, a beauty and greatness of soul, and he liked to repeat his words: "Only he who believes knows and only he who is humble is great."[23] Charles de Mazade was struck by the man himself, by the contrast between his absolute doctrines and his character, full of ease and kindness; it was his superiority without haughtiness and his genuine simplicity, along with his sparkling and ingenious wit, that made him liked and esteemed in the world of Paris.[24] Still others commented on his brilliance, charm, lack of vindictiveness, ingenuous frankness, glowing eyes, and fascinating conversation.

[20] This portrait is reproduced in Schramm, *Vida y pensamiento*.

[21] Joseph A. Hübner, *Neuf Ans de souvenirs d'un ambassadeur d'Autriche à Paris sous le Second Empire, 1851–1859*, I (Paris, 1904), 130.

[22] Montalembert, XV (II), 189.

[23] L. Veuillot, quoted from a letter of October 27, 1849, in Donoso Cortés family archives (Schramm, *Vida y pensamiento*, p. 320); Veuillot, quoted by Juan Manuel Ortí y Lara, *Obras de Juan Donoso Cortés*, I, cvi (a reply from D. to V. in 1851); also see Veuillot, I, lx–lxii.

[24] Charles Mazade, "Chroniques de la quinzaine," *La Revue de Deux Mondes*, 33e Année, seconde série, X (1853), 855.

In his later years Donoso made friends among all ranks and walks of life, from kings and nobles to bourgeoisie and paupers, and of all nationalities—French, German, Russian, Austrian, English, Italians, Scandinavians, at least one Jew (Baron Rothschild), and one American.[25] Despite his political and religious views, as Mazade observed, he made friends more easily than enemies among politicians, diplomats, journalists, litterateurs, philosophers, bankers, engineers, and artists, whether their politics were absolutist, Caesarian Bonapartist, conservative Legitimist, liberal Orleanist, democratic republican, or ex-Saint-Simonian socialist. None of his friends did he esteem more highly than Count Charles de Montalembert, a refined aristocrat, and Louis Veuillot, a brusque plebeian, but it was difficult for this bourgeois to be on good terms with two such different personalities at the same time. After 1849 Veuillot received him into his home and family; they loved to exchange ideas, and sometimes shared their spiritual lives—visits to the Carmelites or walking on pilgrimage to Argenteuil in 1851 through torrents of rain that, joked Donoso, could still not wash away his sins.[26] Montalembert and he were much the same in age, tastes, eloquence, and burning faith, so despite some differences in temperament and politics, they considered living together at Paris and going on a grand tour of Europe.[27] Although Frédéric Ozanam visited Donoso in 1851, we know nothing of the personal relationship of these two social Chris-

[25] Juretschke, II, 233, 774. He mentions his "rich" American friend from New York, at whose hotel-residence he stayed at first, in an unpublished dispatch (July 17, 1852) but does not give his name. A few English names appear on his invitation and visitor lists, but most were of British origin and title, for example, Hamilton and Douglas, but others are not so certain: Webb, Thayer. He visited Rothschild's house in 1849, carried a letter of reintroduction to the brothers in 1851, thereafter invited Baron Rothschild to dinner, and Rothschild attended his funeral.

[26] See Eugène Veuillot, *Louis Veuillot*, II (Paris, 1913), 513. Louis Veuillot, I, lxiii. Letter, Veuillot to Donoso (August 25, 185[?]), Donoso Cortés family archives.

[27] R. P. Lecanuet, *Montalembert*, III (Paris, 1902), 139–40. The letters from Montalembert in the Donoso Cortés family archives are eloquent witness to deep friendship.

tians whose politics were so opposite. Both promoted the Saint Vincent de Paul Society, which Ozanam had founded in Paris and which Donoso helped start in Madrid. They also worked among the poor of the Mouffetard quarter of Paris with the same persons.[28] Fellow ambassadors with whom Donoso was particularly friendly after 1849 were Raczynski of Prussia and Bulwer of Britain at Madrid; Meyendorff of Russia at Berlin; and Hübner of Austria, Hatzfeld of Prussia, Bois-le-Comte of Switzerland, and Brignole of Sardinia-Piedmont at Paris. Raczynski, whose discretion and sober judgment Donoso prized, found Donoso not only charming, interesting, and engaging but also came to admire his prodigious imagination, originality of forms, goodness of heart, and devotion to principles.[29] Admiring him as a profound and original spirit, Hübner often came to discuss all manner of topics in Donoso's plain room at the embassy, where he slept, worked, thought, prayed, and smoked countless cigarettes.[30] Río, his *ami de coeur* and a part-time diplomat who, in Montalembert's words, virtually worshipped him, also sought him out to talk, especially on Plato. In Río's judgment, Donoso resembled Plato in lofty approach to great questions, but he could also tease Donoso about his friendly walks with Madame Thayer in Paris.[31] Hübner is our best witness to Donoso's social life as Spanish ambassador in the gilded Parisian world of court, salons, and the whirl of dinners, festivities, ceremonies, and affairs of legation of which he complained.[32] Among the glittering throng of princes, nobles,

[28] Schramm, *Vida y pensamiento*, p. 319. L. Veuillot, I, lix-lx. J.P. Derum, *Apostle in a Top Hat, the Life of Frederick Ozanam* (New York, 1960), p. 193. Letter, Valmy to Donoso (August 8, 1851), Donoso Cortés family archives; as president of the Saint Vincent Society in Paris, Valmy wrote to thank Donoso for his "influence" and "zeal" in getting the authorization of his government.

[29] Juretschke, II, 795. Comte Adéhemar d'Antioche, *Deux Diplomates*, p. 164.

[30] Hübner, *Neuf Ans*, pp. 129, 130.

[31] Letters, Río to Donoso (June 4, 1851; September 7, 1852), Donoso Cortés family archives; also Montalembert to Donoso (January 4, 1849).

[32] Juretschke, II, 806, 821.

ministers of state, and politicians, Donoso was one of those foreigners of distinction who mix well in any company, although sometimes he was too depressed to put on a display of wit and charm. "Certainly," said Hübner, "he was little given to enjoy the 'small talk' of the salons" of Mme. Swetchine and Princess de Lieven, which he attended out of a sense of duty. "One day, when I met him on the stairs at a ministry, . . . sighing in Spanish accent, he said to me: 'When I die, St. Peter will ask me: "Donoso Cortés . . . what have you done" and I shall answer: "I have gone calling." ' "[33]

Public social events and dinner parties in Paris or the unavoidable visits, clubs, and drives in Madrid scarcely qualified Donoso as a social Christian. This other religious side of his life he kept as secret as possible. He admired Saint Vincent de Paul so much that he referred to himself as a mere loafer; he was very generous in his contributions to both the French and Spanish branches of Ozanam's Society.[34] "I have never seen a poor man at my doors," he confided, "without seeing in him a brother."[35] He believed in charity, practiced it, and preached it. When he advocated it in a speech of 1850 as the only just solution to the ill distribution of wealth short of socialist confiscation, *El Heraldo* had mocked, "Are you an almsgiver?" Donoso had modestly refused to answer.[36] Montalembert, however, knew that in Madrid he gave a sixth of his income to the poor, and Veuillot recorded that in Paris he gave generously to the Little Sisters of the Poor, the nuns of Saint Augustine, and the sisters of Saint Vincent de Paul, as well as working in the hovels of the poor with the then famous Sister Rosalee.[37] Once, when he had nothing else, he gave an expen-

[33] Hübner, *Neuf Ans*, p. 17, 46, 62–63, 130.

[34] Juretschke, II, 205; this letter is misdated; it should be 1850; II, 318. Santiago Galindo Herrero, "Donoso Cortés en la última etapa de su vida," *Arbor*, 25 (May, 1953), 6. Montalembert, *Oeuvres*, XV (II), p. 201.

[35] Quoted by Bois-le-Comte, in Schramm, *Vida y pensamiento*, p. 191.

[36] Juretschke, II, 339f, 589.

[37] Montalembert, XV (II), 201. *El Faro* (May 22, 1853), p. 587ff. L. Veuillot, I, lix–lx. Letter to Sister Julie Marie (January 2, 1852) from

sive shirt, and even from his death bed he sent out anonymous alms for the poor.[38] All of these outlays overburdened his ambassador's salary of 300,000 reales a year, so the difference had to come out of his properties in Spain.[39] He was prosperous financially but not rich, and he saw his total worth decrease by about a quarter during the last year of his life. Charity was only one of his solutions to the uneven distribution of wealth. Like Ozanam's friend, Melun, so-called minister of charity, he also wanted to institutionalize public assistance.[40]

Private works of charity were Donoso's compensation for his busy life in the world. Beginning in Germany in 1849 he experienced a world weariness and strong desire to retire into a private life of study, writing, and good works, possibly into religious life and meditation. Again in Paris in 1851 he was so worn out in mind and body that he wanted to quit diplomacy and politics before a year was out—"all this glory is smoke" and "vanity."[41] As soon as the grave political crisis passed, he hoped to withdraw, but events moved too rapidly from dictatorship to empire. He agonized over whether to take the step and then perhaps regret it or to remain in the world and work for its betterment in diplomacy and active politics. "With one foot I am in the world, with the other in solitude; with one in politics, with the other in religion, so that my soul is becoming a sea of confusion." Why, he asked, "is it not possible to serve God in politics as well as outside it?"[42] Even though he dis-

---

Donoso as "debtor of the poor," Donoso Cortés family archives. *L'Assemblée Nationale*, quoted by L. Veuillot in *L'Univers*, 123 (May 9, 1853).

[38] L. Veuillot, cited by Salvador Minguijón, in *Centenario del fallecimiento de . . . Donoso Cortés*, p. 42. *L'Univers* (May 5, 1853).

[39] A paper in the archives of the Spanish Ministry of Foreign Affairs in Madrid gives his salary as 200,000 reales at Berlin and 300,000 reales at Paris. See Santiago Galindo Herrero, *Donoso Cortés y su theoría política*, pp. 148, 151, 136, for letters and details pertaining to Donoso's property and wealth and his problems with it.

[40] Gordon Griffith, *Studies in Modern European History in Honor of F. C. Palm* (New York, 1956), pp. 141–56.

[41] Juretschke, II, 227, 773; 793f. Valverde, II, 477.

[42] For this letter, see Galindo Herrero, "En la última etapa," p. 8; also Valverde, II, 477–78.

liked the intrigues and feared the evil passions of political life, he honestly admitted how hard it was to close the heart to vainglory, and the desire to count in the world, to pass for an orator and *savant*, and sometimes even to control the will for revenge. Self-interest and ambition, however, would not hold him in public life, because fortune favored only those without conscience or honor. "The Christian, equally with him who is not so, has self-love, but with this single difference: the one has it at his feet, the other in his head. . . . I shall succeed in overcoming it, if I am a true Christian."[43]

Worried that his desire for the contemplative life might be only dangerous illusions of fantasy, he unburdened himself about his moral uncertainty to several spiritual advisers. Almost all of them urged him to stay in the world, not to bury his talents in the country or a monk's cell. Veuillot urged him to light lamps and cry out in the dark, post-Christian world, especially in Paris, the capital of revolutions. Montalembert also advised him to stay in Paris to study the men and politics of Europe. That "necessary science will serve you well all the rest of your career," a career that "will be militant, because with a voice and fame like yours, you will never be allowed to shut yourself off in study and solitude." Raczynski also warned him not to withdraw, "because your spirit is a volcano and your imagination will never know rest."[44]

Whatever his final intentions, Donoso remained in the world, but he lived almost like a monk. Hübner described him as a "hermit lost on the parched steppes of the diplomatic world, an apostle preaching to the savages in the salons, an

[43] Juretschke, II, 796.

[44] Juretschke, II, 318. Letters of the self-seeking Franciscan Serra to Donoso (May 9, May 12, October 1, 1850), in the Donoso Cortés family archives, urged him to forsake the world; Donoso ignored him. Letters of Veuillot to Donoso (October 27, 1849; January 13, 1851), Donoso Cortés family archives. Letter of Montalembert to Donoso (September 26, 1851), Donoso Cortés family archives. Raczynski, in D'Antioche, p. 163.

ascetic in the gilded garb of the ambassador."[45] As he began reading the works of mystics such as Kempis' *Imitation of Christ* (*De Imitatione Christi*), his moral temperament took on a rather medieval character: His new outlook expressed itself in a variety of penances and good works, for example, his pilgrimages to Saint Theresa's Avila and to Argenteuil (the Holy Shroud).[46] Like Thomas More, he even wore a hair shirt and other irritants; he confessed and took the Eucharist frequently, prayed at least a half-hour daily, and visited the poor in their homes and in the hospitals on Sundays.[47] He performed these deeds because he was convinced that there was no salvation without suffering, and he wanted to unite his own suffering with Christ's. Besides, he relied on the prayers of the poor, whom God always heard.

Apart from his conversion, the character and intensity of Donoso's private religious life reflected certain Spanish and Quixotic traits that lay just below the polished surface of his Frenchified and European public image. If he loved his sunny, easy-going country with infinite tenderness, he readily admitted to sharing Spaniards' indolence, pride, fatalism, and extremism, which somehow put Spain beyond the bounds of moral Europe. "The historical character of the Spanish," he said, "is exaggeration in everything: we exaggerate the virtues and the vices, the great things and the small." Because of its fatalistic tendencies, Spanish Catholicism seemed to him as similar to Africa and the Orient as to France and Northern Europe.[48] He exaggerated ideas into absolutes, gloom into despair, and faith almost into fanaticism. By turning to the dead

[45] Hübner, *Neuf Ans*, p. 129.

[46] Juretschke, II, 318, and Galindo Herrero, "En la última etapa," p. 3.

[47] A gruesome sight, the hair shirt and barbed harness are in Don Benito, at a school patronized by the Donoso Cortés family. Letters from Juan to Paco are in the Donoso Cortés family archives, especially Legajo 56, although this one, of June 3, 1850, was published in Galindo Herrero's article, "En la última etapa."

[48] Juretschke, II, 817, 205, 318; 785f; 66.

or dying past for ideals and inspiration, by girding himself confidently in the armor of faith, and by assaulting modern errors and corruption with simple conviction and reckless courage, Donoso reminds one of Don Quixote tilting at windmill–giants without regard for human opinion. Barbey D'Aurevilly, however, compared Donoso to the Saint Augustine of the *Confessions*, as a personification of tenderness and courage; he believed in what he said and would not bend for all the popularity in the world.[49] Like Don Quixote, Donoso's fervent commitment to the absolute and ideal was unshakable by everyday realities or the contempt of men, and like the knight errant, he died defeated by the real world, although, looking to the far future and eternity, he died with hope and expectation. Like Saint Augustine, the ex-Manichean African who died before the final collapse of the Roman City of the World, he also still awaited the City of God, but only after an Armageddon and Apocalypse of world war and world revolution. A modern Christian novelist later appropriately picked Donoso, as an archetype or exemplary Christian, to confront Rousseau in a dialogue high in a cathedral tower overlooking northern France in 1914. It was a "salvation story" with dualistic (if not Manichean) contrasts of good and evil, in a three-dimensional cosmos beyond the bounds of space and time.[50]

Donoso's deep, dark apocalyptic pessimism after 1849 was due perhaps not only to traces of Spanish fatalism and extremism or to a studied intellectual persuasion but also to periodic physical and emotional illness, which induced deep melancholy and depression. His glowing, luminous eyes remind one of the sad, mystic visages of El Greco, who repeatedly modeled saints from madmen, supposing a close affinity between insanity and great sanctity. Those possessed of charis-

[49] Jules Barbey D'Aurevilly, *Les Oeuvres et les hommes; Philosophes et écrivains religieux* (Paris, 1912), pp. 36–38.

[50] Anthony W. Riley, "Elizabeth Langgasser and Juan Donoso Cortés: A Source of the 'Turm Kapitel' in *Das Unauslöschliche Siegel*," *PMLA*, 80 (May, 1969), 357–67.

matic powers have often possessed such a piercing gaze or magnetic manner, the physical expression of highest emotional intensity and conviction, such as Luther, Napoleon, Rasputin, and Hitler—spiritual as well as secular figures, both good and evil geniuses. Such were the fantastic eyes of Tassara's Donoso-Amadeo, weeping eyes that saw a future of horrors. Apologizing for his black prophecies, Donoso confessed, "I believe that I am attacked by a true moral disease, whose effect is to see political affairs in the most somber colors. But, as you know, everything looks sad to one who is ruled by sadness." To another he admitted that the catastrophes he foresaw filled him with great sadness but also inspired him with highest joy as manifesting truth and providence. Usually, however, he contrived to be lighthearted and gay with his companions, even while announcing dire calamities to the public. "If Valdegamas is a Jeremiah, he is a good-humoured Jeremiah," observed Guizot, who previously regarded him as *un homme d'esprit.*[51]

CHRISTIAN 'POSITIVISM', LIBERALISM, AND SOCIALISM

As part of his anticipation of a normal era, Donoso studied religion, particularly Christianity and Catholicism, ever more intensely both before and after his conversion. Like Saint-Simon in the *New Christianity* (1825), he was convinced that the new organic epoch must have an organized and independent religious and moral order to balance and instruct the new commercial and industrial order of the bourgeoisie. Regardless of his early opposition to inquisition, Jesuits, and mortmain, he believed much more strongly than Saint-Simon that the traditional Christianity could serve that purpose or could be liberalized and modernized to do so. By 1838 Donoso had popularized from Vico's *New Science* the idea that religion

[51] Gabriel García y Tassara, *Poesías*, p. 405. See Valverde, II, 38, 122. Guizot, quoted by J.M. Villefanche, *Dix Grands Chrétiens du siécle* (Paris, 1892), p. 79.

was a perpetually necessary social bond and restraint, without which society would decay and decline into bloody class war, anarchy, and disintegration before the cycle began again in a new divine age. Believing that Europe's ultimate survival depended on her return to religious faith, he searched for religious knowledge relating to social history. At first Ballanche's *Essais de palingénésie sociale* (1829), which was a liberal, progressive, and Christian extension of Vico's ideas, greatly attracted him, as it did the Saint-Simonians and the historian Ozanam. Soon he was interested in Bossuet's *Universal History* (1681), from which he moved back to Saint Augustine's *City of God*, theologies of history in which he saw the "finger of God tracing the circles" of history.[52] By the early 1840s in Paris, perhaps partly due to his interest in Saint-Simonian thought, he took another look at the traditionalist romantic conservatives and this time liked what he read, especially de Maistre's *The Pope* (*Du Pape*, 1819) and *Soirées de St. Pétersbourg* (1821) and Lamennais's *Indifference* (1823) and many others of his works on into the *l'Avenir* and liberal period.[53]

[52] Saint-Simon, *Selected Writings*, pp. 85–86; cf. 21, 27. Juretschke, I, 98, 558, 573ff; cf. G. B. Vico, *The New Science* trans. T. G. Bergin and M. Y. Fisch (New York, 1961), pp. 377 (par. 1100), 382 (1107), 383 (1109). Juretschke, I, 318. *The Doctrine of Saint-Simon*, p. 223. Albert J. George, *Pierre-Simon Ballanche, Precursor of Romanticism* (Syracuse, N.Y., 1945), p. 117. Juretschke, I, 792. Donoso's surviving notes on Saint Augustine's *City of God* are in Tomo D, in the Donoso Cortés family archives.

[53] Juretschke, I, 790, 778ff. Some of Donoso's notes from *Soirées de St. Pétersbourg* and *Du Pape* are in Tomo D, in the Donoso Cortés family archives; other notes on de Maistre (now lost) were in Tomo A. Also see Schramm (p. 44). From 1837 Donoso had also read de Maistre's *Considerations sur la France* ("revolution is a crime" and a "punishment"; see Juretschke, I, 347, also 809), and his early constitutional doctrine of 1834 (Juretschke, I, 118ff) reflects de Maistre's *Essai sur le principe générateur des constitutions politiques* (1808) even before it reflects Bonald's *Théorie du pouvoir politique et religieux dans la société civil* (1796) on unity of power (cf., Juretschke, I, 241, and 334f, 339ff; II, 638. Notes on Lamennais from a variety of works (*L'Indifference*) and articles (*L'Avenir*) are also in Tomo D (pp. 205–379), where they constitute an extensive section. See Juretschke, I, 790.

From this time until after 1848, he also began to read the works of other liberal and social Catholics, first of France and later of Germany and England. Among them were Ozanam, Montalembert, Buchez, Döllinger, Görres, and Newman. The book lists he compiled after his conversion indicate a marked preference for religious works of history and history of the Church, theology, pathology, hagiography, lives of Christ and Mary, devotions and spiritual guides, and the Bible in eighteen volumes.[54] Most numerous were the lives of the saints, ranging from the ancient Fathers of East and West on through the Middle Ages and early Modern times, including such contemporary works as Montalembert's *St. Elizabeth* and J. A. Moehler's *St. Athanasius*. As his *Essay* shows, Donoso had a high regard for these saints or citizens of the higher heavenly city henceforth than for the heroes or elite of the lower city of the world.[55] Besides Rohrbacher's twenty-eight volumes and other histories of the Church, he purchased quite a few studies of Moses and of Jewish history and several works of an irenic purpose such as Leibniz's *Thoughts* on religion and morals. As early as the mid-1840s he was buying the works of Tertullian and other ancient Fathers, as well as Suárez and Molina, but particularly after 1847 he obtained a number of solid works in theology, not simply newer editions of Bossuet and of Saint Augustine's *Soliloques* and *City of God*, or Saint Thomas' *Summa* in ten volumes but also works in mysticism by authors such as Luis de León and Luis de Granada, and in Scholastic theology, such as Louis Bail's three volumes on Saint Thomas and Cardinal Gousset's eight volumes of *Moral Theology* (*Théologie Morale*) and *Dogmatic Theology* (*Théologie Dogmatique*, Paris, 1848–1851), from which he took nearly seventy pages of notes, especially on religion as the necessary basis of society and of individual virtue.[56] Donoso's tomes also contain

[54] These book lists are in Legajo 25, Donoso Cortés family archives, and they appear to date from 1847 to 1853, with several in 1849.

[55] Juretschke, II, 539–41.

[56] Tome C, Donoso Cortés family archives.

lengthy extracts which he made of the writings of Augustine, Thomas, Luis de Granada, de Maistre, and Lamennais.[57] Evidently he was not just posturing when he said that Saint Augustine and Saint Thomas were his ideals in Christian philosophy.[58]

The overriding intellectual purpose of Donoso's religious studies from 1838 to 1848 and beyond was a new dogmatic synthesis, not only of a historical, philosophical, political, and social nature but also of a religious and theological type. This was an aim he shared with Saint-Simon, Comte, and the Saint-Simonians: to create a new positive system culminating in a religion for the long awaited organic, or normal epoch.[59] Inspired by Saint-Simon's *New Christianity*, the Saint-Simonian *Doctrine* (1829) had explicitly rejected Comte's earlier scientific positivism as atheistic and negative. In *The Doctrine*, Comte's famous theological, metaphysical, and scientific stages were given a cyclic twist. Instead of ending with atheist scientism, the final stage was an organic epoch that would be theological and religious; there was no radical scientific distinction between natural and supernatural in laws, causes, and beliefs, because man was naturally a religious being and science properly embraced the totality of human knowledge.[60] All of this early criticism of Comte sounds very much like Donoso's *Essay* of 1851, where the Saint-Simonians are the most prominent of the socialist schools. Comte, whose *System of Positive*

[57] Tome A (Augustine, Thomas, Bossuet, and de Maistre) is lost, but Tome D has Augustine's *City of God*, Lamennais's *Indifference*, and de Maistre's *Du Pape*, and Tomes C and E have Luis de Granada (also Legajo 14).

[58] Juretschke, II, 222.

[59] See Iggers, *The Cult of Authority*, pp. 1–6, 189f, where he distinguishes the "Saint-Simonism" of Comte from that of the Saint-Simonians, whom he considers 'anti-positivist' because antiscientistic and proreligious (*Doctrine*, xxxix–xl); however, this was positive in both Saint-Simon's sense and the later Comte, and this is the sense in which the term is used here—which was not Littré's meaning.

[60] *The Doctrine of Saint-Simon*, pp. 222–24, 324–25; Igger, "Introduction," p. xii.

Politics (*Système de politique positive*) was begun in 1851 and whose *Positivist Catechism* (*Catechisme positiviste*) was published in 1852, never formally admitted a cyclic view, although these later volumes actually had as little to do with politics as Donoso's *Essay*. Comte's works had a great deal to do with propagating his positive morality and Godless cult of Humanity and Science, however, so his positivism, like Saint-Simon's, finally terminated in a religion which was far more absurd in its details than the master's.[61]

Perhaps to conceal his debt to the Saint-Simonians, Donoso rarely used the term *positive*, and never *positivism*, but rather *affirmative* and *affirmations*, to describe his doctrines from 1847 to 1851. They amounted to the same thing, as did his use of the expressions *critical* and *negative*—key words used regularly by Saint-Simon and Comte—for the positions he rejected.[62] Despite his continuing affinities with Comte and the Saint-Simonians, his positivism remained uniquely Christian. Even though he still borrowed from contemporary liberal and social Catholics, such as Montalembert and Ozanam, and from the traditionalists de Maistre and Bonald, he never quite belonged to either camp but instead stood alone as a Christian positivist. He anticipated by a half-century the Catholic conservative positivism of Ferdinand Brunetière, an associate of Charles Maurras in *Action Française*, who apparently was unaware of Donoso or his work but echoed his doctrines and positions, especially that of solidarity.[63] Donoso differed from any of the positivist thinkers of this period in his utilization of Vico's cyclic conceptions, as well as Saint Augustine's dualism of the two cities. His dogmatic synthesis was unique as a whole but not in its components, which were liberal—

[61] See Kolakowski, *The Alienation of Reason*, pp. 46f, 65, 71ff, on the religious and millennialist side of Comte.

[62] See Juretschke, I, 416–17, 533–34; II, 83, 150, 207–8, 307–8, 606, 619, and many times in the *Essay*, for affirmation, or negation.

[63] On Brunetière, see W. M. Simon, *European Positivism in the 19th Century* (Ithaca, N.Y., 1963).

conservative, positivist, and traditionalist, with added influences from both democratic and socialist thinkers.

In philosophy, Donoso has usually been placed with de Maistre and Bonald as one of the three great traditionalists, but more recent critics have detected traces of existentialist and positivist thought in his work.[64] Because traditionalism was a religious philosophy which extracted certain premises from the Bible and religious dogmas, Donoso found it convenient to use some of its leading ideas as principles for his new dogmatic system of religious positivism. However, he also drew upon Saint Augustine, Bossuet, Leibniz, Pascal, the mystics, and even Saint Thomas and the Scholastics. Such specifically traditionalist ideas of de Maistre as the purifying efficacy of suffering and bloodshed, for example are in Donoso's *Essay*, but more fundamental are Pascal's pessimistic idea of human nature and Leibniz's thought on the problem of evil, unity and diversity and perhaps the questions of materialism and the nature of the Trinity. At any rate, because Donoso did not have a metaphysical system of philosophy, he borrowed basic notions of the older traditionalists for the social sciences of politics, sociology, and philosophy, where Comte is

[64] José Ferrater Mora, "Tradicionalismo," *Diccionario de filosofía*, 3d ed. (Buenos Aires, 1951), p. 941. Usually the earlier Lamennais is ranked third, as by Lucien-Bruhl, *History of Modern Philosophy in France* (Chicago, 1889), p. 320. Edgar Hocedez treats Donoso as the outstanding traditionalist ("unfortunately"), "the Spanish de Maistre." See his *Histoire de theologie au XIX siécle*, II (Bruxelles, 1952), p. 83; also pp. 187–89 for an analysis of the *Essay*. See Rodrigo Fernández Carvajal for an unsupported allegation that Donoso's philosophy was existential: "Las Constantes de Donoso Cortés," *Revista de estudios políticos*, 95 (1957), p. 160. Actually, Donoso did share certain existential qualities with Kirkegaard, Dostoevski, or Sartre; such as 'alienation' from bourgeois society, class, and values; 'despair' of the world and of reason; acceptance of "suffering" as the human lot (not only as inevitable but as purifying); perhaps even eventual commitment ('decision') and 'action'. However, his fervent adherence to traditional Catholic Christianity gave an anchor, identity, and sense of community and belonging ('solidarity') usually considered alien to a true existentialist. Carvajal also sees positivist elements in Donoso's thought, but again without demonstration (pp. 84, 87–88).

also regarded as being almost as much traditionalist as scientific.[65] The major differences between the traditionalism in Donoso and the residue of it in Comte is that the former definitely used metaphysical principles and theological elements that the latter formally rejected. Comte's system may have terminated in a religion but not in a theology, not in anything like Donoso's Augustinian theology of history or his so-called political theology. Like the Saint-Simonians,[66] and owing to Vico's influence, Donoso had made Comte's three stages of mind and history cyclic and recurring. Consequently, he expected before very long the reemergence of a synthetic theological mentality, after both metaphysical and scientific stages had run their courses. He wanted to update and elaborate on the old religious philosophies from Augustine through Leibniz and the traditionalists in a constructive and affirmative spirit, as a basis on which to build a new body of positive Christian social, political, and historical thought. Traditionalist ideas of monarchy, society, solidarity, corporatism, and war could be extended in the newer social sciences.[67] Absolutism, either traditionalist or Saint-Simonian, was necessary only in temporary crisis situations, however, and was unsuitable for normal times. Because he accepted social and political change and reform much more readily than they, he was far from being just an echo of de Maistre and Bonald. He was so much more than they that he was really less a traditionalist than a Christian positivist.

[65] Jean La Croix, *La sociologie d'Auguste Comte*, 2d ed. (Paris, 1961), pp. 20–25. Noting "les similitudes profondes entre le positivisme et le traditionalisme," La Croix believes that Maistre's and Bonald's influence on Comte's sociology and politics outweighed that of Saint-Simon. See Hans Barth, "August Comte and Joseph de Maistre: the System of Positivism as Theocracy," Ch. 5 of *The Idea of Order* (Dordrecht-Holland, 1960), pp. 112, 121ff; also, Jack Lively (ed.), *The Works of* Joseph de Maistre (N.Y., 1965), p. 3.

[66] *The Doctrine*, pp. 224–25.

[67] Tome D has notes from *Les Soirées de St. Pétersbourg* relating to war and bloodshed; also notes from *Du Pape* relating to "the institutions of the European Monarchy" (Ch. 4) and sections on Russia.

Apart from earlier tentative reflections, Donoso began his general intellectual reorientation with some unpublished "Sketches" or "Outlines of History" in 1847, a seminal work that was almost opposite in spirit and content to Condorcet's liberal–rationalistic *Sketch for a Historical Picture of the Progress of the Human Mind* (*Esquisse d'un tableau historique des progrès de l'esprit humain*, 1793). His study was a theology of history in the tradition of Saint Augustine and Bossuet, with a theological approach to basic sociological problems reflecting Bonald and de Maistre. For world history he rejected Condorcet's idea of indefinite progress for a concept merely of continuity like Comte's. Temporarily he also gave up Vico's classical cycle, except as a very broad and infinitely varied pattern of growth and decline applicable to all societies. As yet his new sociology dealt with little except the nature and origins of man and society, questions Comte dismissed as games fit for theologians and metaphysicians but not for the scientific–historical method of positivism. Donoso did not reject the Comtean type of laws of society, but we see his philosophy of history related closely to sociology in Comte's fashion only later in the *Essay*, which incorporated several of these unfinished themes, including his newly voiced opposition to both liberalism and socialism. In these historical "Sketches" Donoso for the first time connected secular liberalism and socialism and supposed them absolutely contradictory to Christianity on their view of man and society. He held that they were kindred ideological systems, linked logically and successively through common principles as the political and social schools of rationalism. When he had first studied socialism in 1836–1837, he had felt that it might be a passing phenomenon and that a chasm separated it from eclectic liberalism. Now, however, it was not so much the socialism of the Saint-Simonians but of Proudhon from which he feared new and more radical revolutions in the name of progress and social contract. The liberalism he feared might lead into socialist revolution was neither the Christian variety nor the eclectic type, which he had now abandoned as sterile and out-dated for a normal epoch; it was the radical, progressive type.[68]

ROME, JERUSALEM, AND THE CITY OF GOD

While Donoso was thinking out the theoretical foundations for a positive Christianity, the new pope, Pius IX, by appearances a liberal nationalist, surprised the world and dismayed Metternich by initiating amnesty and reforms in the Papal States, thus ending the negative alignment with Austria and the reactionary powers. The pope's action not only pleased Donoso because it coincided with his new line of thinking, it inspired him to preach a heady millennialism: Make way for the City of God! As the era of transition with its moribund eclectic liberalism was about to pass, here was the leader of Catholic Christianity uniting with liberalism and nationalism. This combination might be just what the new normal epoch would need as a model for reconstructing an organic society. Apparently inspired by Saint-Simon's pretended pleas in *New Christianity* for the popes to lead a positive program to uplift the masses of the world's poor both morally and materially, as much as by de Maistre's *Du Pape* or Gioberti's *Il Primato morale e civile degli Italiani* (1845), Donoso hailed Pius IX "the Great" as heaven-sent to give an affirmative Christian answer to modern religious, political, and social problems. Let him show both revolutionaries and eclectics how to unite order indissolubly to a Christian liberty, in place of violent revolutionary liberty or the anaemic philosophical liberty.[69]

Enthusiastically welcoming "The Reforms of Pius IX" in this way, he began a series for *El Faro* from September of 1847, in which he discussed the positive principles and ideas that he hoped the pope would act upon as president of a federal liberal

[68] See Juretschke, II, 128–39 (a development of de Maistre's idea of war) and 145ff, where Donoso partly disagrees with Bonald on the idea of human nature and the origin of language; II, 112f, 122, 149, 156; I, 148–50; 315; II, 106, 108.

[69] Juretschke, II, 82–83; 87, 98ff. Saint-Simon, *Selected Writings*, p. 100ff.

and united Italy to be an example to the world. Elaborating an unusual viewpoint that Comte had also advanced in *Social Physics* for very different reasons, he claimed that "none of the fundamental and constitutive ideas of modern civilization" had originated in modern rationalism; "they all derived from the Christian religion." The two most basic ideals, he believed, were liberty and fraternity, which arose from Christian freedom and brotherhood and from which developed such secondary principles or truths as the unity of mankind, free will, reciprocal independence of the religious and civil powers, equality and democracy. In contrast to the theocratic republics and despotisms of the ancient and modern worlds, including the theories of Hobbes and Rousseau as well as the Jacobin experience, the papacy even under Gregory VII had never been a true theocracy. Accordingly, Pius IX could establish the mutual independence of Church and State in Italy as the palladium of personal freedom, from which could grow a genuine liberty, equality, and fraternity, such as had never yet come from revolutions or parliamentary politics. Indeed, if there were a voluntary return to such religious ideas, he expected a veritable City of God to extend eventually over the whole earth, as a consequence of papal teaching in Christ's name the unity, brotherhood, and equality of mankind. "Slavery disappears, and the citizens of that vast city, of the holy city, recognize each other as brothers, equal and free. That democracy is so gigantic, so universal, that it extends even to the limits of the world." This vague millennialist vision, truly worthy of Saint-Simon's *New Christianity*, was not very specific about democracy, but the City of God would seem also to be a Kingdom of God, where the order and hierarchy of monarchy would balance the freedom and equality of democracy because anarchy prevails unless some command and others obey. Apparently he had in mind his ideal of a liberal–conservative and social-democratic Christian monarchy as the means to harness the soaring utopian ideas of that era to the restraints of the monarchic and Christian traditions for the expected organic era of normalcy and stability. However, he had some reservations about the continuing dangers that could result from popular revolutionary liberty, as well as from the egotistic interests of the great powers. He feared not only arch-reactionary Austria but also liberal England, both Metternich and Palmerston's Minto mission. Still, he urged all Catholics to trust in God and support the pope, whether or not he was immediately successful against the forces of revolution and reaction.[70]

Just before the February revolution of 1848 broke out in Paris and set off a chain reaction in Europe, Donoso published a two-volume *Choice Collection* of his own works. He did this to mark the end of one era of his life and thought and the beginning of another in which he promised to pursue "new paths and routes in the social and political sciences."[71] What he really meant was that he had abandoned eclecticism and its transitional doctrinaire liberalism as sterile skepticism and out-moded politics and that he was developing an affirmative Christianity and positive politics for a new religious and political epoch of normalcy. Already some Moderates had noticed with displeasure his change of position on eclectic liberalism in his articles on Pius IX,[72] but nevertheless the Moderate party chose to honor his past merits as one of its leading thinkers and writers. The Ateneo elected him president, a position he soon declined because he was too busy to perform its duties; the Spanish Royal Academy, which he had attacked as a romantic youth, now elected him as a member.[73] At a colorful reception on April 16, 1848, before his friends Bravo Murillo

[70] Comte, *The Positive Philosophy*, pp. 440, 458, 603ff. Juretschke, II, 82ff; 88ff; 85–86; 101–6; 109.

[71] Donoso quoted in Gabino Tejado, ed., *Obras de don Juan Donoso Cortés*, I, lxviii.

[72] Tejado, p. lxiv. These articles had practically none of his usual "middling" expressions of eclecticism.

[73] Letter, at the Ateneo, Madrid. Tejado, p. lxviii.

and Pacheco and other leaders of the Moderate party and government such as Narváez, Martínez de la Rosa, and Sartorius,[74] Donoso was inducted after delivering a beautiful "Discourse on the Bible," a pronouncement suitable for his new position but a bit unusual for a liberal and secular era, even in Spain.

In Donoso's academic address on the Bible the style was no more eclectic than the subject matter, but was, as Schramm says, a luxuriant poetic prose.[75] He regarded his mode of expression as a positive romanticism that matched his positive Christianity; it was a new style charged with religious exaltation and dogmatic outlook which one can see later in his speeches of 1849–1850 and in the *Essay* of 1851. He declared that the Bible, the book par excellence and treasure and poetry of the Jewish people, was not only the sublime inspiration of great Western poets and writers, such as Petrarch, Dante, Tasso, and Milton but also a perennial source of fundamental truths for society. Actually his discourse was a kind of poetic history of the Hebrews and Jews of ancient Israel, "a nation worthy of perpetual memory" and a "marvellous people"—an outlook directly opposite to Voltaire's antisemitic "philosophy of history." Analogous to Vico's divine, heroic, and civil epochs of the Roman City of the World, he discerned three epochs, promise, warning, and chastisement, to comprise the tragic drama of the City of God, or Jerusalem, whose long, tragic history he surveyed to apostolic times. The epoch of promise he equated with Abraham and the patriarchs; that of warning with Moses, the law, and the prophets; and that of chastisement with the Christ–Messiah, the destruction of Jerusalem, and the dispersion. Israel was distinguished as superior to all pre-Christian peoples and as the only nation "chosen and governed by God," the only one to discover "the unity of God and the unity of mankind," as compared to the idolatrous, Manichean, or pantheistic Greeks, Persians, and Indians. It was, moreover, the only nation to recognize the dig-

[74] Juretschke, II, 159 (note): *El Faro*'s account.
[75] Schramm, *Vida y pensamiento*, p. 163.

nity of woman in Rebecca, in Deborah, and finally in Mary, "more beauteous in herself than all of creation." The prophets of Israel evoked Donoso's profound admiration, as "poets, tribunes, and orators all at once" and thus greater than Homer, Demosthenes, or Gracchus of Greece and Rome. "The prophet was the man who despised every gratification of the flesh and all love of life," a messenger of God, who was duty-bound to threaten, curse, and execrate in the presence of the people, priests, and kings. "I do not know, gentlemen, if history offers a more beautiful sight than that of the prophets of the people of God, armed only with the mystery of the word, fighting all the powers of the earth." After the warning of the prophets came the era of chastisement. "Over Jerusalem the mystical, the glorious, fell the veil of mourning" and death, "a tremendous catastrophe." "Jerusalem, Jerusalem, weep for your children," "the Oedipus people," to whom finally was left nothing but hope.[76]

Lessons Donoso drew from the Bible were mainly prophetic and apocalyptic in nature but modern in implication. The Bible, he said, "contains what was, what is, and what will be," from the Genesis to "the end of things" in Saint John's Apocalypse, which "is as sad as the last heartbeat of nature, as the last ray of light." Although he had previously compared Jews and Spaniards as elect and predestined representatives of religious ideas in their respective ages, he considered the Jews the image and figure of all peoples, notably for the Christians, especially those of the post-Christian City of the World of modern Europe. This perspective may seem a peculiar one for a Spaniard, who, thanks to Philip II, perhaps never saw a Jew until he met Baron Rothschild in Paris. When the revolution of 1848 broke out even in papal Rome, however, his worst fears seemed realized. All his hopes vanished for a return of Europe to Saint-Simon's genuine Christianity in an organic and normal epoch, as a modern City of God and mil-

[76] Juretschke, II, 159–62 passim; 162–78 passim; 165–77, 163; 173; 177; 178–81.

lennium growing out of papal leadership, and he beheld apocalyptic visions instead. He never regretted supporting Pius IX's reforms, because they had presumably demonstrated to the world that even the contemporary Catholic Church could be approached in freedom and could be as universal, or catholic, as its name implied. The liberals, however, had repaid the pope's effort at rapprochement with revolution, and, so far as he cared, they should be called but once before the end of time, like Christ's call to the Jews. But, blackly pessimistic now, he feared that the end of time was not so far away; he foresaw great apostasies and far greater catastrophes than the fall of ancient Jerusalem or modern Rome.[77]

[77] Juretschke, II, 160; 27, 168; 185–86; 322; 219–20, 223.

Chapter V

1848
REVOLUTION AND DICTATORSHIP, SOCIALISM AND RUSSIA

1848! After February 22 crowds marched and demonstrated with cries of "Down with Guizot!" Popular revolution swept Paris and spread through much of Europe like a great, gathering storm, unleashing destructive winds and waves of liberal democracy, republicanism, and nationalism with peals of socialist thunder, shaking thrones or sweeping them away in the flood. The magnitude and suddenness of the general upheaval surprised and frightened everyone who was devoted to monarchy or to moderation, including Donoso, whom Tassara depicted as:

> Prophet of that vast cataclysm,
> But terrified to behold its abyss. . . .[1]

Even *Le National* of Paris recorded its astonishment on February 25; "Never has a revolution been so sudden, so unexpected."[2] In Germany a radical republican, Gustav von Struve, exclaimed, "A tremendous revolution has transformed France. One idea has flashed across Europe. The old system is fading and falling into ruins."[3] While Mazzini exulted, Louis Philippe gave up and trod Charles X's bitter path into exile, Met-

[1] Gabriel García y Tassara, "Prólogo" to "Un diablo más," in *Poesías*, pp. 361–62.

[2] *Le National* (February 25, 1848), quoted by E. Labrousse in "1848–1830–1789: How Revolutions are Born," in *Essays in European Economic History, 1789–1914*, ed. by F. Crouzet et al. (New York, 1969), p. 2.

[3] Koppel Pinson, *History of Modern Germany* (New York, 1956), p. 83.

ternich fled Vienna, Frederick William IV fraternized with Berliners to save his throne, and Pius IX very reluctantly made more "concessions." Nicholas I, however, prepared to order his cossacks to mount up, while General Narváez smashed any stirrings. Between the Pyrenees and the Niemen, Europe was embroiled in general revolution, already over the brink or about to fall.

Early in 1847, Donoso may have believed that Spain and Europe were attaining internal stability. Six months later, however, he had begun to worry about revolutions in Italy and the boredom and decadence of bourgeois France, and he had predicted that the polyglot Hapsburg empire could not last long against the forces of liberalism and nationalism. Only Britain with her Roman political virtues seemed to him really stable and secure late in 1847. Despite these second thoughts he had braved the future, imagining nothing like universal and simultaneous revolution in Europe.[4] When it came, it struck him as a providential cataclysm in which plans and intentions of men counted for nothing. From the first he deplored the revolutions as a great catastrophe prefiguring future revolution that would be even more universal and radically socialist.

ORATOR AND "PROPHET"

After a brilliant and dazzling harangue on nationalism in 1847, Donoso delivered two magnificent speeches on the themes of dictatorship and revolution in 1849 and 1850. He suddenly became famous in Europe not only as an orator but also as a prophet, an oracle of the counterrevolution, a voice of doom for the future. His "Speech on Dictatorship" of 1849, observed Montalembert, instantly made Donoso one of the great orators of Europe. Metternich believed his "Speech on Europe" in 1850 established him as the greatest orator since antiquity.[5] Certainly he was Spain's greatest, exceeding Joa-

[4] Juretschke, II, 103–8; I, 948; II, 192.

[5] Montalembert, Oeuvres, XV (II), 203. Metternich, quoted by Gabino Tejado, ed., *Obras*, I, lxxi. Tejado apparently quoted Metternich out

quín María López, whom Tassara likened to a mere "silver bell" compared to Donoso, whose "marvellous voice . . . rang like a golden bell."[6] Although Donoso admired Demosthenes as the world's greatest orator, he had also studied the rhetoric of Mirabeau, Chateaubriand, O'Connell, Lamartine, and Guizot. "Those kings of word and rostrum are kings for me forever, however fallen," he said. O'Connell's magnificent voice reminded him of Paganini's violin for subtlety and for range: "It sings like a harp, roars like the wind, swells with the enthusiasm of a hymn." He preferred such a romantic style to the magistral coldness and gravity of Guizot's parliamentary "lectures,"[7] but he endeavored always to temper his own verbal splendor, paradox, and hyperbole with challenging ideas expressed with the classical, epigrammatic brevity of a Disraeli. His self-conscious, moralistic tone, however, resembled that of a Gladstone, with no time for the type of banter or levity for which Disraeli became famous. Like a modern Demosthenes, or maybe Jeremiah, he felt compelled to warn Europe of impending catastrophe and conquest, unless it would abandon its errors, reform its vices, and restore good order.

Despite his recent profound admiration for Israel's prophets as orators, Donoso had never expected to cast himself in such a role. Disclaiming any personal mystic, heavenly illumination, he declared: "I should protest, and I do protest against the idea that places me among those who see the future." No gift of prophecy was necessary for him to make his sad prognostications of the catastrophes toward which Europe was rushing after 1848. He explained that he simply pondered the "terrifying conjuncture of human events," as a man of "sound reason, common sense, and an ability to see through things." The

---

of a letter from Meyendorff to Donoso (April 1, 1850), in the Donoso Cortés family archives, Legajo 56. Metternich added that it had "a certain stamp of originality, produced by the Spanish genius, which one may call monumental and primitive, like the walls of the Cyclops."

[6] Tassara, *Poesías*, p. 364.

[7] Juan Juretschke, ed., *Obras completas*, I, 752f, 761; II, 649; I, 753; 805.

symptoms he described were "blindness of mind, rancor of will, pointless discussion, purposeless strife," and above all a rage for economic reforms, in brief, materialism, corruption of mores, unbelief. Although his outlook here reflected Vico's cycle, one should refer to Bossuet and Saint Augustine his remark that his method in judging things clearly, even in politics and diplomacy, was very simple: "I raise my eyes to God and in Him I see what I seek in vain in events, considered in themselves." But, he added, lest anyone think this departure either recondite or mystical, "This method . . . is within the reach of everyone." He looked at things, he said, "from the only true point of view, from the heights" of Christian revelation and prophecy. He may have denied that he had been "so rash as to announce the final catastrophe of the world" in his speeches, but he had indeed viewed the apocalyptic end of time, if not the final day, as no longer very far off, and he reaffirmed his conviction. Like all apocalyptic fantasies, this notion would seem to be very dubious speculation, even if it were a purely rational and historical aproach to Biblical prophecy.[8]

As Tassara noticed, Donoso was a biblical type, whose oratory sometimes sounded more appropriate to a Savonarola or hellfire-and-brimstone preacher than to a nineteenth-century parliamentarian.

> Mind astounded
> Before the rising wave
> Which smashed the hallowed safeguards
> Of aged nations,
> And roared on to engulf the altars
> Of Christian saints;
> Soaring up on wings of spirit,
> Begging God for vengeance
> He announced to us mortals
> The sum of all our evils,
> And brandished 'gainst the new paganism
> The Cross of a vengeful Catholicism;

[8] Juretschke, II, 177–78; 230; 197, 299; 309; 804; 197; 320; 197, 218, 623.

And later from the Spanish rostrum
He hurled forth those biblical harangues,
Grand triumphs of human eloquence. . . .[9]

He had a definite purpose for studying and taking notes on the style and content not only of Demosthenes, Aeschines, and Cicero but also of the great court preachers, Bourdaloue and Massillon.[10]

For a man so small in stature, Donoso commanded a tremendous voice and dramatic presence. An American who witnessed his speech on Europe called it "a singular discourse—full of thought and power, rhapsody, and rant. Its forms were stately, imaginative, and oratorical—its expressions glowing with intense conviction. The orator had enthusiasm, grace, boldness, fire—all the volatile elements which evaporate after a moment of inspiration, yet make that moment glorious."[11] It was the thought and power of the speeches that attracted readers around the Western world when the performances that had captivated his live audiences had long faded away. Even those who despised his ideas at least admired his courage or his virtuosity with words. Yet, his art was not theatrical pose, pretense, and pomposity, nor was it the strained artificial pleading of his youth. His mature oratory was the polished fruit of a decade of preparation and the natural expression of his sincerest conviction.

His two great speeches have survived misuse by exploiters of fascist mentality in the 1920s and 1930s to become world classics of oratory. No English translations of his orations have been made recently except for the "Speech on Dictatorship," which has appeared in three different books.[12] The "Speech on

[9] Tassara, *Poesías*, p. 362.

[10] Donoso's notes on these great orators and preachers are in Tomos C and E, in the Donoso Cortés family archives.

[11] S. T. Wallis, *Writings of Severn Teackle Wallace*, IV (Baltimore, 1896), 153–54.

[12] See the Bibliography for translations of this speech by Bela Menczer (1952), Eugene N. Anderson (1961), and Manfred P. Fleischer (1970). Fleischer's context (*The Decline of the West?*) is especially appropriate for this speech.

Europe," which was the greater and more universal of the two, has been ignored ever since an English rendition of 1850. There have been German translations and Spanish reprints of both speeches since 1918.

"SPEECH ON DICTATORSHIP": SOCIALISM AND A TOTALITARIAN WORLD STATE

Donoso's first impressions of the revolutions of 1848 appear in a letter to Isabella II in which he urged her to study history, because it could be very helpful to heads of state in such dangerous times.[13]

> In this universal shipwreck one can scarcely make out one monarchy from another as standing strong against the impetuous whirlwinds which all at once, and as if they were obeying a mysterious command, have been rising in the world. Those lay strewn on the ground which had their foundation in legitimacy; those are broken to pieces which prudence had raised, and those are leveled to the earth which were founded on glory.

He drew a dark, providential, catastrophic perspective on Europe in 1848, a frightful and tremendous spectacle, a great cataclysm.

> When the transformations which peoples undergo are deep, radical, universal, and simultaneous, . . . they draw their source from further off and higher up; . . . they have their source in God and their preparation in history, since those are precisely the marks which serve to distinguish the works of God from those of men.

Knowing that Narváez had suppressed two disorders in March, he warned the queen that her throne could fall unless she were careful. For the present, she should abide scrupulously by the

[13] Juretschke, II, 947–53. Juretschke, following Schramm, misdated this letter; for its correct interpretation, see Valverde, II, 226 (note), who places it in 1847—where it belongs—and properly compares its style and theme with Bossuet, in whom Donoso then had an extraordinary interest. The ideas on monarchy are noticeably similar to Bossuet, but more modern and more flexible. The precise date of the letter, as given by the Index to the Donoso Cortés family archives is April 26, 1848.

sacred and inviolable terms of the middle-class constitution that limited her sovereignty. Nevertheless, she should see that the monarchy accommodated itself in time to new and imperious needs and changes in society, perhaps prepare for something so new as even to become democratic. Such advice was wasted on poor Isabel.[14]

His recent high hopes for a new positive, Christian liberalism to harmonize liberty and order soon came crashing down when revolution broke out in Rome. In November of 1848 Pellegrino Rossi, papal premier and a doctrinaire liberal, was assassinated. Pius IX fled, leaving the way open for the Roman Republic of Garibaldi and Mazzini. This radical turn horrified Donoso, pushed him into the camp of reaction, and goaded him to condemn vehemently the whole European revolution. Picturing the wide rampage of revolutionary democracy through Europe as an apocalyptic nightmare, he prayed for a reaction to suppress what he called demagogism before it destroyed society.[15] "Irreconcilable enemy of the human race, . . . its gigantic struggle will be its own end or the end or time."

Since 1837 he had preached reaction and dictatorship for revolutionary crises as a just and effective means to save society and to reform bad laws or corrupted mores.[16] Reiterating and expanding his old ideas into a theory of dictatorship in a parliamentary speech of January 4, 1849, he suddenly found himself famous as the spokesman for a European reaction. To prevent revolution, General Narváez had already suspended constitutional guarantees of individual liberties and instituted a virtual executive dictatorship. Before such a ruthless opponent, Progressives prudently limited themselves to attacks in parliament on illegal and unconstitutional acts and called for government by law only. In front of a nominally liberal Cortes, Donoso defied the principles of the Progressives and offered a reasoned defense of the legitimacy of dictatorship as a tempo-

[14] Juretschke, I, 947–48; 951.
[15] Juretschke, II, 183–86.
[16] Juretschke, I, 326f.

rary safeguard for society against revolution. But besides upholding political reaction, he called for a general moral and religious reaction as the only permanent remedy against the disorder of revolutions and the tyranny of dictatorships.

Without personal ambition for power and avowing himself incapable of governing, he assured the chamber that he was not made of "the wood of dictators." He nevertheless declared himself bound in conscience not to leave society defenseless when it was so barbarously attacked by revolution. Dictatorship was a legitimate, good, and rational government in revolutionary circumstances.[17] Having always opposed the abstract principle of legality as a viable basis for society, he restated his conviction that instead the condition of society was the basis for legality. "Laws have been made for society, and not society for the laws." "When legality is enough to save society, legality; when it is not enough, dictatorship," a terrible word, but not so terrible as *revolution*. A sensation swept the Cortes on hearing Narváez's arbitrary government so frankly supported as a dictatorship.[18]

Every society, he claimed, made provision for dictatorship in times of crisis. The Roman senate had delegated the office of dictator, and the Athenian people had held the omnipotent power of ostracism. Going on to identify modern examples, Donoso adverted to the French First Republic as a gigantic dictatorship, full of blood and horrors, and to the English parliament as a permanent dictatorship in its potential powers. Progressives roared with laughter, however, when he extended his argument to call God a dictator for suspending the laws of nature by miracles.[19]

Examining the causes of the revolution of 1848, he again called them manifestly providential, because they were univer-

[17] Juretschke, II, 188–89.

[18] The reactions of the Cortes to his several speeches are given by Juretschke in context, information apparently based on the parliamentary record or published accounts in the press. The "bravos" and applause were frequent.

[19] Juretschke, II, 190f.

sal, unforeseen, and simultaneous. Their really basic human cause, however, lay not in alleged defects of government, political tyranny, or economic misery, but in envy, especially class envy, that agitators had stirred up. The February revolutions in France had been more social than political, for demagogues like Proudhon had turned the masses against the wealth of the bourgeoisie. Donoso felt that because the Spanish middle classes were primarily interested in material security, they would accept dictatorship to keep the socialist formula of revolution from spreading to Spain. He warned of the "power of those magnetic currents which break loose from the centers of revolutionary fever and go infecting the whole world."[20]

To persuade the deputies that danger enough existed to justify dictatorship, he recalled Spain's unsettled problems, which, he implied, Palmerston might exploit to stir up revolution. The traditional and providential roles of England and France had been for the conservatism of the one to offset the revolutions of the other, but, he alleged, they had reversed their roles since 1830.[21] A mere hint then was enough to bring to all lips the name of "Bulwer!" the British ambassador, whom Narváez had unceremoniously expelled for suspicion of revolutionary conspiracy in 1848.

Doubting that present dangers would in fact make the Progressives stop protesting against dictatorship in the name of individual liberty, he cried out an electrifying judgment.

> Liberty, gentlemen! Do those who say that sacred word know the principle they proclaim and the name they utter? Do they know the times in which they live? Has not the clamor of the final catastrophe reached even you . . .? Gentlemen, dreadful is the word, but we ought not shrink from uttering dreadful words if they say the truth, and I am determined to say it. Liberty is dead! It will revive, gentlemen, neither on the third day nor the third year, nor perhaps the third century.[22]

[20] Juretschke, II, 192–93.
[21] II, 194–96.
[22] Juretschke, II, 197.

Pandemonium greeted those dire words, which seemed to project the revolutionary crisis into the indefinite future and predict death for modern liberty.

After the commotion had ebbed, Donoso began to prophesy. He dismissed the complaints of the Progressives as petty and their faith in progress naïve. "You believe that civilization and the world are going forward when they are going backward. The world strides with very swift steps to the establishing of a despotism, the most gigantic and desolating" in the history of man. He implied that this universal tyranny would be a demagogic and socialist world state. The chief cause for its establishment would be growing moral anarchy, which only political despotism could check. Greater individual liberty guaranteed by new constitutions was not the remedy for Europe's troubles, because it was an unruly, individual liberty that made dictatorship necessary. To stave off revolutions, governmental resistance was more effective than additional liberal concessions; Louis Philippe had fallen by not resisting, and Pius IX, by granting concessions.[23]

The only real alternative to either revolution or dictatorship was a religious and moral reawakening of the peoples.[24] To emphasize this idea, he used the analogy of inversely related thermometers, one religious and the other political, which operated by a moral "law of reactions": as one went up, the other went down.[25] One represented individual self-control, and the other, external repression by the state. He equated voluntary restraint with the true liberty that Christ had made known to the world. With the decline of self-discipline, only more political force could keep order in society.

[23] II, 197, 201; 203.

[24] Besides Vico (see Juretschke, I, 568, 570, 577–82), perhaps Balmes inspired this parallel conception of religiously based mores and the state of government among peoples. See Jaime Balmes, *European Civilization, Protestantism, and Catholicity* (Baltimore, 1868) in Bela Menczer's *Catholic Political Thought, 1789–1848* (London, 1952), p. 187: "When no moral influence exists, its absence must be supplied by physical force."

[25] Juretschke, II, 197–203.

His idea of political–moral parallels, which applied poignantly to modern times and pointed to a totalitarian future, greatly impressed Montalembert and all who read it. Donoso portrayed the outcome of administrative centralization, police systems, and modern armies, which established social control, along with the annihilation of time and distance by the great new inventions of steam power and electricity in transport and communications, when coupled with a continuing moral deterioration. With neither physical nor moral obstacles left, he warned, the way was already being "prepared for a gigantic, colossal, universal, immense tyrant."[26] Only a wide religious reaction among the nations, the occurrence of which he thought unlikely, could prevent the advent of a socialist, totalitarian world state some time in the future.

Finally, to make clear that he justified dictatorship only under crisis conditions as a temporary safeguard of social order, he avowed that were there any choice between liberty and dictatorship, he would never "bend the knee" before a dictator. He felt that he had no choice, since liberty did not in fact exist in Europe. "The constitutional governments which used to represent it in years past are now nearly everywhere nothing but a framework, a lifeless skeleton," characterized by "legal majorities always overcome by turbulent minorities; . . . responsible ministers who responded in nothing; . . . inviolable kings, always violated."[27] The only choice left was between "the dictatorship of rebellion and the dictatorship of government," that of "the dagger" or that of "the saber." The Progressives would always vote for the former as the more popular; the Moderates would choose the latter as the more salutary. "Bravo, Bravo!" echoed the Chamber.

Both in Spain and abroad the reception of this speech on dictatorship and reaction was astonishing. A great flurry followed, while the orator received congratulations from nearly all the deputies. Properly gauging the speech as anti-Progressive

[26] Juretschke, II, 199ff; 201.
[27] Juretschke, II, 203–4.

more than antiliberal,[28] his party had approved exuberantly again and again during its course, and *El Heraldo* hailed his "inspired" words and rhetorical flashes. Because he had diagnosed a general malady and prescribed a general remedy, most of Europe soon knew of his speech. When Louis Veuillot, conservative director of *L'Univers* of Paris, printed the speech, he found it "immediately repeated in a hundred echoes."[29] It was translated into several languages and printed in France, Prussia, and Austria, and was both widely praised and widely damned. Orestes Brownson observed that the speech had a marked effect even in America.[30] Veuillot claimed that almost instantly it became "the formula of conservative instincts which fought without doctrine against the domination of revolutionary dogmas."[31] Metternich, Nicholas I, Pius IX, and Louis Napoleon all took note of him for this speech. Even Montalembert, who had been a sincere liberal until the revolutions struck, wrote to acknowledge the profound emotion and admiration this "incomparable" speech had aroused in him.[32]

[28] In Madrid, *El Heraldo* (January 6, 1849) described the speech on page 1 as "inspired words . . . in which each argument is a revelation and each rhetorical figure a luminous flash to guide us through the intricate labyrinth of modern politics." This paper carried the whole speech, verbatim. Veuillot and nearly everyone since then has wrongly interpreted this speech as making a complete break with liberalism (*Oeuvres de Donoso Cortès*, I, i–iii). Donoso had for long been making such attacks on radical liberal principles, had preached dictatorship during earlier revolutionary crises, as at the Ateneo, 1836–1837. As Peter Viereck notes (*Conservatism*, p. 67), at this time (1849) he was truly chagrined at the plight of moderately liberal constitutional governments. He did not break with moderate liberalism until several months later, while in Germany. *El Heraldo* then changed to enemy and critic, detecting "errors" among "the flowers" of his "admirable eloquence" (July 1, 1849, p. 1).

[29] Louis Veuillot, ed., *Oeuvres de . . . Donoso Cortès* . . . I, iii–iv.

[30] Brownson, "Church and State," *Catholic World*, 5:25 (April, 1867), 2. I have not been able to discover where it was then translated and printed in English.

[31] Veuillot, I, vi.

[32] Letter of Montalembert to Donoso (May 7, 1849), Donoso Cortés family archives.

"I have never read anything clearer or truer [in] parliamentary eloquence." Referring both to this speech and to a later famous letter from Donoso, he averred: "You get to the bottom of things, [and after] plumbing the abyss, [you] rise to a height where none have gone before."[33] With this one oration, he claimed, Donoso, like Edmund Burke after 1789, suddenly "darted into fame."[34]

RUSSIA AND THE SOCIALIST WORLD REVOLUTION AND WORLD STATE

Materialism, or an intemperate devotion to things economic, would assure the eventual world triumph of socialist revolution and domination by a vast Russian world state that itself would soon thereafter face destruction from materialism. This was the essential message of Donoso's great "Speech on Europe" (1850), wherein he drew upon a year's experience as an ambassador observing the revolutions in Germany and Central Europe. He did not reveal his concern about future world wars as well as world revolutions, so this speech seemed to be largely a development of the themes of his "Speech on Dictatorship."

While the Cortes was debating the government's budget and financial policy, he seized the opportunity to moralize and prophesy to Europe on a grand scale. On January 30 the post of honor, immediately ahead of Premier Narváez, was given to Donoso because of his reputation as an orator. "Great expectations," wrote an observer, "were formed of his effort and crowds went to hear it."[35] From the very outset he captivated his audience by announcing that he had more gloomy predictions for them. A painful era was beginning for Europe, and its

[33] Letter from Montalembert to Donoso (June 1, 1849), in Donoso Cortés family archives, partly published in Juretschke, II, 211 (note).

[34] Montalembert, *Oeuvres*, XV (II), p. 203; also in *Correspondant* (Aug. 25, 1853).

[35] Wallis, *Severn T. Wallace*, IV, 146, 148.

most patent symptom was in the universal madness for economic reform, which was a "sure omen of great catastrophes and ruin."[36]

It was neither wise nor expedient, he warned, to spend too much time on purely economic problems. Let the Cortes beware of three current misconceptions about reforming the economy through parliament: It should not consider this task first in importance, timely, or easy to realize. To put economics ahead of political, social, and religious problems would not defeat socialism but only propagate it, because socialism was an economic sect. At present, all the states of Europe were still too shaky to place material interest above moral and political questions. Spain, "like an oasis in the middle of the Sahara desert," was itself hardly stable. She could afford to make no great cutbacks in government spending. On the contrary, he feared that bankruptcy must someday seal the fate of constitutional and republican governments. Only by disbanding the standing armies could they bring temporary financial relief, but this action would instead render society bankrupt, because the armies were the last dike against the barbarism of revolution and socialism.[37] Without that extreme measure, he laughed at their economies as utopias.

He went on to prophesy darkly on the perils of revolution and socialism still facing Europe. Despite appearances, the conservative reaction would ultimately be a failure. Even the "supreme concentration" of all social forces had barely checked the monster of revolution. The victory over socialism, too, had been specious. "The awful sphinx is before your eyes, . . . the enigma . . ., the tremendous problem stands, and Europe does not know how to solve it." He looked for a dreadful crisis to arise from the general situation in Europe. "Today, gentlemen, all roads . . . lead to perdition." Neither economic nor political reforms were the essential remedy to ward off the cataclysm of

[36] Juretschke, II, 299.

[37] Juretschke, II, 302–3; 304, 313–14.

revolution and socialism, because they did not fit the cause, which was moral and social. "The evil is not in the governments; the evil is in the governed, . . . who have become ungovernable." The very idea of divine and human authority was disappearing. As a consequence the democratic republic, with its pantheistic deification of the general will, was becoming a necesary form of government. Eventually there would come a final, atheistic phase of anarchy, where no government or authority would survive.[38]

Apart from the internal dangers that faced Europe, there was also the eventual, external threat of Russian dominance. Assuming that Russia would supplant Britain as the hegemonic power of the Asian land mass, he felt that she could conquer Europe only if and after three conditions had been fulfilled. First, Europe's standing armies would have to disappear as a result of revolution. Second, socialism would have to extinguish patriotism by despoiling property owners. Third, Russia would have to place the Slavic peoples of Eastern Europe under her influence and protectorate.[39] "Then, gentlemen, Russia's hour will strike on the clock of time, then Russia will be able to march peacefully, arms at rest, through our Spain."

Russia's vast empire would suffer swift corruption and decline after establishing domination over Europe and Asia, however, because of the susceptibility of her half-civilized and half-barbarian population to the poisonous influence of Europe's higher civilization. Meanwhile, he doubted that Russia could continue to defend her frontiers successfully against the revolutionary influence from Europe. After Russia would undergo her revolution (sooner or later), he said he knew not "what universal cautery God has in store for that universal putrid mass." He did not say it in this speech, but he looked for a demagogic communist despotism of spectacular, world propor-

[38] Juretschke, II, 304; 305; 306, 308–9.
[39] Juretschke, II, 309–11.

tions, a "most dark and bloody" gristmill chewing up all classes, races, and nations, to emerge before a final collapse into barbaric anarchy throughout the world.[40]

"The knot of the future is in England." If she would desert Palmerston's liberal, prorevolutionary foreign policy and head a monarchic and conservative diplomacy for all of Europe, Britain could prevent the triumph of revolution and socialism, two of the preconditions of Russian conquest.[41] If she did not act, eventually she would suffer the tremendous chastisement of the swift collapse of her own colossal empire. Britain's great strength and advantage lay in her people, the Anglo-Saxon race, the "most noble, generous, and valiant in the world," and the most politically stable. "I believe a revolution easier in St. Petersburg than in London." Prophetic words! Even if she chose to play a conservative role, however, she could do no more than temporarily provide a palliative against the external manifestations of doctrines she was powerless to destroy. For a definitive remedy England needed a counterdoctrine that was absolutely opposed to the "pride and barbarism" of socialism. This need, he averred, could be supplied by no political ideology but only by the "wisdom and humility" of Roman Catholicism. But, although he was interested in the reunion of Rome and Canterbury from Newman's Oxford movement and Wiseman's impending reestablishment of a Roman hierarchy in England, he did not reveal that hope.[42]

He had no more confidence in the efficacy of merely political reaction than he had in economic reforms as a cure for revolution and socialism. The only real remedy, the only salvation

[40] Juretschke, II, 794, 310; 311; 622f, cf. 201.

[41] Juretschke, II, 312.

[42] One account has it that Newman visited Donoso later in Paris: Joaquín Iriarte, "Un Donoso romanticamente filósofo," *Razón y fe*, 148 (September–October 1953), 130. Donoso was certainly aware of Newman and of Wiseman's efforts (Juretschke, II, 581). In a booklist of 1852, Donoso wrote Newman's "Conferences Preached at the Oratory in London" (in French) and his library has Wiseman's *Discours sur les rapports entre la science et la religion révélée*, 3d ed. (Paris, 1843).

for European civilization, was a moral and religious matter of social virtue and truth. What was needed were those ideas with which Christianity had once civilized Europe but which "are not now in civil society," "the ideas of the inviolability of authority, of the holiness of obedience, and of the divines of sacrifice."[43] Only in the Church and in the armies could one find these ideas, and they remained the only guardians of Europe's civilization against revolution and socialism. The priest and the soldier were alike in personifying the dedicated and disciplined spirit of self-denial, self-sacrifice, and obedience to lawful authority that this civilization seemed to have forgotten but would have to learn again if it were to survive.

His prophetic analysis of Europe won magnificent plaudits from fellow deputies and from the public. An American witness, S. T. Wallace, admitted, "The speech was eminently successful." The newspapers, he said, "glorified it exceedingly," and he saw "the orator, three nights afterwards, at a ball, . . . still receiving congratulations, like a bridegroom in the first quarter of the honeymoon."[44] After it was all over most people thought that the speech was *un poco metafísico* (a bit metaphysical) but still very sublime. Quoting an old Carlist general who opined that Donoso was "a *pedante*, with his head in the clouds!" the practical Wallace thought that it really was not much to get excited about, when one troubled to read it. Later Cánovas del Castillo echoed a similar judgment, but at the time he was greatly moved.[45]

Readers, statesmen, and scholars abroad also applauded the speech during the next two months. Translations appeared in

[43] Juretschke, II, 313–14.

[44] Wallis, *Severn T. Wallace*, IV, 153, 154.

[45] Antonio Cánovas del Castillo, *Problemas contemporáneos, II: Colección de escritores castellanos*, 18 (II), 177. Later, he said, when he could listen and judge more dispassionately with the reason instead of with the imagination, Donoso's ideas did not seem so valid and compelling. He admitted, nevertheless, that because of the two great speeches, "Catholics, monarchists, and conservatives everywhere began the work of erecting for him the granite pedestal on which his personality rested at the end of his life."

French, English, German, and Italian, and many foreign journals published, excerpted, or commented on it, beginning with *L'Univers* of Veuillot, which distributed fourteen thousand copies and claimed that the speech addressed the entire world.[46] He congratulated Donoso on the "European success" of his marvellous speech. Extrolling it as "one of the most eloquent and philosophical harangues" ever "uttered on the modern rostrum," Metternich called it "a masterpiece in the sphere of principles," "a *tableau* made by the hand of a master."[47] "After what Cortés says, one can lay down the pen, for one cannot possibly place himself at a more elevated point of view."[48] In Paris, Herzen observed, "All the royalist and Catholic journals join in one great chorus of praise," although an arch-reactionary and Bonapartist, Romieu-Trimaleion insisted that, besides Church and army, the guns of Nicholas I were Europe's best guarantee of order.[49] French President Louis

46 Veuillot, "Preface" to Donoso's *General Condition of Europe* (Liverpool, 1850), p. 12. See Edmund Schramm, *Donoso Cortés, su vida y su pensamiento*, pp. 224–27, on Veuillot's response and activity to advertise the speech.

47 Metternich, quoted by Tejado, p. lxxi. Metternich-Hartig, *Ein Briefwechsel des Staatkanzlers aus den Exil. 1848–1851*, ed. Franz Hartig (Vienna and Leipzig, 1923), p. 53, letter of April 4, 1850, from M. to H. Metternich compares Donoso's lofty speech with a petty pamphlet by Mazzini (*Le Pape*). Unable to rise above detail, Hartig liked Donoso's treatment of budgets relating to armies (p. 57), which were the means by which the Austrian government suppressed the revolutions of 1848.

48 *Mémoires, documents et écrits laissés par le prince de Metternich* . . . , ed. Prince Richard de Metternich, III (Paris, 1884), p. 251, Letter to M. of March 3, 1850, from Brussels, to unnamed person. Metternich says that Donoso's speech "contains, in magnificent language, a very accurate picture [*tableau parfaitement exact*] of the period of transition through which Europe is passing. The German question in 1814 and 1815 is the only one which the author has grasped poorly." He could find, he said, no parliamentary orators in Vienna or Kremsier to compare with him (p. 252). Later, at Brussels in 1851, Metternich informed Donoso at length on the Congress of Vienna; see Juretschke, II, 585.

49 Alexander Herzen, "Donoso Cortés . . . and Julian, Roman Emperor," *From the Other Shore and the Russian People and Socialism* (New York, 1963), p. 152. Friedrich Heer, *Europe, Mother of Revolutions*, trans. from German by Charles Kessler (London, 1971), p. 258.

Napoleon was impressed, and Frederick William IV of Prussia repeated Donoso's description of the Frankfort Assembly as a once august senate which had, "like a whore in a tavern," talked itself to death.[50] Harsher than Donoso, Bismarck condemned this "Frankfurterei" as a vile swindle.[51] Meyendorff laughed to see the French nation depicted as "the central club of Europe." Then Russian ambassador at Berlin Meyendorff sent a copy of the speech to Nesselrode for Czar Nicholas I, as previously he had sent the "Speech on Dictatorship." He informed Donoso that "the success and applause were general. Everybody admires the eloquence, the elevation, and the profundity of your thought."[52] Among scholars, he reported, "Schelling, the Nestor of the philosophers, has read with great satisfaction the comparison between republicanism and pantheism; the historian Ranke values above all, for its novelty and fecundity, the distinction between the peoples of ancient culture and the peoples who received civilization through Christianity."[53]

Those whom the speech most directly challenged, the socialists and the British, did not entirely ignore it. Alexander Herzen, the expatriate Russian social anarchist and friend of Proudhon, found much to coincide with his own dark judgment on the history, present character, and future of European

[50] Juretschke, II, 315. Schramm, *Vida y pansamiento*, pp. 225, 227. Donoso's famous characterization of the Frankfort Parliament surely contributed to that "conservative myth" which Theodore S. Hammerow has attacked in *Restoration, Revolution, Reaction: Economics and Politics in Germany, 1815–1871* (Princeton, 1958), pp. 124–25.

[51] Werner Richter, *Bismarck* (New York, 1965), p. 55; also a reference to Donoso.

[52] The letters to Nesselrode of 8/20 March 1850 and of 22 March/3 April 1850 are in Otto Hoetzsch, ed., *Peter Von Meyendorff; Ein russischer Diplomat an den Hofen von Berlin und Wien; Politischer und Privater Briefwechsel, 1826–1863*, II (Berlin and Leipzig, 1923), 274, 283.

[53] Letter (April 1, 1850) in the Donoso Cortés family archives, published in part in Schramm, *Vida y pensamiento*, pp. 226–27. Meyendorff, in reference to Donoso's "magnificient speech," observed, "If there is no more faith in the authorities, the authority of talent still counts."

civilization. His cogent critique, which Proudhon approved, sold forty thousand copies, thanks to royalist and police opposition. Herzen praised the speech as "really . . . remarkable in many respects," but he ridiculed Donoso's belief that priests and soldiers, religion and armies, were the last best hope for preserving a rotten civilization against the triumph of Russia, socialism, and barbarism.

> Donoso Cortés has diagnosed with unusual accuracy the present terrible condition of the European states; he has seen that they are on the edge of an abyss on the eve of an unavoidable, fatal cataclysm. The picture he draws is terrifying in its truth. He depicts a Europe which has lost its way, impotent, drawn rapidly toward disaster, dying for lack of order, and over against it, the Slav world ready to overwhelm the Germano-Roman world.

Herzen agreed with the diagnosis of the illness, but he blushed to repeat the proposed remedy. Donoso was as absurd to seek a return to a real Christianity as Julian the Apostate in his time had been foolish to oppose its triumph.

> To save the world by memories, by violence! The world is saved by "good tidings," not by *rechauffé* religion. . . . How much blood must be shed to return to the happy days of the Edict of Nantes [sic] or the Spanish Inquisition! . . . To sacrifice thousands of men, the development of a whole epoch, to a Moloch of statehood as though that were the whole purpose of our life. . . . Have you thought about it, you Christians who love mankind? To sacrifice others and to be self-sacrificing on their behalf is too easy to be a virtue.

The similarity of priest and soldier was not in their virtues of self-sacrifice and obedience but in their willingness to sacrifice others. "Upon the ruins of a dying world, to encompass its salvation, the last representative of intellectual slavery unites himself with the last representative of physical coercion." Why, Herzen wanted to know, had not Donoso also mentioned the hangman, whom de Maistre had made the bulwark of social order.[54] Unlike the crude Veuillot or the benighted

[54] Herzen, "Donoso Cortés," p. 152; quotations from pp. 152–62, passim.

Carlists, Donoso wanted no return of the Inquisition, but in the *Essay* he soon defended capital punishment as socially and politically necessary. Otherwise, he foresaw a day when, under criminals and communists, "blood would flow even from the hard rocks, and the earth would be changed into a hell," when the only crime would be innocence. "Away there on the far-off horizon new and more bloody auroras begin to dawn. The new gospel of the world is perhaps being written in a prison; the world will only get what it deserves, when it is evangelized by the new apostles."[55] This statement might be applied to some of the liquidations and final settlements of Stalin, Hitler, and Mao.

Impressed that such a speech could still be delivered in a parliament, a Tory Anglican, Francis Sitwell, translated it into English. He agreed with Donoso that "religion and politics go together inseparably" ("radicalism and dissent"), but he had no use for either the politics or the religion of the Spaniard. Understandably he was not enthusiastic for the proposition that England become Roman Catholic to save the nations from apostasy and ruin. He did not believe that the nations could be saved anyway; there existed only a remnant out of each whom a moral message like Donoso's might reach. Nevertheless, monarchy and the established churches should be defended as an obstacle to the anti-Christ.[56]

Unquestionably the "Speech on Europe" was Donoso's greatest, and it was one of the most eloquent, prophetic, and universal of modern parliamentary orations. Besides its intrinsic merits of thought and oratory, perhaps Donoso himself best explained the reason for its success three months later. "I have done nothing but say out loud what everyone has been murmuring. I have said that the world's affairs today have

[55] Juretschke, II, 524.

[56] Francis Sitwell, *Donoso Cortés, General Condition of Europe* (Liverpool, 1850). To this day Sitwell's is the only translation of this speech into English, although it is greater oratory than the "Speech on Dictatorship," which has been translated twice in recent years. Sitwell's introduction, pp. 6–12.

taken a very bad path, and that if they continue in the same direction, we are irremediably headed for a cataclysm."[57] He summed up with exaggerated but magnificent analogies, metaphors, and epigrams what others were then half thinking or fearing. Moreover, the speech so sparkled with striking phrases and assessments that everyone found something to please his taste or stimulate his imagination, whether or not its general theme appealed to him.

Donoso was not vain about his oratory, for he recognized the limitations of the medium. Living before the age of mass propaganda by radio and television, he acknowledged that the effect and influence of a speech were evanescent. To convince and to move people to action, he said, one needed to repeat an idea over and over, until it finally stuck in the public consciousness.[58] For that reason, he rated the daily or weekly press more effective than the rostrum for dispensing ideas or propaganda. His two great speeches of 1849 and 1850 were then resounding triumphs also in the international press, and they remained among the great classic orations of modern times.[59]

"SPEECH ON SPAIN": MATERIALISM AND SOCIALIST REVOLUTION

Less well known than his other two famous speeches was his "Speech on Spain," delivered December 30, 1850. Here he addressed Spaniards specifically instead of Europe in general, although the message was little different. A new era of materialism was now beginning, which would produce such corruption of mind and heart that it could only end in socialist revolution.[60] Fearing that his dictator, Narváez, would not let

[57] Juretschke, II, 320.

[58] Juretschke, II, 209.

[59] See the discussion of his great speeches by Julio Burell, ed., in the prologue to Donoso Cortés, *Discursos parlamentarios*, Grandes Oradores series (Madrid, 1915), pp. xix–xxiv. Since 1914 the speeches have been reprinted numerous times in Spain and Germany and, since 1952, the "Speech on Dictatorship" in the United States. See the Bibliography.

[60] Juretschke, II, 329–40 passim.

the "Speech on Spain" be published because it also condemned the existing government as corrupt and materialistic, Donoso mailed a copy to Paris, where *L'Univers* published it on January 13. Ferrère, one of the editors, reproduced it as a brochure to send to a long list of notables, including Tocqueville, Thiers, Guizot, Hugo, Lamartine, Changarnier, Morny, and Drouyn de Lhuis.[61] Their reactions are not known, but Spaniards of his party, including Narváez, and the liberal press were very angry with him. Not until far into the twentieth century did many Spaniards have any praise to accord that speech which struck too close to home. Nevertheless, it belongs with his two famous speeches of 1849 and 1850 as a development of their themes.

[61] Unpublished letter of Aristide Ferrère to Donoso (February 6, 1851) in the Donoso Cortés family archives.

Chapter VI

GERMANY AND RUSSIA WORLD WAR AND WORLD REVOLUTION

When Donoso predicted the rise of a totalitarian world state in his speech on dictatorship, he was playing the prophet by updating Vico. He expected a new Rome to impose its crushing yoke on these rebellious Europeans, so like the unruly Greeks of old. In the German revolutions and struggle for national unity he equated militaristic Prussia to Sparta. Prussia's ambitions he expected to upset the old European balance of power and to lead to suicidal general wars like the Peloponnesian War and those of the Hellenistic empires. As Russia entered the stage, he saw her as a new Macedonia if not also a new Rome.

When he was sent as ambassador to Berlin to make a contact there with Russia, he found that the heady experience and milieu sharpened his sixth sense, but it left his health and morale undermined. His gloomy forebodings about the future of Europe were reinforced, and he remained a deeply pessimistic prophet of doom. He saw a Europe ruined by gigantic, catastrophic wars and by revolution, but most basically of all, he continued to insist, by the corruption of the popular mind and mores.[1] Even his reports on the revolutions of 1848 and the prospects of German unity vis-à-vis Berlin, Vienna, and Frankfort were perceptive and prophetic. Strange to say, the bulk of his "black prophecies" he communicated with apologies to the

[1] Juan Juretschke, ed., *Obras completas,* II, 784. See Carlos Valverde II, ed., *Obras completas,* 907.

Prussian ambassador at Madrid, Count Raczynski, who was disturbed and shaken by them. Out of respect to his friend Raczynski, as much as from deference to his own official position, he refrained from denouncing Prussia along with Russia in his parliamentary speech on Europe in 1850.[2] Germans have not yet appreciated the starkly prophetic character of these reports.[3]

PRELIMINARY IMPRESSIONS

Before his "Speech on Dictatorship" had suddenly won him an international prestige, Donoso was appointed ambassador to Prussia to treat with the Russian envoy there over restoring diplomatic relations, which Russia had broken when Spain became constitutional. Although he was not enthusiastic about the task, Donoso feared imminent revolution in Spain and was relieved to be able to leave. Carrying letters of introduction from Count Raczynski to Savigny, the famous historian of the law, and to Prince William, the future emperor of Germany, he set out for Berlin late in January of 1849. After a stopover at Paris, Donoso blithely wrote the foreign office that, without neglecting Spanish interests when he had gotten to Berlin, he was "going to sleep, which is what one does there," so dull was it reputed. His diplomacy there served no purpose, but he would learn much and report rather well, at least until his prophetic sense ran out of control.[4]

[2] Juretschke, II, 788; 817.

[3] On Donoso's ambassadorship at Berlin, see Edmund Schramm, *Donoso Cortés. Leben und Werk eines spanischen Antiliberalen* (Hamburg, 1935), Ch. 6, pp. 63–90, 135 (Ch. 7 in Spanish translation); Carl Schmitt, "Donoso Cortés in Berlin," in *Wiederbegegnung von Kirche und Kultur in Deutschland* (Munich, 1927), reproduced in *Donoso Cortés in gesamteuropaïsche Interpretation.* Neither grasped his prophetic thought on Germany. Also see Ernesto von Hippel, "Donoso Cortés en Alemania," *Informaciones* (1953), cited by Galindo Herrero, introduction to P. Dietmar Westemeyer's *Donoso Cortés, hombre de estado y teólogo*, p. 27.

[4] Juretschke, II, 770; 790; 248.

Owing to a death in the royal family, Donoso could not present his credentials to Frederick William IV until two weeks after his arrival. On March 6 in the customary half-hour audience, tiring of pleasantries and small talk, Donoso broke protocol to praise the conservative and monarchical sentiments of the rural population of that part of Europe. He even had the admitted temerity to exhort the king to save his throne by taking energetic action against the demagogues and traitors.[5] "You are right, you are right," nodded the king, but Donoso soon learned just how noncommittal was the royal assent. Apparently he displeased Frederick William, for he was never granted another conference. Much though he wanted to offer advice in the following months, he had to complain in September that "in Berlin diplomats never see the king." What he learned of the Prussian monarch was through hearsay and information from other diplomats and ministers like Arnim and Radowitz, both of whom he came to know personally. He shortly concluded that the king would not accept advice. "How could he give an ear to the counsels of men when he is convinced that he receives such directly from God? His council of ministers is in heaven, and God himself presides over it. If he has a minister here below, it is only for form; because he despises everyone with a sovereign disdain."[6]

Outside the court he soon established very agreeable and friendly ties with other foreign diplomats, including Nothomb of Belgium and Osson of Sweden but especially Baron Meyendorff of Russia.[7] He wrote to Madrid that, owing to his recent "Speech on Dictatorship," he had been given an extraordinary reception. "Never has any diplomat been received here as I have been: I know neither wherefore nor what for, but the idea

[5] Juretschke, II, 770. This story is from a letter to Raczynski (March 15) and is fuller than the account he gave in an unpublished dispatch, No. 1 (Berlin, March 1, 1849), archives of the Ministry of Foreign Affairs, Madrid. Donoso tells here of his reception and recounts Frederick William's words, as he remembers them.

[6] Juretschke, II, 790; 248.

[7] Juretschke, 770, 774.

they have formed of me here is better than I hold of myself."[8] Above all others in the diplomatic corps he liked Meyendorff, who spoke Spanish like a native, was very friendly, could talk well on all manner of subjects, and was highly regarded at Saint Petersburg. Donoso struck up close relations with him, and he undoubtedly profited from Meyendorff's knowledge of Central and Eastern Europe.[9] Meyendorff was equally impressed with Donoso. He enthusiastically conveyed the Spaniard's ideas and speeches to Saint Petersburg.

A few days after arriving in Berlin, Donoso described the nature of the reports he intended to send to Madrid. He promised to "study attentively the political movement of this great part of the world, where, if I am not mistaken, will come good or ill for Europe."[10] Because he knew little about central Europe or the German tongue, he soon admitted how difficult was political analysis and how inadequate he felt to understand this "German chaos" of "variety, multitude, and confusion."[11] For two crucial months, while both revolution and reaction came to a head in the new Austrian, Frankfort, and Prussian constitutions, he reported events, "letting them speak for

[8] From an unpublished dispatch of March 4, in Santiago Galindo Herrero, *Donoso Cortés y su theoría política*, p. 146, note.

[9] Juretschke, II, 770. Already conferring with Meyendorff by March 15 or 17, according to his unpublished dispatch No. 2 (March 6, 1948), which deals with Russia's announced intention to intervene in Transylvania. Archives of the Ministry of Foreign Affairs, Madrid.

[10] Juretschke, II, 232f.

[11] Dispatch of March 14, 1849 (Juretschke, II, 238): "Considered from the religious viewpoint, Catholicism, Protestantism, mysticism, rationalism and atheism coexist, . . . from the political viewpoint, constitutionalism, absolutism, and demagogism, . . . from the social viewpoint, feudalism and socialism." To Raczynski on March 1 (II, 767), Donoso admitted his lack of confidence: "This is a new country for me; I have been here only a few days, and I have seen only a small number of persons. Are these not reasons enough to make me timid and reserved in my estimates?" As late as March 23 (Valverde, II, 368) he said that the "German chaos grows darker and more intense daily." It is apparent that he read and studied while he was in Germany, on Germany and things German, if not in the German language itself. See Joseph A. Hübner, *Neuf Ans de souvenirs* . . ., I, 130—on Görres.

themselves," as he said, before venturing boldly into interpretive projection on the grand scale.[12] Even his preliminary efforts, however, were penetrating, as he repeatedly reminded the Ministry of Foreign Affairs. His observations covered Berlin, Frankfort, and Vienna and included Denmark, Hungary, and Russia in their relation to German affairs. Much of the information and opinion on which he based his analyses he undoubtedly drew from Meyendorff, Raczynski, and other diplomats who were more versed in German personalities and affairs than he. Long preoccupation with constitutions, revolutions, and political parties in France and Spain also helped shape his views. Thus, in the old doctrinaire way, he classified all political factions in Prussia in three main groups: reactionary right, moderate center, and demagogic left.[13] At first his sympathy went to the small moderate party of the wealthy classes, who stood for a "constitutional liberty wisely progressive." The reactionary Junkers, he said, were opposed to all social reforms, as devoid as the Carlists of ideas for adjusting society to new conditions. During the summer, however, he despaired of moderates all over Europe.[14] With increasing pessimism he dreaded truly apocalyptic events and feared catastrophe and cataclysm from passing crises. Although his responses were thus too often spasmodic and extreme, his analysis of Prussia and of the future of Germany was sharp, penetrating, and prophetic.

[12] Juretschke, II, 245.

[13] Juretschke, II, 234. In the ranks of the "demagogic" or democratic (also socialist and republican) group he saw Poles, Jews, proletarians, university students, and men of letters. He thought the proletarians more materialistic here than in France; they "refuse to admit the existence of God in order not to recognize the authority of the king." The students and litterateurs were corrupted by "the philosophical doctrines of the Hegelian school," for which he blamed the radical aspect of the revolutions in Germany. Further use of these already current political terms, "right, left, extreme right, and extreme left," appears in his unpublished dispatch No. 20 (April 5, 1849), Ministry of Foreign Affairs archives, Madrid.

[14] Juretschke, II, 233–36; 781f.

SCHEMES FOR GERMAN UNITY

The most crucial issues on which Donoso reported were the schemes to unite Germany into one nation, at first through the Frankfort Parliament, then Prussia's Erfurt Union plan, and finally the more distant prospects. In sharp contrast to his enthusiasm for Italian unity in 1847 and his past sympathy for divided and oppressed nationalities, Donoso feared the idea of German national unification. "That very famous Assembly [at Frankfort] the center of all hopes and all fears," he wrote, was fostering "projects of devastation and ruin."[15] Central to Frankfort's scheme, of course, was Prussia, which he believed controlled the fate of Germany.[16] He did not think that political unity in Germany under any system was then either possible or desirable, but he expected that in the future, both imperial and republican forms would be employed, one after the other.[17] He opposed German nationalism, or the unitary idea, for two reasons. First, it was too closely connected with demagogism in the Frankfort Assembly.[18] Secondly, after the Frankfort scheme failed, only Prussia was strong enough to bring national unity in a federal state, and he deeply disliked and distrusted Prussia.

Even while he recorded that Prussia had rejected Frankfort's offer, he noted that she "would like to set up to her own advantage a great Protectorate in agreement with the German princes. This is what Prussia calls the *Federal State*."[19] At first he noted the king of Prussia's offer to become provisional director of Germany with the consent of the other princes, a move which Austria quashed swifty and rudely.[20] Then, Gen-

[15] Valverde, II, 368.
[16] Juretschke, II, 233.
[17] See the summary of his dispatch of June 12, 1849 (Juretschke, II, 276, 240ff).
[18] Juretschke, II, 238ff.
[19] Juretschke, II, 253.
[20] He communicated Frederick William's diplomatic circular (Apr. 3),

eral Radowitz emerged as the guiding genius of what became Prussia's Erfurt Union plan for German unity. Donoso had been favorably impressed by reports of Radowitz at first and described him as a very important person for Prussia, Germany, and Europe. Evidently he hoped the Prussian Catholic Radowitz might emerge as military dictator, a strong man to restore order; to his chagrin, the general proved to be a constitutionalist instead of a reactionary. Comparing Radowitz's proposed constitution for Germany with that of Frankfort, he noted that Radowitz too envisioned a German empire, but with a president instead of an emperor. Government would be by the will of the princes, and popular sovereignty would be nullified.[21] Monarchic and antibourgeois, favoring socioeconomic reforms for the masses, Radowitz was much like Donoso in political outlook, but Donoso never believed that Radowitz's German plan would succeed.[22] After meeting Radowitz, Donoso disliked both him and his ideas, those for nationalism as well as those for constitutionalism. At present, he argued, "unity is entirely impossible in this country." In September he noted that "the negotiations between Prussia and Austria have a very bad look" on this matter and that even Hanover and Saxony were trying to extricate themselves. "For my part I foresaw this from the first." Two weeks later he wrote Raczynski, "This tower of Babel of our Radowitz you can consider destroyed before it has been built." Neveretheless, the king "believes

which proposed a "provisional directorate" of Germany, if the other princes agreed (unpublished reports No. 19, April 4 and 7, 1949). Later (April 15), Donoso recorded that Austria had informed Prussia in the most "openly hostile manner" possible in diplomatic communications that Vienna not only declined to recognize the Frankfort Assembly or any constitution or central government it decreed, but also refused to accept the Prussian king as a "provisional director of Germany" (Valverde, II, 380ff). On the federal problem vis-à-vis Prussia and Austria, see Hans Rothfels, "1848–One Hundred Years After," *Journal of Modern History*, 20 (December 1948), 309ff.

[21] Juretschke, II, 245f; 266.

[22] On Radowitz, see Koppel Pinson, *History of Modern Germany* (New York, 1954), p. 89.

himself bound to other combinations which unfortunately are not worth much more."[23] Actually, it was not until the next year when Austria threatened to declare war that the Erfurt Union plan was finally and completely abandoned. Radowitz fell, but his ideas made a lasting impression on Bismarck.[24]

From the first Donoso thought it unlikely that the Prussian king would accept the imperial crown from Frankfort, however much he wanted it, because it carried the grave danger of international war and of more radical revolution.[25] He noted that Frederick William vacillated because he was reluctant either to go back on his previous declarations and ambitions, despite his fear of democracy, or to ignore the opposition of Austria and other German princes and of foreign powers. The empire the Frankfort Assembly offered was not a true empire but a republic in disguise with direct universal suffrage and a merely suspensive veto for the emperor. "Their idea is to reduce the Monarchy to a single head, so as to be able to cut it off more easily than before." Frederick William he likened to Molière's *Le Médecin malgré lui* (*The Doctor in Spite of Himself*); they would make him an "emperor in spite of himself."[26] "I can assure you that the king of Prussia has understood perfectly that the imperial crown would be for him a crown of thorns," he wrote to Raczynski.

Once he had reported how the king had refused Frankfort's crown and constitution in April, Donoso, feeling that the only possible way for immediate unity in Germany now was through a democratic republic, began to hope for a slow res-

[23] Juretschke, II, 276; 788–90.

[24] See Priscilla Robertson, *The Revolutions of 1848* (1960), p. 152; closer to Donoso than Radowitz on the German question were Raczynski and Constantin Franz, who also wanted a dual Germany and opposed constitutionalism, parliamentarism (separation of powers), and secularism (See Pinson, pp. 119–20).

[25] See Juretschke, II, 242; also dispatch No. 11 of March 19, 1849, in which he predicted that, regardless of the king's answer, the question of German unity was to disturb the peace of Germany and of Europe for many years to come (Valverde, II, 367).

[26] Juretschke, II, 243; 772; 769; 773.

toration of order.[27] "The head of the Republic is in Frankfort, and you can be sure that the kings are going to cut off that head" by withdrawing their delegates. Nevertheless they should be wary, for the revolution still lived in the popular assemblies, in the German masses, and in Hungary and its army. He hoped that Prussia and Austria would bury their differences to work with Russia to suppress the revolution and to assure the triumph of monarchy throughout central Europe.[28]

Despite the failure of the Frankfort and Erfurt plans, Donoso suspected that Prussia intended eventually to unify Germany by stages, as Bismarck in fact did. In the more immediate future he thought that there would emerge two Germanies, a Protestant North under Prussia and a Catholic South under Austria. Prussia had ambitions, he suspected, to absorb Saxony, Hanover, and surrounding states in the North, and if her leaders had any sense, that should be the limit of her aspirations. "Prussia cannot be less, but she cannot be more" for the near future. Bismarck's North German Confederation included precisely this territory in 1867, and one of Donoso's final predictions was that Prussia would take the first opportunity to overrun the small Northern states around her.[29] In this professedly rational calculation, he even allowed for the unforeseen

[27] See reports Nos. 12 and 14 of March 23 and March 29 (in Valverde, II, 368–70) and unpublished report No. 17 (archives of Ministry of Foreign Affairs) of April 3, as well as an unnumbered communication of April 4 containing Frederick William's measured reply to the Frankfort delegation. After the king's rejection of the crown he expected "commotions and upheavals" from "German demagogy" (Valverde, II, 368f). In an unpublished report, No. 5, March 8, 1849, he had noted that at a review, the troops shouted "vivas" only for the king, so he tended to discount rumors that the revolution would be renewed on its anniversary, March 18.

[28] Juretschke, II, 251; 258. As late as April 15 (Valverde, II, 382) he deplored Prussia's "policy of pessimism" as a "disastrous" and negative principle, "which consists in seeking to derive the common salvation from the common ruin." Despite grave risks, he wanted an end to her "wait and see" policy for active intervention on the side of the monarchs against the revolutions.

[29] Juretschke, II, 257, 276, 819; 742.

through a stroke by a "man of daring." He may or may not have met Bismarck, but he could not foresee how by shrewd diplomacy such a man could exploit the Prussian Customs Union, militarism, and German nationalism to go still further and snatch the Catholic South out of Austrian and French hands. Nevertheless, after talking with Donoso on his return from Germany, Veuillot predicted that the king of Prussia would indeed someday become emperor of Germany but would eventually fall as a victim of revolution.[30]

"The aggrandizement of Prussia" in a form of German unity that excluded Austria, however, struck Donoso as an extremely serious question. Such a development would gravely upset the balance of power not only in Germany but also in all of Europe. It would lead to "terrible revolutions and gigantic catastrophes." All the great powers, he held, would fear or oppose a Prussian German empire. Russia would regard it as a barrier to her expansion; Austria, as the end of her traditional preponderance in Germany; France, as a threat to her possession of Alsace and Lorraine; Britain, as a potential threat to the supremacy of her sea power. A Prussian Germany would provoke "general war," against Germany.[31]

If Prussia's king were to become Germany's emperor, Donoso looked further ahead to a cataclysm, in which revolutionary democracy would renew its strength and sweep all thrones before it. Despite the temporary victory of the conservative reaction in Central Europe, he was sure that "the revolution will triumph all along the line and most completely in Germany." When Frederick William IV rejected Frankfort's empire, Donoso predicted that eventually "the form of German unity" would be a demagogic republic, for demagogism was seeping into the very "marrow of the bones of the German people."[32] He was very apprehensive about a united front of republican, demagogic, and socialist forces forming

[30] Eugene Veuillot, *Louis Veuillot*, II (Paris, 1913), 426.
[31] Juretschke, II, 787; 241, 772.
[32] Juretschke, II, 259; 791; I, 251, 257.

someday to exploit and to combine with German nationalism. He believed that demagogy and Germanism would remain very strong, that the revolutionary movement would become socialist, and that "only by being republican can Germany be one." These forces, in a sense, were not fused until Hitler.

DONOSO'S FEAR AND DISLIKE OF PRUSSIA

Another reason he strongly opposed German unity under Prussia was that he distrusted and disliked the Prussian state as a whole, even while he admired its success and its "marvellous adaptability." His attitude toward Prussia was a kind of love–hate ambiguity comparable to his view of England. He made a very perceptive historical analysis of the Prussian dynasty, state, and Customs Union.

> Prussia is a marvel in the history of nations, and the family of its princes is another marvel in the history of reigning houses. There is no nation and no dynasty but what has reached greatness by one specific road; only Prussia and her family of princes have come to greatness by all roads; by treaties, by conquests, by wars, by purchases, and even by disasters. When they have not risen by great virtues, they have risen by great treachery; when their aggrandizement has not come from the nation, it has come from the kings; to climb to the summit where they are now, they have been favored with equal success, yesterday in absolutism, today in the revolutions.[33]

He clearly approved of the Prussian manner of reform implemented from above, from the monarchy, such as the administrative, economic, and social reforms by Stein and Hardenburg after 1807. His summary of the recent advances of Prussia was especially discerning. "From 1815 to the present, two great events have changed the face of Germany, and both have favored the ever increasing aggrandizement of Prussia:" political revolution and economic Customs Union. "The Customs

[33] Juretschke, II, 277.

Union gave Prussia the economic direction of Germany;[34] the revolution, which consumed other states, has placed in her hands the scepter of political domination."[35]

By contrast, sensing a mystical significance in the origins and destiny of Prussia, he was very critical of her championship of Protestantism in the past and of her constant political opportunism in the present. Three years later he confided to Raczynski, "I am not a friend of Prussia, not even of her very existence."[36] Vaguely he saw her destined to become a power of satanic and fatalistic proportions. In 1870 Bismark would recall his hostility as a religious–political fanaticism,[37] but he misunderstood Donoso's prediction of a future decisive battle being fought out "on the sands of the March of Brandenburg." Donoso did not foresee it as a confessional (or *Kulturkampf*) struggle between Protestantism and Catholicism but as one between the mammoth powers of Germany and Russia for the domination of Europe, a Europe perhaps no longer even Christian.

Donoso also quickly became disillusioned with the Prussian king for his absolutist and nationalist ambitions. By mid-April he wrote that Frederick William was of such a character, "a

[34] On the Customs Union, see the dispatch of July 2, 1849 (Juretschke, II, 282–97). Donoso assigns the inspiration for it especially to Frederick List, whom he said proposed it as a means to the political unification of Germany (284f). This report grew out of a request from the Spanish Government (March 17), and Donoso utilized the consuls and a variety of written sources for "plentiful and certain" facts of an economic character, on which he gave preliminary reports on April 18 and 24, and June, 1849 (unpublished papers in Donoso's personal file, Ministry for Foreign Affairs, Madrid).

[35] Juretschke, II, 281. This viewpoint elaborated his first impression of March 7 that "Prussia, by her advanced civilization, by the material forces of which she disposes, by her daring mercantilist conceptions, by her growing prosperity, and by the faith which she has and has inspired in others in her destiny and fortune, holds in her hand today, up to a certain point, the fate of Germany" (II, 233).

[36] Juretschke, II, 281f; 817.

[37] Carl Schmitt, "Donoso Cortés in Berlin," in *Donoso Cortés in gesamteuropaïsche Interpretation*, p. 44ff.

mystic in religion and an absolutist in politics," that he could not be wedded to a genuine constitutional government in Prussia.[38] The constitution which the king had granted "by the grace of God" after dismissing the constituent assembly was meant by him to be not the democratic and constitutional government most people expected but was intended to reinforce an absolute government. With his fondness for paradoxes Donoso pointed out that this constitution established a democratic absolutism: "an exalted throne and a great people, and nothing between" them.[39] In this way, he explained, the king expected to rid himself of unwanted checks on his authority by the administration, nobility, and middle classes, while he had a constitutional power of dictatorship and the army to use against democracy in emergencies. Although he decided that absolutism or authoritarianism of the Prussian and Austrian type were the only kinds of government still

[38] Juretschke, II, 247. "Frederick William IV is a mystic in religion and an absolutist in politics. Endowed with a strange genius and a lofty and persuasive eloquence, he is the wonder of those who see him, and the charmer of those who hear him. In conversation he says things and discloses knowledge which leaves everyone astounded for not knowing how, when, or where he came by it. Despite these outstanding gifts, he is quite lacking in common sense and his reason swings forever between the sublime and the ridiculous. He thinks himself predestined, and he is, but for an end different from what he imagines in his day-dreaming. He believes that he is in direct communication with God, and when he speaks and when he acts he thinks that he is obeying divine inspirations. When, surrendering himself to the inspiration which assails him, he utters eloquent words, if perchance those around him compliment him, he raises his eyes to heaven and thanks the Lord for the words He has put on his lips. Lifted up in spirit above those lower regions and placed in those highest regions where neither the world's passions, nor its rumors, nor its commotions reach, he lives here as in a foreign land, and he watches men and events, deputies and ministers, assemblies and crowds, princes and revolutions, royalists and demagogues pass by with indifferent gaze."

[39] Juretschke, II, 249–50: Dispatch of April 15, 1849. One wonders if such a political system—"the king above and the people below" and those two in mutual contact without need of mediators—was what he meant in 1842 when he described Guizot's methods as "Protestantism in the state of government," for he also had criticized Guizot for destroying the intermediate bodies of society (I, 799, 801ff).

possible in Europe's crisis after 1848, he did not like the polarized system he saw developing in Prussia. He seemed to sense that it prefigured a terrible totalitarian state. In 1849, a Prussian arch-conservative, Leopold von Gerlach, understood Donoso to have predicted a future military despotism of a Caesarian ("praetorian") type which surpassed anything in the European or Prussian experience.[40]

Although Donoso admired the very loyal Prussian army and the efficient bureaucracy as dikes against revolutionary chaos in 1848–1849, in a longer perspective he had also regarded these things as instruments of state oppression and as potentially the means of totalitarian power in the future. In the "Speech on Dictatorship" he saw that the soldier might be either a defender of necessary social order or "a slave in uniform," one of the "million arms" of despotism, as the police were its "million eyes," and the centralized bureaucracies its "million ears." The evidence strongly suggests that he believed the situation in Prussia prefigured the type of militaristic totalitarianism in Germany that Hitler established.[41]

[40] The contrast is so surprising as to seem hypocritical and religiously biased, when his attitude on the Prussian constitution is compared with his approval of Schwarzenberg's new unitary constitution for the Austrian empire, which he admitted was so stacked in the emperor's favor that it amounted to a veritable coup d'état restoring "the absolute monarchy." He thought it nevertheless necessary for the "salvation of Austria" and for the safety of Europe. However, at least in the way it promised to solve the problems of nationality and local rights, he considered it "unity and diversity conjoined." In other words, despite its high degree of centralization, it supposedly preserved local and corporate barriers to absolute power, which he thought would safeguard due liberty and balance (Valverde II, 357–59: March 10, 1849; cf. Juretschke, II, 638, 645). Nevertheless, it proclaimed "the unity and indivisibility of the Empire" and the "radical unity and permanent indissolubility of its races and nations," so that it is hard to see how he could approve of it, except as a temporary answer to the crisis. Such a centralized and absolute construction otherwise violated his political principles. Leopold von Gerlach in *Von der Revolution zum Norddeutschen Bund. Politik und Ideengut der Preussichen Hochkonservativen 1848–1866*. Aus dem Nachlass von Ernst Ludwig von Gerlach (Göttingen, 1970), II, 622.

[41] Juretschke, II, 248ff; 199f.

GERMAN, SLAV, AND WORLD WAR

During his four months in Germany Donoso made some remarkable predictions about the decline of France, the rise to European hegemony of Prussian Germany and Slavic Russia, and the prospects of horrible general war arising out of the conflict between Eastern and Central Europe, and involving the Western nations too. He asserted that "the scepter of European dictatorship" had passed from France and the Latin nations to the Germanic and Slavic. France was entering into an era of "prodigious decadence," regardless of whether her government were republic or empire. "It is possible that she may still have moments of repose, but these moments will be ephemeral. Her role has ended in history." "Nevertheless, she will continue to be called a nation of the first rank for some scores of years yet; but that is because names last longer than realities. . . . Henceforth, Europe will have to take everything, the good like the bad, from the races which are disturbed on this side of the Rhine," the Slavs and the Germans. "Today, as in other times, these will be the races of the great solutions."[42] In particular, he feared that Russia's intervention to crush the revolution in Hungary in 1849 might touch off either a new general revolution or a general war in Europe.[43] Should these circumstances arise, there would be a "universal cataclysm, the greatest . . . that the nations have seen." Europe would come out of that cataclysm as Napoleon foretold: *republican* or *Cossack*, unless, because of the great chastisement, it returned to Christianity.[44] However, he did not really believe that Europe

[42] Juretschke, II, 253; 233; 253f; 255.

[43] This armed intervention early in May coincided with a new insurrection at Dresden in Saxony and acute unrest in the Prussian Rhineland at Cologne, soon followed by proclamation of a republic in Baden. He reported these events while he fretted that Russia's failure to get a quick victory in Hungary would unleash a new "flood of revolution," which would sweep over the Rhine and engulf all the rest of Europe. Unpublished dispatch No. 37, May 4, 1849. On Baden, see his unpublished dispatch No. 41, May 16, 1849, in Ministry of Foreign Affairs archives.

[44] Juretschke, II, 258f.

would fall under the hegemony of either Germany or Russia very soon. A revived revolution would have to triumph in Germany or a general war break out in Europe, but neither of these conditions occurred until the twentieth century when one introduced the other.

The temporary war scare prompted Donoso to write from June to August a series of communications concerning the prospect of general (world) in Europe. At that time the Spanish foreign office considered them so unrealistic, so impossible, so naïve, that the papers were marked "*Sobre la guerra por el fuego*" ("On the war by fire"), secreted in Donoso's personal file, and have not been released to this day. Consequently there is a gap of three months in his published reports on Germany.[45] Those reports very probably contained dark prophecies of later world wars, especially relating to conflict between Germany and Russia. One may guess at their content from his letters of that summer. Just as Russia was intervening in May, he wrote: "The imagination boggles" at the prospect of European society in the agony of a "shameful and premature death" from general war and revolution. Such was the bitter fruit of

[45] This packet of unpublished reports was contained in the archives of the Spanish Ministry of Foreign Affairs in Madrid in 1960, in one of the bundles of Donoso's papers pertaining largely to Prussia. On that very hurried visit I used that bundle and abstracted or transcribed various other papers in it, such as footnotes 54–56 of this chapter, but had time only to note the description on the packet in question. After thorough search for the missing documents in the summer of 1968, I failed to find them in any of the bundles of "Política" or "Correspondencia" for any of the years or countries in which he worked. I presumed they were lost in the archives until, in 1971, finding that (despite Valverde's publication of 1970 of some of Donoso's unpublished dispatches for Germany) the bundle "Política" was still short a large part of its contents, I then asked if Donoso might not have had a personal file. Out came the same collection of papers I had recorded in 1960 but had not since seen, but the packet "Sobre la guerra . . . " was not in it. None of my inquiries or searches have turned it up again, and the dispatches are still missing, lost, or secreted—how or why, I cannot fathom. The archives were reorganized after 1968 but this packet of reports stays "lost." Apparently no one, at least no outsider, has read them since they were bound and labeled after 1849, for no editor or published account makes any reference to them.

this materialistic "human civilization." In August he developed further his presentiment of the European cataclysms: "We are touching with our very hands the greatest catastrophe in history. At the actual moment what I foresee clearly is the barbarization of Europe and her depopulation not long afterward. The land where philosophical civilization has reigned will be the land of corruption and blood." [46] He did not think that world war and revolution were then imminent, however, for in July he said that he expected a breathing spell for some years. Though he could not determine whether it would be "ourselves or our children who will take part in the great catastrophe," he felt crushed with a sense of the "omnipotent force of evil in . . . history."

VISIONS OF WORLD WAR AND WORLD REVOLUTION

One must either leave Donoso's black outlook on the future at this point or turn to other sources than his lost diplomatic reports. Some other records of his visions of the end of Europe's secular civilization are his reflections on war, his "Letters to Montalembert" (June, 1849) on "world revolution," and Tassara's fantastic "Un diablo más" on world war, which Donoso inspired. Donoso never explained how the one presumed fate related to the other, in sequence or simultaneous, but he implied that war would come first, revolution later. Both visions were the fruit of this summer in central Europe.

War always fascinated Donoso, and he often tried to explain its causes and role in world history.[47] Because war was both providential and caused by the very nature of man, he thought it was inevitable. Even though a particular war could be prevented, it was a modern illusion to hope to abolish all war. If one long prevented violent and bloody conflicts of arms, war

[46] Juretschke, II, 269; 228; 780.

[47] On war, see Juretschke, I, 133, 135f, 575, 591ff, 766ff; II, 95, 138f, 411ff.

would erupt as a spiteful, enervating conflict of spirits. Essentially war was struggle or competition, always present in a variety of forms that are all very evident in the relations of modern nations and empires: industrial, commercial, and even cultural or intellectual, as well as military. Too early for social Darwinism, he still believed in a kind of moral "survival of the fittest" in world history. War's ultimate purpose was to secure ever broader organizations of human unity, to consolidate tribes, nations, empires, regions (East and West), and eventually the world, into a material unity of mankind under a new Rome. Morally speaking, the bloodshed and suffering of war also served to chastise and to purge civilizations of the errors and poisons of overrefinement and materialism. Where societies were too stubbornly corrupt, they would be subjected to hardier peoples, or even be exterminated. At basis, Donoso's grim conception of the world–historical role of war was not Hegel's nor Montesquieu's but Vico's. It was an expectation of great wars accompanying both the rise and the decline of world states or civilizations, Greece and Rome, imperialistic Europe and the West, and presumably Russia in the future.

Donoso wrote to Tassara asking him to prophesy once again in verse the approaching death of the modern European world civilization and the birth of a new Middle Age, a new Vicchian divine age, a new and universal City of God.[48] Tassara reluctantly complied with some disconnected stanzas on world empires, world wars, and "vast hecatombs of mankind" (p. 393 of Tassara's *Poesías*), which he called "Un diablo más." Apparently he (or Donoso) foresaw more than one such cataclysm

[48] Tassara, *Poesías*. Tassara wrote some parts of this long poem in 1851–1852, under the collective name of "Luzbel" (Lucifer) including "Hymn to the Messiah" and "The New Attila," but Donoso conceived his vision mostly in the summer of 1849. Tassara acknowledged that this was not the first time (previously after 1840) that Donoso had made the request and that he had complied, without really knowing what he was doing, since they were Donoso's ideas. See *Poesías*, pp. xiii, 364–65, 374, 376.

of war, which involved Russia, Germany, Great Britain, France, America, and the rest of the world. At first, Tassara described Europe as an armed camp.

> There arose, the lance of Attila brandishing,
> The Scythian giant of the icy North;
> There was seen anew the burnished German
> Breastplate of Arminius gleaming,
> And with countless ships girding her isle
> The Carthage of Europe, England. (p. 409, Tassara, *Poesías*)

Too weak to conquer but still pretending new empire were Paris and France: "the new Babylon, / The cemetery of old Europe." There behind her "unbreakable shield of Pyrenees," stood Spain on guard, ready "to renew her history." A wan sun bathed in livid rays the tents of the great "City" like "a lamp o'er the tomb of nations" (p. 409, Tassara, *Poesías*).

Then horrible world war began, "catastrophe on earth," "the hurricane which sweeps away the nations," "the two barbarities" confronting each other over the body of Europe, preparing that now "toothless monster" for burial. But the agony was not yet ended. There stood Russia threatening: "Yes, I am Attila: I hold here in my hand *the flash of light which annihilates*" (p. 449). And tomorrow, waging new war arises "the Leviathan of the Ocean." "And the waves wash to shore / The final, last human corpse" (p. 419). Then even Nature added holocaust to calamity, "a wandering comet" that was "unexpected, horrendous" encircled and blanketed the earth with its fiery tails and shattered the solid crust "like a broken vase" to pour out floods of molten "prime matter." "Unhappy world! not even your name will survive" (p. 419).

By then the old Europe, "the people whom God forgot" (p. 435, Tassara, *Poesías*), would be dead beyond resurrection, and with her, her liberalism, parliamentarism, and socialism (p. 428f). Tassara invoked Dante for a "canto" to echo through "her vast mausoleum": "Abandon all hope, ye who enter here" (p. 458). "Darkness now is Europe: / She drained the draught of science, / cursed her belief" (p. 463). In her pride she rose up and boasted: "I am Lucifer!" And now, "There is nothing left but the hymn of human grief / And the sempiternal *adios* to hope" (p. 460). The world was surfeited with her "poison" and the centuries of her dominion (p. 460), and "those terrible days / Of mourning and agony / Of death and orphans" were upon her (p. 404). "HERE LIES THE DEAD BODY OF EUROPE" (p. 444).

If there were any hope for Europe, for an end of the agony of all humanity, short of despair and extinction, it was by suffering, expiation, and religious faith revived in a new divine age under Russian domination. The Russian Attila was a barbarian but also a "son of Europe," "suckled at the sickly breasts of France." "But my barbarism is not decrepitude, is not the agony of death, / Is not your barbarism," but a "fruitful barbarism," disdained by haughty Europe (p. 435, Tassara, *Poesías*). The Russian was the Hun, the Vandal, the Goth, the Scythian, who revives; the European was the degraded Greek of Alexander the Great, the "infamous Latin of Ravenna, / Vile Greek of vile Constantinople." The sun of the former was rising, while that of the latter was setting. Indeed, the Russian was "the Attila eternal," the Nebuchadrezzar, the Cyrus, the Alexander to all corrupt, decrepit civilizations. "I am your death" (p. 449f).

Europe's fate would be subjection to the vast world empire of a Russian Rome, of a new and greater Constantinople. "I am the mighty. Asia is mine / The scepter of hundred empires is my sword / The labarum of a hundred Romes my standard" (p. 453, Tassara, *Poesías*). The Russian saw himself as another Constantine "gathering the great races of mankind," joining East and West in a flood of bloodshed and tears. But the Russian was "not now the savage horde" of the Attila of old, who burst suddenly from regions unknown "to mow down generations with his scythe." "God sent me not . . . / to destroy you, but to save you" (p. 453). At the hands of the Russian Attila as the instrument of Providence, Europe would nevertheless suffer an "enormous, tremendous, funereal tragedy" and be dragged back into another Middle Age of prolonged war, suffering, and expiation (pp. 450, 452).

And what of America, that land of nascent peoples, that "sun to come," hailed by "the blest siren of the Atlantic"? Would America perish in the holocaust, be swallowed up in Russia's world empire, or survive to become yet another "new Europe," a "new West" to confront the "new East"—a new home of freedom and brotherhood in a new Middle Age? Tassara seemed in doubt and his devil–muse, Donoso–Asmodeo, was enigmatic: O Liberty, "Spread your powerful wings / To the cradle of infant America" (p. 435, Tassara, *Poesías*). There in the far West was the future of humanity, "the peoples of the future," there "the fraternal peoples." "And there will be neither slaves nor tyrants / And the earth will be one great people." But cynical Asmodeo abruptly switched his mood to wonder if that "vision of the age which lies ahead" of freedom and humanity were not just a myth, a dream which must vanish, if indeed the people (every people apparently) were not simply "a big boob," a tyrant destined for the yoke of tyrant, in the Americas even as in Europe (p. 436f).

Rather than despair, Tassara entoned the Messiah's second coming, as "into the human chaos / God descends."

> The heavenly curtains are parted
> And the prophecies ring out
> And the gates of heaven open
> And the Messiah comes down to earth.
> No, the peoples do not die. Raise them up,
> Apostles, prophets,
> Martyrs, heroes! Raise them up, you athletes
> Of enervated humanity! (p. 452, Tassara, *Poesías*)

"And His word filled the hemisphere / And atheist Europe returned to her God" (p. 453). In the twenty centuries since the Crucifixion and the destruction of Jerusalem, Tassara sensed a fullness of time, when he prayed: "Come down again, O Messiah!" "As anew are the days / Of Thy sublime calling." Behold the grief and pain of all humanity blindly crawling to its own Calvary and groaning for redemption (pp. 462–64). "Yes, you will come." Foresakers of "the flock" would be confounded with the atheists / The new pharisees of the fallen law" (p. 465). "Human destiny is not / a Godless humanity." "Finally you will return, O Messiah! / In glory and majesty" (p. 465). Donoso saw and approved of at least part of Tassara's poetic version of Donoso's wild vaticinations of 1849.[49]

In his "Letters to Montalembert," which provoked much controversy in Paris and Madrid that summer, Donoso described two civilizations, one Christian (or Catholic) and the other philosophical, in terms of Saint Augustine's two cities. These civilizations were respectively modern forms of the purely naturalistic City of the World, with its triumphs here and now in this world and in time, and the City of God, with its triumph apparently only beyond time and supernaturally. The total victory of the modern worldly civilization would necessitate the progressive growth of evil and error until they became nearly absolute. Mankind was destined finally to reject all forms of authority, so that no family, no property, no government would survive, and man would be crucifying man. This utter freedom of the final anarchy would be more than even Proudhon could imagine in his "insane pride."[50]

How did this final world revolution of anarchy fit with Europe's future general revolution of anarchy and Russia's appropriation of a Europe embroiled in anarchy? Donoso did not demonstrate, but in his "Speech on Europe" he had also

[49] Donoso saw and liked (Tassara, *Poesías*, p. 376) his "New Attila." It is very doubtful, nevertheless, that the part about an "age reborn," a "New Middle Age" for Europe under Russian–Slav domination was really Donoso's idea then. It was probably a carryover from the version of 1841 (p. 364), because it is, oddly enough, too optimistic in comparison with others of his statements about "the end of the world."

[50] Juretschke, II, 207–9; 208–10.

said that the despotic Russian conqueror would quickly suck corruption from such a vanquished Europe, which could only mean that Russia's communistic world state would itself slide into socialist anarchy.[51] His answer to this question perhaps appears more clearly in the ideological dimension in his *Essay*, which he wrote in the following months. In that work, total anarchy succeeds the despotic communistic state before the universal City of God appears.

MISSION A FAILURE

It was not the cholera, which forced him to flee from Berlin to Dresden, that helped to ruin Donoso's health that summer in Germany but his feverish, overexcited imagination. Physically and emotionally ill, he asked on September 10 for a leave of six months to recover his rapidly failing health before the harsh northern winter thoroughly destroyed it.[52] Besides, he now knew the futility of his mission; all that Meyendorff and Raczynski could do was not enough to interest Nicholas I and Nesselrode in reopening relations with Spain at that time.[53] Turning over affairs to the secretary of the legation, he left for Spain around November 1.[54] Clearly not intending to return,

[51] Juretschke, II, 311. Note that when Donoso spoke of "general war" in this speech, he rejected the likelihood of it being very soon, in which case it would mean a disastrous defeat for Russia, since it would precede the necessary conditions of anarchic and socialist revolution in Western Europe, plus a Russian "protectorate" over Eastern Europe (II, 310–11).

[52] Unpublished dispatch (September 10, 1849), archives of the Ministry of Foreign Affairs, Madrid.

[53] Comte Adéhemar D'Antioche, *Deux Diplomates, le Comte Raczynski et Donoso Cortès . . ., dépêches et correspondance politique, 1848–1853*, pp. 27, 151–52. It is interesting to compare his stated reasons for seeking the renewal of relations with Russia at the beginning of his mission (Juretschke, II, 773)—as a possible alliance with Russia to free Spain "from the clutches of England, that eternal instigator of revolutions"—with what he later told Drouyn de Lhuis for Napoleon III's ears, when it looked as though relations and alliance might be established (Valverde, II, 907): that Spain had no need of Russia's recognition, much less an alliance directed against France, "her best friend."

[54] Unpublished dispatch (November 1, 1849).

he shipped back such diplomatic essentials as his two carriages and harness on the pretext that he could not sell them in Berlin.[55] On December 19 he asked the Secretary of Foreign Affairs to extend his leave of absence for another four months, because of the continued bad state of his health.[56] Never did he go back to Berlin.

During his brief stay Donoso anticipated by a century what Sir Lewis Namier said of the revolution of 1848, especially in regard to Germany. It was "a seed plot of history," which "projected the pattern of things to come."[57]

Aside from his wild apocalyptic and millennial fantasies, his speculation on the rising power and impending clash of Germany and Russia were starkly prophetic. Perhaps nothing illustrates better than his diplomacy in Germany the curious compound of immediate practical realist and long-range idealistic visionary in Donoso. Only compare his capable analysis of Prussia, the Zollverein, and the question of German unity with his speculation on European hegemony by Slav or Teuton via general war and revolution. Three years later he continued to oppose any unification of Germany under Prussian domination. He still recommended that Germany be reorganized into two great states, a Prussian North and an Austrian South, as the safest way to placate nationalistic aspirations without wars and revolutions that would gravely endanger European peace and stability. Despite his fundamental antipathy toward Prussia, he did not want to see her humiliated by Austria or by Europe, but rather "to gain her for the good cause, by assuring her the place which suits her as a nation essentially military and warlike," and thus "to use her forces when the great complica-

[55] Unpublished letter (June 11, 1850), archives of the Ministry of Foreign Affairs, Madrid.

[56] Unpublished letter (December 29, 1849), Donoso's personal file, Ministry of Foreign Affairs, Madrid.

[57] Sir Lewis Namier, "1848: Seed-Plot of History," *Vanished Supremacies, Essays on European History, 1812–1918* (New York, 1963), pp. 29–30. Also see François Fejtö, ed., *The Opening of an Era: 1848–An Historical Symposium* (London, 1948).

tions arise," meaning, presumably, threats from Russia and from socialist revolution. This kind of solution of the German question seemed to him "reasonable, just and practical."[58]

[58] Juretschke, II, 819; 818.

Chapter VII

REALPOLITIK IN FRANCE DICTATORSHIP TO EMPIRE

MASTER DIPLOMAT AND OBSERVER

With an apprenticeship at Berlin and writings and speeches on diplomacy and foreign affairs, Donoso proved to be a master in the art of diplomacy at Paris from 1851 to 1853. He was the only diplomat who helped arrange the coup d'état, which he both recommended to Louis Napoleon and helped to finance. Although he very soon ceased to be a Bonapartist and predicted a second Waterloo for Napoleon III, his reports were masterful analyses, and his "plans" were of considerable interest and importance for French and European history of that era.

In that "golden age" of amateur diplomacy when men of literature, culture, and learning served as ambassadors alongside aristocrats of birth and blood, Donoso was in fact as well as name an "envoy extraordinaire," but he was a quiet mole compared to his sensational friend Henry Bulwer. To an unusual degree he possessed many of the gifts desired of an ideal diplomat, despite some grave shortcomings.[1] He had a voice that compelled his listeners in conversation as well as in oratory. He possessed the modern social qualities which Callière, the arbiter of the art of diplomacy of the eighteenth century, had defined as nobility of spirit, dignity, and courtesy, plus

[1] On the qualities of diplomats, historic and ideal, see: Harold Nicholson, *Diplomacy* 3d ed. (London, 1965), pp. 21–22, 31–32, 71, 75; E. Wilde Spaulding, *Ambassadors Ordinary and Extraordinary* (Washington, D.C., 1961) viii–lx, 94, 128, 282ff (on François de Callière's *Practice of Diplomacy*).

affability, friendliness and "fertile wit." Moreover, as courtier and politician, marquis and bourgeois, he had developed an assurance with princes and a democratic ease with all classes, for he possessed the "genius for getting to know people, working with them, and persuading them." But he was more distinguished for prized qualities of mind—intelligence, observation, judgment, and penetration, projection or prophecy—than for his appearance or parentage. With a scholarly interest in the history and principles of diplomacy, he was also well grounded in European history, politics, and social thought over and above philosophy and literature. As a positivist of sorts he brought with him a realistic political theory of crisis, transition, and normalcy. Because of his apocalyptic sense of urgency and alarm, however, together with a mystical inclination and a pessimistic cyclic philosophy of history, he overreacted in the real crisis of the French coup d'ètat of 1851.[2] Moreover, if he had the requisite ability to keep secrets, he also had an almost Byzantine penchant for quiet intrigue and covert schemes, notably in the coup itself. According to his view of the situation, he worked more for the common European good than for the narrow national interest or personal caprice with which Palmerston was charged. His diplomacy was a strange combination of romantic idealism and cold realism.

Having watched at close hand the mistakes of Bresson and Bulwer in Spain, Donoso thought he knew what diplomats ought and ought not to do to be effective: "I believe that diplomats are the men most ignorant of what really goes on in nations; preoccupied exclusively with *the life of relation* between peoples, they never fasten their eyes on their true life, on their interior life; and that explains why all revolutions take them by surprise."[3] Neither coup d'état nor Empire took him by surprise. He knew France, and he got to know the French.

Any diplomat would have admired Donoso's perceptive

[2] Juan Juretschke, ed., *Obras completas*, II, 803f.

[3] Carlos Valverde, ed., *Obras completas*, II, 132.

analyses and remarkable predictions, quite apart from his style of political prose. While one scholar rightly praises his masterful power of political analysis, another ranks him with Chateaubriand as a new light in diplomacy for the literary quality and imagination of his letters and reports, although they were neither light nor anecdotal.[4] Refusing to compete with telegraph or newspapers in merely reporting events, Donoso concentrated on evaluating them as a diplomatic analyst and on anticipating developments as close as the coup d'état and as far in the future as the fall of the Second Empire and beyond.[5] While admiring his intuition, a fellow conservative diplomat in Madrid, Raczynski of Prussia, nevertheless admired in him the balance of idealistic visionary with realist, and of principles with necessity, and Hübner of Austria, viewing him as a misplaced ascetic, still consulted him frequently and admired his remarkable force of logic and *perspicacité*.[6] Strange to say, however, scholars have ignored his inside reports as sources for the history of the era. Where ambassadors Hübner and Cowley, or Victor Hugo, Tocqueville, Bagehot, Proudhon, and Marx, are often cited on Louis Napoleon, the coup d'état, and Second Empire, Donoso remains unknown.

Donoso's reports on France compare very favorably with famous contemporary works on the coup and its consequences by Proudhon, Marx, Hugo, and Comte. In a new edition of his *Confessions of a Revolutionary* (*Les Confessions d'un révolutionnaire*) and in his *Coup d'État*, Proudhon reacted angrily to Donoso as the chief intellectual and formulator of

[4] Edmund Schramm, *Donoso Cortés, su vida y su pensamiento*, p. 292. Bela Menczer, "A Prophet of Europe's Disasters," *The Month*, 183 (May, 1947), 269, 274. Comte Adéhmar d'Antioche, *Deux Diplomates*, p. xxxi. Queen Isabella II was delighted with the clarity of his periodic general summations on the situation in France and in Europe, and she instructed the foreign minister to write Donoso that she wanted more of them. Unpublished letter from the Palace, Madrid, January 16, 1852, in the archives of the Ministry of Foreign Affairs.

[5] Juretschke, II, 651.

[6] Raczynski, quoted in Antioche, p. 164. Joseph A. Hübner, *Neuf Ans de souvenirs*, II, 26, 129, 130.

a theocratic utopia for the so-called Catholic party, which then included not only Louis Veuillot of *L'Univers* but also Count Montalembert, all "Jesuits" to Proudhon and to Hugo, who borrowed that epithet from historians Quinet and Michelet.[7] Compared to Veuillot, however, Donoso was almost a conservative social revolutionary, for whom it was not enough for Louis Napoleon to be a new Constantine unless he were at the same time a bit of "Saint-Simon on horseback." Proudhon rejected Louis Napoleon as Caesar, but he wanted him to become virtually "Proudhon on horseback"—the "chief of socialism," "general" and consummator of "the democratic and social revolution," champion of anti-Christianity, antitheocracy, anticapitalism, and anarchy. Such naïveté, to Marx, constituted an "historical apologia for the hero of the coup." Later, in *Appeal to Conservatives* (*Appel aux Conservateurs*, 1855), Auguste Comte also urged Napoleon III to desert the retrograde theocrats and to undertake a positivist reconstruction of society in France and for the world in the areas of science, industry, world religion of Humanity, and elites. Both Proudhon and Comte now forsook their former romantic trust in contagious appeal to the masses by deed or dogma as the way to inaugurate a new order and, like Donoso, turned instead to a dictator–hero to impose their own utopian schemes by the brute force of realism. Counting on dictatorship, but not on dictators, Marx scorned Louis Napoleon as a fake, "hero Crapulinski," "chief of the *lumpenproletariat*," Bohemian roué. The disillusionment of Donoso and the others came sooner or later. As Sidney Hook observes, in *The Hero in History*, men tend to look for "a savior, a man on horseback,

[7] P.-J. Proudhon, *Oeuvres Complètes* . . . , C. Bouglé and H. Moysset, eds., I: *La Révolution sociale demontrée par le Coup d'État* (Paris, 1936), pp. 178ff on Donoso and "the Jesuits"; also p. 191 on Louis Napoleon. George Woodcock, *P.-J. Proudhon* (London, 1956), p. 136 on Donoso's *Essay*, pp. 179ff on Proudhon and the coup d'état and p. 182 for Marx on Proudhon's book. Victor Hugo, *Les Châtiments* (Paris, 1932), pp. 81–83, 279f.

prophet, social engineer," in times of "sharp crisis in social and political affairs."[8]

Toward Louis Napoleon as a savior on horseback, Donoso was perhaps the most realistic prophet of the lot in the long run; certainly he had much more experience with dictators. Having already interpreted Napoleon Bonaparte as a strong man and savior of society,[9] and having helped raise up Narváez as well as knock him down again, he now hoped that Louis Napoleon would surpass Napoleon I in resolving the revolutionary crisis and in peaceful social reconstruction, while avoiding war with the rest of Europe. He expected Louis Napoleon to use authoritarian democracy to introduce enough social-economic reforms to ward off socialism from France and Europe, and he hoped he would inaugurate a new conservative social program to serve as a model for the reconstruction of the rest of Europe. What Napoleon III actually undertook was more similar to Donoso's scheme than to any other, but it was not enough to satisfy Donoso. Bismark, if not Disraeli, later more nearly enacted the kind of new social conservatism Donoso advocated.

SIZING UP THE SITUATION

What diplomatic post could have suited Donoso so well as the one in Paris? As a youth he had admitted an "irresistible, instinctive inclination" for France, and as late as 1850 he still confessed that he was "French in thought."[10] Leader of civilization, or bourgeois and decadent, France had often been the object of his study, hopes, and despair. When the Parisian *grand monde* now greeted this famous orator so graciously, he

[8] Auguste Comte, *Appeal to Conservatives*, trans. T. C. Donkin (London, 1889), 147ff, 157–82. Karl Marx, *The Eighteenth Brumaire of Louis Bonaparte* (New York, 1963), pp. 24, 75, 85. Sidney Hook, *The Hero in History. A Study in Limitation and Possibility* (New York, 1943), p. 12.

[9] Juretschke, I, 302, 328.

[10] Juretschke, I, 465; II, 205.

wondered if a foreign diplomat had ever before been so well received by the press and especially by the upper classes.[11] His previous trips and contacts and his years of study in both doctrinaire-liberal and conservative French thought and politics made him easily conversant with leaders of center and right.

As ambassador, Donoso consulted a wide spectrum of the political, social, and diplomatic world at Paris, from Louis Napoleon downward, including Guizot, the Broglies, Molé, Montalembert, Ozanam, Veuillot, Tocqueville, and many others. From fellow diplomats, especially Hübner of Austria, he obtained valuable news and exchange of opinion. He attended the salons of Princess de Lieven and Madame Swetchine; he both gave and frequented social affairs and dinners for the famous and the amusing.[12] His long guest lists read like a *Who's Who* of high society and notables, and include princes, dukes, counts, and marquis, as well as many of the bourgeoisie from within and outside of political circles, generals galore, and ministers of governments. Aside from social engagements with close friends and fellow diplomats, just a few of his dinner invitations were to or from such notables as Guizot, Rothschild, Molé, Merode, Decazes, Barthélemy, the archbishop of Paris, Drouyn de Lhuis, Maupas, Princess Mathilde, and Lady Douglas. His list of visits, besides all of the above, contained such names as Ozanam, Ravignan, Persigny, Fould, Villemain, Bonnety, Mme. Swetchine, Mazade, and Bulwer. In one concentrated period, to which no definite date was assigned but which probably related to December 2, 1851, he visited the President of the Assembly, the general of Paris, the prefect of police (Maupas), and the prefect of the Seine.[13]

[11] Donoso makes it very clear in an unpublished dispatch (No. 494) of August 10, 1852, that he maintained "fine relations with notable persons of all the parties, especially with the most monarchical of all of them," particularly with the aristocratic "notables of Faubourg Saint-Germain."

[12] Juretschke, II, 572. Schramm, *Vida y pensamiento*, pp. 189–90.

[13] These lists of invitations and visits at Paris are in Legajo 25, Donoso Cortés family archives.

Hübner admitted that he had better official connections, was also more "in" with Louis Napoleon ("*très bien en cour*"), than himself.[14] Moreover, Donoso soon enjoyed the confidence of the monarchists, both Legitimists and Orleanists of the party of order and, particularly, of the clerical Catholic party. Most important, of course, was his special relationship with Louis Napoleon.

When he presented his credentials on March 27, 1851, he departed from strict protocol to commend the President for his support of order in France and Europe; Donoso was pleased to hear himself praised in speeches for service to the same cause.[15] Over the next two years he was to obtain a number of personal interviews, in which Louis Napoleon more or less openly confided in him. He in turn offered sometimes unasked advice. He was scarcely the *éminence grise* of Louis Napoleon—that was the role of Persigny or Morny—but he cultivated an influence with him in politics and diplomacy that was both conservative and reformative. As the Empress Eugénie later confirmed, a strangely confidential relationship grew between them; Louis Napoleon liked and trusted him above other diplomats.[16] In 1852 Donoso wrote to the foreign minister of Spain: "The Prince, whose dominant mark, according to everyone, is circumspection, is accustomed to being completely forgetful of it when he speaks with me, even to the point of committing what, if it were known to others, could pass for inconceivable imprudence."[17] What he did not learn from hints or even from the silence of Louis Napoleon, he guessed from studying his character, his writings, and the career of his uncle, Napoleon I. He claimed to base his own judgment of the Prince "on the knowledge I have of his person

[14] A. Hübner, *Neuf Ans de souvenirs*, II, 26, 115, 129, 130.

[15] On the first meeting of Donoso and Louis Napoleon on March 27 at the Elysée, see Schramm, *Vida y pensamiento*, p. 237, and Valverde, II, 782–83.

[16] *Lettres familières de L'Emperatrice Eugénie* . . . , publiées par les soins du Duc D'Albe (Paris, 1935), p. 85.

[17] Juretschke, II, 746.

and of the way he has of approaching his object."[18] Like Tocqueville, Thiers, and others since, he noted the superstitious imitation of the policies, constitutions, acts, and anniversaries of Napoleon I.[19] Donoso felt that Louis Napoleon was a prisoner of the very Napoleonic legend he had helped to create. While others were perplexed by the contradictory statements Louis Napoleon made from day to day, Donoso disregarded those remarks and instead searched his speeches and writings for more permanent underlying purposes, for his fixed ideas, in short, for his "Napoleonic Ideas." "Whoever proposes to divine what the Emperor is going to do by what he says," he warned in 1852, "is sure to fall into the grossest mistakes; the important thing is not to listen to what he says but to determine what he thinks, because there is undoubtedly a unity of thought amid this diversity of speech."[20]

One of his first dispatches from Paris (April, 1851) was a masterpiece of analysis and prognosis, which showed that he had already acquired a good grasp of French problems. He described France as a nation deeply divided, as tormented by a double and contradictory character, doomed to a "sterile struggle" likely to end in suicide; her instincts were still monarchic but her defects and qualities were demagogic and republican. Any restored empire or monarchy could only be a shadow of its former self. He accurately predicted that the solution to the impass between Assembly and President would come within the year (1851). Looking into the remoter future, he asserted that any kind of restoration, whether Legitimist,

[18] Valverde, II, 875.

[19] On Tocqueville's opinion of Napoleon III as "essentially a copyist," see Sir Lewis Namier, *Vanished Supremacies* (New York, 1968), p. 56—a view which Namier shares (pp. 54, 63) of this "first mountebank dictator." Namier also thinks, like Donoso, that due in part to "imitation," "recurrent situations in history reproduce analogous forms," (p. 54). Adolphe Thiers also came to a very similar view of Louis Napoleon as an "imitator" of his uncle by 1852; see William Nassau Senior, *Conversations with M. Thiers, M. Guizot, and other distinguished persons, during the Second Empire*, I (London, 1878), 115.

[20] Juretschke, II, 728, 735; 740.

Orleanist, or Bonapartist, would be ephemeral, only "different phases of the great republican epoch which will stretch indefinitely through the bloody annals of France." Since 1849 he had expected a presidential coup d'état, but since 1850 he had feared a republican and socialistic wave in France again and in Europe. Although his ideas on the specific type, time, and chances for a coup varied, he soon became convinced that a socialist revolution would sweep everything before it in 1852 unless the president acted to become a dictator before the end of his term.[21]

Until the coup was at hand, his most interesting speculation was on the future of monarchy in France. In his "Speech on Europe," he had said that France's salvation depended on the dissolution of the Bonapartist, Orleanist, and Legitimist parties "and the formation of one single monarchist party." Because of the continuing division between Legitimists and Orleanists in the monarchical majority in the Assembly, he now rightly judged the prospects of restoration as a fatal illusion. "Never will France turn her eyes toward the monarchy unless a deluge of blood comes over her; it is necessary for France to be socialist before again being monarchical."[22] Whereas he was certain that a monarchy could not directly emerge from a republic, he believed for a while that a dictatorship could issue from a republic and might carry out a restoration.[23] But such a dictator would have to be the Legitimist General Changarnier rather than Louis Napoleon, who would restore nothing except the

[21] Juretschke, II, 652ff. See Donoso's letter to Raczynski (February 12, 1849); here he predicted both coup d'état and Empire: Juretschke, II, 765–66, 305–6; 655f, 664f, 672.

[22] Juretschke, II, 306; 667.

[23] Donoso felt that when they had the chance the monarchists should have used the "iron hand of the dictator" (Changarnier) to destroy such prominent liberal and revolutionary institutions as unrestricted freedom of the press, purely secularized education, and the National Guard as invincible obstacles to a monarchy (Juretschke, II, 667). Also, his apparent approval of the decentralizing schemes of the Count of Chambord should be considered, although this was not conceived as a program for crisis. Unpublished report No. 425, July 10, 1852.

Empire. "The monarchy is the revolution defeated and the Empire has not been and will not be other than the revolution crowned." Later, however, he returned to his original idea that a monarchy which was restored even by the sword of a dictator would after all be no more than a passing phase of the republic. Socialism had to bring bloody misery before Frenchmen would accept a lasting restoration. In September he absolutely dismissed the monarchists' fortunes, because the traditions of those "glorious fourteen centuries" of monarchy were dead in French memory. "France for the Frenchmen of today began only in 1789, . . . the generations which have seen her enter into the bottomless sea of the Republic will not see her emerge."[24] After the coup d'état, however, he encouraged the monarchists again by participating in Guizot's fusionist scheme to reconcile the feuding parties of the Count of Chambord and of the princes of Orleans. He had decided there might be a chance for a restoration after the fall of the empire, which was not yet proclaimed, if only the monarchists were united instead of in their present hopeless disarray.[25]

In regard to the constitutional struggle, he judged in June that peace between president and Assembly, as two equal, divided, and checkmated powers, was thenceforth entirely impossible, and that one had to succumb and the other become dictatorial master of France. Better the president than the Assembly, he decided, but he would have preferred that either a king or a general rule. Already in April he had predicted that if Louis Napoleon did not get a legal extension of his term, he would probably resort to the heroic remedy of a coup d'état. Louis Napoleon would wait for the supreme moment, however, since he expected "everything from time" as his "true minister." Later, noting the great enthusiasm of his popular support, Donoso thought that the Prince would be tempted to wait "in hope that the people will make a coup for him in the final hour." Having observed, however, that universal suffrage

[24] Juretschke, II, 672; 671; 690.
[25] Unpublished report of July 10, 1852; Juretschke, II, 680.

was "the mace of Hercules" with which the masses would exercise the "omnipotence of their will" to install their own "tyrants-for-a-day," he expected that they more likely would send him a "red Assembly" in May. He feared that for Louis Napoleon to attempt a coup before the end of the Assembly's summer session would be disastrous but that to wait until the end of his term would be to court socialist revolution by the masses. After the Assembly refused to revise the constitution and had adjourned, Donoso observed that "there remain but two personages standing: Louis Napoleon and the Mountain," a situation which must end in new revolution or in dictatorship. A monarchic restoration was no longer possible, for General Changarnier's reputation was now too tarnished. The Legitimists could not rely for support on the peasants nor the Orleanists on the bourgeoisie. Although Donoso was bourgeois, he noted that the egotistic and timid middle class was, "naturally, contemptuous of abstract principles and friendly to the victorious feat." He looked for it to support whomever could promise the material order and peace which commerce and industry required. Of these two contending forces, the revolutionaries promised a future of ease to all the proletarians, while the Bonapartist official propaganda called for order, concord, and union of "all social forces and of all conservative passions." If Louis Napoleon acted soon and boldly for a coup d'état while the Assembly was prorogued, then the cause of order should triumph; the longer he delayed the more doubtful the outcome, for time and illegality now favored the revolution.[26]

COUNSELLOR OF THE COUP D'ÉTAT

Even while Donoso wrote these lines of August 1 and 15, Louis Napoleon told Morny that he had decided on a coup, and he intended to make it on September 17.[27] When no ac-

[26] Ibid., II, 671; 658; 674; 652, 675; 664; 680–82; 684–85.

[27] On the timing of the coup and different dates (for example, September 17), see M. de Maupas, *The Story of the Coup d'État*, trans. A. D.

tion had been taken and as the rumors flew, Donoso wrote to Madrid on October 1 that the president had been thinking about a coup for the past month and had backed away from it only because he lacked bold helpers. His ministers and General Magnan, the commander of the Paris garrison, failed him not because of any "love of legality," but only for "meanness of soul." Heroic force, either for good or evil, was impossible in the France of that day. But, "the French, my friend, know very well that they must die, and they are becoming resigned to it; they only pray God to let them die peacefully. I rather doubt that God hears their prayers."[28] For having tipped his hand, he feared, the president's star was starting to decline and that of the revolution, to rise.

On October 11, Donoso's uncertainty ended when he learned directly from Louis Napoleon in an interview that he still intended a coup d'état. Henceforth, Donoso was in on the plot. When the president wanted to know the opinion "of a man like you" on the situation in France, Donoso reported that he had replied very frankly, but not in his official capacity: He forthright urged a coup d'état. The monarchists were powerless. Nothing was left between the president and the revolution, he asserted, and time was on the side of the revolution. "Every legal and peaceful solution is impossible here, and . . . force alone can loosen France's Gordian knot." As France went, Europe would follow. Presidential force could save order in Europe; otherwise, Europe would be lost to the

Vandam (New York, 1884), pp. 139–42. From what Maupas reveals of Louis Napoleon's mind in late September and early October, Donoso's encouragement came at a very opportune time to galvanize him to act with "courage and decision" to "save" France. Maupas's rationalization of the coup (pp. 139–40) was very like Donoso's. It is entirely possible that Donoso was in on the coup before even Louis Napoleon knew it, because a letter from Río (an intimate personal friend of Donoso and perhaps his agent), dated Strassburg, 27 August 1851, makes mysterious reference to "la chose en elle-même" and "comment M. Persigny a pris la chose." Letter in Donoso Cortés family archives, Legajo 57.

[28] Juretschke, II, 693.

revolution. Finally, he cautioned Louis Napoleon against trying to rule by popular suffrage after abrogating the law of May 31. He should do no more than base his own authority on the strength that it would give him, then annul it, and dismantle the revolutionary institutions. According to Donoso's report, the effect of his words on the prince was impossible to describe, except as evoking joy and pleasure. "Thanks be to God," he had replied with equal candor, "that I have found a man, and him a foreigner, who is more informed than the French on the condition of France. . . . I congratulate myself on being in complete agreement with a man like you." He affirmed that he meant to use universal suffrage precisely as the Spaniard advised. Then he ended with an affectionate squeeze of the hand. Donoso was sure that Louis Napoleon would now force his ministers to resign unless they cooperated with his plans, and he was confident of his own influence. That same day he wrote to Madrid to Raczynski: "I expect a coup d'état, and if it comes, it will be repeated everywhere to reestablish order by force everywhere. But if the coup d'état miscarries, Europe will enter into a period of confusion such that the devil himself would be unable to foresee the end to which it will go."[29]

As late as January 12, 1852, Donoso could still write to Vicomte de la Tour: "I advised the coup d'état, I approved of it from the first, and every day I am more satisfied in having advised and approved it." Not only did Donoso know the coup was coming, he helped to finance it, with a few others whom Louis Napoleon trusted most.[30] If we cannot be sure what else he contributed, it appears he continued to advise. A week be-

[29] Juretschke, II, 744; 745; 797.

[30] Rosemary Pflaum, *The Emperor's Talisman, the Life of the Duc de Morny* (New York, 1968), p. 107. "Prince Louis was begging funds for the coming enterprise wherever he could. Mlle. Henriette mortgaged her London properties, the Princess Mathilde pawned her jewels, *and the Spanish ambassador advanced money*." (My italics.) These efforts to raise funds took place during the month of October. Donoso never adverted to his underwriting of the coup, but his total wealth showed a precipitous drop at about this time.

fore the coup he confided cryptically to Raczynski that, although Louis Napoleon had his bad side, "someone [he almost certainly meant himself] has acquired influence at the Elysée, [whose] advice carries great authority."[31] Louis Napoleon followed Donoso's advice to confide to Montalembert early in 1852 that his intent was conservative, to defend civilization and order, and he would not let himself be ruled by the universal suffrage he had restored. "I accept it as the source of power, not as the organ of government."[32] At the least Donoso provided encouragement, money, and a convenient rationale for the coup and dictatorship.

In his next communication to Madrid on October 24, Donoso defended dictatorship as necessary remedy for France's "actual circumstances." Louis Napoleon intended a "saving dictatorship," that is, a conservative one. A dictator had a right to seek power from the masses, because a ruler had to have some source for his authority. If he did not inherit it from an ancestor, then he should acquire it from everybody. "The king receives his authority from his father, but the father of the dictator is the people." There was nothing anarchic or revolutionary for everyone "to elect him who, once elected, is going to govern everybody." France, he argued, could not be saved from socialist revolution except by dictatorship, and no dictatorship was possible or durable "unless it comes from the people and is based in the people." Since the president had not yet acted, however, he feared that anything was still possible except the "constitutional government of the middle classes." Noting that "There is never a revolution which does not make something impossible," he observed that "the revolution of February [1848] is to the middle classes what 1789 was to the aristocratic classes." A bourgeois constitutional monarchy was now as impossible in France as the old absolute monarchy. If

[31] Juretschke, II, 801.

[32] G. P. Gooch, *The Second Empire* (London, 1960), p. 241. *Notes et lettres de Montalembert* (1848–1852) ed. André Trannoy (Paris, 1942), p. 75.

the monarchy were ever to return, it would have to become democratic. Nevertheless, the monarchist parties were clinging to the past, refusing to face even the immediate future. "The month of May," he warned, "is tomorrow," when "three million proletarians" would try by force and revolution to recapture their constitutional right to vote. The unrealism of these parties which refused to admit this peril put them "out of the game" in Donoso's eyes. The bourgeois and doctrinaire party, the so-called great party of order, he said, "neither knows what order is, nor is a party, nor is great." It could only prevent until too late a solution to the explosive stalemate; it could not possibly restore the monarchy, which could only follow "military dictatorship or revolutionary despotism."[33]

Never was he more hostile toward parliamentarism than in November of 1851. As the Assembly first refused to restore universal suffrage and then tried to seize control of the army by the Questors bill, his exasperation mounted. These "angry and ephemeral coalitions" were subjecting France to a "capricious, absurd, blind, mad" game of chance, in which "authority, religion, order, family, property" and her very existence were gambled frantically on a throw of the dice in an "insane lottery" with "the god of chance." Although he had expected the President to keep his head—but to attempt his "eighteenth Brumaire" at once, if he should fail—he was jubilant when the Assembly lost the cast. Had it won, he reasoned, its deep divisions would have left it in paralysis and sterility. "There would not have been a majority for anybody or anything, and the ship of state would have been left to the mercy of the waves." A national convention would have had to be held, ending in devastating tyranny or utter anarchy. Of one thing he felt sure, "the parliamentary power is going to end, be it victor or vanquished: vanquished, it will die at the hands of the president's dictatorship; victor, it will be transformed into a convention, to die at the hands of a revolutionary dictatorship." But whatever happened, France should not again have to pass through

[33] Juretschke, II, 696; 697; 695, 705; 697f; 695, 705; 799, 801.

the parliamentary phase. "France is destined to save the world," he wrote confidently. Six months later, however, forced to acknowledge that parliamentary Britain had regained a dominant influence in European affairs, he admitted, "We have not seen, nor will we see the true death of parliamentarism." Nevertheless, reflecting on the experiences of November exactly a year afterward, he wrote a classic analysis of the weaknesses and failures of parliamentarism, which Metternich called a masterpiece: With an unworkable equal division of powers, parliamentarism was eventually fated to die, either peacefully by the democratic ballot elevating "envious mediocrity" to supreme power, or "violently" by the "wrathful hand" of revolutionary masses or of a dictator, as in 1848 and 1851. He added, however, that he did not reject parliaments, only parliamentarism.[34]

For very different reasons Marx and Proudhon took fairly similar views of the last days of the Republic. "You did not want the Republic, honest, moderate, conservative, progressive, and free," taunted Proudhon. "Therefore you must choose between the Emperor and the Social Revolution." In *Eighteenth Brumaire (Der 18. Brumaire de Louis Bonaparte, 1852)* Marx heaped contempt on the Legitimists and Orleanists who had combined into the "party of Order" in the terrible June days of 1848 to crush the "proletarian party of Anarchy, of Socialism, of Communism," in order to save society, property, family, religion, order. Observing that it had carried the game of division of powers to the point of *va-banque* (all or nothing), he thought that it deserved to be annihilated at the mere touch of a "three-cornered Napoleonic hat" on December 2. "We wish it a happy journey." Beaten by "a card sharper's trick"! "Easy come, easy go."[35]

When Louis Napoleon had not struck by the last week of

[34] Juretschke, II, 703; 705, 801; 706, 801–2; 815; 648.

[35] Proudhon, *Coup d'État*, p. 294. Marx, *Eighteenth Brumaire*, pp. 19, 31ff, 40.

November, Guizot, Molé, and other Burgrave leaders (as Victor Hugo called them) of the Party of Order relaxed. They were convinced that he lacked the capacity to seize power by a coup and by December 1 the public in general had dismissed the likelihood of a coup until after the business as usual of the holiday season. Victor Hugo asked, a coup? "By a dwarf?" "What a farce!"[36] Donoso saw it differently. After November 25, concluding that everything hinged on the attitude of the army, he decided that the probabilities favored the president.[37]

By December 1 Donoso *knew* that the stage was set for a coup d'état. "Everything is happening here as I foresaw," he wrote to Raczynski; "the parliament has expired, its leaders are terrified and some have already obtained passports. The President is master of the situation: he will give the coup d'état on the day he determines, and it will be soon." Very probably he attended the president's reception at the Elysée that night, as he had done previously. It is unlikely that he was invited to the meeting of conspirators afterward, however, when Louis Napoleon gave the orders and assignments for the coup.[38] That same date, however, he wired in code to Madrid as certain and official the news that Louis Napoleon "has decided to give the coup d'état" and that the President had just written to Pius IX to ask him to persuade the French bishops to lend the coup their moral force.[39] Who but Louis Napoleon could have given him that news?

Louis Napoleon carried out the coup during that night and on the day of December 2, 1851. It was a lucky date for the

[36] Victor Hugo, *History of a Crime*, trans. H. Smith, I (New York, 1888), p. 1.

[37] Juretschke, II, 702ff, 802. Adrienne Dansette, *Louis Napoleon, à la conquête du pouvoir* (Paris, 1961), p. 337; Pflaum, *Duc de Morny*, p. 110; T.A.B. Corley, *Democratic Despot, a Life of Napoleon III* (London, 1961), p. 101.

[38] Juretschke, II, 802; 703–4.

[39] Valverde, II, 830. René Rémond, *The Right Wing in France* (Philadelphia, 1966), pp. 147–49. The hierarchy gave servile support to the "new Constantine"; a few who did not were replaced by the papacy.

Bonapartes, the anniversary of Austerlitz and of the coronation of Napoleon I.[40] Donoso promptly telegraphed to Madrid, "Paris is in a state of siege: universal suffrage has been reestablished and the people are called up for the 14th" to vote on a new constitution. "We are in full revolution," he told his government the next day, referring to the several barricades, but by the seventh he wired: "Complete tranquility reigns."[41] He defended what he called the most daring seizure of power in history as entirely necessary under the circumstances.[42]

On December 3 Donoso wrote a letter to Raczynski to boast about the accuracy of his predictions, which had been fulfilled in the "most skillful coup that history records: a man who a short while ago passed for an adventurer yesterday turned the key which locks up the most eminent political and military personages of France."[43] Marx observed that they had been "hauled out of their beds in the darkness of night, . . . their mouths sealed, their pens broken." The minister of police, Maupas, was more laconic: "Jugged." By some oversight Proudhon had been released from prison on a pass on December 2; in vain he advised Hugo and the Mountain not to resist, because the people would follow the dictator. Then he cursed universal suffrage as an absurdity. Soon he was roundly cursing "the Jesuits," a reference to Donoso, Veuillot, and Montalembert, in Morny's very presence. "The sabre and the cowl" ruled, noted Marx.[44]

The naïve enthusiasm with which Donoso hailed Louis Napoleon as the invincible "instrument of Providence" is almost comical and is entirely pathetic, but he was not alone.[45] Delighted and full of enthusiasm, Veuillot stoutly defended the dictator's coup and absolutism in *L'Univers* from the first

[40] Juretschke, II, 805.

[41] Unpublished telegraphic dispatches of December 2 and 7, 1851.

[42] Juretschke, II, 706.

[43] Juretschke, II, 803.

[44] Marx, *Eighteenth Brumaire*, pp. 25–26, Hugo, *History of a Crime*, p. 36. Woodcock, *Proudhon*, pp. 176–78. Marx, p. 18.

[45] Juretschke, II, 803.

day. Even the sober-minded Walter Bagehot, however, thought like Donoso that the coup had prevented the outbreak of socialist revolution in 1852, so did the British ambassador Cowley, and, strangely, so did Palmerston too.[46] Even Proudhon then hoped that Louis Napoleon might yet serve the social revolution, but, with more perspective, Marx dismissed the prospects of May, 1852, as millennial illusions.[47]

What Donoso demanded of the coup d'état was "a new social epoch," namely a dictatorial reform and revitalization of French and European society. He wanted Louis Napoleon to base his regime on "the three most vigorous and expansive forces in the world: religion, the army, and the people."[48] Foolishly he hoped that France could now do what he had thought virtually impossible under British domination in 1850, take decisive positive and preventative action to avert another great revolution and socialism. Could the French dictator, like Vico's Augustus, Diocletian, or Constantine, save society and turn Europe back from a final rendezvous with catastrophe? Donoso soon discovered he could not. He could have profited meanwhile from another talk with Ozanam, who had written that very year: "We are always hoping for a Constantine, who at one blow and with one effort would bring back the people to the fold. The trouble is that they do not really know the history of Constantine."[49]

While he still exulted over this "saving" dictatorship, how-

[46] R. P. Lecanuet, *Montalembert*, III (Paris, 1902), 25–36. See R. W. Collins, *Catholicism and the Second French Republic* on the sycophancy of Veuillot and the conservative clergy, pp. 317–25, 331; on the "discreet silence" of the "social Catholic party" of Ozanam, Lacordaire, de Melun, and Maret, pp. 329, 333f; on the opposition of Dupanloup, p. 327. Franklin C. Palm, *England and Napoleon III* (Durham, N.C., 1948), pp. 69–70, 73–78, 91f. Donald Southgate, "*The Most English Minister . . . ,*" *The Policies and Politics of Palmerston* (New York, 1966), pp. 286–89.

[47] Woodcock, *Proudhon*, pp. 176, 180. Marx, *Eighteenth Brumaire*, p. 20.

[48] Juretschke, II, 711.

[49] Quoted by Virginia M. Crawford, *Frederick Ozanam* (Oxford, 1947), p. 108.

ever, Donoso declared that the coup had defeated parliamentary liberalism, settled the lingering crisis of 1848, and prevented the triumph of socialism in 1852. A month later he summed it us in a more sober mood:

> This coup d'état either is nothing and means nothing or it means the simultaneous suppression of the revolution of 1789, of 1830, of 1848, and of 1852: the suppression of *liberalism*, which had its origin in the first; . . . of *parliamentarism*, which had its origin in the second; . . . of *republicanism*, restored in the third; and . . . of *socialism* which would have come to the world with the fourth.[50]

In his own resumé of the course of revolution since 1789, Proudhon's anarchist and optimistic expectations agreed with Donoso's fears.

> Personal, or despotic, government is impossible; [1789, 1830]
> Representative government is impossible; [1848]
> Government is impossible. [1852]

Let Louis Napoleon be a revolutionary dictator; let him accept as his destiny the revolutionary idea and anarchy or else fall by it. For Donoso, as for Proudhon and for Tocqueville, the revolutionary movement that began in 1789 was one throughout its length, through all of its phases.[51] This dictator-

[50] Juretschke, II, 707, 709; 717.

[51] Proudhon, *Coup d'État*, pp. 286–87, 174–75. P.-J. Proudhon, *General Idea of Revolution in the 19th Century*, trans. by J. B. Robinson (London, 1923), pp. 40f. The subtitle is very revealing: "Law of Tendency in Society—The Revolution of 1789 has done only half its work." Tocqueville: "There is but *one revolution, the same under all the changes of fortune, of which our fathers saw the beginning, and of which we ourselves in all probability shall not see the end*"—quoted by J. P. Mayer, *Political Thought in France from the Revolution to the Fifth Republic* (London, 1961), p. 53. Donoso: "The Republic is not an arbitrary nor accidental institution; it is the logical, invincible consequence of the great syllogism which began to establish itself in 1789, and which today shows its consequence after having fixed its premises. The marvelous unity of the revolution in all its successive transformations and the necessity of denying it with an absolute negation or of accepting it in all its various manifestations was demonstrated . . . by the orator of the Mountain." (Juretschke, II, 679; August 1, 1851).

ship, thought Donoso, would render the conservative reaction triumphant, through the French example and leadership, in all of Europe. If not, ultimately it was destined to be insignificant in history. As he had reflected on the general effect of a permanent French Republic or socialist state, so it should be with a new conservative regime: "Never has an institution been consolidated in France . . . which . . . has not finally been changed into a European institution. The destinies of Europe are those of France."[52] Before long, hard facts convinced him that this dictatorship was destined to be ineffectual but for the moment he dared almost to hope for miracles.

CONSOLIDATING THE DICTATORSHIP

At first the domestic threats to the new dictatorship worried him more than its foreign problems. For a short while he was disturbed at the continuing hostility of the liberal middle class. Their participation at the barricades, although it was easily put down, was for him a sign of the incurable blindness and the radical incapacity of his own bourgeois class to govern. He felt that had the coup of Louis Napoleon failed, socialistic mobs would have fallen on the bourgeoisie like mad dogs. Nevertheless, he knew that the dictator would suffocate in a vacuum without the "moral assistance of notable men" from the middle and upper classes. "The wealthy citizens are incapable of governing, and nevertheless it is a certain and verified thing that no kind of government is possible today unless it is composed of the most notable among its individuals." The thorny problem was how to isolate these notables from their class sentiments and loyalties.[53]

Soon he warmly praised the heroic conduct of Montalembert as the first eminent man to proclaim support, by December 10, for the new regime.[54] Having wrestled with his conscience and principles for several days, having consulted with

[52] Juretschke, II, 672; 779.
[53] Juretschke, II, 709f; 707; 710.
[54] Juretschke, II, 603.

Donoso, Veuillot, Guizot, and Pasquier on a course of action, and having been assured by Louis Napoleon that the coup was intended for the sake of order and religion, Montalembert proclaimed that this conservative dictatorship was preferable to the "red" dictatorship of socialism, and he urged a favorable vote in the plebiscite.[55] "To vote for the prince is to arm the power to quell the army of crime, to defend your churches, your homes, your women."[56] Donoso was also a very ardent advocate of his accepting a place on Louis Napoleon's advisory commission, a decision Montalembert regretted ever afterward. Like Donoso, Montalembert was to be very bitterly disenchanted in less than two months and within six months showed his hostility publicly in the Legislative Assembly.[57]

Since Louis Napoleon had promised a new constitution after the coup d'état, Donoso waited to see what it would reveal about the nature of the regime. He had correct inside information ten days before the document was released that it would set the foundation for an authoritarian democracy.[58] It "constitutes absolute power" in place of liberty; the prerogative of the dictator to use the plebiscite as a last resort reduced the legislative body to a mere shadow parliament.[59] Although "the whole government is concentrated in the President," Donoso still considered it a good constitution for a people who were as sick to death with constitutions as he thought the French were. However, such a constitution (which changed little when the Empire came a year later) was in his outlook only

[55] André Trannoy, ed., *Notes et lettres de Montalembert* (Paris, 1942), pp. 71–75.

[56] Montalembert, quoted by Gustave Aubry, *Le Second Empire* (Paris, 1938), p. 82. On the reactions of Montalembert and Veuillot, see Eugène Veuillot, *Louis Veuillot*, II, 468; Roger L. Williams, *Gaslight and Shadow, the World of Napoleon III, 1851–1870* (New York, 1957), pp. 78f; G. P. Gooch, *The Second Empire*, pp. 241f, 246.

[57] Unpublished dispatch, No. 385, June 24, 1852, archives of Ministry of Foreign Affairs, Madrid.

[58] Unpublished dispatch, No. 24, January 14, 1852.

[59] Unpublished dispatch, No. 45, January 24, 1852.

suitable for the existing crisis, not as permanent.[60] Normal, stable government had to be limited in power.

Despite middle-class hostility to the new regime, Donoso was greatly impressed by the solidity of the dictator's power over the masses. "Among absolute powers none is more tremendous than that which the masses delegate to their darling lovers; these powers, however, are accustomed to be as ephemeral as they are formidable."[61] He explained where the dictator's short-range strength and long-range weakness lay.

> His strength consists in having made himself the representative of the universal reaction against the exclusive preponderance of the middle classes and against the parliamentary theories, . . . and in having sought his support in the army and in the Church, the two greatest instruments of organization and of conservation in the world. His weakness consists in the fact that he neither seeks nor finds men, that he is in the middle of a vacuum.[62]

He was right to prescind from the middle class, but he was wrong to do so without eminent individuals from that class. A nation like France, Donoso warned, would not long consent to being governed "by people of little worth, come forth from who knows where," men like Morny and Persigny, one his parrot and the other his puppet.[63] Nevertheless, he advised, the dictatorship was secure for some time to come because of its solid support from the masses.

Closing the Pantheon, cutting down liberty trees, and erasing "*Liberté, Egalité, Fraternité*" from public buildings pleased Donoso, but when the dictator confiscated property of the Orleans family late in January to distribute it among the lower classes and to bribe the Church, he was astonished and cha-

[60] He indicated such in his dispatch of December 24, 1852; Valverde, II, 894.

[61] Juretschke, II, 721.

[62] Juretschke, II, 717.

[63] Valverde, II, 898. Baron D'Ambes, *Intimate Memoirs of Napoleon III*, I (Boston, 1912), 375, cited Thiers that Morny was Napoleon III's "pet vice" and called Persigny "the pitiless." Juretschke, II, 721.

grined and wondered if the hostility of the bourgeoisie were not justified. "*This is socialism clearly characterized.* . . . To attack property at this moment, when his only title is in having rid us of robbers [the socialists], is an act of madness that confounds human understanding." The dictator had stupidly pulled a coup d'état against himself.[64] Perhaps he had even "signed his death warrant."

This seizure of property, Donoso feared, might portend other acts of Bonapartist socialism that would alienate the rest of Europe and deprive the coup d'état of any general conservative influence on the Continent. At that time he was very involved in Louis Napoleon's foreign policy, trying in vain to get him to resurrect the old Concert of Europe and to lead a counterrevolutionary front of continental nations. Having failed to get him to act by April 1, he reluctantly resigned himself to the prospect of the Second Empire, for which he had not the least enthusiasm.

After four months of the dictatorship Donoso was too disillusioned to offer more than a feeble protest when Montalembert, professing "I love liberty," wrote to plead with him not to let his name and talent be exploited by Veuillot's "nasty little school" of absolutists and clericals. He reminded Donoso that he had won his own glory under a parliamentary regime, whose abuses and dangers he preferred a thousand times to those of absolute government. Refusing to stand with the courtiers of force, he declared, "I prefer the *Chamber* to the antechamber."[65] Not wanting to offend Donoso or to break with him, but only to warn him, Montalembert was convinced

[64] Juretschke, II, 711, 720; 808f. Unpublished dispatch, No. 45, January 24, 1852. Compare with the attitude of Hübner, quoted by Aubry, p. 87. Among those in on the coup, General Flahault's reaction was also very much like Donoso's: Philip Guedalla, *Secret of the Coup d'État* (New York and London, 1924), pp. 271ff. A large packet of Donoso's correspondence on Montpensier and the Infanta continues through 1852, and deals with this confiscation in part (Legajo 22, Donoso Cortés family archives).

[65] Letters of Montalembert to Donoso (July 30 and November 11, 1852), Donoso Cortés family archives.

that their disagreement was only superficial, a matter of words. "I shall never see you among the flatters of force, among those who compromise . . . the Church by seeking to identify . . . her cause with that of the winners." Donoso was conciliatory, but he refused to identify either liberty or Church with parliamentarism any more than with absolutism, since neither was his ideal.[66]

THE SECOND EMPIRE

Already in April of 1852 Donoso announced, "We are in the eve of the Empire." Ever since 1849 he had believed that Louis Napoleon intended to reestablish the Empire, and he personally preferred such a monarchy to the Republic. With no exciting developments to report, however, during the summer of 1852 he watched Louis Napoleon's triumphal journey to Strassbourg, his frustrating search for a bride, and his speech at Bordeaux. In all of these actions he sought hints about the time and character of the Empire and the probable reaction of the great powers.[67] From "the superstitious veneration with which the Prince always regards certain anniversaries" and acts of Napoleon I, he guessed four months ahead of time that Louis Napoleon would proclaim the Empire on the next December 2.[68] He repeatedly and urgently advised Madrid on

[66] Juretschke, II, 633–34, 606, 610–11.

[67] On Donoso's early anticipation of the Empire, see Juretschke, II, 728, 733, 765. On the trip to Strassbourg, see Valverde, II, 871–73, where he notes that Louis Napoleon had been received by the masses with such festive celebration as if he were a conquering hero on triumph and a savior of the state, although he noted ominously that both Charles X and Louis Philippe had previously been acclaimed there by the fickle masses. Unpublished dispatch, No. 536 (August 24), described the boredom and cold indifference of France after several months of dictatorship. On October 10 (Valverde, II, 881) he interpreted the Bordeaux speech as signaling that "we are touching the Imperial epoch."

[68] Juretschke, II, 747 (August 30, 1842), also II, 749. On September 10 (Valverde, II, 874–75), observing that the empire already existed "except for the name," he again predicted that the empire would be formally proclaimed on December 2, next repeating precisely the same rea-

how to act and how to derive the most from the inevitable by granting the Second Empire immediate recognition and thus gaining the emperor's very useful friendship. The queen promised him new credentials beforehand to avoid any embarrassing interval,[69] but when the time came, Donoso had to watch several other powers precede him, while he waited for Madrid to send his papers.[70]

Donoso's first public function after the proclamation of the Empire was to represent Isabel II officially at the marriage of the emperor and Eugénie of Montijo, a beautiful Spanish countess. Napoleon III had suddenly determined on this unlikely match, he pointed out, for three reasons: "love, defiance, and illuminism."[71] The despised parvenu defied both the old dynasties and the French middle class by taking a spouse without royal blood, and superstitiously he had read some coincidences as portents to guide his choice and even the day of the wedding. Donoso accompanied his bride in the coach from the palais de l'Elysée to the Tuileries for the civil ceremony.[72] The next day he assisted at the religious rites at Notre Dame, which he described as "solemn and majestic." "The Empress was beautiful but exceptionally pale; the Emperor exuded joy and gaiety. Both participated in the ceremony with open devotion, especially the Empress, who let neither her eyes wander nor her knees rest." Yet, for all the vast crowds, the parades, the social color and glitter, the banners with "N" and "E," he

---

sons. These predictions were made months ahead of those by Lord Cowley (see Palm, *England and Napoleon III*, pp. 107f, 110). On Donoso's prediction of the Empire, Tassara wrote: "Donoso with his gift of prophecy / Time and again foretold me it." Gabriel García y Tassara, *Poesías*, p. 365.

69 Unpublished letter to the queen (undated) in the archives of the Ministry of Foreign Affairs. He repeatedly warned against a delay of recognition (Valverde, II, 875, 880).

70 Unpublished telegraphic dispatch, December 11, 1852; also see Valverde, II, 891–92.

71 Juretschke, II, 757, 759.

72 Robert Sencourt, *The Life of the Empress Eugénie* (New York, 1931), pp. 84–87, mentions Donoso's role on the night of January 25. Juretschke, II, 762–63.

noted that only a cold silence greeted the new Spanish empress.

Since the coup d'état Donoso had learned much about the new dictator–emperor. Having been disappointed first by Narváez and now by Louis Napoleon, he should have learned something about the danger of trying to utilize for social purposes the passion for power of ambitious and unscrupulous adventurers. His excessively realistic description of the new emperor in January of 1853 was the fruit of bitter disillusionment. Besides putting a fatalistic "complete trust in his fortune and in time," Napoleon III had revealed himself as a "great master of the political science of Machiavelli and of the governing art of the Borgias," for he understood the human passions and how to exploit them.[73] He was a character against whom everyone must stand on guard and fear anything.

Speculating on the domestic and foreign policies of the Empire, which he believed were intimately connected, Donoso observed, "With Louis Napoleon anything is possible in Europe. . . . The future is as obscure for him as for everyone else." Precisely because of the ambivalent character he assumed as heir of Napoleon I, he poses as "champion of order" within France, but in foreign relations with the Poles and with Piedmont he was potentially a fomenter of revolutionary war.[74] Donoso considered him monomaniacal about his Hamlet-like double character and role. He is "a man who believes himself, and who is, at the same time authority and revolution incarnate, who today talks peace to Europe and tomorrow, to the electors, talks of reaction against the affronts to the Empire, who leaves hanging the questions of peace and of war with neighboring nations."[75]

Now that the Empire had come, he distinguished between Napoleon's immediate and long-term domestic and foreign objectives. For the moment he detected a policy of peace and material interests, which was like that of the July Monarchy.

[73] Valverde, II, 896.
[74] Valverde, II, 883.
[75] Unpublished dispatch, No. 757, November 24, 1852.

It depended on middle-class prosperity and on an English alliance "without cordiality" in place of the former *entente cordiale*. In the future, however, the emperor's true policy would emerge; Donoso called it quasi-socialistic internally and quasi-warlike in foreign policy.[76] By experience he came to know long before Bismarck detected it, that Napoleon III was "a sphinx without a riddle," full of doubts, fears, contradictions, and half measures rather than such a decisive man of action, after all.[77] Nevertheless, Donoso still feared his caprice and cunning. He observed that his foreign policy was a combination of prudence and daring, that is, "daring in design, prudent in action."[78] He feared that before long Napoleon III would attempt some kind of European coup d'état similar to the one in France. War, whenever and wherever it came, territorial or revolutionary, would be the inevitable result of the new empire.[79] Already in 1852 he declared that wars and conquests would certainly follow in the train of the Empire and would just as certainly destroy it. "A peaceful, popular Empire would be something new under the sun, and there are no new things under the sun." Of Louis Napoleon he had observed, "The idea of revenge for Waterloo and of aggrandizement are as rooted in him as the imperial ideas." Europe was justified in fearing any action he might take almost anywhere Napoleon I's ambitions had turned: a strike in Africa, Belgium, Britain, or Italy. Donoso actually predicted the participants and the

[76] Juretschke, II, 740; 741. On March 10 he had said much the same: "The prince president who is a compound of conservative and revolutionary, who on the one hand loves absolute power passionately and on the other goes into ecstasy in the presence of the masses of the people; . . . who, swinging between all contradictions, can be God knows what, can take the bad road on seeing that, on the one side, while the great monarchies hesitate in coming to his aid, England unfurls the conservative banner and, on the other, that he remains the object of unrelenting opposition from the conservative parties of France" (Juretschke, II, 726).

[77] Juretschke, II, 648.

[78] Unpublished dispatch, No. 536, August 24, 1852; also Valverde, II, 896.

[79] Valverde, II, 897; this is in part repeated from his dispatch of December 15, 1852 (Juretschke, II, 738–42).

general Near Eastern locale of the Crimean War early in 1853.[80]

Donoso surpassed all of his contemporaries, including Marx and Proudhon, not only for force of expression but also for rapidity of sizing up Napoleon III and foreseeing his doom.[81] For example, he described the constitutional changes that came with the Empire as placing even greater power at the top and leaving even less significance for the Senate and Legislative Body than in the dictatorship. "Never has any man, . . . neither in ancient nor in modern times, concentrated in his hands so gigantic a power in Christian Europe. The most absolute divine-right monarchies encountered certain effective barriers in the great corporations of the State and in the proud spirit of the nobility and aristocracy. The new Emperor finds no resistance anywhere."[82] It was the closest approach to the

[80] Juretschke, II, 750; 728, 754; 742f, 750f.

[81] G. P. Gooch, *Second Empire*, p. 17. The phraseology of these five critics is often very alike; that of Donoso, Hübner, and Cowley may owe something to their mutual conversations. On Bagehot, see "Letters on the French *Coup d'État*" and "Caesarism after Thirteen Years" in *The Works of Walter Bagehot*, II (Hartford, Conn., 1891). Thiers (1852): "He will *probably* perish by war, and he will *certainly* perish by peace"—(Senior, *Conversations*, II, 118). Senior quoted Cousin as saying (1858): "The institution which France wants more than any other is that of a dictator—a temporary despot, legally appointed—who can remedy evils which ordinary authorities cannot reach. From time to time we have a self created one; he cannot depend on our obedience unless he performs the duties we expect from him; *Celui-ci* [Napoleon III] was submitted to because we expected him to put down the *Rouges*" (Senior, II, 185). General Lamoricière's view of the bourgeois opposition in 1852—"Not for action, they will talk against him."

[82] Valverde, II, 892 (December 10, 1852). His view of the regime considerably antedates similar ones by Bagehot and Victor Cousin. Looking backward from 1865 Bagehot saw Napoleon III pretty much as Donoso saw him in 1852–1853. Bagehot recognized that this empire was something new in European history, something comparable to the old Roman Caesars. Here was a "Benthamite despot . . . for the greatest happiness of the greatest number . . . the best finished democracy which the world has ever seen" in the material sense—"an absolute government with a popular instinct." Its great failing was in what Tocqueville or Donoso would have called its egalitarian "mediocrity"; it inculcated dullness by refraining to assist the people's "future elevation" (Bagehot, pp. 441–43).

totalitarian state that Donoso would ever see, but he was sure that it could not last. "That which characterizes the present Power is that it is omnipotent and unstable. No one thinks that it can be resisted and no one believes that it will last. It is always the nature proper to powers which rise suddenly from popular acclaim; everyone obeys them until everyone resists them."[83] This type of system was "necessary in certain circumstances," such as the current moment of crisis, but "by its very nature the future is denied to it."[84]

Shortly before his death in 1853 Donoso described the nature of the Second Empire as essentially a dictatorship still, partly conservative, partly revolutionary." Here is the great, the immense revolution which was worked in our presence: . . . to the bourgeois Monarchy has succeeded a great democratic Empire, which is nothing other than a great Republic directed by a dictator with a crown."[85] The Emperor alone, he said, knew the importance of this revolution; at the same time he represents both "authority against internal revolutions and revolution against the European monarchy."

Politics aside, however, he did not think that Napoleon III would be an old-style conservative in domestic policy, but quasi-socialist, whom he called a "socialist after his fashion."[86] He knew such former Saint-Simonians as Fould and de Lesseps, who supported and served the regime, and he believed that he might very well undertake the 'gigantic internal works' of a Saint-Simonian kind which he had once promised.[87] In his social-economic policies, Louis Napoleon in fact was to show a concern not only for the prosperity of the bourgeoisie but also for popular welfare by employment on great public works projects, trying to improve working conditions, beginning public

[83] Juretschke, II, 739.

[84] Valverde, II, 894.

[85] Juretschke, II, 759.

[86] Valverde, II, 889. Montalembert's view was similar: "His habits are despotic, but his instincts are socialist." Senior, *Conversations*, p. 314.

[87] Those names appear on Donoso's lists of invitations or visits more than once; Legajo 55, Donoso Cortés family archives. Juretschke, II, 750.

housing, and encouraging workers' mutual aid societies.[88] In so far as he can be considered a conservative, Napoleon III was ahead of both Disraeli and Bismarck with a program of reforms to assuage popular discontents in the social-economic order. One cannot prove that Donoso's pioneering ideas in this area were known to him; however, Donoso had the ear not only of the emperor but also of the new empress.[89] Possibly he urged on Eugénie what he recommended to the Spanish queens: a lavish and well-advertised public charity, which in fact became conspicuous in the Second Empire, as an initial fanfare to precede a more institutionalized program of social-welfare reforms.[90]

In assessing the future career of Napoleon III, Donoso noted that he was as "fatalistic as a Turk" about his star and destiny, and he thought that there was good reason for his superstition. "This man is in the hands of fatality, . . . a series of successive fatalities." He did indeed have his star, but it was leading him to a sad end. "I know none of the providential men whom history honors, who, for a longer or shorter time, has not been such a success. The truth is that afterward comes another period during which he errs in everything, do what he will; this is the fatal period of his decadence and death."[91] The time would come, he predicted, when "the dispersed elements of opposition will begin to draw together and take shape; the necessity to distract France will come to be imperative; war will then be inevitable."[92] This situation was to exist in 1859 in

[88] See David L. Kulstein, *Napoleon III and the Working Class* (Los Angeles, 1969) for a discussion of the origins of "social Bonapartism" and for the acts and propaganda of the Second Empire in behalf of workers, pp. 23–28, 97–100. Kulstein finds a wide gap between promise and action, a promise of cradle-to-the-grave assistance, but more emphasis on imperial and private charity, public works employment, and public housing.

[89] Hübner, *Neuf Ans de souvenirs*, p. 115.

[90] Kulstein, *Napoleon III*, pp. 97–98. Juretschke, II, 598–99; also see Ch. 10.

[91] Juretschke, II, 760, 750; 733; 740.

[92] Valverde, II, 889–90.

respect to Italy, and to an even greater extent in Prussia and Germany in 1870. Donoso predicted in 1852 that the actual situation would move fatally into a "hereditary Empire," from that "to conquest" and "war," from war into "another Waterloo," and finally after renewed attempts to restore the monarchy, into another democratic Republic. "The history of the future will be the history of the past. For me it is self-evident that experience does not profit anyone, neither individuals nor nations." (Donoso himself never did learn from his experience with dictators.) He thought, however, that there would be one signal difference between the course of the First and Second empires. He knew that Napoleon III, unlike his uncle, was no soldier and had neither the stomach nor the genius for the wars which he was doomed nevertheless to pursue. The end of the Second Empire, therefore, would lack the glory of Waterloo; Donoso predicted that it would be another Novara, like that ignominious rout of the Italians by Austria in 1849.[93]

At the end, Donoso considered that through the coup d'état both Louis Napoleon and the rest of Europe had bungled an opportunity to regroup the monarchist, clerical, and conservative forces of the old Europe. They could have sapped the strength of the revolutionary movement by capturing the popular mind and loyalty through social-economic reforms and plebiscitary democracy and thus could have averted later socialist revolutions, totalitarian states, and ultimate anarchy. It also appears that, through his disappointment, he sensed that the new Napoleonic regime might after all be something significant in history as a weak harbinger of the totalitarian state of which he had forewarned in 1849. One of the supreme ironies of history, moreover, is the fact that his own arguments against socialism, liberalism, and parliamentarism were later to be utilized by fascists and Nazis, who distorted his words to their purpose.

Although many observers besides Donoso, including Proudhon and Marx, noticed parallels between the two Napoleonic

[93] Juretschke, II, 733; 736.

careers, the cyclic outlook which Donoso applied to French history and politics was more highly developed that one finds anywhere else in the literature of the period.[94] Marx's and Proudhon's view of world progress, however, like Hegel's and Comte's, excluded any real belief in cycle, recurrence, repetition, or retrogression in history. No new Caesar for Proudhon; but, if Louis Napoleon would not be a revolutionary, the only apt historical analogies were monsters like "Caligula, Heliogabalus, and Commodus."[95] More cynically dispassionate and realistic, Marx quoted Hegel that all great personages and events occur twice in world history, but, he added, "the first time as tragedy, the second time as farce." He saw the superficial phenomenon of imitation, if not repetition, in history in the classical Roman style of the French Revolution and Napoleon I ("Caesar himself") and again of the style of the revolution of 1789–1800 in the parodies of February, 1848, to December, 1851. Because conditions were premature for a true proletarian revolution, only the aimless ghost of the old bourgeois revolution masqueraded. And the petty knavery of Louis Napoleon completed the farce—the cycle from bourgeois monarchy, to bourgeois republic, to bourgeois dictatorship—the last act of a "comedy in the most vulgar sense."[96] Paraphrasing Donoso, the poet Tassara put it in almost the same words, "a mad farce": "Mireabeaus, Ciceros, / Caesars, Napoleons / Are all the same . . . actors / In different costumes."[97] After the farce, however, all expected eventually another tragedy, socialist revolution. The result would be progress and utopia to Marx and Proudhon but to Donoso, retrogression and doom for modern civilization. Right after the coup d'état, however, Donoso had predicted that the dictatorship would lead to the

94 Donoso's cyclic interpretation of general, or world, history is far more subtle and complex than his application of the cycle to France, where he scarcely went beyond Marx in noting historical imitation and political cycle.

95 Proudhon, *Coup d'État*, p. 176.

96 Marx, *Eighteenth Brumaire*, pp. 15–20, 23–24.

97 Gabriel García y Tassara, *Poesías*, p. 439.

Empire, and the Empire, to the monarchy: "all of this by reason of the perpetual law of rotation, to which all things human are subject"—"that great circle."[98] Later he added socialist revolution to the cycle again, as he lost hope for any real restoration.

Apart from any cyclic theory of history, Donoso's evaluation of Napoleon III compares well not only with the views of his noted contemporaries but also with later interpretations by historians up to the present.[99]

[98] Juretschke, II, 712.

[99] Recent historians generally emphasize Napoleon III's superstitious faith in his star and Providence. Namier, *Vanished Supremacies*, pp. 58, 63. A newer view of Napoleon III, strongly attacked by Namier, which closely resembles Donoso's interpretation of the man, his policy, and regime, is that of Albert Guerard, *Napoleon III* (Cambridge, Mass., 1953). Even in the terminology used, except that after the coup d'état, Donoso became more like Namier in his judgment of the man and his role. Donoso's final view, in fact, supports the detractors and critics who maintain that Napoleon III's ultimate future was inevitable, according to "the logic of the situation," to so speak, and the emperor's personal defects and characteristics. Donoso was not, however, contemptuous of the man, in the sense of Hugo's "Napoleon le petit," for he recognized his great capacity for good or ill in France and Europe. Judging by Tassara's picture of Napoleon III as a "modern Caesar" foreshadowing later Caesars and also as analogous to ancient Rome (*Poesías*, p. 411) as well as by Donoso's reflections along the very same line (Juretschke, II, 751), then, like J. S. Schapiro (*Liberalism and the Challenge of Fascism*, New York, 1949), Donoso saw him as a herald of twentieth-century plebeian (fascist) dictators. In fact, Donoso's own defence of Louis Napoleon before the coup, as well as his more hostile description later, goes far to support Schapiro's thesis in regard to the character of propertied and religious support for this "savior" of society against socialist revolution; his posing as democrat and socialist, even while serving bourgeois material interests by an authoritarian (but not totalitarian) government with pretended parliaments and plebiscitary elections—a "pioneer fascism," a Fascist pattern. Nevertheless, he knew well that neither the man nor the regime was the totalitarian state he had envisioned for the future (II, 201). A. J. P. Taylor, in *Rumors of War* (London, 1952), also closely parallels Donoso's judgment of Napoleon III, even to the view that the "man of December" was fated to be the "man of Sedan."

Chapter VIII

SPAIN AND DICTATORSHIP MILITARY AND CIVIL

DONOSO AS STATESMAN

After 1848 Donoso emerged as a statesman, devoted to monarchy, Spain, and Europe. He had often speculated about what distinguished statesmen from mere politicians, "The special character which distinguishes the statesman from everyone else . . . is the instinct which discerns those questions on which there can be compromise, those on which it is possible to yield, and those which can neither be compromised nor abandoned." In other words, statesmanship was more than the pragmatic art of the possible in politics and diplomacy; it also entailed sound judgment about permanent political, national, and social interests according to true principles. He regretted that after 1848 no true statesman emerged, either for Spain or for Europe as a whole, and he was tempted to try the role. After 1850 he almost attained the first rank of power as Spain's premier, and he formed a lofty conception of the position. "The public ministry is not a sinecure. Its very name tells what it is: it is a service, and a laborious service. . . . It is to serve, not to enjoy. It is to row, and to live and die with one's hand on the oar. Such is the price for one who wants to be a minister." He did pay this price, too early, as a statesman and diplomat who advised heads of state in Spain and France on dictatorship, coups d'état, and European diplomacy to reinforce order internally and internationally and to inaugurate social-economic reforms to forfend socialist revolution in the future. Although his intrigues may even have constituted conspiracy, they were within the traditions of authoritarianism and enlightened despotism. At least his actions were motivated by high principles and good intentions, instead of personal ambition and lust for power. In trying to play a European role, despite the weakness of Spain, perhaps he saw himself as a new Alberoni; in trying to remake Spain, he was more comparable to the authoritarian Prime Minister, Bravo Murillo, except that he would not have made his friend's mistakes of 1851–1852. As prime minister, or dictator, he would surely have committed his own errors, but success or failure, he would have been more spectacular.[1]

THE FALL OF NARVÁEZ: "SPEECH ON SPAIN"

Donoso had supported General Narváez both before and after his "Speech on Dictatorship" in 1849, because for him any government was better than revolutionary anarchy.[2] "I am a man of government," he explained, "before and above everything." Nevertheless, still fearing revolution, he was glad to leave Spain in 1849. The slow restoration of political order in Europe could not dispel his feeling that Spain was corrupt, and doomed sooner or later to revolutionary upheaval, ultimately to socialism. Narváez was his hope and his despair. Previously he had told Raczynski how much he disliked the general personally. "You know that between Narváez and me there can exist neither friendship nor sympathy; by our characters, by our tastes, by our way of seeing and appraising everything, we are at opposite poles."[3] He considered the general a mere opportunist, and he feared that his cabinet coterie of inept parasites would ruin Spain. Nevertheless, he admitted, "Narváez is the column which holds up the edifice; the day the column falls, the whole building will crumble." At that time Donoso could not see that he would be the one to play Samson in 1850.

[1] Juan Juretschke, ed., *Obras completas*, II, 69; cf. I, 165, for a similar statement in 1835. II, 811f; 800; 341; 799; 74.

[2] See Raymond Carr, *Spain, 1808–1839* (Oxford, 1966), pp. 242f, for a very unflattering description of Donoso's defense of the dictatorship: "Hot air."

[3] Juretschke, II, 325; 775–85; 789.

He had supported the dictator in 1849 not just to uphold the established order but to inaugurate reforms to eliminate the causes of revolution. As the immediate crisis passed and no reforms were forthcoming, he could no longer justify this liberal dictatorship. He was especially disillusioned when official venality culminated in the scandalous elections of 1850, a corruption that he believed had involved his own brother Eusebio and had sullied the family name.[4] "Shame forbids me to tell what goes on in Spain," he wrote Veuillot. "Prior to February [1848] you had an incorruptible but corrupting ministry [Guizot's]; but we . . . have a corrupting and corrupted ministry."[5] Foreseeing a break, Raczynski wrote to Berlin:

> The ministry of Narvaéz has also lost the support of the Marquis of Valdegamas, who seems to be, despite his immense talent and the firmness of his political principles, left without a cause. He has no view in common with the liberal party. Fate has tied him to the Moderates, but his conscience forbids him to serve their cause; his conscience and his honor also always separate him from the partisans of absolute power, because they are the enemies of the queen.[6]

Not entirely isolated, Donoso joined Pacheco and Bravo Murillo on *La Patria* after April of 1850 in their fight as a conservative opposition to Narváez's "dismal policy."[7]

In parliament on December 30, 1850, he delivered a blistering moral indictment against the Narváez government. It was the kind of attack to which an effective reply can never be given. Unlike most denunciations of this kind, however, this speech was instrumental in bringing down the government. This "speech on the situation in Spain," the last of Donoso's great orations, was also his most completely antiliberal blast,

[4] Eusebio Donoso Cortés to Juan Donoso Cortés (Badajoz, 30 August 1850); Eusebio denied the allegation. Letter, Donoso Cortés family archives.

[5] Juretschke, II, 344.

[6] Comte Adéhmar d'Antioche, *Deux Diplomates*, p. 38.

[7] Pedro Gómez Aparicio, *Historia del periodismo Español*, I (Madrid, 1967), 372–73.

where at last he openly condemned some of the most fundamental principles and practices of liberalism. It was even more strongly against materialism in a world that seemed to him to be going crazy over economic considerations, the same theme of his famous "Speech on Europe" earlier in the year. Alleging capital disagreements with the erroneous and dismal system of the Narváez cabinet, he declared that his opposition was a matter of conscience, a personal vote of no confidence.[8] Since 1844 the cabinet had been its own sovereign master and could have introduced true principles of order and reform into things political, social, and religious, but instead it had pursued material order alone.

This speech was a biting condemnation of materialism, ambition, and corruption in places high and low, in the government and in the whole country. He accused the government of flagrant corruption among its officials, especially in the last elections, where its highest agents were the buyers and sellers of consciences.[9] Everywhere he saw boundless ambition. "There is no Spaniard who does not think that he hears that prophetic voice . . . : 'Macbeth, Macbeth, thou shalt be king!' " All office-holders wanted to climb, the elector to deputy, the deputy to minister, the minister to "I don't know what." For him this ambition was proof of an all-pervading ill. "The dominant fact in Spanish society today is that corruption which is in the marrow of our bones" and "in the air we breathe."

The most general cause of this decay, he charged, was the prevailing liberal ideas and sentiments: "All the capital ideas that dominate at the moment are false." He meant first of all the parliamentarian principle of ministerial responsibility, at least as Spain used it, as part of the system of constitutional guarantees against the abuse of power. To be responsible for everything, he explained, one had to be omnipotent, hence arbitrary and tyrannical. Like Marx he also condemned liberal economics as tending, even through freedom of competition,

[8] Juretschke, II, 325–27.
[9] Juretschke, II, 329–31.

to end up eventually in a monopoly of wealth. He prepared but spared the Cortes an attack on the elective principle and against freedom of the press. Still, he condemned the existence of neither institution, only their abuses, corruptions, and failings, which he thought a religious influence could remedy. Finally, he had meant to strike at the very heart of liberalism in the middle class as the "most corrupt and corrupting personage" in Spanish society.[10] At least, he outraged the liberals of both parties by declaring that "everything you hold for truth is a lie."

The government's financial policy he flayed with merciless sarcasm. He charged the ministry with trying to deceive people by juggling contrary systems of deficit spending and retrenchment.[11] The priorities for spending and saving piqued him, especially the building of an expensive state theater and the withholding of funds that were needed by the Church. The *Teatro de Oriente*, a "monument erected only for material pleasures," symbolized the present age of materialism, just as Philip II's austere Escorial had symbolized the excessive moralism of the Habsburg era. The "policy of material interests" was now reaching the point where among decadent peoples material pleasures were the supreme interest.

Nothing but catastrophe, he warned, could come from materialism. Had Spain all the armies of Russia, the fleets of Britain, and the gold of Peru and California, corrupted sentiments and wrong ideas would destroy such power. He did not need to be a prophet to predict the sad future for Spain from the past history of the July Monarchy, which had pursued commerce and industry so successfully, only to have moral disorder poison everything. The "great republican flood" in February of 1848 had given a definitive answer as to whether "society is safer and stronger when it is based on material order

[10] For a recent description of the irresponsible "new plutocracy" that ruled Spain, see: V. G. Kiernan, *The Revolution of 1854 in Spanish History* (Oxford, 1966), p. 23. Juretschke, II, 330–40, passim.

[11] Juretschke, II, 334–36.

or on moral order," on industry or on virtue. Spain had begun to follow the same path as Orleanist France in giving worship to the material order. Since 1848 "an industrial and commercial fever inflamed our blood." The ministry had not only failed to fight the contagion but had even encouraged it. "To-day . . . all these things—corruption, error, industrial fever—have reached their apogee."[12] Socialist revolution would finally result from this materialism.

With his Southwestern rural origins and professional career, Donoso was ill prepared to understand or to sympathize with an industrial revolution for the Northeast, but he did not really oppose it in itself. What worried him was the intense public response to this economic revolution, such as he observed in the great London Exhibition of 1851. He pleaded for a "balance between material interests and those which are moral and religious." It was not railways or industry he opposed but the spirit of materialism so evident in the avid pursuit of these things.[13]

He was not so naïve as to suppose that the social-economic problem, which he called the greatest "problem of Humanity and of History," could be ignored or wished away, but he held that it was more social and moral than strictly economic or political. Here in parliament, well ahead of J. S. Mill, he openly agreed with the socialists that the chief problem was "to regularize in society the most equitable distribution of wealth." He anticipated Marx in predicting that there would develop a monopolistic trend in the liberal competitive economy to concentrate wealth in ever fewer hands, until revolution broke out.[14] Of course, he did not favor the socialist solution of "universal confiscation, placing all public wealth in the hands of the State." This approach would simply effect another and a worse monopoly. Instead he proposed what sounded to his audience as a very naïve and outdated answer, a Christian

[12] Juretschke, II, 335–38.
[13] Juretschke, II, 620, 656; 824; 327.
[14] Juretschke, II, 339.

solution consisting of the spirit of charity and justice. Unless men were moved by these ideals in their social-economic relations, he warned, the problem was insoluble, and socialist revolution was the certain outcome.

Anticipating an objection that Spain faced no danger because she had no socialists, he asked: "What would you say, gentlemen, if I were to assure you that the country of socialism is not France, but Spain?" In words that evoke the social anarchists of twentieth-century Spain, he had remarked: "The day when the dikes break you will see more socialists here than in Paris . . . In Spain every novelty is admitted instantly and everything that penetrates Spain immediately arrives at the furthest limits of exaggeration." He charged that the poor of Spain had been socially and economically degraded in the revolutionary land settlement during the 1830s and were ripe for the growth of socialism, which Spain's inclination for one-party rule would merely conceal until the moment of explosion. With the very phrases of the socialists, he held up the specter of class war and expropriation before the bourgeois deputies, who, since they had won control of the government, had taken the motto: "All for the rich." "How do you wish, gentlemen, that this thesis not beget its antithesis and the defeated class in turn not cry out in the roar of war: all for the poor?"[15] He blamed this potential class war on the greed of the rich, whom he accused of exploiting and robbing the peasant masses after seizing Church properties. More scholarly views from the twentieth century strongly supported Donoso's picture of mid-nineteenth-century Spain, its government, its middle class, and their legislation.[16]

If the government wished to avert a socialist revolution at some time in the future, it must begin now to quell the forces

[15] Juretschke, II, 338; 785f; 340.

[16] A. Ramos Oliviera, *Politics, Economics, and Men of Modern Spain, 1808–1946*, trans. Teener Hall (London, 1946), pp. 55ff; V. G. Kiernan, *Revolution of 1854*, Ch. 1, "The Condition of Spain at Mid-Century," pp. 19–23, 35.

of corruption to put order and concert into public expenditures and to place a rein on appetites and wants. Because such a good fight would require forceful means, he was again ready to sanction dictatorship. However, let it be proclaimed as such, so Spain would not have to suffer the intolerable situation of a *de facto* dictatorship in the guise of constitutional government, where "liberty, instead of serving as a shield, serves then as a decoy."[17]

What Narváez would have done, had Donoso actually delivered the character sketch he had prepared, but prudently omitted, one can only guess. This general reputedly had boasted that he had no enemies because he had shot them all. Objectively Donoso admired his talent for command, decision, and action, but he criticized his lack of firm principles and program, his policy of expediency and improvising, his impatience with long-term reforms and his demand for quick results, his reliance on subservient but worthless parasites, his skill at persuading critics and so deferring important questions.[18] Donoso admitted that such techniques worked in the short run. "I myself have been seduced a score of times with a salute." "But to put off questions is not to answer them; the day will come" when they would trip him up. "There is not in Spain nor in Europe a person more convinced than he that material order is nothing without moral order," but, because he could not accomplish so slow and difficult a task "with a decree," he had not the patience even to try.

Abroad there was little interest in this speech; all its effects were at home. Added to the impact of his "Speech on Europe," Donoso now helped induce a temporary mood of deep pessimism in both the liberal and conservative presses about future class war and revolt by barbarous, socialistic masses.[19] Not until

[17] Juretschke, II, 340–41.

[18] Juretschke, II, 342f; 785.

[19] Kiernan, *Revolution of 1854*, pp. 30, 34, mentions Donoso as one of "the hysterical reactionaries," who caused much stir by writings that preached "a combination of religion with bayonets to save order and property," but he does not advert to Donoso's two great speeches of

the twentieth century, however, did the trenchant and prophetic character of the oration come to be acknowledged by Spaniards. At the time, he said, deputies applauded his brave eloquence, but there were no tempestuous "bravos" as before, because of his overt antiliberalism. Although he appealed to "the voice of your fathers and to conscience above interest," only twenty-two deputies voted with him.[20] Understandably, the government was quite unhappy. Martínez de la Rosa attempted a feeble answer, but Narváez was so piqued by this "shot in the back," as he called it, that he soon resigned and went off in a huff to France.[21] Donoso was very surprised to learn that he had helped to bring down a cabinet. Now, however, he began to incur bitter enmity in a "war of pin pricks and daggers" from Narváez's supporters and from the liberals, Moderates, and Progressives. He had to pay this price for descending from his so-called politics in the clouds into the dirty arena of day-to-day politics.[22]

BRAVO MURILLO, DONOSO, AND AUTHORITARIAN REFORM

Probably it was on Narváez's resignation that Donoso was asked to become premier and to form a cabinet, but he demurred. As he told Tejado shortly afterward, he did "not want to be minister so as not to do anyone even that ill which many times is just and necessary in those who govern."[23] Instead, the

1850, which preceded his mood of pessimism, nor realize how his "neo-Catholicism" attacked bourgeois mores.

[20] Juretschke, II, 344.

[21] Ángel Salcedo y Ruiz, *Historia de España* (Madrid, 1914), p. 713. There were reasons for Narváez's resignation other than Donoso's speech, but Julio Burell also affirms its effect in *Discursos parlamentarios* (Madrid, 1915), pp. xxi–xxii. Bravo Murillo also took credit for his opposition to Narváez in the cabinet and in *La Patria*; see Gómez Aparicio, *Historia*, I, 376. As for its being due to Bravo Murillo and Donoso, see Diego Sevilla Andrés, *Historia política de España, 1800–1967* (Madrid, 1968), pp. 126–27.

[22] Gabino Tejado, ed., *Obras*, I, lxxii.

[23] Juretschke, II, 572.

former Minister of Finance, Bravo Murillo, a politician from the Moderates' right wing and Donoso's long-time friend, now became president of the Council of Ministers. He had an ambitious program to put the public debt in order, to terminate political domination by the generals and by the middle class, to build a national system of roads and railways, and to correct what he and Donoso deemed the abuses of the liberal press and parliamentarism.[24] Naturally the new premier bid for Donoso's support and the votes of his faction. Aside from being equally reactionary and authoritarian, however, Donoso had more daring and more positive plans than Bravo Murillo. He proposed a social-economic program for the masses, resting on the support of both the army and the people, through cooperation by generals and by a democratic electoral law, or plebiscite. Instead of entering the cabinet or staying in Spain to help, therefore, he removed himself by accepting the diplomatic post at Paris in February of 1851, when Santomayor was dismissed for welcoming Narváez with state honors.[25] He might have helped Bravo Murillo even from Paris, if he had been willing to cooperate with *El Orden*, which belonged to the new president and represented almost his only support from the press. Instead, he seems to have encouraged Gabino Tejado, who was Bravo Murillo's editor but Donoso's disciple, in an independent and critical policy at times.[26]

While he was waiting for Louis Napoleon's coup and dictatorship in Paris, Donoso suffered unbearable anxiety and embarrassment from the actions of ex-dictator Narváez. De-

[24] Antonio Ballesteros y Bereta, *Historia de España*, VIII (Madrid, 1936), 32.

[25] Kiernan, *Revolution of 1854*, pp. 33–36. Carr, *Spain*, pp. 244–45. For an interpretation that views Bravo Murillo as trying to carry out Donoso's program, see Modesto Lafuente, *Historia general de España*, VI (Barcelona, 1890) p. 538. Galindo Herrero, *Donoso Cortés y su theoría política*, properly objects to so close an identification. Also see Luis Sánchez Agesta, *Historia del constitucionalismo español* (Madrid, 1955), p. 271.

[26] Gómez Aparicio, *Historia*, I, 383–85.

spite his repeated disillusionment with Narváez, the general now became his greatest hope for perhaps pulling off a coup d'état in Spain similar to the one in France and introducing the reforms he wanted.[27] Once more he had to learn the hard way that Narváez did not intend to be the executor of his ideas.

In September Narváez left him in a quandary by asking for a passport to go back to Spain. Personally unwilling to withhold it, he nevertheless knew that Bravo Murillo dreaded the general's return to active politics. Donoso also knew that even though a military strong man might be useful to the reactionary regime, his value would be destroyed by his intrigues once he were back home. Accordingly, he advised the government to get ready to use the general when Bravo Murillo had to step down, but to let him return only if firm pledges "for the good of the State" could be extracted from him beforehand. When Raczynski reproached him for playing at such a dangerous game, he replied that he was no child but was acting like one serpent with another; Narváez would have to conform to Donoso's principles and to give an exchange of guarantees.[28] In order to get the passport the general proved to be the more slippery snake. Privately assuring the ambassador that he was a partisan of his ideas, Narváez convinced him of his good faith. Later he would boast that he had never read a single phrase of Donoso.[29] For his part, Donoso tried to show this ambitious opportunist that his personal interest lay on the side of good principles, and he hoped that he had persuaded

[27] All the information on Donoso's involvement in the Narváez affair comes from his letters to Raczynski and from Raczynski's replies or reports to Berlin. Donoso's official dispatches to Madrid do not advert to the matter, so his letters to the government on this subject have either been destroyed or remain unpublished, except one (note 28).

[28] Juretschke, II, 795. Carlos Valverde, ed., *Obras completas,* II, 814–15. Juretschke, II, 801; 799. Valverde, II, 829. Donoso stamped Narváez's passport on November 11, 1851, with reference to Isabel's orders.

[29] Andrés Revesz, *Un dictador liberal. Narváez* (Madrid, 1953), p. 191; cited by Galindo Herrero, *Theoría política,* p. 111.

him.[30] In fact, he had just been seduced again by a strong man who felt only contempt for men of ideas.[31]

His hope that he could handle Narváez took a hard blow in November, when the general broke all his promises and returned forthwith to Spain. Donoso learned at last that he could never rely on him. He expected Narváez soon to exceed the limits of moderation in Spanish politics, and feared, besides, that his own reputation would be compromised.[32] Although the queen had but recently awarded him the Grand Cross of Charles III and made him a senator, the Spanish court was indeed angry on learning of his dealings with Narváez.[33] For a time it appeared that he would be ordered home, but he weathered the storm.[34] Despite the bad outcome, he refused to think that he had acted unjustly or imprudently in trying to convert to good principles a man who could have been so useful.[35] On the day before the coup d'état in France he had to dismiss Narváez as an incorrigible.

During November and until after the coup d'état of December 2 in France, Raczynski repeatedly told Donoso to expect a summons either to join Bravo Murillo in power or to form a new cabinet to enforce his own ideas.[36] He said that Donoso's opponents, dreading to see him take charge of Spain's affairs

[30] Juretschke, II, 804.

[31] Stanley G. Payne affirms that Narváez particularly scorned lawyers and clerical reactionaries with advanced ideas. Interested only in keeping order, he could not cope with wider problems or creative solutions, or grasp political theory. *Politics and the Military in Modern Spain* (Stanford, 1965), pp. 24–26.

[32] Juretschke, II, 800f.

[33] The royal decree and a letter of acknowledgment (October 26, 1851) from Donoso, who expressed his deepest thanks, are in the archives of the Ministry of Foreign Affairs, Madrid. Also see his letter to Raczynski (November 14, 1851), Juretschke, II, 800.

[34] See his letter to Raczynski (November 25, 1851), Juretschke, II, 801–2. Unpublished documents in the archives of the Ministry of Foreign Affairs reveal further details of his troubles with the Queen over Narváez and his resulting insecurity in office in October and November of 1851.

[35] Juretschke, II, 802.

[36] Antioche, letter from Raczynski to Donoso (November 9, 1851), p. 164.

for fear that their ambitious projects would be ruined, were raising "a very lively opposition" against him. "When the wolves howl against a dog, it shows that he is a good watchdog." Donoso professed to have no such hopes, "You deceive yourself when you say that *my time will come*." At first he told Raczynski that order could never be reestablished in Spain without a violent reaction, and for that task power would not be conferred on him. He claimed that he had no current offers and, moreover, that there would not be any. If he were approached, he could not accept because there was no disposition to follow his system. In addition, since Narváez had proven false, he had no sword to lend him support. Finally, in December, he told his friend to quit "building castles in the air." "I am rigid enough, absolute and dogmatic enough, to suit nobody and so that nobody may suit me. I know very well the imperious need which everyone feels of compromising, of plying to windward, of yielding to overcome obstacles; but I despise this as much as another despises virtue." Raczynski then let the matter lay, and, as a matter of fact, Bravo Murillo clung to power for another year. Nevertheless, the Prussian provoked replies that make one wonder whether in fact Donoso really were not "of the wood of dictators," whether he actually was morally incapable of being one. Not two months passed before he ardently wished to be minister so as to impart a counterrevolutionary direction to international affairs, and, beyond question, already in November he had a plan for a "reaction" and some basic internal reforms, with or without Narváez's help.[37]

Despite the anger toward him at court, he had addressed a letter on November 26 to María Cristina, the real power behind the throne, to recommend a new social, economic, and political departure in Spain. His plan was both reactionary and positive, or forward-looking. As preparations were beginning for a costly festival to celebrate the birth of an heir to the throne, he wrote to oppose it altogether, unless it were given

[37] Juretschke, II, 800–801; 804f; 189; 812.

for the sake of the poor by means of a very munificent public almsgiving.[38] Perhaps, he reasoned, the example of the queen would shame the wealthy to forsake their excessive egotism and voluntarily to redistribute some of their wealth to alleviate the distress of the poor. If the situation of the poor were not relieved, socialism would come to promote class war between rich and poor, would destroy the monarchies, and would sack the nations by confiscation of private wealth.

Giving alms, however, was only to be a first step, for he recognized that the selfishness of the rich could be countered only by institutionalizing a new order. His scheme called for removing what remained of the revolutionary edifice in Spain and for restoring institutions it had destroyed. While he deplored the revolutionary spirit of recent political and economic legislation, the only liberal institutions he wanted to destroy were the sovereignty of the middle class, the restricted electorate, and the parliamentary prerogative, which the wealthy had exploited against the interests of the poor, the monarchy, and the Church. Still, he had no specific proposals for replacing them. He was perplexingly vague about exactly what he wanted to restore; it entailed neither absolutism, alienated Church properties, nor the Inquisition. His way of reform, as he had explained earlier, was to plant a seed and let it grow spontaneously and ripen in due season. He had always distrusted neat schemes of constitutional planning as contrary to the nature of man and society. Praising the new Concordat of 1851 as a point of departure, he asked that the spirit of Catholicism be restored to Spain's economic and political legislation and to education in order to ensure justice and to preserve society. He was in favor of making a beginning on a general reform of a popular and welfare type which only time could finish. The state could provide the right external conditions, but the Church must reach for the minds and hearts, which really counted.[39]

[38] Juretschke, II, 595–96ff.

[39] Juretschke, II, 599ff; 343; 599. Jerónimo Becker considers the con-

Although he counted on the friendship and confidence of both Isabel and María Cristina, he was not so blind to their incompetence and corruption as to entertain much hope for his proposals.[40] He was embarrassed by the deluded miracle monger, Sister Patrocinio, who had deceived the credulous queen in a scandalous fashion before she had fled to Paris to plague him.[41] The plain facts which Raczynski related to him about palace intrigues and deals could only have diminished what little esteem he had left for the royal family, if not for the monarchy itself.[42] Despite his chagrin, he remained loyal, for he could never bring himself to embrace the blindly reactionary Carlists as an alternative.[43] When his plan of reform got nowhere, his instinct, reason, and the evidence combined to convince him that Spain was in for very bad times. "Things go from bad to worse; the liberal reaction is inevitable; . . . the outlook of the palace, wretched and pointing to catastrophes; . . . every day, under the impulse of detestable and guilty intrigues, the moment of falling apart approaches by long

cordat as simply a development of the principles of the Constitution of 1845 and as representing the dominant thought of the majority of the nation at that time. *Historia de las relaciones exteriores de España durante el siglo XIX*, I (Madrid, 1924), 214–16. The agreement promised a partial restoration of nationalized lands not yet sold to the third parties and otherwise a recompense similar to Donoso's scheme of 1845—a guaranteed income for the clergy from the interest on State securities. Also see Kiernan, p. 30.

[40] Juretschke, II, 796. The day before he sent this letter to María Cristina, he wrote to Raczynski: "I am completely indifferent whether or not the court takes my advice seriously, so long as I always find in my conscience the testimony that in all things I have counselled what is most fitting for my country and the monarchy" (II, 802).

[41] The Ministry of Foreign Affairs in Madrid preserves a fair number of communications from the Spanish embassy in Paris on the ridiculous affair of Sor Patrocinio, and several bear Donoso's signature. See Valverde, II, 870–71, 873–74, 899.

[42] Juretschke, II, 813.

[43] There are many unpublished reports relating to the activities, conspiracies, and attempts of Carlist émigrés in France as well as many petitions in behalf of repentant, homesick Carlists, and Donoso processed a large number of these.

strides." Reading María Cristina's thoughts from afar, he observed that she wanted to seem liberal while preferring reaction. "Today she is less liberal than ever, because under a liberal regime her husband [Muñoz] could not play the role to which he aspires." Her shortsighted cunning left her blind to the inevitable consequences of her intrigues, which must be a restoration of liberal parliamentarians to power. "Hence, I deduce that everything is lost and that her own downfall is certain."[44] Donoso could not depend on her, and neither could Bravo Murillo "in the pinch."

BALMES, DONOSO, AND PARLIAMENTARY REFORM

Apart from becoming premier with dictatorial powers to enforce reforms, Donoso could still have had resort to the parliament. In its halls he had first imagined himself a statesman, fighting, sacrificing, and dying to lead Spain to her rendezvous with destiny.[45] He remained a deputy and the nominal leader of a small right-wing group whom others called "Neo-Catholics" or "absolutists," depending on whether they looked at their religious or political views.[46] While Donoso was in Paris he kept well informed on Spain and the Cortes. "Distance," he argued, was "necessary for perspective," but it also diminished his influence. All his clients had been squeezed out in the scramble for office, and his ability to sway parliament had also dwindled. Whether or not Bravo Murillo needed his support, he decided that to go back and mix in any more parliamentary debates would be an unpleasant waste of time.[47]

[44] Juretschke, II, 810; 818; 821.

[45] Juretschke, II, 165.

[46] Ballesteros y Bereta, *Historia*, VIII, 32. Ballesteros calls them "absolutists"; *El Heraldo* then called them "Neo-Catholics." Donoso rejected both names publicly as inappropriate (Juretschke, II, 606, 214). *El País*, 103 (June 30, 1849), p. 1, "La Escuela Neo-Católica"—comprising Bossuet, Montalembert, Lacordaire, etc.; "theocratic" and dualistic.

[47] Juretschke, II, 582; 577f; 580–81. Letter to Raczynski (October 11, 1851): "I consider the time that I devote to it as lost; between the Chamber and me there is an incompatibility; and I even feel an unpleasant

Still, a sense of duty tormented him, for he complained repeatedly in 1851 that he had not nearly enough backing in parliament. If he had but a dozen Catholic deputies, he would fight for his ideas in the Cortes, even though they could not triumph until after the flood. As it was, however, he had not even four sure followers, "because it is not enough to follow me, it is necessary to follow me with conviction and to fight gallantly. Not counting on this, why give battle?"

Donoso was not interested in expanding his influence and faction within the existing Moderate party. Instead he wanted to build a distinctly new political party, which would be not only Catholic but also authoritarian without being absolutist, somehow social and democratic, and decentralizing.[48] If the Moderates were "a glorious party in times past," he now regarded it as fated soon to dissolve impotently into quarrelling factions, like other moderate parties from before 1848.[49] He detected a transformation afoot in Europe's political parties to create a new polarization of conservative right and democratic left. The Spanish Progressive party seemed to him to be rapidly becoming democratic as a whole, realizing at last an old tendency in its principles and in its radical minority.[50] The new conservative party he contemplated would have sought the support of both Carlist right and popular left to found a potent national movement.

Did he try to woo Balmes's "social Christian" followers to his banner, even as Blanche-Raffin strongly urged him to do after Balmes's death in 1848? Acknowledging their marked

---

sensation when I hear parliamentary debates mentioned" (Juretschke, II, 797).

[48] In contrast to the centralized absolutism, which he accepted as temporary crisis regimes for France, Austria, and Prussia, he now rejected the policies of the Spanish Moderates and supported the Basques' fueros and municipal corporations against the omnipresent current of centralization (Juretschke, II, 656, 720, 824). In Viluma he apparently attracted some of Balmes' "social Christians."

[49] Juretschke, II, 587.

[50] On the democratic movement after 1849, see Kiernan, *Revolution of 1854*, pp. 31–32.

similarity in ideas, Donoso said that they had not known each other personally, but "I esteemed him and I know that he esteemed me." "Balmes is an honor to his country: a man of clear, sharp, and solid genius, firm in the faith, agile in the fight." Raffin deplored the breaking up of Balmes's "little school" and asked Donoso to take it upon himself to reorganize that group of young writers. If he were too contemplative to head it himself as *chef d'école*, at least he could find someone capable to organize the action while he provided inspiration.[51]

What little Donoso and Viluma attempted was enough to attract the attention of the Görres circle in Germany, which praised him as a great statesman and a man of the future for having conceived of such a specifically Catholic party, long before Windthorst's German Center party appeared.[52] Regrettably, he pronounced himself finished irrevocably with parliament a month before the coup d'état in France. At the end, however, he admitted that parliamentary government itself was far from finished, and his little party survived and fought, but in vain.[53]

FAILURE OF THE MODERATE DECADE

The crisis of 1851 in France soured him on liberal parliamentarism. He thought this system was an even greater danger to Bravo Murillo than Narváez. Little more than a month after

[51] Letter from Blanche-Raffin to Donoso (December 25, 1849): "Votre doctrine se rettache à la sienne." Donoso Cortés family archives. Juretschke, II, 226; letter to Raffin (July 21, 1849). Letter from Raffin to Donoso (May 18, 1850), in the Donoso Cortés family archives.

[52] *Historische-Politische Blätter*, 29 (1852), p. 601; 34 (1854), p. 478.

[53] Juretschke, II, 799; 822. Donoso's friend Tassara later described him as "the true intellectual leader finally of this new party of political and militant Catholicism, which with the name of Neo-Catholicism at this time presented itself in the hopeless fight; a party which . . . powerless and too late, [was a] protest of the past and of traditional Europe against the modern and revolutionary Europe of our day" (Introduction to Gabriel García y Tassara, *Poesías*, xii–xiii). Without Donoso, however, it failed to develop a social and democratic content and was thus still-born. For a view of its brief upsurge in 1851, with Donoso, as its "prophet" see H. B. Clarke *Modern Spain* (Cambridge, 1906), p. 219.

Donoso wrote what he hoped was an obituary on parliamentarism in France for *Revue des Deux Mondes*, Bravo Murillo's would-be authoritarian regime fell at last before the parliamentarism he had been trying to bridle. Not at any time during 1852 had Donoso looked for success against the liberal opposition, but, even while he called the ministry moribund, he admired its chief's perseverance and *sang-froid*. When he learned in May of a scheme for a ministerial coup d'état, he was not enthusiastic. It would miscarry, because "little will be done and it will not be done in the necessary measure." After the coup failed to materialize, he expected that María Cristina would support Bravo Murillo in office just so long as he did not compromise her appearance as a liberal. With the time at hand for the premier to convoke the Cortes and to present his authoritarian proposals for electoral and constitutional reforms, Donoso, believing that everything depended on the attitude of the army, looked for him to fail.[54] On December 14, 1852, the Murillo cabinet was defeated by the combined opposition of the generals with Progressives and Moderates in parliament. The *Narvaístas* (Narváez's followers) were among the declared enemies of the ministry, and not even Donoso's absolutists voted for it.[55] Bravo Murillo had wanted to end the political power of the generals, but Donoso was sure that the authoritarian changes he wanted could not be carried through against the middle class and parliament without military backing. One other mistake Bravo Murillo had made, said Donoso, was in "not having sought support in the true people," that is, in not having adopted plebiscitary democracy like Louis Napoleon.[56]

[54] Juretschke, II, 795; 810; 816; 817–18. After Bravo Murillo's fall, Donoso pointed out that he had the support of only María Cristina, who had finally abandoned him rather than incur the enmity of the parliamentarians. "She wants the death of parliamentarism, but on the condition that this death be necessary and that she appears to regret it" (II, 820–21). Juretschke, II, 819.

[55] Ballesteros y Bereta, *Historia*, VIII, 32, 35. Sánchez Agesta, *Historia*, pp. 272–73.

[56] Juretschke, II, 819–20; cf. II, 708. See Diego Sevilla Andrés, *Historia*

Apparently Donoso expressed his opinion in much the same fashion on January 15, 1853, to the Paris newspapers, the *Journal des Débats* and the *Revue des Deux Mondes*, and stirred up angry protests by both parliamentarians and monarchists in France, which he expected to be repeated in Spain. Defending his words to Alcoy, the new president of the Council of Ministers at Madrid, he declared himself opposed to Mon's ambitions as a parliamentarian and against the upcoming Cortes as sure to be ungovernable. His opinion of what was going on in Spain was very frank:

> It is neither order, nor liberty, nor government; it is confusion and chaos, and, nevertheless, I say it and shall repeat it a million times: the remedy is easy; the trouble is with a dozen persons and in the fact that the Parliament, instead of being limited, is a power. The day when you are finally convinced of this, you will save the Monarchy.[57]

Complaining that it was hell to fight alone against the whole world, Donoso was determined to continue the fight with bare hands and without illusions. Hard pressed to keep Narváez out of Spain again and out of power, Alcoy replied that he could not abide the *Narvaístas*, "who only seek absolute dominion," and he acknowledged that Donoso had been right about Narváez.[58] "I thank you for your loyalty, your disinterest, your self-denial . . . in sacrificing the combinations which could take place in the politics and cabinet over which I preside." Perhaps the last political report that Donoso received from Spain was a letter from Gabino Tejado of *El Orden* in April of 1853. It

política de España, p. 127ff; this account agrees with Donoso's opinion that Bravo Murillo fell because he did not imitate Louis Napoleon in relying on the army, but it does not mention popular plebiscite.

[57] Valverde, II, 899.

[58] Letter from A. Llorente to Donoso (Madrid; January 9, 1853), in the Donoso Cortés family archives; this letter describes a crisis in government involving Narváez, whom Bravo Murillo had sent abroad again and whom Alcoy wanted to keep out of Spain (see Valverde, II, 899). Donoso cooperated.

was full of alarming predictions that the whole regime would soon collapse.[59]

In 1854, after Donoso's death, Narváez helped overthrow the Moderate regime altogether in a *pronunciamiento*, which drove out María Cristina again and allowed Espartero's return to power for two years before Narváez took over again in 1856. By 1855 there were republican, democratic, and socialist parties in Spain, but democracy in the form of universal suffrage was not proclaimed until 1869 after a revolution, a first republic was not declared until 1873, and Socialists did not come to power before the second republic in the 1930s.

Donoso's fate was much like that of his friend, Bravo Murillo. He had been more of a realist, perhaps, than the economic expert, but he too was wholly isolated at the end from his party, from the army's generals, and even from the Court. Strange to say, he had prophesied his failure years before, when he said, "The statesman who enrolls under none of the banners of interests, opinions, or parties which contend, is alone, and he will die alone."[60] He was a romantic idealist who tried to be a realist, but he learned that for that era at least, it was practically impossible to combine the two. Even as a prophet he was so far ahead of his time in many ways as to prove the biblical maxim: "A prophet is not without honor, save in his own country" (Matt. 12:57).

[59] Letter from Alcoy (Federico Roncali) to Donoso (January 21, 1853), in the Donoso Cortés family archives. Letter from Gabino Tejado to Donoso (April 26, 1853), in the Donoso Cortés family archives.

[60] Juretschke, II, 198.

Chapter IX

EUROPE AND BRITAIN UNITY OR CATACLYSM?

DONOSO AS "GOOD EUROPEAN"

In the crisis after 1848 Donoso tried to put the common interests of Europe as a whole ahead of the particular national ambitions of either France or Spain. The term *good European* as ascribed to Metternich, Saint-Simon, or Comte describes him at this time better than the word *nationalist*. He looked for safety from renewed general revolution or general war only in a common international remedy. Long before Ortega y Gasset, he regarded Europe as a kind of unity and diversity of shared heritage and institutions amid a variety of national cultures, but he favored what he called solidarity among the nations more than political union. His idea of "Europe" was broader than Comte's historic core of the five nations, France, Britain, Germany, Spain, and Italy, which excluded Russia as barbaric. Like Metternich, he wanted both Britain and Russia comprised in any conservative European order, but, if he had to choose, he preferred solidarity for Continental Europe and Russia over the predominance of an insular and divisive Britain. His position on Europe was vaguely prophetic of the twentieth-century experiences, as well as a reaction to the passing crisis of his time. The policy he advocated stood somewhere between Metternich's Concert of Europe and the federal-union scheme of Saint-Simon, or Comte's European community. Without Comte's illusions about abolishing war and armies, however, his idea of international relations was positive in a somewhat different sense.[1]

[1] Without the benefit of practical experience, Comte also theorized on

Donoso's attempt to lead Louis Napoleon into a conservative European diplomacy in 1852 perhaps marks the closest approach to a common counterrevolutionary front against the forces of 1848. Convinced that foreign and domestic policies were interdependent, he tried, with Metternich's encouragement, to revive the moribund Concert of Europe as a counterpart for conservative but reformative dictatorship. Assuming that nationalistic foreign policies were suitable for times of general peace and stability, he advocated that a common policy be adopted in international diplomacy during international crises of general revolution or threat of general war. He urged European solidarity and a unity of policy that was idealistic,

---

international diplomacy and on the future shape of Europe, with results often like Donoso's. Earlier, he too considered Metternich's system as a retrograde reaction from the old feudal-theocratic Europe, but he viewed nonintervention, nationalism, and national independence as an equally outdated metaphysical system that had survived from the transitional era of the previous three centuries. He called for an entirely new diplomatic system to replace the old balance-of-powers system with a positive new European community of nations, in which war would cease (*The Positive Philosophy* . . ., *II*, 412, 772). He proposed to prepare for this new order by a regeneration of minds and morals, to be achieved through a common European education (positive and social) to instill an active European patriotism, all under the direction of a new homogeneous speculative class, the new supranational spiritual and moral authority to fill the vacuum left by the old papacy and clergy (ibid). Later (1855), in a proposal for coordination of the West, which is much closer to Donoso's diplomacy of the few preceding years, he proposed a new spiritual reorganization of Europe to offset the national political centralization, which was obstructing the emergence of "the metropolis of mankind." He too wanted Napoleon III's France, as the central nation of Europe, to play the role of natural leader of the European reorganization, to assume the "normal presidency" of Europe, rather than Britain and the Northern Protestant states, and he wanted the Southern Latin nations of Spain and Italy to be associated with Napoleon III's "organic dictatorship," or "republican monocracy," in the work of reestablishing a "normal program" and "political uniformity" in the West (*Appeal to Conservatives*, pp. 184–93). See José Ortega y Gasset, "Unity and Diversity of Europe," *History as a System, and Other Essays Toward a Philosophy of History*, trans. Helene Weyl (Princeton, N.J., 1941), pp. 51–62. Ortega both predicted European unity and derived his idea of it largely from Guizot, who also originally inspired Donoso's conception of Europe.

political, and counterrevolutionary in place of materialistic imperialism or nationalism for territorial aggrandisement.[2] Once he had predicted that a liberal West, led by France, could check Russian expansion and rule the world. At the end he thought that the Russian "new Rome" would finally win out over the West and Britain, Europe's "new Carthage." In 1850 he had speculated that Britain might yet display her own Roman political virtues to lead Europe in a united conservative policy that could, for a long time, save Europe from socialism and Russia.[3] In the absence of such British initiative, however, he turned to Louis Napoleon in 1852 to lead the Continent, Russia included, in stifling the revolutionary movement everywhere and in shutting out the disruptive influence and hegemony of Britain. Trying to make a Continental union under Louis Napoleon's leadership, however, involved too many contradictions. Consequently, Donoso died expecting the worst: renewed imperialism, war and revolution, and ultimately world war and world revolution.

METTERNICH AND DONOSO

In April of 1851 Metternich let Donoso know through Meyendorff and Hübner that he was anxious to make his acquaintance.[4] So, joining a stream of other notables, Donoso set out on April 27 for Brussels, where the former *bête noire* of liberals and revolutionaries now sojourned, aged, benign, and harmless. Two days later, after being received by King Leopold, the

[2] R. C. Binkley, *Realism and Nationalism, 1852–1871* (New York, 1935, 1963), Chs. 7 and 8, "The Politics of Reaction" and "The Concert and the Crimean War," especially pp. 127, 162ff. A. J. P. Taylor, *The Struggle for Mastery in Europe, 1848–1918* (Oxford, 1954), p. 61. Taylor holds that later, in the Crimean War (after Donoso's death), the British were trying "to substitute 'the Concert of Europe' for the hegemony of Russia," whereas Louis Napoleon was seeking only his own hegemony.

[3] Juan Juretschke, ed., *Obras completas,* I, 135f, 143f, 461; 613ff; II, 66–69; 105, 195, 311.

[4] Carlos Valverde, ed., *Obras completas,* II, 794–95. My own notes give April 26 instead of April 27 for this dispatch.

"celebrated Donoso," as Melanie called him, visited Metternich and her at their house.[5] The interview was mostly monologue by the garrulous oldster reminiscing in "bad French." Metternich had a very high regard for Donoso as he did also for Disraeli. He wanted to continue friendly relations. "I am . . . a voluminous book," he said, "in which are consigned all the great events of this century; when you wish, I shall put myself at your disposal so that you may page me from the first leaf even to the last."[6] Donoso agreed. "He alone possesses in its integrity the history of the present century."[7] After two hours, declining dinner, Donoso took the train back to Paris. He never met the Prince again, but they exchanged letters. Metternich continued to follow his writings with keen interest, while Donoso quietly tried to play arbiter of Europe.

Despite the disparity in age, the interview had been a meeting of two conservatives of complementary minds and personalities.[8] As a statesman, Metternich had actively personified the reaction to the French Revolution; as an intellectual, Donoso represented the second era of reaction and restoration after the European revolution of 1848. Vanished now was Donoso's liberal aversion toward all that Metternich had stood for. The revolutions of 1848 had taught him to appreciate the statesman and master diplomat who had resisted revolution for three decades. Metternich, in turn, already admired the younger conservative for his speeches in defense of traditional society against revolutionary forces which seemed ever more

[5] Metternich, *Mémoires . . .*, ed. Metternich, III, 99 (from Melanie's Diary).

[6] Juretschke, II, 586, an account of the interview sent to Gabino Tejado; also see Valverde, II, 795–99, for a closely similar (but not identical) account written for the Spanish Minister of Foreign Affairs.

[7] Juretschke, II, 792.

[8] See Bela Menczer, "Metternich and Donoso Cortés, Christian and Conservative Thought in the European Revolution," *Dublin Review*, 201 (last quarter, 1948), 19–51. Anton Rothbauer, *Austria, símbolo de la tragedia Europea*, "Crece o Muere" pamphlet, 2d ed. (Madrid, 1956), p. 9. Heinrich Ritter von Srbik, *Metternich, der Staatsman und Der Mensch, III* (Munich, 1954), 184–85.

radical, general, and ominous. He saw in the trenchant phrasing of Donoso his own ill-expressed and misunderstood conservatism.

On that April day they certainly discussed both Germany and the Concert of Europe. But how much did Donoso owe to Metternich for his plan to resurrect a counterrevolutionary Concert under the leadership of a Bonapartist France? After the coup d'état of December 2, he knew that the dictator's popular support in France was then unshakable. Louis Napoleon's reconciliation with Europe, however, would be very difficult, but it was necessary if France were to lead a European reaction. He hoped that the dictator would revive the Concert of Europe rather than pursue empire and glory, which could wreck any chances of antirevolutionary solidarity among the nations. In 1850 he had predicted that Europe would fall to revolution and socialism, unless England adopted a conservative foreign policy, a turn which he did not expect from Palmerston. Now, under a conservative and antirevolutionary dictatorship, he hoped that France could lead the Continent to smother the embers of internal revolution and socialism and to shut out a renewed revolutionary influence from Palmerston's England.[9]

BRITAIN AND THE COUNTERREVOLUTIONARY POLICY

Events did not happen according to plan, however. On the heels of the coup d'état Palmerston astounded Europe and diplomatic circles by precipitously recognizing the dictatorship. Apparently his action had so outraged liberal sentiment in England that he was dismissed.[10] Reactionaries everywhere rejoiced at his fall; Schwarzenberg celebrated with a ball.[11]

[9] Juretschke, II, 585; 724f; 775; 603.

[10] Franklin C. Palm, *England and Napoleon III* (Durham, N.C., 1948), pp. 73–76.

[11] R. W. Seton-Watson, *Britain in Europe, 1789–1914* (Cambridge, Eng., 1955), p. 291. Donald Southgate, "*The Most English Minis-*

Actually, Palmerston had approved of the coup because he had been frightened by the upheavals of 1848, and he expected the dictatorship to prevent a renewed outbreak of revolutions in France and in Europe.[12] He was sacked not because he had recognized a dictator or displeased the liberal *Times* but because he did not first consult the queen and prime minister.

One of the first in Paris to hear of Palmerston's dismissal but misconstruing his motives, Donoso pondered for long nights over the apparently contradictory behavior of the British minister, until he thought he had divined his purpose.[13] His total view of Palmerston as more nationalistic than liberal in his foreign policy may have been more a myth than reality in its exaggerations, but it agrees in its essentials with current scholarly assessments, while challenging the contemporary opinions of Thiers and of Marx.[14] Donoso concluded that Palmerston,

---

ter . . .," *The Policies and Politics of Palmerston* (London and New York, 1966), p. 292.

12 Palm, *England and Napoleon III*, pp. 69–70. Southgate, *Palmerston*, pp. 289–90.

13 Juretschke, II, 806. Valverde, II, 818f. After Guizot, Donoso was first to hear of Palmerston's fall; he thought it was caused by his enraging Austria by welcoming Kossuth and other refugees.

14 W. N. Senior, *Conversations with M. Thiers, M. Guizot, and other distinguished persons, during the Second Empire*, I (London, 1878), 120. Thiers pictured the real Palmerston as vain, vindictive, and rash: "He is always aiming at petty successes and partial triumphs, instead of large objects which are pursued by real statesmen." Seton-Watson concludes that Palmerston made "unnecessary enemies on all hands" by his menaces and by what Prince Albert called his "hobby" of foisting constitutionalism on countries that did not want it (*Britain in Europe*, pp. 251–52). While defending Palmerston's recognition of the dictatorship as an act of statesmanship, Southgate shows that on the question of German unity in 1849 Palmerston had consulted the European balance of power in relation to British interests as much more real and important to him than the question of despotism or constitutionalism (*Palmerston*, pp. 280–83, 289). Also see Taylor, *The Struggle for Mastery*, p. 33. Donoso's working analysis of Palmerston makes interesting contrast with that of Karl Marx. Basing his opinion on the record of parliamentary debates, Marx saw Palmerston's policy up to 1842 as consistently friendly to Russia and to the European reaction. He saw him as a consummate actor and explained the actions of this aristocrat by his class origin as much as by

with penetrating sagacity and intrepid boldness, had acted not for capricious or personal reasons but for permanent nationalistic interests. England's supreme interest, her historic, perennial, and fundamental foreign policy, which Palmerston perceived so clearly, was to divide and rule by preventing a unity of views and action among Continental nations and thus maintaining herself as "peaceful dominator and supreme arbiter." In other words, she wanted to maintain a balance of power favoring British interests and prestige. Donoso decided that Palmerston had encouraged parliamentarism among the Continental nations until 1848 not "because it makes peoples free, but because it weakens authority and divides the continent." England, he believed, before she would allow the whole Continent to exist in harmony as constitutional states, would even resort to absolutist propaganda. Thus, her traditional policy in European disputes had been to support absolutism and revolution alternately, the former during the first revolutionary period and the latter since then. After the conservative wartime policy of the Tories always came a revolutionary peacetime policy by Whigs. In this fashion Britain would determine the dominant policy of the Continent so as to keep Continental powers from being aligned against her. European solidarity would be opposed in England he thought, regardless of whether the government were Whig or Tory. He remarked of Disraeli and Palmerston that "they understand each other." "I cannot account for the blindness of Europe." Because of the coup d'état, he explained, Palmerston knew that England could avoid isolation only by either aligning with France as in the former *entente cordiale* or renouncing his system and humbly seeking reconciliation with all the rest of Europe.[15]

---

personal whim or by national interest. Marx thought that Palmerston's policy, which was of "the essence of Whiggism," had made him both "the *bête noir* of the continental courts" and "the truly English minister at home." Marx, *Secret Diplomatic History of the Eighteenth Century and The Story of the Life of Lord Palmerston*, ed. Lester Hutchinson (New York, 1969), pp. 166–68.

[15] Juretschke, II, 718; 715–16; 729; 816; 718. Valverde, II, 838.

Had Palmerston not fallen, the coup d'état would have lost all its significance for political reaction in Europe as a whole. Now that the man who had unleashed "the winds of revolution" had departed, Donoso hoped that "the wind of reaction" could blow freely on the Continent.[16] Nevertheless, Palmerston's action still posed a great threat, unless England remained isolated.

In keeping with his grim visions of 1850, Donoso wanted above all to see the revolution "beheaded." To achieve this end, he had to maneuver England into political and diplomatic isolation. From the beginning of 1852 he strove to initiate a united Continental policy directed first to check internal revolution and secondly to isolate England as a potential source for a renewal of revolutionary influence. He insisted that to frustrate England's national policy, and with it the revolution, was the supreme and sacred cause. The occasion was never more favorable than now, before the English overcame their momentary indecision. A Tory ministry, he feared, would all to soon lull the Continental nations into a reconciliation and thus erase the bad impression left by Palmerstonian policy. Then he would not be surprised to see Palmerston resume his post and unleash anew the "winds of revolution" over Europe. It was indispensable, therefore, to avert this result "at all cost," and he promised to do everything in his power toward that end. "*I have made the oath of Hannibal against England.*"[17]

The sober Raczynski told Donoso that his hostility toward Britain was extreme and unbalanced; did he want to behead England along with the revolution? Donoso admitted that "the disappearance of England would break the balance of the world," which was precisely what he sought to keep, but he wanted to maintain it against the absolute domination of England. He opposed England not from blind prejudice, for he greatly admired her people and her institutions.[18] His atti-

[16] Valverde, II, 838–39.

[17] Juretschke, II, 722, 807f; 808.

[18] Juretschke, II, 808, 811f; 726. On several occasions he had praised

tude reflected a rational and historical judgment in diplomacy that, given his European purpose, was only partly in error. He was not so wrong in assessing the basic motives and character of Palmerston's foreign policy before 1848. It had indeed been designed to place British interests first and foremost above any common European interests, regardless of whether a particular action favored either a liberal and revolutionary situation on the Continent or a conservative one. However, he oversimplified the past and read too much of it into the future, particularly in regard to an assumed alternation of Whig peace followed by revolutions and Tory war followed by order. Even before Bismarck came along to upset all patterns, these patterns changed. One example of the fallacy in his prediction is the Crimean War, which Palmerston did not start, to be sure, but helped conduct to victory. However, Palmerston was still in power at the time of the revolutionary changes in Italy from 1859–1861, and he gave them his blessing, even though Napoleon III and Cavour were the prime movers.

To establish a European counterrevolutionary policy, Donoso knew that France must be reconciled with the rest of the Continent. To that end he tried in several interviews to persuade Louis Napoleon to take the initiative in European diplomacy in order to reassure the other Continental powers that he would not break the treaties of Vienna or wage impe-

---

the English extravagantly, before he had turned to criticize their foreign policy sharply; see Juretschke, II, 105–6, 640–41. Part of the explanation for this distinction—or ambivalence—was undoubtedly a certain nationalistic pride and resentment, as well as his concern for Europe as a whole. For an excellent example of his ambivalence toward the English, see his dispatch of January 10, 1853 (Valverde, II, 896), in which he says, "I am not a friend of the English people tyrannically treating the continent like a vassal, but I regard with mute admiration the greatness of that race, and I bow low to British patriotism. What impresses me most of all in that nation is its sureness of viewpoint on whatever affects its interests." This is much as the Latin nations and most of the world have recently viewed the United States. See J. Remak, *Origins of World War I* (New York, 1967), p. 75, on Britain as Europe's arbiter.

rialistic wars of conquest.[19] Moreover, he reported someone else with a certain authority in diplomacy, perhaps he was referring to Metternich or Schwarzenberg, had earnestly recommended that the dictator call a congress of Continental powers to prepare for a mutual reconciliation and a common policy against the revolution and England.[20] But, neither Donoso nor anyone else could get decisive action. Preferring to "have his cake and eat it," Louis Napoleon issued contradictory statements. He apparently hoped that his threats against revolutionary refugees in Belgium and Switzerland might persuade the great powers to acquiesce in an intervention that could lead to annexation. Thus he would at the same time deal a blow for counterrevolution and obtain a cheap imperial conquest.[21] Fear of the dictator's imperialistic ambitions made the other nations forget the question of revolution, and Louis Napoleon, unable to decide on one course of action, vacillated.[22] When Britain finally warned him off the border question in March, it was already too late for reconciliation with the Continent. If the issue of territory displaced that of revolution

[19] One such personal conference is known to have taken place on or before January 17, as mentioned in a dispatch of that date, part of which is published by Jerónimo Becker, *Historia de las relaciones exteriores de España durante el siglo XIX* (Madrid, 1924), II, 265–66. At least one more conference took place before March 24, which Donoso mentions (Juretschke, II, 746–48), but by that time he had almost given up hope for a French-led Concert of Europe.

[20] Juretschke, II, 725.

[21] See Palm, *England and Napoleon III*, pp. 82, 88ff, 126–28, on the basic facts of Louis Napoleon's maneuvering.

[22] Donoso particularly feared the bad impression the dictator's "socialistic" seizure of Orleans's property would have on other monarchs and states. "Pirates make difficulties which divide." Letter to Raczynski (January 24, 1852) in Juretschke, II, 809; also, 811. On the same matter, in reference to other monarchs, see the unpublished dispatch No. 45 of January 24, 1852, archives of the Ministry of Foreign Affairs, Madrid. At the time, he regarded Nicholas I as the only statesman of Europe, for his willingness to put his fear of revolution ahead of his suspicions of Louis Napoleon (Juretschke, II, 812). Taylor, *The Struggle for Mastery*, pp. 47–48. Valverde, II, 840, 851.

in international relations, Donoso predicted, England would be able to divide and paralyze the Continent, while she "alone would keep her freedom of action," exercising "her insolent protectorate."[23]

As February passed, Donoso felt very frustrated that there was not a true statesman who could act for Europe to take the initiative to form a "continental league on the basis of the continent's independence and of conservative ideas." "All could be saved, but all will be lost."[24] "If I were minister" he wrote to Raczynski, "Spain would take the initiative in order to fix the boundaries of this problem and England would not forget my name. Nevertheless, in the sphere of my functions I do not cease to work on this formidable power without disturbing her; but of this I cannot speak." The secret action he undoubtedly referred to was to suggest that Louis Napoleon act forceably against England.

After mid-March he made a final effort to turn the dictator toward a "monarchic and conservative policy" against England and revolution, even by war, if need be.[25] In an interview he remarked that it was strange that "France would always be revolutionary in time of war and conservative in time of peace,"

[23] Juretschke, II, 722.

[24] Donoso's lament was very like that of the British diplomat, Sir Hamilton Seymour who, later in 1852, regretted the dearth of European leadership like that of Metternich or Wellington previously (Binkley, *Realism and Nationalism*, p. 128). Juretschke, II, 722, 811–12.

[25] Juretschke, II, 730, and II, 746–47 (dispatch of March 24, 1852). Apart from the contents of the dispatch, which sound like a veiled incitement to war, we have his final official words on the possibility of establishing a common European antirevolutionary policy against Britain's preference for a "territorial" policy (dispatch of April 10, 1852; Juretschke, II, 730): "The only means to avert the catastrophe of eventual revolution through Europe, which would follow England's diplomatic triumph would have been to establish frankly and decisively the revolutionary question and to have come to find its solution, if it were necessary, even in war; war in these conditions would have been good and fruitful, because its outcome would have been the definitive humbling of England and the normal triumph of monarchic and conservative policy." Cf. Palm, *England and Napoleon III*, p. 84, on Cowley's dismissal of the fear that Louis Napoleon intended to invade England (October, 1852).

while England played exactly the opposite role. Such was "the fatality of their traditions," was the reply. However, when Donoso pointed out that such fatality would also result in the overthrow of France again, Louis Napoleon complained that he had tried to obtain the cooperation of Europe to destroy revolutionary germs," but his efforts had been nullified by suspicions of his territorial ambitions. Knowing very well that such suspicions were not baseless, Donoso now hinted that the dictator might pursue his ambitions in a direction opposite from the Rhine, as Napoleon I had tried in vain to do. Why not use the new steamships to cross the channel? An inscrutable and deep silence followed his daring and most undiplomatic suggestion. "I looked at him, but in vain, for he had lowered his eyes."[26] Still, Donoso felt that "a descent upon England" would be tempting to him, for had again laid bare a furtive scheme already forming in the dictator's devious mind. Later on, he observed that if the landing on British coasts were possible, "as the Prince believes, and as England fears," then mighty Britain had an Achilles heel. In January of 1853 he learned that the new emperor had contracted for a fleet of transatlantic steamers based at Cherbourg, which could easily be converted for military use.[27] The potential menace to England was manifest.[28] Before Palmerston, Donoso foresaw

[26] Juretschke, II, 747. When General Flahault protested vigorously to Louis Napoleon against the confiscation of Orleans's property, he met with a similar chilly response, a stubborn "silence of some duration." Philip Guedalla, *Secret of the Coup d'état* (New York and London, 1924), p. 311. Sir Lewis Namier gives the same view: "When argued with he would keep silent without giving in—'he abandoned nothing.' " *Vanished Supremacies* (New York, 1958), p. 63.

[27] Juretschke, II, 756; 760f.

[28] In a dispatch of January 10, 1853 (Valverde, II, 896–98), he notes that the English, now aware of the peril and both parties agreed, were undertaking "gigantic preparations" to defend their coasts, even while they were ready to make an alliance with Napoleon III. At this time (January, 1852), Palmerston told Flahault that such rumors of war and projected invasions were absurd, but William Nassau Senior more than a year later affirmed that the English had finally decided that events at Cherbourg meant that he had been planning war against them soon after the

the threat of the new steam navies to the "splendid isolation," security, and power of "that queen of the seas and lord of the nations."

Even before the interview Donoso sensed that England had won the race to define the dominant question in European relations, and he was sure the consequences would be bad for France and worse for Europe, a doubly horrible catastrophe.[29] Louis Napoleon had not been sufficiently skillful to call a congress of Continental powers to guarantee the treaties of Vienna. "The Prince vacillated, lost time, did nothing" to secure unity against England and "someday he is due to weep over his vacillation with tears of blood." He foresaw England achieving a universal domination with revolution eventually following as an "imprescindible consequence."[30] On the other hand, Donoso feared that when Louis Napoleon realized that he was deserted by the conservative and monarchist parties and powers, he, a curious "compound of conservative and revolutionary," would turn on Europe to spread revolution by war, before he himself would be overthrown in a second Waterloo. He reported a conversation in which the dictator "in a moment of abandon gave me to understand that the French army was

coup, and he remembered that Guizot (like Donoso) had thought so a year earlier. *Conversations with M. Thiers, M. Guizot, and other distinguished persons, during the Second Empire*, I (London, 1878), 142, 148.

[29] Juretschke, II, 725, 727, 728. "The Conservative Lord Derby in a recent speech before Parliament," he said, "has come to sanction all my principles, to confirm all my predictions, and to strengthen all my assertions. I have said that England had an enormous interest in putting an emphasis on the territorial question and in obscuring with shadows the revolutionary question, and that is exactly what, a few days after I said it, England has done through the mouth of her prime minister" (II, 725). Derby had restated Britain's old position of nonintervention in the internal affairs of other nations (which Donoso had espoused in 1834 against the conservative powers of the Concert of Europe) and had refused to yield to Louis Napoleon's blandishments against her asylum for refugees, and he had on the other side reaffirmed Britain's commitment to the treaties of Vienna, which hemmed in France's boundaries, and had spoken out for armaments.

[30] Juretschke, II, 813; 726.

not truly heroic except in propagating revolutions."[31] Europe, therefore, faced a hopeless and chaotic future. She would be chastized for her common failure to form a conservative union. If war came from French imperial projects, Europe would suffer sooner than if peace continued.[32] He meant, apparently, what he said to Louis Napoleon: France would promote revolution in other nations by war, and England would favor revolutions during times of peace.

Among the great powers he thought quite rightly that only Schwarzenberg's Austria could be an ally for Louis Napoleon's policy of imperialism because of a coincidence of their political and territorial interests in Switzerland and the Rhineland.[33] Donoso opposed any imperial ventures on the Continent, but otherwise he and Schwarzenberg had much the same view of the situation. This Austrian minister had told Russia and Prussia after December 2 that Louis Napoleon had done them "a great service by putting down parliamentarism and that the policy of the continent should be to countenance him, and to isolate England" as a foyer of the anarchical principles of constitutionalism.[34] When Schwarzenberg died suddenly on April 5, Donoso correctly estimated that Louis Napoleon would now find himself isolated in a Europe that was hostile to his imperial ambitions.[35] In fact, the dictator thereafter concentrated on finding a bride and proclaiming the Empire, where he expected more opposition from Russia than from England.

[31] Unpublished dispatch, No. 319, May 24, 1852. Cf. Juretschke, II, 727 (March 10); unpublished dispatch, No. 319.

[32] Juretschke, II, 730.

[33] Juretschke, II, 738, 729, Palm, *England and Napoleon III*, pp. 127ff. A. Debidour, *Histoire diplomatique de L'Europe*, II (Paris, 1891), 73–74. This dated work is one of the few which cite Comte Adéhmar d'Antioche's *Deux Diplomates* (Donoso and Raczynski) as a source. Also on Schwarzenberg, see Viet Valentin, *1848; Chapters of German History*, trans. E. T. Scheffawer (Hamden, Conn., 1965), pp. 333–35; R. A. Kahn, *The Multinational Empire*, (New York, 1950), 68–71.

[34] *Correspondence and Conversations of Alexis de Tocqueville with Nassau William Senior, from 1834 to 1859*, II (London, 1872), 172. Letter of S. to T. (January 5, 1852); Senior's words quoted.

[35] Juretschke, II, 729.

Donoso keenly regretted this shift in emphasis, because any opportunity to establish a conservative concert of the Continent against England and revolution had been thrown away for dynastic and territorial interests.

In May Donoso wrote to Metternich in despair over the prospects of anything resembling a renewed conservative Concert of Europe. If a general counterrevolutionary policy had ever been possible, it no longer was.

> I wish with all my heart that I were able to speak with Your Highness about the present state of Europe, but . . . I shall take the liberty to say one thing only . . . that the territorial question is beginning to take the place of the revolutionary question, or . . . by one of those transformations which its evil genius usually inspires in it, [it] is seeking to turn itself into a territorial question. After things have gone on in this fashion for a while, the revolution will raise its head before us again, and it will answer the question to its own profit, by taking over all territories.[36]

Apparently Metternich could offer no remedy, and Donoso had exhausted his own plans and ideas. Now his fever of diplomatic Anglophobia quickly cooled down. Nine months later he noted that Napoleon III's relations with the Continental nations had improved but would always lack solidity and firmness, because the other powers would always have to fear that he would turn into an aggressive, revolutionary prince.[37] At the same time, he noted the breakup of the old Tory and Whig parties into unstable coalitions. This development persuaded him that England was developing a Continental style of parliamentarism, and if Europe ever became solidarious, it would be in this fashion, all finally suffering the "same end," the "same fate"—tyranny or revolution.[38]

36 Juretschke, II, 561.

37 Juretschke, II, 821. Valverde, II, 910–a "union" and "concert" plea.

38 Valverde, II, 894–95, dispatch No. 24, December 24, 1852. He believed that the shift of Palmerston to the Tories and of the "Peelites" to the Whigs was already a *fait accompli*. Compare his view of English parliamentarism here with a very similar judgment in a letter of November 15, 1852: Juretschke, II, 641 and 648, on the "death of parliamentarism."

FROM CONCERT OF EUROPE TO SOLIDARITY AND UNITY

Let us now take stock of Donoso's analysis of the attitudes and foreign policy of Louis Napoleon and of Palmerston and England. Certain judgments, hopes, and fears were exaggerated, but, over-all, his analysis was cogent and coherent for its time. His was a genuine diplomacy of counterrevolution, which in one way or another was shared by various statesmen and governments.[39] In several ways it was a continuation, yet an adjustment and modernization, of Metternich's policies. Moreover, his search for a conservative yet reformative solidarity of European nations to forestall eventual socialist revolution and conquest by Russia, his wish to isolate England as the historic foe of European unity under the hegemony of any Continental nation (especially France), and his support for Louis Napoleon's authoritarian–democratic regime as hopefully the model of consevative reform and the leader of the Continent are similar enough to our recent experience with de Gaulle to give them a vaguely anticipatory character. Donoso's policies suggest de Gaulle's recent movement for European unity that sought both to counter Russian and communist domination of Europe and to shut out Anglo-American hegemony from the Continent in favor of European independence the French leadership of an authoritarian regime in France.

Donoso's efforts in behalf of France during these months were not meant for the profit of Louis Napoleon, as Schmitt

39 Cf. Taylor, *The Struggle for Mastery*, especially Ch. 2, "The Diplomacy of Reaction, 1849–1850," and Ch. 3, "The End of the Holy Alliance, 1852–1853." According to Taylor, a romantic scheme like Donoso's European policy of conservatism, solidarity, and counterrevolutionary principles, in a renewal of Metternich's Concert system or in a kind of second Holy Alliance, would have had much more attraction for Nicholas I and Russia than for the new realists, Louis Napoleon, Schwarzenberg, or Radowitz (pp. 22–26, 32). But Donoso, unlike Taylor's Nesselrode and other statesmen of the time (p. 32) looked ahead to consequences that matured in 1854 and 1914.

thinks, but for the interests of Spain and especially of Europe as a whole.[40] Several prominent political figures, including Schwarzenberg, Nicholas I, Metternich, and even Palmerston, shared in part his estimate of the French and international situation.[41] He did not underestimate nor ridicule the suspicion of Louis Napoleon's imperialistic ambitions on the Continent, but he was foolish even to hope that a Bonaparte could either change his coat or quickly overcome the inherent hostility of Prussia and Russia. Donoso wanted France to take the leadership of a conservative Europe, because her influence still reached into all parts of Europe. Might she not inspire imitation again, as she had in past eras, if she were revitalized by a Christian conservatism under a decisive government? This type of leadership, however, was impossible for devious Louis Napoleon in 1852. Like Carlyle, Donoso sought heroes to lead when there were no heroes. Nevertheless, he may have influenced Napoleon III's later foreign policy of advocating settlement of problems of peace and war by international congresses: in 1856 at Paris to end the Crimean War, in 1863 to discuss Poland and the general political structure of Europe, and in 1864, the Schleswig–Holstein problem.[42] At any rate, that portion of Metternich's Concert of Europe to which Castlereagh had always agreed, conferences to safeguard or restore the general peace, survived the confusion of 1848 to

[40] Throughout this crisis Donoso repeatedly stressed European (chiefly Continental) interests above those of England or France (Juretschke, II, 727, 729). Where Spain was concerned, he recognized her weakness vis-à-vis the great powers, but, after reassuring Louis Napoleon about new fortifications in the Balearics, he wrote, "One thing consoles me, and it is that he [L.N.] will not try anything against Spain. He knows that Spain was the occasion for the disastrous end of his uncle" (ibid., II, 748). Reminding Louis Napoleon in February, 1852, of "my adhesion to the coup d'état which has saved Europe," Donoso still upheld Spanish interests (Valverde, II, 850).

[41] See Palm, *England and Napoleon III*, pp. 73–78, 82, 88ff, 91–92, 126–28; Southgate, *Palmerston*, pp. 286–89; Seton-Watson, *Britain in Europe*, pp. 249, 252, 290–91.

[42] See Taylor, *The Struggle for Mastery*, pp. 25 and 61.

work intermittently until 1914. That portion which Metternich and Alexander I had built up, which called for intervention in the internal affairs of nations to stamp out liberal and revolutionary movements, could not be resurrected in 1852. The new liberal principles of nonintervention and national self-determination to which Donoso had appealed before 1848 at last had won the field outside the multinational empires.

Donoso's vision of a European solidarity and concert, or a continental union was a kind of unity in diversity. It was more similar to the earlier conservative ideas of Metternich and Alexander I than to the several positivist, revolutionary, liberal, nationalistic, or socialist schemes for European unity like those of Comte, Saint-Simon, Hugo, or Mazzini.[43] He wanted a unity that still preserved the nation states, but he was afraid that rampant nationalism in Central Europe, Italy, and the Balkans would eventually produce terrible world wars which could destroy Europe. For that reason, he now regarded the existing great empires as useful for maintaining stability and peace in the world, provided they followed a common conservative, cooperative foreign policy.

With prophetic insight, he had imagined in 1849 what a democratic and socialistic union of Europe that was based on the predominance of France and Germany might be in the future. It would be:

> One of the most marvellous events of history: the coming to the world of a great socialist and demagogic empire, which, considered geographically, would have the same extension, would embrace the same races and would be bound by the same fron-

[43] See C. G. Haines, ed., *European Integration* (Baltimore, 1957), p. 19; he attributes the ideas of a "United States of Europe" to Carlo Cattaneo and Victor Hugo in 1848. Also see H. A. Schmitt on the "pioneers of European union," in *The Path to European Union* (Baton Rouge, La., 1962), Ch. 1; René Albrech-Carrie, *One Europe* (New York, 1965), pp. 124–41; A. J. P. Taylor, *The Trouble Makers* (Bloomington, Ill., 1958), pp. 67–68, on the European scheme of Harrison and the English positivists.

> tiers as the great Empire of the West, which Charlemagne founded. The Rhine would be the great artery of the one as it was of the other; both would contain the Latin and Germanic races. There would be left outside the compass of the latter, as of the former, only the Slavic race and the Anglo-Saxon. . . . God spare us that frightful catastrophe.[44]

Now that this unification has evolved in part a century later, but largely under Christian democracy and revisionist socialism, and with British membership and possible *détente* with Russia, it is not at all clear that it must end in catastrophe. Like de Gaulle, Donoso was more suspicious of the British role in Europe than of the Russian; he too opposed any centralized, unitary state that would override national bounds and differences. On the other hand, like Saint-Simon he admired American federalism as a new principle of political organization more than did de Gaulle, with his idea of a "Europe of the fatherlands." Emphasizing the existence of nation states as an unavoidable fact, Donoso wanted a Europe of Christian monarchic nations to cooperate on common problems, to become at most a federal association but no super-state of a republican, socialist–democratic kind.[45] For him the revolutionary problem was paramount, and it embraced both the internal and external relations of the nations. To cope with the problem, he advocated governments and foreign policies that were conservative, even repressive where necessary. He also urged timely social-economic reforms and a new foundation of authoritarian democracy to remove the causes of popular revolutionary discontent. Hence, neither in foreign nor domestic policy was he an old-style reactionary. Metternich and he parted company here, unless the old statesman really meant it, when he referred to himself as a "Christian socialist."

[44] Juretschke, II, 263.

[45] Donoso was interested in American federalism as a new form of organization in history (Juretschke, II, 209), and he observed the attempt to apply the federal principle to German unity. On the widespread interest in federal organization for nations and for Europe at that time, see Binkley, *Realism and Nationalism*, pp. 158ff, 181f.

THE UNITED STATES AND CUBA

Even while Donoso worked for Continental solidarity in a counterrevolutionary Concert and tried to turn France against Britain, he illogically pursued a nationalistic and territorial policy for Spain against the United States in a way that had to undercut his European policy. From 1851–1853 he was involved in negotiations over filibustering expeditions, which followed a Cuban revolt in 1850 led by advocates of union with the United States.[46] From September of 1851, when he forwarded to Madrid a dispatch about the execution of the López band, he considered himself the only one able to settle affairs with the United States.[47] In fact, he played an important role in Paris by getting Spain the support of Louis Napoleon and of French power and prestige. For more than a year he worked to get a tripartite convention, wherein England and France would join Spain to protest the filibustering and to demand a formal guarantee of Spain's right to Cuba.[48] Palmer-

46 Ballesteros y Bereta (*Historia de España*, VIII, 396) calls Donoso's dispatches on Cuba "*españolista*." They are, but not immoderately so; they manifest nothing beyond a natural indignation at the United States' designs on Cuba—nothing like his anger at British foreign policy nor his deep dislike of Prussia—at least nothing that I have seen. These dispatches, which seem to be contained for the most part in the bundles of "Política" and "Correspondencia" for the United States, are still unpublished, except where they are cited by Jeronimo Becker, *Historia de las relaciones exteriores*. The last dispatch before Donoso's death (unpublished, No. 283 of April 25, 1853) was on U.S. foreign relations: on President Pierce's inaugural address, which seemed especially truculent to Madrid in reference to the rights of U.S. citizens on foreign soil. It was too like Palmerston's "civis Romanus sum" speech of 1850, which had so irritated the Continent. Donoso sought and obtained the promise of a French protest on this matter. Early in the negotiations over Cuba, Donoso was so angered at the handling of a French dispatch he had forwarded to Madrid that he was on the verge of resigning. Dispatch of October 11, 1851; Juretschke, II, 796. Also see A. A. Ettinger, *The Mission to Spain of Pierre Soulé, 1853–1855* (New Haven, Conn., 1932), pp. 59, 65–67, 78.

47 Antioche, *Deux Diplomates*, p. 162; Juretschke, II, 796; letters, Legajos 22, 56, Donoso Cortés family archives.

48 Becker, *Historia de las relaciones exteriores*, p. 232. Isturiz's unpublished letters, replying to Donoso from London (September 27, October

ston was willing, but foreign minister Turgot of France was not, for he counted on establishing an alliance with the United States in case of a break with England. By appealing directly to Louis Napoleon in February of 1852, Donoso circumvented Turgot. "You have obliged us, Monsieur le Marquis," Turgot warned him, "to do a thing rather dangerous for France." It was all very inconsistent with Donoso's own effort to isolate Britain and to turn France against her. American Secretary of State Everett rejected the convention in December of 1852. When the Crescent City filibuster came on the heels of this rebuff, the Spanish government instructed Donoso to find out whether France would aid Spain, if she had to use armed force to "guarantee justice and right." He therefore conferred with the emperor in January and February of 1853 to ask if and where France would help Spain "in the probable case of conflict with the Federal Government." Napoleon III was not sure enough of the French people to commit himself on the extent of aid, but Donoso said that he definitely promised to help in the event of war.[49] The danger, before it evaporated, was felt much more keenly by Spain than by the United States. If such a war had come, however, it might have diverted Louis Napoleon from his imperial projects in the Crimean War, which so deeply divided Europe as to preclude any new conservative Concert or Holy Alliance.

FUTURE IMPERIALISM AND WORLD WAR

In predicting the international war that would soon break out because of the predominance of divisive territorial interests over common political interests, Donoso foresaw clearly the outlines of the Crimean War of 1854–1856, of Cavour's

7, 1851), already concerned the "triple guarantee." Isturiz relayed his request to Palmerston, who previously had told Isturiz that he could not participate because he lacked support for it in Parliament; now he demurred because the U.S. Senate and American public opinion could not accept it (Donoso Cortés family archives).

[49] Becker, *Historia de las relaciones exteriores*, pp. 234–35; 264–66.

war for Italian unity and independence in 1859, and of later European imperialism as well. Late in 1852 and early in 1853 he considered the prospects of war in the Near East over the Turkish question.[50] If this conflict took place, France and England would probably align together against the Northern powers of Russia, Austria, and Prussia. On the other hand, the latter two powers, he felt, might stay neutral, much to Russia's chagrin. Napoleon III could have no motive except material aggrandizement. Donoso also worried that a war might break out in Italy before long, if Sardinia–Piedmont continued to oppose Austria by championing the rights of the Milanese. In this case, both Napoleon III and England might intervene in the dispute on the Italian side.[51] The international grab bag that he envisioned in an explosion over the Eastern Question was actually a preview of the seizures or frustrations connected with nationalism and imperialism for the next half century. Russia would try to take Constantinople; Austria, the Danube provinces; Prussia, the smaller German states; England, Egypt; and France would take everything that fell to her hand.[52] His present and past predictions, he thought, must necessarily occur according to the "natural order of things," but he admitted that they might well be forestalled by what he called one of those *coups d'état* of Providence, commonly known as

[50] Juretschke, II, 742ff. Valverde, II, 911.

[51] Unpublished dispatch No. 226, March 30, 1853. He found ominous "revolutionary" implications in Piedmont's effort to gain European interest in her favor, especially France and Britain. This dispatch, which vaguely anticipated Cavour's policy, was Donoso's last personal report. Also see Valverde, II, 909–10 (February 24, 1853), in which Donoso refers to the Italians allegedly sending an assassin to Paris, also Mazzini's presence there, events which, he said, momentarily convinced the other great Continental powers that a universal conspiracy was afoot and caused them through their ambassadors at Paris to try to convince Napoleon III "of the necessity of union and concert in such critical circumstances." The emperor demurred, refusing to become their policeman or gendarme while they refused to accept him as an equal in formulating general European policy. All of this meant, to Donoso, that nothing had really changed, he would "never break absolutely with the revolution."

[52] Juretschke, II, 742.

coups of fortune. "There is always at hand a pernicious fever, a rebellious army, a coup by a daring man, a sudden change of opinion." As it turned out, more than Cavour or Napoleon III in Italy, Bismarck was the "daring man" who changed the balance of power in Europe and altered the order of events that Donoso had predicted, including the fact that it was not England but Germany which gave Napoleon III his Waterloo.

The nightmare that haunted him to the end of his life was a horribly destructive world war arising from a major upset in the European balance of power that would have resulted from a new Prussian German Empire. The future clash of German and of Russian leviathans, which he had envisioned in 1849, flashed again across his mind as he surveyed the areas of potential conflict in the forthcoming "dismemberment of the Ottoman Empire": "The pretensions, on the one side of Russia and, on the other, of Austria" in Southeastern Europe would be "the gravest of happenings which seriously compromise the general peace and which are taking on gigantic proportions."[53] But the incidents at Sarajevo were more than

[53] Juretschke, II, 742. Also see Valverde, II, 911, for a previously unpublished dispatch of February 24, 1852, which in parts almost exactly duplicates the wording of the earlier dispatch (in Juretschke) of December 15, 1852, on the Eastern Question. Similarly a still unpublished dispatch of December 24, 1852 (archives, Ministry of Foreign Affairs, Madrid), repeats exactly much of the wording of the report of December 15 on other matters. This repetitiveness is strange—very unlike Donoso. However, see also Valverde, II, 912–14 (March 24, 1853), on "the great Eastern Question," where he says, in reference to the decline of the Turks and the rise of the Russian Empire, that Nicholas I truly "believes himself the legitimate successor of the Eastern emperors," although he did not want war and sincerely desired "to preserve the peace of the world." He also noted that in Germany the great powers of Prussia and Austria had settled their differences, that "the revolutionary effervescence has passed," and that Austria was taking an "arrogant initiative" in reference to Montenegro and the Adriatic, in rivalry with Russia. Finally, he noted that Napoleon III had been all ready to launch his fleet at Toulon eastward to Salamina, in cooperation with the British fleet of Malta and to the Dardanelles, except that England was not ready and the Russians wanted peace. Hence, he concluded that, for the present, there would be no general European war. At least, if war came soon over the Eastern Ques-

sixty years away. Donoso was almost always ahead, sometimes far ahead, of events. He was an observer who read the auguries, a statesman and diplomat who was also a prophet. He was not alone, of course, in foreseeing future general wars against a background of Near Eastern conflict or the roles of Russia or the United States in deciding the fate of Europe.[54] Nevertheless, he was also a realist at the end, as appears in his letter to Raczynski only three months before his death. "In summary, things are going badly: they follow a road worse than before, outside of the one we would like, and I fear that they have left the right path never to return to it. The world will go on as before, struggling with obstacles, without our ever seeing either its downfall or its salvation."[55]

---

tion, Russia could not count on Prussia and Austria's aid against France and Britain, which is precisely what happened in the Crimean War.

[54] See Senior, *Conversations*, I, 126, 282–83, 402–3, 411ff on the opinions (1853–1854) of Thiers, Dumon, Manin, and Circourt. Thiers: "Then in the next war America and Russia will play a great part. They are the only young nations, France and England cannot boast of more than a green old age" (p. 126).

[55] Juretschke, II, 822. See note 53.

Chapter X

CATHOLICISM, LIBERALISM, AND SOCIALISM

APOLOGIST, ULTRAMONTANE, "PROPHET"

Some nineteenth- and twentieth-century writers have regarded Donoso as an important religious thinker and figure for his *Essay* and letters. Around 1860 Barbey D'Aurevilly ranked him with de Maistre and Bonald as a virtual lay Father of the Roman Church, and Menéndez y Pelayo considered him and Balmes as Spain's leading apologists. Tassara revered Donoso as the "Augustine and Bossuet of the Godless century," and before 1900 a French author also compared him with Bossuet and Saint Augustine as a transcendent theological synthesizer. More recently a few clerical scholars have devoted books to his theology of history.[1] Whether or not he had any real merit in this field of religious literature as apologist, ultramontane, or apocalyptic prophet, his *Essay* and letters gave him a considerable influence in the Roman Catholic Church in his time and for years afterward. After he had become conservative, he urged the defensive and antagonistic posture against modern forces and ideas, which triumphed in 1870 at Vatican I. Because of the impact of the *Essay*, when he died he was a central figure in a bitter dispute between liberal

[1] Jules Barbey D'Aurevilly, "Philosophes et écrivains religieux," in *Les Oeuvres et les hommes (XIXe siècle)* (Paris, 1912), pp. 35–41. R.P. At, *Les Apologistes espagnols au XIXe siècle: Donoso Cortès* (Paris, n.d.), pp. 14–17; published before 1898, which is the date of his *Apologistes français*, which refers to the earlier work. Marcelino Menéndez y Pelayo, "Principales apologistas," in *Historia de los heterodoxos españoles*, VII, 407–23. See Bibliography for later works by Westemeyer, Chaix-Ruy, and Monsegú on Donoso's theological thought. Gabriel García y Tassara, *Poesías*, p. 393.

and conservative Catholics, which prefigured later such conflicts up to the present. The reactionary *Syllabus of Errors* of 1864 reflects to a degree his attitudes and writings. Because of his influence on Pius IX and on Veuillot, he also contributed to ultramontanism and infallibility in de Maistre's tradition of spiritual dictatorship.[2] Nevertheless, for the extended crisis of authority and liberty, which he foresaw for both Church and State, he was as close to Montalembert, Ozanam, and Leo XIII on tactical accommodations as to Veuillot and Pius IX on doctrinal intransigance.[3] Finally, his dark, pessimistic visions of the ultimate in tyranny and anarchy inspired not only Tassara's "Lucifer" and "Messiah" and Bloy's apocalypticism but also anticipated the upsurge of the genre of secular and religious apocalyptic thought in the twentieth century.[4]

THE ESSAY AS PHILOSOPHY OF HISTORY AND SOCIOLOGY

The *Essay on Catholicism, Liberalism and Socialism* (1851) was Donoso's greatest claim to fame as a religious thinker and writer, but it was not just a narrowly religious work. A Christian theology of history that incorporated sociological principles of conservative order, the *Essay* not only directly

[2] See Alejandro Pidal y Mon, "Balmes y Donoso Cortés: Orígenes, causas del ultramontañismo," *España del siglo XIX*, III (n.d.), p. 441. Natalicio Rivas Santiago, *Anecdotario histórico* (Madrid, 1951), p. 515. In 1845 Donoso had disavowed both the regalist and ultramontane positions for mutual independence. However, he admitted a supreme spiritual power for the papacy, which properly amounted to an intellectual and moral dictatorship of hearts and consciences because it did not include a temporal power of physical or political "dictatorship" (Carlos Valverde, ed., *Obras completas*, II, 116–20). Moreover, in Donoso's papers (Donoso Cortés family archives) is an unfinished treatise on the supranational papal spiritual prerogatives and jurisdiction, which is clearly ultramontane.

[3] Juan Juretschke, ed., *Obras completas*, II, 629ff; cf. 632f.

[4] On León Bloy's debt to Donoso, see P.E. Charvet, *A Literary History of France*, V (London, 1967), 113; W. Waren Wagar, ed., *European Intellectual History Since Darwin and Marx* (New York, 1966), especially Chs. 6 and 7.

challenged liberalism and socialism but also indirectly Comte's scientistic positivism, which became the characteristic European outlook for the next half century. If Metternich, Veuillot, and Pius IX thought it marvellous, most of his contemporaries regarded it as a beautiful but excessive polemic against liberals and socialists by a clerical conservative of de Maistre's school—a Quixotic joust not in the best of taste and judgment. A century later it was reassessed as a modern version of Saint Augustine's *City of God*, to which he once or twice adverted.[5] He may have more modestly intended either a new version of *The Genius of Christianity*, one which added to romantic beauty the logical demonstration and social dimension that Chateaubriand regretted having left out, or a positive Christian response to Saint-Simon's *New Christianity* in opposition particularly to the socialism or positivism and the cults of humanity in the Saint-Simonians and Comte.[6] It accomplished all of these purposes and more, for it is one of those rare works which moves in concert and harmony on several levels at once. Beginning with an assessment of European history that resembled Comte and Saint-Simon more than Guizot, Donoso also incorporated into the *Essay* the dualism of Saint Augustine's two cities, the sociohistorical cycles of Vico and the Saint-Simonians, and the philosophical principles of Leibniz,

[5] Ludwig Fischer, ed. and trans., *Der Staat Gottes* (Karlsruhe, 1933). J. R. Mayer, "Donoso Cortés' De Civitate Dei," *Dublin Review*, 225:451 (Spring, 1951). Juretschke, II, 368, 409, 437.

[6] Donoso once rated Chateaubriand "the greatest of all" the modern philosophical historians for his *The Genius of Christianity* (Juretschke, I, 934). Only to peruse this work is to realize the great impact it had on Donoso's mind, methods, and conceptions in regard to Christian history, oratory, and philosophy, especially in Augustine, Bossuet, Leibniz, and Pascal. See *Le Génie du Christianisme*, 2 vols. (Paris, 1966), especially I, 54, 419, 433–35, 447; II, 9, 236–37, 266, 274–76. Donoso took up where Chateaubriand left off—with the social structure of Christendom and its social benefits and services. For Chateaubriand's reconsiderations from *Mémoires d'outre-tombe* (1849–1850), see Eugen Weber, ed., *Paths to the Present* (New York, 1969), p. 35: "I would show that Christianity is the thought of the future and of human liberty; that the redeeming and messianic thought is the only basis of social equality."

Pascal, and de Maistre. Finally he used logic and Hegel's dialectic to combine all of these elements into a lofty theological and ultrahistorical synthesis. No one at that time recognized the work for what it was. It became almost a world classic in its genre; it was work of beauty, power, and originality but was also simplistic and dogmatic.

Because the *Essay* is the most perennial and vital of all Donoso's works, as well as the most synthetic and the easiest to obtain in translation, many scholars have foolishly studied it alone for the quintessence of his thought. Even though it epitomizes his philosophical, historical, social, and political thought, it is too condensed, diverse, and subtle, and too florid, exaggerated, paradoxical, partisan, and polemical, to reveal Donoso's thought as a whole. No one can understand the *Essay* by itself, apart from his tacit and unidentified sources, his developing system of thought, and his milieu or world. The *Essay* reveals his newer social theory much more completely than his long-established political thought. Even as a romantic philosophy of history, its daring ideological projections suffer for lack of the specific details and political realism that are contained in the letters, reports, and speeches he wrote throughout his career. It remained for Tassara to put into verse that grim vision which Donoso developed from Vico, in which not only ideologies but also specific nations and empires, Germany, France, Britain, Russia, and America were locked in mortal world combat and dissolved in world revolution, before the new City of God arose. Only in the "Letters to Montalembert" (1849) can one clearly see him turn Augustine's two cities into rival civilizations, one of modern philosophy and one of Christianity, which were competing for the minds and souls of mankind.[7] Most of these notions, which Vico and Saint Augustine inspired in Donoso, are present in the *Essay* only implicitly. Properly understood, the *Essay* can be an introduction to Donoso, but the *Essay* itself requires an extensive introduction.

[7] Juretschke, II, 207ff.

Character and Purpose. Louis Veuillot encouraged Donoso to write his only book, but as publisher he also shares responsibility for some of its worse defects. At Paris in 1849 Veuillot asked him to compose a little volume for his "New Library" of Christian apologetics. This pamphlet series for simple souls was meant to be a kind of counter-*Encyclopedie*, with pretensions to universal knowledge at which even Diderot or Comte might have blushed! As a polemicist de Maistre's mentality, Veuillot wanted Donoso to write something timely on protestantism, socialism, and revolution addressed to ordinary lay Catholics, "children from 15 to 70 years of age."[8] Donoso, however, preferred to write on rationalism, liberalism, and socialism, and in the context not just of 1848 but of centuries of Christianity and civilization. Although he preferred to write two or three solid volumes for a more intellectual audience,[9] he had to accept Veuillot's limitations and dash off a slender, popularized essay with a dogmatic and combative tone that was suited to the mass mind in an era of crisis.

It was a struggle to start the book, but once begun, he polished it off quickly. At first he was too sick to do anything at Don Benito except peruse religious works, such as Fray Luis de Granada, ascetic of the age of Philip II and author of an Augustinian theology of history.[10] Later in Madrid, amid political and social distractions, he read the works of the socialists with pen in hand. He studied Proudhon most thoroughly as the acid critic of all the other socialist philosophers, and Donoso regarded him as intellectually the most formidable. "I lack time: in order to write, one ought to take leave of the

[8] Eugène Veuillot, *Louis Veuillot*, II (Paris, 2d ed., 1913), p. 426. Ludwig Fischer, *Der Staat Gottes*, p. 43ff. The prospectus accompanied a letter from Veuillot to Donoso (February 20, 1850), Donoso Cortés family archives. Veuillot, quoted by Edmund Schramm, *Donoso Cortés, su vida y su pensamiento*, p. 238f; similar in content to the Veuillot-Donoso letter.

[9] Juretschke, II, 554.

[10] Juretschke, II, 317f.

world," he complained, and to labor "from sunrise to sunset, wholly absorbed in his work." "We are only improvisers."[11] In a mere four months, from April to August of 1850, he had finished. Protesting that it was incomplete, that its theology was uncertain, and that its scholarly and literary merits were dubious, he sent the manuscript to Veuillot to have it checked carefully, translated into French, and readied for publication.[12]

From Paris Donoso wrote candidly to Gabino Tejado in Madrid, where Moderate papers did not even want to advertise his book, that he expected the *Essay* to be universally impugned. "If I go against all, why should not all go against me?"[13] Opposition, however, should exalt it more than hurt it. What interested him most was to see whether critics recognized any "genius or power" in it: "These two points constitute the greatest eulogy of an author."

Because it tried to do so many things, the *Essay* immediately provoked disputes about its character and purpose that have not ceased to this day. Still wanting religious apologetics, Veuillot anticipated "a great deal of good" from it. While he did not expect to "convert Europe . . . by books," he did expect to influence individuals.[14] But Donoso himself remains our best authority on the nature of his book.

> I could not compress into so small a volume what I had to say on Catholicism, Liberalism, and Socialism. . . . I have only sketched the preface of the real work which I shall write when things allow it. That does not keep the *Essay* from forming a whole

[11] Letter to Veuillot (April 6, 1850), given in L. Veuillot, *Oeuvres de Donoso Cortès*, III, 520; letter to Veuillot (August 7, 1850), also in Veuillot, III, 520. See Fischer, *Der Staat Gottes*, pp. 46–47 for details on the composition and publication of the *Essay*.

[12] An unpublished letter from Veuillot (February 22, 1851) sent notes for theological revisions with an eye to future controversies; Cardinal Fornari, he said, had recommended DuLac, a Benedictine of Solesme for this task.

[13] Juretschke, II, 575.

[14] Letter, Veuillot to Donoso (April 20, 1850), Donso Cortés family archives.

considered in itself. It contains the general principles which will serve as a starting point for my later works: it is a stepping-stone.[15]

He did not say how it formed "a whole," but it was most nearly complete as a Christian theology of history and it was a prospectus for a new body of social and political thought which he did not live to finish.

Positive Catholicism. Although it was a kind of modern *City of God*, Donoso's *Essay* was for his own era more comparable to Comte's older *Social Physics* (1842) and newer *System of Positive Politics* (1851–1854), which were also a synthesis of religion, sociology, and politics resting on a philosophy of history. The tacit Comtean character of the *Essay* may be seen in the very title. Although the term *Catholicism* implied a sectarian tract of apologetics, Donoso actually employed the word according to its broad root meaning, as did Comte, who, finding *Christianity* too vague and factious, preferred *Catholicism* because "it is more universal."[16] In place of *Christianity* and *Christian civilization* Donoso (like Comte) had used the terms *Catholicism* or *Catholic civilization* since 1847 to signify both medieval Western Christendom and a future universal religious civilization, besides the existing reactionary Church of Pius IX.[17] Both for its concept of the Middle Ages and for its prospectus of a positive (or 'affirmative') social-political system for a universal normal epoch in the future, the *Essay* truly resembled the works of Comte. However, Donoso's methods, values, and conclusions about the future of knowledge, society, and the world were generally opposite to Comte's.

Throughout the *Essay*, beginning with a perplexed remark from Proudhon on page one, he appealed to theology, claiming

[15] Louis Veuillot, *Oeuvres de Donoso Cortès*, III, 520.
[16] Comte, *Positive Philosophy*, p. 599.
[17] Juretschke, II, 82, cf. 98f; 130, cf. 150, 153, 157.

it contained and embraced all the sciences in the same manner that Comte elevated science as the center and circumference of human knowledge.[18] Not only a political theology but also a social and historical theology emerged as he sought to correct and complete the rational and the natural, the metaphysical and the scientific, with the supernatural and the theological. In the first of its three "books," the *Essay*'s social-romantic view of medieval Europe's progressive development read much like a paraphrase of the positive view of history that Comte naturally approved and J. S. Mill accepted but that contemporary liberals rejected as outrageous distortion.[19] However, Donoso refused to admit Comte's thesis that the Christian social theology had thereafter become outmoded and retrograde, doomed to be supplanted by a new scientific philosophy or cult in a future definitive reorganization of European and world society. On the contrary, he tried to show that Catholicism was still a theology of life-giving strength for society, a source of perpetually valid *affirmative* principles and laws of social order and progress. In contrast he pictured rationalism as permanently negative and destined to end in nihilism and social anarchy. He condemned not only liberalism and socialism but also Saint-Simonian positivism as schools of what Comte himself had described as the critical and negative philosophy of rationalism, which for three centuries past had worked to de-

[18] Juretschke, II, 347.

[19] Except for condemning the eighteenth century, he actually held Comte's positivist view of the past, of which Comte naturally approved; see Comte's *Appeal to Conservatives*, trans. T. C. Donkin (London, 1889), p. 98. John Stuart Mill, in turn, praised Comte's view of history as essentially correct but not likely to please English readers; see Mill's *August Comte and Positivism* (Philadelphia, 1866), pp. 106–16. On Comte's philosophy of history, see Karl Löwith, *Meaning in History* (Chicago, 1949), pp. 67–91; J. S. Mill, *Comte and Positivism*, pp. 106–17; also F. S. Marvin, *Comte, The Founder of Sociology* (New York, 1937), Ch. 7, pp. 100–121. Ordnarily, liberals have been more repelled than attracted by the *Essay*, but Donoso had a fairly reasonable answer to chidings of his historical distortions by such liberals as Montalembert and de Broglie; see Juretschke, II, 629ff.

stroy the old Catholic order and to prepare for the future positive order.[20] In the last third of the *Essay*, beyond a materialistic epoch of science, industry, prosperity, and presumably peace and progress, Donoso foresaw no normalcy. Instead he predicted a new general crisis of apocalyptic nihilism and regression succeeded by the triumph of a new world religious civilization and world peace in Saint Augustine's City of God instead of in Comte's City of the World of atheistic "Humanity."

As an intellectual *tour de force* Donoso's theological inversion of Comte's positivism was comparable to Marx's materialistic upending of Hegel's idealistic dialectic. This tacit, inverse relationship, however, was difficult to recognize, for the historical similarities at the beginning of the *Essay* soon gave way to patent contradiction, especially in the cyclic ending. As a whole, the book related to Comte much like the photographic negative to the positive. Whereas contours were much the same, positive became negative and negative, positive. The paradox in this inversion was too clever. The Saint-Simonians had already constructed it and although Comte recognized it, the French intellectual community as a whole failed to see what he was doing. Although Donoso failed even to refer to Comte by name here, de Maistre's name was never mentioned either, and everybody detected his influence in the *Essay*. Whether or not Donoso intended it, Saint-Simon and Comte contributed as much to the substance of the book as de Maistre and Saint Augustine influenced its spirit. Besides, although Donoso twice mentioned Saint Augustine, not even Brownson then saw that the *Essay* was a Christian philosophy of history comparable to the *Civitas Dei*. Consequently, its status as beginning a new Christian sociology also was lost to readers, ex-

[20] Comte, *Positive Philosophy*, pp. 402f, 538ff, 796; pp. 401, 406–11. Frank E. Manuel, *The New World of Henri Saint-Simon* (Cambridge, 1966), pp. 354, on the 'affirmations' of the Saint-Simonian "nouveau Christianisme," and 362–63 on Saint-Simon's positivism.

cept for J. F. Buss and La Tour du Pin who did not relate it to Comte.

Liberalism and Socialism. After Catholicism, Donoso's chief concern was not liberalism but socialism. He viewed socialism less as a secular ideology than as an incipient new theology or secular religion, destined to drag civilization down through a more than Saint-Simonian communism into a more than Proudhonian anarchy. The liberalism and socialism depicted in the *Essay* pertained not only to Donoso's era, for he projected their future development dialectically out of their fundamental principles.

What he criticized as "liberalism" in the *Essay* was mainly the middle-class variety of the European continent, which the July Monarchy, the eclecticism of Cousin, and the doctrinairism and parliamentarism of Guizot had typified, the sort Donoso himself and the Moderates had represented in Spain. From twenty years of experience, he described this bourgeois liberalism as inherently unstable and transitional, unable to establish a viable synthesis of liberty and order and fated to end in democracy and socialism either by revolution or by evolution. He agreed with Proudhon and the socialists that a common revolutionary tradition and common rationalistic principles, especially equality, bound parliamentary liberalism to socialism as its logical and ideological heir, which would some day overthrow liberal parliamentarism violently in instances where it could not succeed it peacefully via democracy.[21] Bourgeois liberalism, he concluded, was both shallow and contradictory; it generally addressed itself to little but politics and always stopped short of developing its rationalistic premises to

[21] Juretschke, II, 445, cf. 339f, 648. P. J. Proudhon, *The General Idea of the Revolution in the Nineteenth Cenutry*, trans. J.B. Robinson (London, 1923), p. 40: "Law of Tendency in Society—The Revolution of 1789 had done only half its work." G. D. H. Cole, *A History of Socialist Thought*, III (London, 1956), p. 289, for revisionist Eduard Bernstein on socialism as the legitimate heir to liberalism.

their equalitarian, much less nihilistic, conclusions. Socialism was already more logical than liberalism and would become more so in the future. "The right of victory belongs to the more logical."[22]

His main adversary, socialism, was not just the utopian communism of Robert Owen, the Saint-Simonians, Fourierists, and Blanc, but also the anarchism of Proudhon and, indirectly, even the system devised by Karl Marx.[23] For his knowledge of the socialists' doctrines, Donoso made use of Proudhon's caustic criticisms, but he also consulted other works written by Socialists or about them.[24] Proudhon's capricious use of the

[22] Juretschke, II, 446, 450, 513; 495f.

[23] Although he identified none of the masters of the liberal school (Guizot, Constant, Cousin, and Royer-Collard were too obvious to readers), among the socialists be placed Owen, Saint-Simon, and Fourier and their followers as communistic. He considered Proudhon—now as anarchist, now as "communistic,"—the most formidable thinker among them, but Marx was still too obscure to merit attention. See J. B. Wolf (*France*, pp. 138–39) on Proudhon as indeed the keenest mind. Through reading Proudhon, Donoso knew of other communists, for example, Cabet and Blanc, whom Proudhon effectively excoriated. Indirectly, through the same source, he at least knew of Marx's doctrines, but Proudhon, out of pique, refused to use his name. See Proudhon's *Les Confessions d'un révolutionnaire*, in *Oeuvres complètes de P. J. Proudhon*, VIII (Paris, 1929–1946), p. 82, and *Système des contradictions économiques, ou philosophie de la misère* (same series), 265ff. Pierre Hauptmann, *Marx et Proudhon* (Paris, 1947), pp. 76, 79, 81, 92. For some lines in Donoso's *Essay*: Juretschke, II, 503.

[24] In the *Essay* itself, Donoso cites Louis Reybaud's *Études sur les réformateurs ou socialistes modernes* (Paris, 1841), 2 vols., which treated the Saint-Simonians ("communists" and "humanitarians") and also Owen, Cabet, and Fourier, with a bit on Proudhon and one reference to Comte. He treated the socialists in the context of utopian and millennialist traditions of thought—obviously a very important source for Donoso. Reybaud even discussed Proudhon's use of the dialectic and the idea of solidarity. However, Donoso's library contains another such work: Alfred Sudre's *Histoire du communisme, ou réfutation historique des utopies socialistes* (Paris, 1849), which covered thought on these subjects from Plato to More, to Babeuf, as well as Owen, Saint-Simon, Fourier, Cabet, Blanc, and Proudhon. Probably too late for the *Essay* or for Donoso's great speeches was Abbé Philippe Gerbert's *De Rapports du rationalisme avec le communisme* (Paris, 1850), although Donoso's notes from it, arranged in parallel columns (for example, *rationalisme athée—communisme*

dialectic in *The Philosophy of Poverty* (*La philosophie de la misère*) provoked Marx to reply with *The Poverty of Philosophy* (*La misère de la philosophie*). Also critical of Proudhon's version of the dialectic, Donoso observed that "the pontiffs and masters" of socialism were German, that the French were only disciples. He foresaw clearly the two mainstreams into which socialism later flowed, anarchist and state-communist. Like Marx, Donoso anticipated a successive development in which a despotic state socialism (communism to Donoso) would come first; afterward socialist anarchy (communism to Marx) would arise in reaction to it, as a radical antithesis. Thus, although he thought that Proudhon's immediate schemes would necessarily entail communism, Donoso nevertheless presented him as a prophet of the ultimate anarchy in which he thought modern world civilization was fated to end.[25]

A Synthetic Philosophy of History. The *Essay* is most nearly a synthesis of all the elements in Donoso's philosophy of history, Augustinian dualism, Vicchian cycle, Hegelian dialectic, and positivist view of history. In it, however, he dealt only with the ideal, abstract level of history, with the conflict of principles, religions or ideologies, and civilizations. He reserved for other works the more concrete movements such as the nations and empires of Hegel and the socioeconomic and material forces of Marx. Augustine's *City of God* is foreshadowed at the beginning of the *Essay* and hovers over the end. First it appears as an affirmative but imperfect civilization of Germano-Latin Christendom in medieval Europe similar to Comte's positive Catholicism, and finally it is described as a universal (truly catholic) Christian civilization, or the Kingdom of God in Christ. For Donoso, the initial and final religious civilizations were also equivalent to Vico's divine epochs. In between them stood Vico's civil epoch of European civilization in its decline

ánarchique; rationalisme panthéiste–communisme égalitaire) are either sources or confirmations of his political theology. (Tome C, Donoso Cortés family archives.)

[25] Juretschke, II, 413f, 304; 503, 622.

through liberalism and revolution to a despotic communist world state which was finally destined to end in anarchic self-destruction. This so-called philosophical civilization was equivalent to Saint Augustine's City of the World and Comte's metaphysical and scientific stages of civilization, which Donoso represented as failing ever to turn from its negative stage to a truly positive one. He used Hegel's dialectic to account for the regressive or progressive development from one epoch to another: from the synthesis or thesis of a religious Christian civilization in the Middle Ages to the antithesis of a neopagan, rationalistic, and secular civilization in modern times. The regression had begun before the Renaissance and continued through the Enlightenment and nineteenth-century liberalism until it would climax in a communistic world despotism and ultimately disintegrate in universal nihilistic anarchy. Because it was more radically negative, logical, and theological than liberalism, socialism was due to develop into this full and final rationalistic antithesis and negation of the old Christian civilization. Presented at the end as the antithesis of terminal socialism, is the ultimate universal, supreme synthesis of natural and supernatural, liberty and order, in Christ. It is the City of God fulfilled in a concluding divine age and universal Christian civilization, a closing of the divine and cosmic circle, the point at which the alpha becomes the omega. The supreme affirmation would succeed the supreme negation of history. At this stage the highest unity, a universal extension, and the resolution of all contradictions would be achieved in a cosmos in which an infinite contraction of divine love would succeed to the infinite expansion of rebellion.[26]

Donoso accepted the assumption of Hegel and Marx that the dialectic, or the human potential for contradiction and rebellion, could at some time terminate. If he understood Hegel's theory correctly, however, should not he have combined Christianity with liberalism and socialism in his final synthesis instead of assuming that liberalism would disappear

[26] Juretschke, II, 501f, 511–14; 467f, 495f; 436f, 528–30, 533.

and socialism destroy itself prior to the rise of a Christian world civilization? He did consider such a synthesis possible, but not probable, because he was not concerned with accommodation in externals, but with fundamental principles about God, man, and society. On these basic essentials he would not compromise. A rapproach, he thought, would require liberalism and socialism to "pass through the rollers," to shed their negative principles and become assimilated to Christianity in a Christian social democracy. Actually, for Donoso, Christianity was properly not a thesis to oppose with an antithesis but was potentially "a synthesis that covers all, contains all, and explains all."[27] Ultimately it could be overcome only by a similar but opposite synthesis, a negation so complete that it would be nihilism and the end of everything. Nevertheless, he feared that future nihilists and anarchists would at least approach such absolute negation before the final positive synthesis of Christian universalism emerged.

By its nebulous, abstract ending, the *Essay* suggests a vague, timeless, eternal dimension of reality. Not so cautious in his "Letters to Montalembert" and to *El Heraldo* in 1849, he had claimed that within time and the natural order, total victory belonged to the philosophic civilization or "City of the World," which would pursue freedom to the point of utter breakdown and anarchy, or absolute evil and error, a grand catastrophe on a universal scale. The triumph of the City of God, or universal civilization in Christ, and of absolute truth and goodness could not come except supernaturally. This ideal —within time—had been achieved only imperfectly in past history by means of grace or miracle, but in the not-so-distant future, he clearly expected the end of time and therefore a perfect realization. For him, the whole philosophy of history was finally contained in this simple formula: "the natural triumph of evil over good" in time, and "the supernatural triumph of God over evil." He rejected the principle of Vico's eternal cycle in favor of this formula. Nonetheless, he insisted

[27] Juretschke, II, 469f, 514; 502, 514; 515.

that he was neither fatalistic nor Manichean, because (with divine help) man could save himself if he would. Donoso simply did not think that he wanted to do so.[28]

A Sociology of Order. Besides philosophy of history, Donoso also used the *Essay* to set forth a sociology of fundamental principles for social and general order, which, despite its theological and deductive method, was often like Comte's sociology in its historical approach, supposed laws, and emphasis on order.[29] His great worry in 1850 was the increasing materialism reflecting the advance of science and industry, which put material order and technological and economic interests ahead of social, political, and religious order. He had stressed religious and moral order more emphatically than Comte as ultimately the only source of true freedom and the only escape from alternating state despotism and revolutionary anarchy.[30]

The sociological problem of order involved not only princi-

[28] Juretschke, II, 207–10; 216–20. Also see Donoso's letter to *La Revue des Deux Mondes*, II, 632–33, in which, after describing the social renovation under the Christian church in the Middle Ages as a kind of second creation out of chaos, he stated that no such thing would be seen again, "because there will not be three creations." Hence, the social reconstruction that Tassara sketched out in "Un diablo más" as a unity of Europe and Russia, of science and faith—an age reborn was the invention of his hope, not of Donoso's words or mind, although the Messianic stanzas are faithful to Donoso's vision. See, Tassara, *Poesías*, pp. 452–53, 462–65. Juretschke, II, 209; 215–16, 318–19.

[29] See Jean La Croix, *La Sociologie d'Auguste Comte*, 2d ed. (Paris, 1961), pp. 1, 3, 21, 61. He affirms the influence of de Maistre's "theological sociology" on Comte's "sociology of order." Donoso's sociology fits somewhere between de Maistre's and Comte's, more historical in method than the former, more theological than the latter. Marvin (*Comte*), notes that the root idea, or starting point, of Comte's sociology was the existence of laws of social phenomena (p. 47ff), or the discovery of evolutionary laws in history (p. 61f). "In sociology he draws his method and his supreme authority from history" (p. 99). "Sociology thus becomes, not exactly a philosophy of history, . . . but certainly history philosophically considered" (p. 100). Almost the same thing can be said of Donoso's sociology, except that the ultimate touchstone, even of his philosophy of history, was theology.

[30] Juretschke, II, 303, 327; 200.

ples and laws but also such related basic questions as: the nature of man and God and society; the problems of good and evil, which reformers logically had to face; the relation of man and society, as liberal individualism, socialist organicism, or Christian solidarity; and the problems of suffering and perfectibility, or redemption. Underlying the entire structure of universal order Donoso found Leibniz's natural and divine law of unity and variety everywhere observable: in the cosmos, God, man, the family, society, and government. Next in importance was Newton's "law of action and reaction"—also a basic law of Saint-Simon and of Comte's social dynamics—which he expressed here in terms of Hegel's dialectic. The most basic moral law of order was man's freedom just as the most basic cause of human disorder was the sinful abuse of it. A principle of solidarity was the fundamental law of structure, or social statics for mankind and society, followed by principles of hierarchy and corporatism.[31] This and other presumed natural laws, had their less obvious supernatural side, where they concerned the unity, elevation, and salvation of the human race, through a common imperfection, heritage, and destiny involving an original sin, expiatory suffering, and the perfecting and saving effect of grace through Christ.

Clearly Donoso was consciously defying the vogue which Comte and Spencer typified, of seeking purely natural laws of order for man's ethical, political, social, and economic life, to the exclusion of any supernatural laws, order, or dimension. Besides logic, science, philosophy, and history, he drew upon theology. Although he had a dualistic outlook, he admitted no rigid distinction between matter and spirit, natural and supernatural. Like the Saint-Simonians, he viewed them instead as different aspects or modes of one universal reality, but he did not fall into the romantic pantheism of the Saint-Simonians. Since it was then deemed superstitious nonsense for an intellectual to speak of the supernatural, much less original sin, Donoso admitted that his views would strike the petulant

[31] Juretschke, II, 370ff, 438; 397ff; 487ff.

sophists of the day as "inexcusable madness."[32] His pessimism and idealism came between Hobbes and Freud, Pascal and Barth, at the beginning of an unsympathetic era of optimism and materialism, which he expected to end in the antithesis of order, in socialism and anarchy.

Compared to Christian sociological affirmation, the purely natural and rationalistic explanations of the nature and destiny of man and society by liberalism and socialism seemed to Donoso only partial at best, or disastrous nihilistic negations at worst. The *Essay*'s fundamental proposition was to either return to religion or await the anarchic ruin of modern society and civilization. Basically this was Comte's message too, although the religion was different.

***Reactions to the* Essay.** Since the original editions in Spanish and French, the *Essay* has appeared in several editions in German, English, and Italian translations, from 1851 up into the twentieth century, altogether enough to qualify it as an international classic.[33] The praise and the criticism have also been international and generally have divided, respectively, along political lines of left and right. In 1851 Metternich was full of admiration, Pius IX was inspired, Guizot was cool, Comte was perplexed, and Proudhon was scornful. Today Julian Marías is still scornful, most are indifferent, and hardly anyone is enthusiastic. Nevertheless, the work survives as viable, and understanding of it increases.

When the *Essay* came out in Madrid early in June of 1851, Tejado was shocked at the "gross insults, bold calumnies, ma-

[32] Juretschke, II, 388; 397.

[33] See the Bibliography for most of these editions. Schramm supposed that Reiching's poor translation (Tubingen, 1854) was due to Metternich's initiative, but if so, Fischer says that Metternich regretted it as a disservice to Donoso (p. 9). J. B. Mortier of Brussels brought out a Belgian edition in French in 1851, according to Fischer; another was published by Lardinois at Liege in 1851. Italian editions came out in the Papal States at Foligno in 1852 and at Rome in 1860 and in Austrian-held Milan in 1854. Goddard's American translation came out in 1862 under Brownson's guidance, and McDonald's version in Dublin in 1874.

lign reticence" with which Spanish liberals received it. The oversensitive Tejado said that they did not even want to hear this retrograde theocrat. In reference to *El Heraldo* he remarked, "*Blasphemisti,* they have said; and to excommunicate him, they called him an absolutist."[34] Donoso had to remind Tejado that he had expected nothing less.

> The case is reduced to the following: You meet someone in the street and say to him: "You are very ugly." I ask: Will that person thank you and tell you that he is pretty good? You would be crazy to expect it. Well, consider the story. I told the liberals: "You are very ugly." How the deuce do you want them to endure me and to thank me besides?[35]

The Spanish liberals, he told Raczynski, were so stung to fury that they would like to annihilate him, yet their hostility proved to him that he had hit the right spot. Unfortunately his book had been published "out of time": If only it could have come after instead of before "the flood" of revolution, democracy, and socialism.[36] With such sublime self-assurance, opposition could only exalt.

Donoso found that preliminary comment in the press in Paris made happy contrast to Spain. The *Gazette de France* in "News of the Day" (June 21) welcomed it in the name of logic and reason. Such praise from "the daily of universal suffrage" struck him as curious but not inappropriate, since the *Essay* did support popular suffrage, precisely with logic and reason.[37] Surveying several newspapers, he proudly claimed that his book had caused an explosion, a great sensation. Only the *Journal des Débats,* the "last representative of Voltaireanism and of European liberalism," had shown animosity by apparently by studiously ignoring the work. The general difference in attitude from Spain, he thought, was due to "some waves of the flood" having passed over France already.

[34] Gabino Tejado, ed., *Obras,* I, lxii–lxiii.
[35] Juretschke, II, 578.
[36] Juretschke, II, 793; 578.
[37] Juretschke, II, 579.

To liberal Catholics of the 1850s like Montalembert or de Broglie, the *Essay* was a seductive but unconvincing effort to bind Catholicism forever to a medieval past, to monarchy, and to conservatism. Thus Juan Valera would call it "one of the most sublime and one of the most absurd books" of the century.[38] As late as 1853, however, Montalembert still praised the *Essay* as "an admirable book, in which the obscurities, contradictions, and exaggerations are left drowned in a sea of splendor," but he no longer accepted its conservative outlook.[39]

Guizot, once Donoso's mentor and lately his friend, took amicable exception to the *Essay*. Among liberal masters, he alone had been criticized by name in the book for his purely naturalistic view of the historical role of medieval Catholicism in regenerating European society.[40] As a Protestant liberal historian, however generously disposed, he could not assent to Donoso's supernaturalist view. Without having read his courtesy copy entirely, Guizot observed wisely that the Catholic Church, however she deemed herself changeless in essentials, moves historically, and "in order to rejoin human society in our days, she still has to take a step."[41] Would Donoso influence his church to take that path? (Both men had thought that Pius IX was taking such a step in 1847, but now Donoso judged the step as essentially mistaken, whereas Guizot felt it had merely been too hasty.) Donoso answered that his church already possessed the intellectual and moral forces of revelation and charity that were capable of saving European society if hostile governments would cease blocking her.[42] Guizot promised that his own *Meditations and Moral Sketches* (*Médi-*

[38] Juan Valera, *Estudios críticos sobre filosofía y religión*, in *Obras completas*, 34 (Madrid, n.d.), p. 19.

[39] Charles Comte de Montalembert, *Oeuvres de M. le Comte de Montalembert*, XV; *Oeuvres polémiques et diversés*, II, 212.

[40] Juretschke, II, 557; 394ff.

[41] Letter from Guizot to Donoso (July 3, 1850) in Donoso Cortés family archives. Juretschke gives an excerpt of it in Spanish translation which is not very accurate (II, 556, note); also see Tejado, V, 131.

[42] Juretschke, II, 557.

tations et Études Morales) would arrive at the same conclusion as the *Essay* by a different yet parallel path regarding Europe's need of moral regeneration.[43] Albert de Broglie, a liberal Catholic who criticized Donoso's *Essay* as medieval and utopian, had lyric praise for Guizot's book, whereas Donoso refrained from comment.[44] Apart from an introduction, Guizot's book was just a repetition of his pre-1848 views.

Comte's ideas were not distinguished in the *Essay* from the Saint-Simonianism from once been derived, and Donoso did not mention him by name in the book. If only by hearsay, however, Comte was aware of Donoso's book, because he was still very interested in the current retrograde Legitimists who exalted it. Intentionally or not, he finally answered Donoso on essential points in *Appeal to Conservatives* (1855), which defined for true conservatives the proper approach toward the 'theologism' of those reactionaries who, lacking a doctrine of their own, had combined divine right with popular sovereignty. Comte claimed to offer them a better theory of spiritual reorganization and a more coherent synthesis of history, humanity, and belief. His doctrine of continuity was "superior to mere solidarity," and the ultimate unity he projected would offer no

[43] See Tejado, V, 134, for the letter from Guizot to Donoso (November 24, 1851), which accompanied a copy of his *Meditations*. Guizot assured Donoso of his "great regard and profound esteem. . . . We two have thought much on the same things, and we both approach the same end by paths, if not identical at least parallel." See Guizot's *Meditations and Moral Sketches*, trans. John Butler (Dublin, 1855), in which Guizot too emphasizes that the greatest question of the time is "between those who acknowledge and those who deny a supernatural . . . order of things," which—given freedom and free inquiry—he acknowledges (pp. 5–14) and even insists on (pp. 27–28).

[44] Juretschke, II, 558. Albert de Broglie, "Le Moyen'Âge et l'église catholique," *La Revue des Deux Mondes* (November 1, 1852), 411, 413. He felt that Donoso's "*piquante* originality" and oratorical skill made his criticism of the liberal principles of discussion all the less justified and the more paradoxical by the parliamentary orator, the man of discussion par excellence. His ideal political system was a misreading of medieval history as too theological and theocratic a view of authority, although Donoso was a "political man [*politique*] above all." For Donoso's cogent reply, see: Juretschke, II, 631–49.

stationary or absolute harmony but would incorporate "all phases whatsoever of the human evolution." The reactionaries, he said, "mistake the fundamental condition of the order they preach," for, although "they estimate aright the Middle Ages," they break the continuity and progress of humanity by rejecting the eighteenth century and pagan antiquity.[45]

In this *Appeal* Comte sought to outbid Catholic 'theologists' for a dominant influence with Napoleon III's imperial dictatorship. He wished to promote a transitional program of order and reform which could end the long revolutionary crisis of the West and introduce a positive and a normal state, which would include a purely natural "Universal Religion." During the transitional period, the theological reactionaries and modern Catholicism could help the dictatorship restore the conditions of moral and political order and to maintain the continuity with the past. Then a positivist–scientific priesthood of his "Religion of Humanity," in alliance with the "better" revolutionaries, would take charge and proceed to reconcile proletariat and capitalists and to regenerate the West morally and intellectually. Catholicism, Protestantism, and Islam would be absorbed into a new synthesis as a new positive and catholic, or universal, religion of all-embracing and all-uniting love and brotherhood, which would stand independent beside a political construction of order and progress. Let future generations know that according to the law of human evolution, "Man becomes more and more religious."[46]

To secular liberals and socialists the *Essay* was the work of an arch-reactionary bigot whom they ignored or ridiculed. Only derision and mockery came from Proudhon, echoing Herzen's query of 1850: Why not return to the Inquisition and the hangman for order? Proudhon ignored Donoso's valid criticism of the contradictions and inconsistencies in his theories, including his use of the dialectic. Instead he pounced upon Do-

[45] Comte, *Appeal to Conservatives*, p. 29; 98.

[46] Comte, *Appeal to Conservatives*, pp. 11ff, 21–22, 38–40, 96–98, 117; 100–104, 114–19, 127, 144ff, 151, 154, 159–60; 123.

noso's unfortunate rhetorical question about his frenzy of negation and pride: Was he "possessed of a devil"? He scorned Donoso as a pharisaical Jesuit and fanatical Spanish inquisitor, ready to put him in a *san-benito* and consign him to the flames in an *auto da fe*! "After the Jews, the pagans used the same argument to make martyrs of the first Christians, the Church to burn heretics and witches."[47] Where Henri de Lubac, examining the residue of Christianity in Proudhon, agreed that the *Essay*'s florid rhetoric was abusive, Karl Löwith had justified Donoso because Proudhon's mind was decidedly theological.[48] On one issue Donoso, Proudhon, and Herzen agreed: Western civilization was decaying and headed for dissolution. Donoso, however, pointed to anarchy as the destroyer, and he deplored the collapse which they eagerly awaited.

Captious and caustic criticism like that of *El Heraldo* of Madrid, which immediately disparaged both work and author, did not disturb Donoso greatly. "It says that my book is worth little and that I am worth less than my book. . . . And in all of this it speaks truly."[49] He did not even want to be defended in *El Orden* unless the paper would observe the bounds of temperance and avoid giving injury. After a year's time really bitter opposition arose from French liberal Catholic clergy in the "Donoso Cortés affair," which was largely provoked by Louis Veuillot. Years later, Menéndez y Pelayo would claim: "Today all that was written against the *Essay* is dead and forgotten, and the *Essay* lives on with all the beauteous youth of its first day."[50] Menéndez y Pelayo was a dedicated conservative, however!

[47] P. J. Proudhon, *Oeuvres complètes de . . . Proudhon*, Vol. VIII, *Les Confessions d'un révolutionnaire* . . ., 202–3 (footnote by Proudhon). Juretschke, II, 503: cf. II, 622.

[48] Henri de Lubac, *The Un-Marxian Socialist: A Study of Proudhon*, trans. R. E. Scantlebury (New York, 1948), p. 173. Karl Löwith, *Meaning in History* (Chicago, 1960), pp. 64–66.

[49] Juretschke, II, 588, 591.

[50] Marcelino Menéndez y Pelayo, *Heterodoxos*, VII, *Obras completas*, 2d ed. (Madrid, 1932), 413.

Conservatives, led by Veuillot, were loud in praise of the *Essay*. Metternich called it admirable; "everything is severe like your thought and luminous like your intellect."[51] As one of "your most enthusiastic admirers," he promised in conscience to have it published in Germany. Certainly the *Essay* stimulated conservatives, especially clericals, and helped the cause of reaction in the world of both politics and religion, not only then but for decades afterward. Pleased with the *Essay*'s harsh judgments of the modern world and its liberal and rationalistic movements, Pius IX had it republished at Rome in 1860, and his *Syllabus of Errors* (1864) soon reflected Donoso's harsh rejection of modern civilization. The *Essay*'s continuing influence on clerical conservatives appeared in the new editions of the 1920s and 1930s in Italy, Germany, Argentina, Britain, and the United States.

Donoso's dogmatism, intransigence, and hyperbole—more than his subtlety—concealed the greatness in the *Essay* from all its readers. Without these flaws, it might have remained a world classic for its beauty of prose and lofty universal themes. Thus, in 1926 a British literary historian characterized the *Essay* as justly renowned but intensely intolerant. Donoso had written "with eloquence and fire" but "with a belief in his own infallibility that has no parallel in literature. This self-arrogance would be ridiculous in the majority of people: it is not so in Donoso Cortés. One feels behind it all the convictions and strength of the man."[52] Critics have rarely judged the *Essay* by any measures other than literary taste or partisan bias and have long overlooked its historical and social ideas; even the great

[51] Letter from Metternich to Donoso (August 5, 1851), given by Juretschke, II, 558 (note). Also see Tejado, V, 177. Donoso's reply to Metternich (Paris, 27 August 1851), in the Donoso Cortés family archives, expressed his pleasure and pride a such praise: "It is for me the proof that I have not deluded myself: I can hope now that I have not labored in vain. A book which you deem useful will of necessity make its way *dans les esprits.*"

[52] James Fitzmaurice-Kelly, *A New History of Spanish Literature* (London, 1926), pp. 463–64.

Menéndez y Pelayo, who warmed to its "words of fire," neglected it as serious thought. Recently, however, Valbuena Prat has seen in the dialectical romanticism of Donoso's *Essay* a "gift of prophetic intuition of the historical convulsions of the future," and, owing partly to his theology, "a powerful capacity for organization" to balance his "verbal richness."[53] Perhaps, as Donoso hoped, critics may come to recognize some genius in the *Essay*, along with its glaring faults and beauty of style.

LIBERALS *VS.* CONSERVATIVES

In the last years of his life Donoso became deeply embroiled in a rising controversy between liberal and conservative Catholics, lay and clerical, over his religious, philosophical, historical, and political doctrines. This dispute began with his famous "Letters to Montalembert" in 1849 and ended with a rancorous contest over his *Essay* in 1853. His efforts to befriend both Montalembert and Veuillot, who were usually on opposite sides of any issue concerning Church and State, typified his dilemma. He understood and sympathized with the liberal Catholics because of old ties and a once common cause; his convictions after 1848, however, drew him toward the intransigence of Veuillot and the conservative Catholics and aroused the animosity of the former.

Veuillot and Montalembert were divided as much over method as over ideas. Veuillot was too violent, pugnacious, vindictive, and unyielding for almost anyone's taste. Victor Hugo detested him and his newspaper as a venomous serpent. "*Serpent cracheur, jetant son venin à distance.*"[54] For Montalembert, Ozanam, and other liberal Catholics, who favored conciliation and moderation in relation to the secular world in the tradition of Chateaubriand and Ballanche, he was a painful embarrassment who attacked them and refused to

[53] Ángel Valbuena Prat, *Historia de la literatura española*, III, 7ª ed. (Barcelona, 1964), 353–56.

[54] Victor Hugo, *Les Châtiments* (Paris, 1932), pp. 300–301.

sacrifice an epithet "for anyone or anything."[55] A victim of Veuillot's diatribes in 1849, Ozanam scorned him for making his church look ridiculous by defending the Inquisition. His school of apologists, he charged, followed "de Maistre, whom it exaggerates and garbles." "It presents truth to mankind, not by its attractive but by its most repulsive side."[56] Blanche-Raffin called Veuillot a buffoon.[57]

Although Donoso half belonged to Veuillot's school and admired his tireless energy, he was not blind to his faults. To Pius IX in 1853 he defended *L'Univers*'s fight against Gallicanism and the democratic spirit in the French clergy, but he conceded its defects, especially lack of charity.[58] Where Veuillot relished invective, Donoso always avoided personal attacks. Ardently wooing Donoso's help, Veuillot urged him to light a torch in the darkness, to make truth ring out, and to cast "some solid rocks into the foundation of the future edifice" for the sake of a posterity which "will know nothing of it." "With all the power of your lungs, cry out that we are no longer Christians, for that is what ails us."[59] Certainly such crusading spirit and proud self-righteousness, however, worried Donoso when Veuillot puffed himself up to assume the role of stalwart champion of Church, pope, and authority.[60]

Montalembert noted that his friend had some belated misgivings about Veuillot's extremism. In a letter of January 3,

[55] Montalembert, *Notes et lettres de Montalembert (1848–1852)*, ed. André Trannoy (Paris, 1942), p. 56.

[56] Kathleen O'Meara, *Frederick Ozanam* (London, 1878), p. 340.

[57] Letter, Raffin to Donoso (October 13, 1850), Donoso Cortés family archives.

[58] Juretschke, II, 572; 569.

[59] In three letters of 1850 (September 5, September 21, and October 12), Donoso strongly supported Veuillot on the question of freedom of the lay Catholic press against hostile episcopal authority; Bibliothèque Nationale in Paris, in manuscripts entitled "Fonds Veuillot, VI. Correspondance adressée à L. Veuillot, 1839–1852." Letter, Veuillot to Donoso (October 27, 1849 and undated, but 1850), Donoso Cortés family archives.

[60] Letter, Veuillot to Donoso (January 22, 1850), Donoso Cortés family archives.

1853, Donoso agreed that there were always men who were "more royalist than the king, more papal than the pope, and more zealous in the service of God than God himself. These are the *enfants terribles* of the Church and . . . of the State."[61] Moreover, in the contest over the Falloux law (1850), Donoso more nearly agreed with Montalembert than with Veuillot; Donoso was more liberal in practical matters than the latter but more conservative in principles than the former. His friendship for Montalembert survived all political and religious differences as long as he lived, for they still experienced a considerable agreement on ideas, which he chose to emphasize.[62] They differed mainly over Donoso's conviction that liberalism could not be separated from revolution and democracy.[63]

In his then famous *Catholic Interests* (*Des Intérêts Catholiques au xixe Siècle*, October, 1852) Montalembert twice praised Donoso's person but was silent about his friend's ideas, which would have embarrassed the liberal spirit of the work.[64] Like Tocqueville and many others, Donoso wrote to congratulate Montalembert; if the letter is ever published, it should reveal how far Donoso deserted liberal form in defending conservative principle.[65] Shortly before, he had written: "Give whatever form you wish to Catholic doctrine, and regardless . . . the face of the world will be renewed." Although liberals seemed unaware of it, he always supported mutual independence of Church and State.[66] Still, he now greatly feared the effect of liberalism, nationalism, and democracy within the Church as inimical to her unity and authority.

Although he did not criticize Catholic liberalism publicly, Donoso privately turned against the efforts of both lay and clerical Catholic liberals after 1848. He had no confidence in their attempt to obtain social reform through political action,

[61] See Montalembert, *Oeuvres*, XV (II), 223, for this fragment.
[62] Juretschke, II, 629; 211.
[63] R. P. Lecanuet, *Montalembert*, III (Paris, 1902), 434.
[64] Montalembert, *Oeuvres*, V (Paris, 1860), 13.
[65] Lecanuet, *Montalembert*, III, 75.
[66] Juretschke, II, 606; 633, 636.

that is, to make a better society by reforming governments. Let them try first to reform society, with private charity and social legislation. Progress, modern civilization, nationalism, and liberalism were also matters for disagreement. Having despaired not only of secular liberalism after 1849 but also of papal Catholic liberalism, he wanted no more such experiments. Henceforth the pope should seek solidarity with the conservatives and monarchists and forget liberalism as essentially negative and naturalistic. The liberal adventures that Bishop Dupanloup of Orleans promoted in *Ami de la Religion* were dangerous.[67]

Liberal Catholics discerned a gloomy dualism and a radical opposition to modern civilization, rationalism, and progress in Donoso's letters, speeches, and *Essay*, which they attributed at best to a dogmatic, absolutist, medieval temperament, and at worst to erroneous doctrines of fatalism, Manicheism, and fideism. Lay opponents, defending what he attacked, usually answered him with moderation; the liberal clergy took after him on a heresy hunt.

Donoso's troubles began when two liberal Catholic journals in Spain, the Moderate *El Heraldo* and *El País*, took sharp exception in 1849 to the theological absolutism in his "Letters to Montalembert." Upholding contrary views on the value of modern rationalism, especially the still-popular eclecticism, they called him a Manichean and a neo-Catholic follower of Bossuet and de Maistre.[68] He rejected the labels, attacked eclecticism, and went on to distinguish at length between the natural and the supernatural, the conflict of good and evil on those two planes.[69] Next, the "Speech on Europe" disturbed the French clerical *l'Ami de la Religion*, which identified fatal-

[67] Juretschke, II, 228, 643; 322–23, 568ff.

[68] *El Heraldo* (July 1, 1849), p. 1; *El País* (June 30, July 4, August 1, 1849) all p. 1. Both papers confirmed the great commotion Donoso's letters had created in literary and political circles in Madrid and the provinces.

[69] Juretschke, II, 213–24. Actually, Bossuet fascinated him.

ism in his dire prophecies, and in Germany F. J. Buss objected that Donoso's catastrophic outlook and despair of modern society amounted to fatalistic quietism.[70] Donoso answered their objections by asserting that one who insisted that the individual is free to lose or to save himself could not be a fatalist.[71]

Donoso's rash exaggerations misled both friend and foe. In April of 1852 *El Heraldo* astonished him by quoting his Ateneo lectures of 1836 against theocracy and divine-right absolutism in an article defending rationalism, liberalism, and parliamentarism. Indignant, he made a testy, unqualified denunciation of those doctrines of his youth and proclaimed that there was a radical contradiction and an invincible repugnance between them and his current principles. "In regard to *parliamentarism*, to *liberalism*, and to *rationalism*, I believe of the first that it is the negation of government; of the second, that it is the negation of *liberty*; and of the third, that it is the affirmation of madness."[72] Nevertheless, he also rejected absolutism as a mere form that was not even necessarily monarchical. It could not therefore be the radical contradiction of those three doctrines; only Catholicism could be so.

When *El Heraldo* countered with a cogent defense of the thesis that Catholicism and liberalism were not incompatible, he was so pleased to be answered with reasons that he replied with restraint, to correct misunderstandings of his position. He condemned the doctrine of parliamentar*ism*, not parliament, a practical institution which he certainly did not oppose. His idea of Christian liberty, which supposed self-restraint in the Christian, was no more utopian than any theory of liberty, none of which can ever be perfectly realized. Men were not

70 See Donoso's letter to Veuillot (April 11, 1850), Juretschke, II, 318 (Champagny's article: "On Fatalism among Christians"). See Schramm, *Vida y pensamiento*, pp. 227–28 on Buss, whose work was *Zur Katolischen Politik der Gegenwart* (Paderborn, 1850).

71 Juretschke, II, 319f.

72 Juretschke, II, 605f.

excused from striving for it, unless they were resigned to "the turbulent ebb and flow of tyrannies and revolutions." When Metternich saw these letters, he suggested that one could avoid misunderstanding by using concrete words instead of these newfangled *isms*, but Donoso upheld the utility of such abstract terms to cope with complex ideas or ideological movements.[73]

In November of 1852 he tried to explain his position further for the *Revue des Deux Mondes* in which Albert de Broglie had criticized him for tying the Catholic Church to the middle ages.[74] While denying that he idolized the middle ages, he regarded certain medieval principles adequate both to render government strong and stable and also to limit it. On the relationship of the modern Church and State he showed himself theocratic only in the metaphysical sense, not in the political. Against de Broglie's call for an "alliance between Catholicism and liberty," he held that true liberty already existed in Catholicism. Most memorable, however, was his classic pessimistic analysis of parliamentarism,[75] which Metternich hailed and which was to seem especially poignant during twentieth-century crises.

In a similar clarification of his political position early in 1853 Donoso engaged M. Villemain, a respected member of the Academy, in a spontaneous public debate on England and the balance and separation of powers of government. "Donoso caught fire and launched a magnificent improvisation against government by the masses and by their instincts, against the omnipotence and infallibility of universal suffrage," said Montalembert. " 'I want,' he said, 'that men govern by light, provided that they seek it where it is, that is, outside the masses, outside the instincts, the prejudices of the mob. I want inquiry,

[73] Juretschke, II, 610f; 558–61. Legajo 56, Donoso Cortès family archives (August 28, 1852).

[74] Juretschke, II, 228, 553. To prove that Donoso was not an absolutist, Montalembert cited from a similar letter of November 12, 1852; Oeuvres, XV (II), 224ff. In brief, Broglie objected to Donoso's theocratic code.

[75] Juretschke, II, 633–43 passim.

discussion, freedom; but inquiry enlightened from on high, discussion tempered by faith, freedom restrained by duty.' "[76]

THE SYLLABUS OF ERRORS AND THE CONCEPT OF INFALLIBILITY

While liberal Catholics were recovering their confidence after 1851, the papacy was also bestirring itself. Pius IX, now a reactionary, was disturbed at the renewed strength of liberalism, secularism, and rationalism. Donoso helped direct him toward what finally emerged as the *Syllabus of Errors* in 1864. Already in 1847 he had called on the pope to initiate a new era of social teaching by word and example to solve the great problem of "the indissoluble partnership of liberty and order." Seeing the errors of rationalism as one of the chief obstacles to achieving the solution, he declared, "Pius IX carries the burden of . . . showing its deceit to the peoples." A long time passed before positive social encyclicals began, however, and a precise answer to the political problem was never arrived at even by Leo XIII. Nevertheless, a signal act in the long prelude to the *Syllabus* was Pius's decision to seek the opinions of prominent Catholic spokesmen about the errors of the age. In May of 1852 Cardinal Fornari, papal nuncio at Paris, requested in the pope's name statements from both Veuillot and Donoso.[77] Since Veuillot's is accounted an important antecedent of the *Syllabus*, so must Donoso's be.[78] Claiming for himself a "certain kind of competence" to expose those political and social

[76] Montalembert, p. 222. Juretschke, II, 634, 649.

[77] Juretschke, II, 82–83; 630.

[78] The original letter to Veuillot is at the Bibliothèque Nationale in Paris; "Fonds Veuillot," 2° série, XIII, Complément des Lettres de L. Veuillot. Donoso's reply to Fornari shows that the two letters were almost identical. Also see the following: Fischer, *Der Staat Gottes*, p. 49; L. Veuillot, *Correspondance*, III, 361; P. Hourat, *Genèse historique du Syllabus* (Paris, 1901); Roger Soltau, *French Political Thought in the 19th Century* (New Haven, Conn., 1931), pp. 84, 193; Luis Ortíz y Estrada, "Donoso, Veuillot, y el 'Syllabus' de Pío IX," *Reconquista*, I, (São Paulo, Brazil), 1950; Gabriel de Armas Medina, *Donoso Cortés, su sentido transcendente de la vida*, pp. 13–16.

doctrines which reflected theological errors, Donoso wrote a personal "syllabus of errors" (June, 1852), which was an epitome of his criticism of rationalism, liberalism, and socialism. Here one may see his so-called political theology, where liberalism connects with deism, democracy and socialism with pantheism, and anarchism with atheism. For his church, Donoso feared not only great persecutions in the future but an eventual carryover of deistic liberalism or pantheistic socialist democracy into the attitudes of both clergy and laity toward the unity and order of the Church. Clerical liberalism might result in episcopal denial of special authority in the papacy, and a democratic or anarchic outlook could lead both priests and people to deny all restrictions in the name of liberty and "the indivisible sovereignty of the mass of believers." Although he reasured Pius IX, he (like Proudhon) expected that in the not too distant future some such anarchic demagogy finally would destroy not only the state but also the papacy. In his political theology, the religious and secular orders were inseparably connected. Both reflected the social and intellectual milieu, which he was convinced would finally end in utter anarchy and nihilism. Equally arresting was his apocalyptic preview of communistic socialism, a grim anticipation of Stalin's bloody purges and Mao's cultural revolution.[79]

For the immediate future, Donoso undoubtedly wanted to

[79] Juretschke, II, 613f; 620ff; 625f; 185–86; cf. 208, 219–20. Proudhon, *La Révolution sociale* (1852), pp. 178–92, especially 183, an alleged conversation with a country priest from his area of eastern France that is so very like Donoso's prior letter to Cardinal Fornari (Juretschke, II, 625f) as to be perhaps more than coincidence. Both may have talked to the same priest, who may have been the curé of Longrey (near Nancy) who wrote to Donoso in 1849 to agree with his prediction of the future "dissolution, near or far of European society" in the letters to Montalembert (Donoso Cortés family archives, Legajo 56). In Proudhon's book, as in Donoso's letter, anarchy is the common end. Donoso's inspiration, as well as that of Proudhon's "priest," was not only de Maistre (p. 185), to whom Donoso's curé also appealed, but Bossuet, in whom both Donoso and Proudhon then had a keen interest, for both the *Universal History* and the *Variations*. Juretschke, II, 622ff.

strengthen papal authority with the principle of infallibility in a manner in which de Maistre perceived that concept, that is, as a power of final decision and as a principle of unity that all kinds of stable government required.[80] As a bulwark against impending anarchy, such an ecclesiastical government for crisis was akin to the temporarily absolute power of dictatorship that Donoso also advocated. Apparently, Louis Veuillot, the zealous champion of infallibility in 1870, owed nothing to Donoso's more pragmatic approach to that doctrine.

THE DONOSO CORTÉS AFFAIR

In 1853 Donoso was swept into an already embittered dispute between France's liberal and conservative Catholics, which was waged especially by the clerical *l'Ami de la Religion* of Dupanloup and the lay *L'Univers* of Veuillot. The liberal clergy was incensed at Veuillot's claims for his *Bibliothèque Nouvelle*, which pretended to refute all the errors of the age and to provide the only true Catholic program for society. Veuillot particularly extolled Donoso's *Essay* as the most influential member of this series. Because of its hyperbole, paradox, and loose theology, however, the *Essay* was easy prey for critics. As a center of public attention, its discredit would redound on Veuillot, *L'Univers*, and the whole conservative camp. Thus began "the Donoso Cortés affair."[81]

Dupanloup authorized his vicar-general, the Abbé J. P. L. Gaduel, to publish a series of articles against Donoso's book in *Ami de la Religion* in January and February of 1853. Despite some just and reasonable objections, Gaduel's criticism on the whole was petty and treacherous. Naturally this professor of theology made Donoso's theology the point of his attack. Ob-

[80] Juretschke I, 683ff. Proudhon, *La Révolution sociale*, p. 178, on Donoso's ultramontane doctrine and theocratic utopia.

[81] The Gaduel controversy was called the "Affaire de Donoso Cortès" by Msgr. Fevre, who follows Veuillot closely for his facts: *Histoire critique du catholicisme libéral en France jusqu'au pontificat de Léon XIII* (Saint-Didier, 1897), Ch. XII, pp. 360–385.

serving that the *Essay* enjoyed "a great vogue, and exercises in minds an influence as considerable as it is dangerous," he promised to expose its "grave and numerous theological and philosophical errors."[82] After saluting Donoso's unblemished reputation and sincerity, he retracted his praise by innuendo and by outright accusation. He charged that lay theologians were always treating problems beyond their depth and leading the people into a torrent of errors. It was necessary to reduce "at last to their just worth all those usurped and seductive reputations."

Practically every theological question in the *Essay* relating to God, man, and Christianity entered into Gaduel's catalog of errors, which ended with "etc." Understandably Donoso believed that he stood publicly accused of multiple heresy,[83] although Gaduel refrained from doing so directly. Instead, Gaduel connected Donoso's idea of liberty with the Lutheran, Calvinist, Bayanist, and Jansenist doctrines as being too hard on human nature and as reflecting fatalism. In fact, Donoso's pessimism about natural man and natural liberty was pretty close to Pascal's, as was his emphasis on the exclusive goodness of Christian man or Christian society and on the expiative purpose of life and suffering.

By late January of 1853 Donoso, alarmed at reports, rejected Gaduel's charges in a letter published in *L'Univers*. Gaduel, however, refused his "simple and vague declaration of submission to the Church" as not a sufficient reply to specifically designated errors.[84] Donoso then submitted his book and Gaduel's criticisms to the judgment of a competent authority, Pius IX. With mordant sarcasm Donoso told Gaduel that he liked bishops and priests who became journalists even less than he cared for journalists who pontificated like bishops, perhaps a reference to Veuillot.[85] Never had Ozanam's plea for charity

[82] Gaduel, in Tejado, IV, 301–5, 313, and 336.
[83] Juretschke, II, 563.
[84] Gaduel, in Tejado, IV, 336.
[85] Juretschke, II, 564–65.

in controversy seemed more pertinent. Although Donoso had never attacked personalities, except for Proudhon, he had assailed beliefs. Now, for adhering to Veuillot, his own beliefs and person were assaulted.

Meanwhile *L'Univers* was so stoutly defending Donoso that their two cases almost became one. Veuillot perceived that Gaduel's attack was actually aimed at him and repaid it with caustic replies, relishing praise of the *Essay* from conservative Italian clergy of the Papal States and Sardinia–Piedmont.[86] Siding again with the liberal Catholics against Veuillot, the archbishop of Paris forbad his clergy and laity to read *L'Univers* on February 17. However, Sibour's hostility did not extend to Donoso, who had often been his dinner guest. Four days later, in a very friendly letter, he informed Donoso that he was ordering Gaduel's charges removed from the diocesan records. A man of "so fine a talent and character," he said, should fear no reproach.[87] Thanking him for such courage and kindness the next day, Donoso revealed how painful it was to be involved "in this sad affair."

In his letter of presentation to Pius IX of February 24, 1853, Donoso complained of Gaduel's lack of charity, claiming that he had been accused before Europe as "a poisoner of souls and propagator of enormous errors."[88] His adversary had wrenched phrases out of context, even looked for errors "in the errata of the printing," but he accused Dupanloup, "that turbulent and bellicose prelate," as the real instigator of the excesses against him. The appeal was made; now the wait for a verdict. By then Veuillot had already gone to Rome for rest and reassurance. In a private audience, Pius IX praised his good work, and in an encyclical letter he pronounced in favor of *L'Univers* and against Sibour by March 21. Staying on to watch the progress

[86] Seven different articles and reprints for Donoso were in *L'Univers* in January–February, 1853; see Tejado, IV, 335ff. Eugène Veuillot, *Louis Veuillot*, II, 537ff.

[87] Letters between Sibour and Donoso, Paris (February 20 and 21, 1853), in Donoso Cortès family archives, Legajo 56.

[88] Juretschke, II, 566f.

of Donoso's case, Veuillot complained of unendurable boredom and sadness from long waits in the antechambers.[89] By March 4 the *Essay* lay before the Congregation of the Index, but Veuillot wrote that there was nothing to fear.[90] The warm praise Pius IX directed to his "beloved son" in a brief of March 23 to acknowledge Donoso's plea was propicious.[91] Pius IX then ordered *Civiltà Cattolica* to prepare an opinion.[92]

Civiltà Cattolica came out on April 16, but the decision was not so impressive as Veuillot pretended.[93] Only an unsigned book review of the Foligno edition of the *Essay* appeared, and it bore no visible mark of authority to connect it to Pius IX.[94] Still, Montalembert, if not Dupanloup, viewed it as official even then.[95] The anonymous reviewer, reputedly Taparelli d'Azeglio,[96] praised the *Essay* highly, but he did not ignore the defects; the flaws he pointed out were chiefly exaggerations in theology and an innate disposition to affirm and dogmatize recklessly. Commending Donoso and other lay theologians for speaking out in times of crisis, he likened him to de Maistre for sowing fertile seed among the laity. Gaduel he found was indeed guilty of petty carping over words taken out of context: He had subjected the untechnical terminology of a layman to a

89 Letter, Veuillot to Donoso (April 11, 1853), Donoso Cortés family archives.

90 Fischer, *Der Staat Gottes*, p. 89.

91 Tejado, IV, 381, gives the brief in the original Latin.

92 Fischer, *Der Staat Gottes*, pp. 89–80. Donoso had predicted this indirect procedure for Veuillot's case of 1850. Letter of September 5, 1850, in "Fonds Veuillot," VI, Bibliothèque Nationale, Paris.

93 Letter, Veuillot to Donoso (April 11, 1853), Donoso Cortés family archives: "We are winners on all counts." A letter from Donoso to Paco (April 24, 1853) says that thanks to *L'Univers*, "I always knew what Rome's opinion was" (Donoso Cortés family archives, Legajo 56). Letter, J.M. Gutiérrez to Donoso (Rome, April 23, 1853), Donoso Cortés family archives; this Spaniard sent a copy of *Civiltà* to Donoso.

94 "Saggio sul cattolicismo, liberalismo e socialismo di Donoso Cortés Marchese di Valdegamas . . . ," *Civiltà Cattolica*, II (1853), 171–88.

95 Montalembert, *Oeuvres polémiques et diversés*, II, 212.

96 P. Letruria, "Previsión y refutación del ateísmo communista en los últimos escritos de Juan Donoso Cortés," *Gregorianum*, 17 (1937), 481–517.

Scholastic inquisition. Although he was not so well versed on Scholasticism, at least Donoso knew his ancient Fathers. His controversial idea of human liberty was that of Saint Thomas Aquinas and of Saint John Damascene.[97]

Donoso barely lived to read this rather ineffectual support. His controversy with Gaduel probably contributed to his death, for the "Donoso Cortés affair" coincided with a rapid and fatal decline of his health.

[97] *Civiltà Cattolica,* 180–81; 183–88 passim.

Chapter XI

A TRAGIC AND UNTIMELY DEATH

From his youth Donoso appeared to have a rather delicate constitution. He left Spain for France in 1839 ostensibly to visit the spas because of ill health. Ten years later in Germany his health deteriorated alarmingly, and he required several months of rest with his family in Spain to repair it.[1] The climate in Germany and France perhaps had a detrimental effect on him; he always detested the cold northern winters.[2] His problem, however, was much more serious than that. It was bound to be fatal, and, if known, acutely embarrassing. Apparently, Donoso had syphilis, in the dreadful terminal stage. He was plagued with many terrible symptoms and debilitating side effects, which finally ended in a heart attack in April of 1853.

Several medical books were on Donoso's booklists or in his library. A list of 1849 included the title *Botanique de la santé* by Dr. Coffin beside which he wrote the words very good. On another list of 1852 or early 1853 appears *Traité des maladies des voies urinaires et des organes générateurs de l'homme et de la femme* by Dr. Tozan (or Jozan?). In 1971 his library still contained another medical book on the urinary tract and genitals by one V. Goery (Paris, 1846), the worn appearance of which implies that it was consulted often. The dates of his

[1] Juan Juretschke, ed., *Obras completas*, II, 317.

[2] Letter (Berlin, September 1, 1849) in Donoso's personal file, archives of Ministry of Foreign Affairs, Madrid. Donoso blamed the "alarming" deterioration of his health on the climate and feared it would become worse with the onset of winter. Juretschke, II, 712.

books and known illnesses suggest that his malady was recurrent over at least several years time, very possibly beginning well before 1846, climaxing in 1849, and finally utterly destroying Donoso's health and killing him in 1853. Among his papers in the family archives is a treatment and diagnostic sheet, which was folded, undated, and unsigned but clearly his handwriting, on which are listed in a series the following drugs: *nostrum carbonicum, bismuthum, hepar sulphuris, brucea Anti-Disenterzea, bryonia albe*, and *tachesis*.[3] Opposite these he listed his varying symptoms and responses during the period in which he administered these nostrums to himself. He recorded observations of general feeling, sleep, appetite, stomach, abdomen, stools, genitals, limbs, head, and temperament, or morale.

The symptoms, which Donoso recorded with almost scientific exactness and honesty, while varying with time and treatment, are simply frightful. Whatever ailed him, he clearly suspected that he at least had gonorrhea, if not syphilis. He recorded instances of blood in the urine, swelling of the testicles, utter loss of control over his sexual appetites and functions at all times of the day, and much pain. These symptoms were accompanied by diarrhea, bloating of the stomach, general weakness, sleeplessness, sharp pains in the thighs and later in the legs, with some paralysis around the knees. All in all, it seemingly added up to a near total physical and nervous collapse, involving stomach, bowels, kidneys or bladder, and genitals. Nor was that all. Since the pain prevented him from stretching out and sleeping, he grew nervous and irascible, and toward the end, unable to do much mental work because of "uncertainty and indecision, great apathy, and extraordinary weakness of memory and a very great nervous irritability."

Only a skilled medical diagnostician could hope to decipher all these symptoms into one or more diseases. If indeed Donoso

[3] Written in French, this technical-looking document has apparently escaped notice until now.

was suffering third-stage syphilis, it seems extraordinarily complicated and diverse in its manifestations.[4] The astonishing thing is that Donoso retained such a written record instead of destroying it. Even more astounding is the fact that he tried to be his own physician for such a ravaging illness. The shame must have been more unbearable than the pain. If his enemies had learned of his predicament, what might they have done with that information?

Perhaps one can estimate from his diplomatic reports the period of time during which the sickness developed. The unusual repetitive character of his reports in December of 1852 may not have been a design to emphasize certain issues but may have reflected simple inability to write entirely new ones. However, another possibility exists. The mere fact that the diagnostic sheet was found in Legajo 55 with so many papers from Paris, proves nothing about the time he began to be affected by the disease; that packet also contains papers from earlier years and from Spain. Possibly this very severe attack was in 1849, beginning in Germany and continuing through the winter at Don Benito. After that time the symptoms may have disappeared, as has been known to happen with this disease, and subsequently may have flared up again in a milder but finally fatal form in Paris, when he sought his second book on urinary and genital disorders.[5] This explanation is not only possible but also probable because his illness in 1849 is the most severe one he recorded. In fact, the next reference he made to bad health was just prior to his heart attack in a letter to Paco, April 10, when he mentioned that he had been suffer-

[4] William J. Brown, *Syphilis and Other Venereal Diseases* (Cambridge, 1970), pp. 15–26. Brown says that, when untreated (or improperly treated), the course of the disease is individually unpredictable. "Infection may heal spontaneously or progress steadily to cause debilitation and death in later stages. Damage can include crippling, blindness, insanity, aortic insufficiency, visceral disorders, loss of nerve and muscle control, and the deterioration of bone and tissue." See pp. 122 and 125 on cardiovascular syphilis and neurosyphilis.

[5] Brown, *Syphilis*, p. 15.

ing "for some days" with "a little gastric fever" which was not serious, but it fatigued him. Right after his heart seizure, in a dictated letter to Paco dated April 14, 1853, he said, however, that he had been ill "for a month past."[6]

Overwork at the embassy or worry about the attack on his *Essay* may have precipitated his *péricardite très aiguë*, as his physician diagnosed it. Dr. Cruveilhier worried about the fever and "oppression" as much as the sharp pains his patient suffered, but after several days he believed the condition had stabilized.[7] Late in the month Donoso experienced a deceptive rally that he described as recuperation in a letter on April 29 to Benita, Pedro's widow. "Give thanks to God for having rescued me from the danger of death. . . . Since the trouble has been so serious, my convalescence will be lengthy and it will be quite a while before I recover all my strength."[8] Then his condition rapidly grew worse, and he died on the evening of May 3, 1853, just short of forty-four years of age.

TO WHAT PURPOSE?

Although Donoso was a sincere man of integrity and therefore painfully embarrassed and even ashamed that he had contracted venereal disease, it is clear that his ailment was far from rare among people of all stations of life in the centuries since the voyages of Columbus. Even one youthful indiscretion could ravage and destroy a person twenty to even thirty years

[6] Letters from Donoso to Paco (April 10, 14, 1853), Donoso Cortés family archives.

[7] The medical reports of the physician Cruveilhier, who diagnosed his condition as a critical heart ailment, are preserved in Donoso's personal file in the archives of the Ministry of Foreign Affairs in Madrid. His first report of April 15 refers to "*un péricardite très aiguë, maladie sérieuse,*" as apparently having occurred the previous day. A death notice in *La Patrie* (reprinted in *L'Univers* on May 5) gives the same description of the disease and says that he had suffered it for more than a month before May 3. Note from Cruveilhier, April 19, 1853, archives of Ministry of Foreign Affairs.

[8] Given by Manuel Mesonero Romanos, *Goya, Moratín, Meléndes Valdés, y Donoso Cortés* . . ., p. 32.

later, regardless of what kind of life one lived afterward—king, cardinal or commoner, rogue or saint. What happened to Donoso afflicted Baudelaire, who was also a prophet of evil in *Fleurs du Mal* (1857), although he appeared perversely to enjoy evil. Had Donoso's malady become known during his lifetime, it could have been severely detrimental not only to his reputation but also to his good influence on others.

During his life, the most damaging charge even his foes alleged against him was to call him a hypocrite, for recommending charity.[9] *El Heraldo* also accused him of hypocrisy for clinging to a privileged class and to well-paid high office, strutting around in "embroidered uniforms, grand crosses and decorations," like something fit for vaudeville or the Italian opera,[10] after he had attacked corruption, materialism, and Narváez in the name of "moral interests."

No evidence exists that the disclaimer of any wrongdoing which Donoso made to Gabino Tejado in 1851 was not perfectly true and just:

> Holy God! and whom do they hate? A man who has never done ill even to his enemies; a man who had not wanted to be minister precisely so as not to have to do to anyone even that ill which is many times just and necessary for those who govern. . . . God forgive them. . . . You tell me of attacks on my morality and that I should get ready to defend myself. Defend myself! Never. My life is too pure for me to defend it.

This biography, which reveals his terrible misfortune, changes none of that. He never claimed such purity for his life before 1847, certainly not in his rebellious, romantic youth, nor in the intervening years of lonely life as a widower. Certainly, we know that in his later years in Paris he enjoyed the company of women in high society such as Amadée Thayer and Marie Douglas. Donoso was not a typical Victorian moralist and never mentioned sexual morality in his analysis of ancient or

[9] Juretschke, II, 588–89.
[10] *El Heraldo* (June 1, 1851), p. 1.

modern corruption and decline, except to condemn effeminacy. Like a typical Latin, perhaps he regarded a modicum of dallying or fornication as normal for a normal society. A recent allegation by Friedrich Heer that Donoso manifested "repressed homosexual tendencies" toward his brother Pedro has no basis in evidence except Heer's too imaginative twisting of Donoso's words.[11]

The document which records his condition does provoke several important questions about the effect his illness had on his thought and actions, especially those profoundly pessimistic visions of the future in 1849 and 1850. There is no question here of madness, for Donoso remained supremely rational and logical in everything he wrote. His black visions and prophecies, he admitted, might reflect some "moral disease" akin to profound melancholy. Knowledge of the probable state of his physical health, nerves, and mentality could affect the interpretation of the following statement, when he envisioned horrible world wars in the future: "Anxiety oppresses my heart when I consider what has been the omnipotent force of evil in the whole course of history."[12] One should not try to determine the worth of his cyclic or dualistic theory of history and civilization only as they relate to his illness because his sources and essential conceptions have their own *raison d'être*. However, his illness may help to explain why a Spaniard could anticipate Spengler, world wars, and totalitarian despotisms seventy-five to one hundred years ahead of time. Why did he always fear the worse, when others expected better or the best? Why did he refuse to accept the highest office of state in such an epoch of crisis, unless perhaps it coincided with his personal crisis and fears of himself? Did he wear hairshirt and harness for masochistic or morbid reasons of pain for pain's sake (or pleasure) or to try to resubject a flesh which refused any longer to obey?

[11] Juretschke, II, 572. Friedrich Heer, *Europe, Mother of Revolutions*, trans. from German by C. Kessler (London, 1971).

[12] Juretschke, II, 780, 788.

The disclosure of the record of Donoso's illness may help provide answers to some of these questions, and knowledge of Donoso's malady does not really damage his reputation at all. Perhaps it makes him more human yet, less austere and less perplexing. Such profound tragedy should evoke sympathy and greater understanding, not guffaws and scandal.

A DEATH WORTHY OF PEDRO

The brave and pious resignation which Donoso showed during his final days and hours deeply impressed all who saw him. But when Cruveilhier declared his patient truly a saint, the dying man instantly and vehemently objected. Apart from his friends' visits, he devoted all his time to prayer and family. In his last will and testament, he begged his family to receive Benita and her children as their own sister and sons, and of Pedro he said: "His life and death have caused me endless tears, which even now I consecrate to his memory and even so cannot repay him: his prodigious virtue, after divine grace, effected my conversion, and, after the mercy of God, his burning prayers will open for me the gates of heaven."[13] Pedro's eldest son was to inherit Donoso's title of nobility.

Visiting him for the last time on May 1, when he took a sudden turn for the worse, Montalembert was deeply moved at what he saw.

> "Alas! he [Donoso] says, this must be our last visit. I find you already very changed, very despondent, choking. . . ." Always his same lively look, tender and sorrowful when looking at the crucifix. . . . He wanted nothing. I tell him that here he is in his true country, better liked and better understood in France than in Spain. I speak to him of the affection which he inspires in us. . . . He says to me: "You have the heart of an angel!" He complains of not being able to pray as much as he wants. I kiss his hand and withdraw, never doubting that it was the last time that I would see him alive. . . . [14]

[13] Given by Mesonero Romanos, Goya . . . y *Donoso Cortés*, p. 33.

[14] *Journal*, May 1, 1853; given in R.P. Lecanuet, *Montalembert*, III (Paris, 1902), 140.

His crisis came about 4:30 P.M. on May 3, at a time when his doctors could not be found.[15] Among those present at the end were Sister Rosalie who looked after his needs, members of the diplomatic corps such as his friends Hübner, Hatzfeld, Brignole, and Bois-le-Comte, and an aide-de-camp for Napoleon III. Having received the last sacraments, he prayed sometimes in French or Latin, sometimes fervently in Spanish—"*Jesús de mi alma! Dios de mi corazón!*" According to Charles de Mazade, his last words were "charged with a religious and mystic exaltation." As they watched him struggling with the mounting pain, he pointed to a crucifix: "Behold the model of suffering."[16] His last audible words were: "My God, I am Thy creature! Thou has said: 'I will draw all things to Myself!' Draw me to thee! Take me!" A mere sigh, and he was gone.

OBSEQUIES AND OBITUARIES

Magnificent funeral rites were held at the church of Saint-Philippe-du-Roule in Paris at noon on May 7.[17] The Emperor did not attend, but the whole French government, the entire

[15] *La Patrie* (May 4, 1853). Montalembert is the best immediate personal source, sometimes an eyewitness, on Donoso's final days and hours (*Oeuvres*, XV, 231ff). Bois-le-Comte also gave an account which mentioned among those present the Marquis de Brignole and Mme. Thayer (Thaer), whose husband was with the postal ministry. Joseph A. Hübner, *Neuf ans de souvenirs* pp. 128–31, gives additional details on the last hours. He and Hatzfeld called late in the afternoon, just as Donoso's final struggle began. At Sister Rosalie's request Hatzfeld ran to fetch a priest to administer the last rites, but he was thereafter so upset that he waited outside the sickroom. Donoso recognized Hübner but did not cease his prayers. "La foi se peignait sur sa figure émaciée, mais tranfigurée par l'expression d'une ineffable douceur" (p. 120). Hübner had to leave minutes before the end.

Only the widespread (then and later) comment on the manner of his passing justifies dwelling on it here. Contemporaries were much impressed.

[16] Charles de Mazade, "Un Penseur catholique espagnol: Donoso Cortés," *L'Espagne moderne*, p. 210.

[17] The following account of the funeral is drawn from a report in *La Patrie*, as reproduced by Juan Manuel Ortí y Lara, *Obras, de don Juan Donoso Cortés*, I, cxi–cxiv; also the *Le Moniteur*, as reprinted by *L'Univers* on May 9, 1853.

diplomatic corps and nearly every Spaniard in Paris assisted. Msgr. Garibaldi, papal nuncio at Paris and the Spanish chargé d'affaires presided at the solemn requiem, while representatives of four nations served as pallbearers: M. Drouyn de Lhuys, French minister of foreign affairs; Lord Cowley, ambassador from England; Count Lowenhielen, minister of Sweden and Norway; and Count von Moltke, minister of Denmark. Among the attending throng were Narváez, Albert de Broglie, Guizot, Montalembert, Gaume, Ventura, Ravignan, Rothschild, Barthélemy, Molé, Mérode, and many other notables of the time, including former ministers of France, the nobility, publicists, artists, and "the very numerous friends" of Donoso. The reporter for *La Patrie* remarked: "In the depth of all hearts there was a profound and sincere grief." Indeed the funeral showed how wide and diverse were the friendships which Donoso had made in all ranks of French society. "One saw there," wrote Montalembert, "the most illustrious servants of the defeated and proscribed monarchies, walking behind the great of the present regime."[18] Conservatives and liberals, Legitimists, Orleanists, and Bonapartists met in momentary peace. Many disagreed with Donoso's ideas, but at least they all respected his sincerity and upright character.

The press of Paris, Madrid, and the rest of Europe honored the passing of a famed author, orator, and statesman. All agreed that his untimely death was a great loss to the political, intellectual, and religious worlds. All regarded him as a great Christian and would have agreed with Donoso's contention: "My life is too pure for me to defend it." More than one student of his writings noticed that his intellectual work was unfinished, incomplete. Veuillot first commemorated his death in *L'Univers* on May 5, extolling him as "a great light," "good, gentle, and charitable," "full of humility and trust."[19] In *Revue des Deux Mondes* Mazade lavished personal praise, and avowed that he "assuredly will hold a place among the eminent

[18] Montalembert, *Oeuvres*, XV, 234.
[19] *L'Univers*, 122 (May 5, 1853).

spirits of French adoption."[20] The liberal paper, *Le Constitutionnel* of Paris, May 4, 1853, remarked that Donoso, "whose beautiful book on Christianity and socialism . . . left such a deep impression, was not only a philosopher, he was more and better than that, he was a true Christian, intelligent and courageous."[21] *L'Assemblée Nationale* saluted his "inexaustible charity" to the poor, and the *Moniteur* expressed the "universal regret" at the passing of a man who held such an "eminent place" in France by his charm, profundity, and intelligence.[22] The German Protestant, arch-conservative *Kreuz-Zeitung* saluted him as a great Catholic statesman and diplomatic representative.[23] Tributes were forthcoming even from his erstwhile foes, *l'Ami de la Religion* and *El Heraldo*.[24] Although still rejecting his ideas, *El Heraldo* acknowledged the legitimacy of his talent and of his European name, honor, and reputation as orator, thinker, and even poet—all for Spain to take pride in.[25] Even England, which almost ignored him while he was alive, observed his passing in the *Times* and in the *Illustrated London News*, but without any real comprehension of the man or his thought.[26] Both Veuillot and Montalembert soon wrote

20 Mazade, *La Revue des Deux Mondes*, 33, an (II) (1853), 855.

21 Quoted by Mesonero Romanos, *Goya . . . y Donoso Cortés*, p. 33.

22 Both newspaper reports were reprinted in *L'Univers*, 123 (May 9, 1853).

23 *Kreutz-Zeitung*, No. 105 (May 8, 1853); see Ludwig Fischer, ed. and trans., *Der Staat Gottes*, p. 3, footnote.

24 Santiago Galindo Herrero, *Donoso Cortés y su theoría política*, pp. 142f. *El Faro* (May 22); *Diario Español* (May 7).

25 *El Heraldo* (May 7, 1853), death notice, p. 1.

26 *The Times* (May 6, p. 6; May 9, p. 5) called him one of Spain's most remarkable men, but it noted only that he was so honest that no shadow of accusation could ever be brought against his character; the *Times* saluted him as a great orator, but it referred only to his part in the debate on the Spanish marriages, oblivious to his later renowned speeches of 1849 and 1850—all of which leads to the suspicion that Bulwer was the source of the paper's statement. *The Illustrated London News* (May 7 and May 14) in "Foreign and Colonial News" merely observed that Donoso was a former advocate of liberal institutions who had reacted in an extreme way to the excesses of the revolutions of 1848. It attributed his death to a rupture of a major vessel of the heart.

biographical sketches in praise of Donoso. Veuillot's was published in *L'Univers* as the feature article on May 22, and for the most part it was later reproduced as a preface to Donoso's collected works. He asserted that in politics and philosophy his and Donoso's ideas were nearly identical.[27] In a fine biographical essay and tribute in *Correspondant*, August 25, 1853, Montalembert admitted some differences of opinion with Donoso, but he thought conservative extremists like Veuillot were unjustly twisting Donoso's ideas and personality to the service of their cause. Confessing "the tender and faithful admiration which I keep for him," he wanted merely to add "a few strokes of the pencil . . . in the interest of truth" while paying "the homage which all Christians owe to a life so pure and to a death so admirable." God bestowed on him two gifts, "the seal of elect souls during their passage on earth: authority and serenity. He renewed them again and again in the humble and generous ardor of his faith."[28]

The imperial court also genuinely regretted the loss. On May 9 Empress Eugénie wrote to her sister, the Duchess of Alba:

> You know about the death of Valdegamas. We have felt it deeply, for you cannot imagine how likeable he was. Against my will he won my heart. Moreover, it is so much the greater loss for Spain to have the number of her outstanding men declining. The Emperor liked him very much. Thus it was easy for him to make certain promises which he would have had difficulty granting to another ambassador.[29]

His bully of a successor, whom she disliked, was the Marquis de Viluma, an associate of Donoso's neo-Catholics in the Cortes.

Spain was tardy in giving full honors to the dead. Donoso's

[27] *L'Univers* (May 22, 1853). This article took up the first two pages of the paper and was the basis for Veuillot's later introduction to Donoso's *Oeuvres*.

[28] Montalembert, *Oeuvres*, XV (II), 189, 235.

[29] *Lettres familières de l'impératrice Eugénie* . . ., publiées par les soins du Duc D'Albe (Paris, 1935), p. 85.

body was provisionally interred in a vault at Saint-Philippe-du-Roule in Paris. The Spanish government, by a royal decree of June 28, 1853, ordered the body transferred to Madrid, where it was placed in a vault at the Collegiate Church of San Isidro el Real on October 12 with fitting official ceremony and attendance.[30] Martínez de la Rosa headed a committee in that year to obtain subscriptions, mostly from nobility and court, to erect a public tomb, but the project was not completed. The very crypt where his bones rested was forgotten and lost until Mesonero Romanos rediscovered it at the end of the century.[31] Not until 1900, in fact, did his remains come to a final resting place in the royal cemetery of San Isidro. He and three other great Spaniards who had died abroad—Goya, Moratín, and Meléndez Valdés—were now finally interred in their homeland on the same occasion, one in each of the four wings of a noble monument crowned by a spire. An appropriate inscription could have been this dramatic elegy by Tassara:

> Valiant champion of the ancient faith,
> Donoso fell, succumbed in the fight,
> and dying, embraced the bloody cross:
> The eagle of the storm vanished,
> Vanished, as in his flight
> He soared to heaven seeking
> Peace, glory, faith, immortality . . . [32]

Instead, a bullet later gouged the marble plaque bearing Donoso's effigy, and Goya's remains were transferred elsewhere. A street in Madrid has been named for Donoso, and Franco's organic law of 1967 incorporates the major constitutional principle he advocated: "unity of power." Street names and constitutions are not such durable monuments, however. Renown too has proved far more inconstant than stone in the case of Juan Donoso Cortés.

[30] Ortí y Lara, *Obras*, I, lxxxvii, cxiii.
[31] Mesonero Romanos, *Goya . . . y Donoso Cortés*, p. 33.
[32] Gabriel García y Tassara, *Poesías*, p. 372.

SELECTED BIBLIOGRAPHY

I

Works by Juan Donoso Cortés

Ensayo sobre el catolicismo, el liberalismo y el socialismo. Madrid, 1851.

Ensayo sobre el catolicismo, el liberalismo y el socialismo. Introduction by Francisco Ayala. Buenos Aires, 1943.

Discursos parlamentarios. Grandes Oradores series. Madrid, 1915.

Donoso Cortés. Selected by Antonio Tovaro. 4th ed. Madrid, 1944.

Ideario de Donoso Cortés. Compiled by Antonio Porras. Madrid, 1931, 1934.

Obras de don Juan Donoso Cortés. Edited with a biographical note by Gabino Tejado. 5 vols. Madrid, 1854–1856.

Obras. Edited by J. M. Ortí y Lara. 4 vols. Madrid, 1891–1894.

Obras completas de don Juan Donoso Cortés. Edited by Juan Juretschke. 2 vols. Madrid, 1946.

Obras completas de don Juan Donoso Cortés. Edited by Carlos Valverde. 2 vols. Madrid, 1970.

Obras escogidas. Madrid, 1930.

Pagínas escogidas de Donoso Cortés. Selection and preface by Jorge Fuenzalida Pereyra. Santiago de Chile, 1945.

Textos políticos. Madrid, 1954. (Series edited by Calvo Serer.)

II

Translations of Works by Donoso

Briefe, parlamentarische Reden und diplomatische Berichte aus den letzten Jahren seines Lebens, 1849–1853. Edited, with a preface by Albert Maier. Cologne, 1950.

Der Staat Gottes; eine katholische Geschichts-Philosophie. Translated and edited by Ludwig Fischer. Badenia in Karlsruhe, 1933.

Des Abfall von Abendland, Dokumente. Vienna, 1948.

Die Kirche und die Zivilisation in Briefen von Donoso Cortés. Translated by H. Abel. Munich, 1920.

Drei Reden: Über die Diktatur, Über Europa, Über die Lage Spanien. Zurich, 1948.

Essai sur le catholicisme, le liberalisme et le socialisme. Paris, 1851.

Essai. . . . Liege, Lardinois, 1851.

Essai. . . . Brussels, Mortier, 1851.

Essay on Catholicism, Liberalism and Socialism, Considered in Their Fundamental Principles. Translated by M. V. Goddard. Philadelphia, 1862.

Essay on Catholicism, Liberalism and Socialism. Translated by William M'Donald. Dublin, 1888.

Essay on Catholicism, Authority, and Order. Translated by Goddard, edited by J. C. Reville. New York and London, 1925.

General Condition of Europe. Translated by Francis Sitwell, with Introduction by Louis Veuillot. Liverpool, 1850.

I. Brani migliori di Donoso Cortés. Edited by B. Sanvisenti. Florence, 1924.

Katholische Politik in Reden von Donoso Cortés. Translated by H. Abel. Munich, 1920.

Oeuvres de . . . *Donoso Cortès*. . . . Edited with an introduction by Louis Veuillot. 3 vols. Paris, 1858–1859; 3d ed., Lyons, 1876.

Saggio sul cattolicismo, liberalismo e socialismo. Foligno, 1852.

Saggio. . . . Introduction by G. E. de Castro. Milan, 1854.

Saggio. . . . Rome, 1860.

Saggio. . . . Traduzione, introduzione di Giovanni Allegra. Milano, 1972.

Scritti vari. Rome, 1861.

"Speech on Dictatorship" (1849). In Bela Menczer, *Catholic Political Thought, 1789–1848*. London, 1952.

"Speech on Dictatorship." In *Europe in the Nineteenth Century*. Edited by Eugene N. Anderson et al. Vol. I, 163–82. Indianapolis, 1961.

"Speech on Dictatorship." In *The Decline of the West?*. Edited by Manfred P. Fleischer. Holt's "European Problem Studies." New York, 1970.

Versuch über den Katholizismus, den Liberalismus und Social-

ismus. Translated by Carl B. Reiching. Tubingen, 1854. (*The Essay*.)

III

Works on Donoso

Aguiar, Fernando de. "Donoso Cortés y el pensamiento contrarevolucionario portugués." In *Informaciones*, 1953.

Alvarez Rubiano, Pablo. "Evolución política de Donoso Cortés." *Revista española de historia*, 11:42 (1951), 202–3.

Antioche, Comte Adéhemar d'. *Deux Diplomates, le Comte Raczynski et Donoso Cortés . . ., dépêches et correspondance politique, 1848–1853. . . .* Paris, 1880.

Araquistain, Luis de. "Donoso Cortés y su resonancia en Europa." *Cuadernos, Paris* (September–December, 1953), 3–11.

Armas Medina, Gabriel de. *Donoso Cortés, su sentido transcendente de la vida*. Madrid, 1953.

———. *Libertad y los caminos de la represión según Donoso Cortés*. Las Palmas de Gran Canaria, 1952.

———. *Porque volvemos a Donoso Cortés*. Las Palmas de Gran Canaria, 1956.

At, Jean Antoine. *Les Apologistes espagnols au XIXe siècle: Donoso Cortès*. Paris, n.d.

Barbey d'Aurevilly, Jules. "Donoso Cortès." In *Les Oeuvres et les hommes* (XIXe siècle); *Philosophes et écrivains religieux*. Paris, 1912.

Barth, Hans. "Donoso Cortés." In *Flutten und Dämme, der philosophische Gedanke in der Politik*, pp. 93–107. Zurich, 1943.

———. "Juan Donoso Cortés und Giambattista Vico." In *Hortulus Amicorum*. Zurich, 1949.

Bernhart, Joseph. "Ein Untergangsprophet vor 80 Jahren." *Münchener Neuesten Nachrichten*, 154–55 (June 10, 1932).

———. "Donoso Doloroso." *Living Age*, 342 (August, 1932), 544–50.

Brief, Goetz. *A Christian Statesman and Political Philosopher: Donoso Cortés*. Saint Louis, 1938. Pamphlet of the Central Verein.

Broglie, Albert de. "Le Moyen-Âge et l'Église catholique." *La Revue des Deux Mondes* (November, 1852), 409–45.

Brophy, Leo. "Donoso Cortés: Statesman and Apologist." *Irish Monthly*, 78 (September, 1950), 416–21.

Brownson, Orestes A. "Church and State." *Catholic World*, 5 (April, 1867), 1–14.

———. "Rights and Duties." *Brownson's Review* (October, 1852), 523–51. Includes Donoso's letter to *El Heraldo* of April 15, 1852, translated.

———. "Philosophical Studies on Christianity." *Brownson's Review* (July, 1853). On the *Essay*.

Buss, F. J. *Zur katholischen Politik der Gegenwart*. Paderborn, 1850.

———. "Donoso Cortés." In *Wetzer und Weltes Kirchenlexicon*, 2, 3 Bd. Freiburg, 1884.

Calvo Serer, Rafaél. "Europa en 1949; Comentario a dos discursos de Donoso Cortés." *Arbor*, 13:39 (March, 1949), 329–54.

———. "El pensamiento contrarevolucionario de Donoso Cortés y la ruina de la Europa moderna." *España sin problema*. Madrid, 1949.

Cánovas del Castillo, Antonio. *Problemas contemporáneos, II: Colección de escritores castellanos*. Vol. 18. Madrid, 1884.

Caturelli, Alberto. "Donoso Cortés en la Argentina." *Sapientia* (April 9, 1954), 88f.

———. "Una Obra francesca sobre D. C." *Sapientia* (April 12, 1957), 279–87.

———. *Donoso Cortés: Ensayo sobre su filosofía de la historia*. Cordoba, Arg., 1958.

———. "Despotismo universal y Katechón Paulino en Donoso Cortés." *Sapientia* (August 13, 1958), 36–42, 109–27.

Ceñal, Ramón. "La Filosofía de historia de Donoso Cortés." *Revista de filosofía*, 40 (August 11, 1952), 91–113.

Chaix-Ruy, Jules. *Donoso Cortès, théologien de l'histoire et prophète*. Paris, 1956.

Copeland, Raymond F. *Donoso Cortés and His Social Thought*. Ph.D. dissertation, Saint Louis University, 1950.

Corts Grau, J. "Perfil actual de Donoso Cortés." In *Motivos de la España eterna*. 9th ed. Madrid, 1946.

Cossio, Alfred de. "Donoso Cortés." *Dublin Review*, 220 (Spring, 1947), 30–47.

Costa, Joaquín, "Filosofía política de Donoso Cortés." In *Estudios jurídicos y políticos*. Madrid, 1884.

Dempf, Alois. *Christliche Staatsphilosophie in Spanien*. Salzburg, 1937.

———. "Die Stattslehre des Donoso Cortés." *Neue Zurcher*

Nachrichten, 152 (July 3, 1937), 39. A chapter of *Christliche*. . . .

Díez del Corral, Luis. "Donoso Cortés Doctrinario . . . ." In *El liberalismo doctrinario*. Madrid, 1945.

Escobar García, Francisco. "Semblanza de Donoso Cortés." *Revista de estudios extremeños*, 9 (1953), 175–225.

Elías de Tejado, Francisco. *Para una interpretación extremeña de Donoso Cortés*. Cáceres, 1949.

Fagoaga, Miguel. *El pensamiento social de Donoso Cortés*. Ateneo, "Crece o Muere" pamphlet. Madrid, 1953.

Fernández Carvajal, Rodrigo. "Las constantes de Donoso Cortés." *Revista de estudios políticos*, 95 (1957), 75–107.

Fevre, Msgr. "Affaire de Donoso Cortès." In *Histoire du catholicisme libéral en France jusqu'au pontificat de Léon XIII*. Saint-Dizier, 1897.

Fischer, Ludwig, editor and translator. *Der Staat Gottes; eine katholische Geschichts Philosophie*. Badenia in Karlsruhe, 1933. Donoso's *Essay* of 1851.

Fraga Iribarne, Manuel. "Donoso Cortés ante la Crisis de España: su visión ante el problema Africana." In *Africa en el pensamiento de Donoso Cortés*. Instituto de Estudios Africanos. Madrid, 1955.

Galindo Herrero, Santiago. "Donoso Cortés y su Pensamiento Político." Doctoral thesis, University of Madrid, 1951.

———. "Donoso Cortés en su paralelo con Balmes y Pastor Díaz." *Revista de estudios políticos*, 69 (May–June, 1953), 111–41.

———. "Donoso Cortés en la última etapa de su vida." *Arbor*, 25 (May, 1953), 1–17.

———. *Donoso Cortés y su theoría política*. Badajoz, 1957.

———. "Donoso Cortés." In *Themas españoles*, 26. Madrid, 1953.

———. "Donoso Cortés, actualidad de su pensamiento." In *El pensamiento Navarro*. Pamplona, 1954.

Gander, Dr. Jacob. "Um Donoso Cortés." *Neue Zurcher Nachrichten*, 235 (October 9, 1942).

García y Tassara, Gabriel. "Un diablo más." In *Poesías de Gabriel García y Tassara*. Madrid, 1872.

Graham, John T. "Donoso Cortés on Liberalism." Ph.D. dissertation, Saint Louis University, 1957.

Herzen, Alexander. "Donoso Cortés . . . and Julian, Roman Emperor." In *From the Other Shore and the Russian People and Socialism*. New York, 1963.

Iriarte, J. "Un Donoso romanticamente filósofo." *Razón y fe*, 148 (September–October, 1953), 128–42.

Javier de Silió, Francisco. "Vico y Donoso Cortés. El influjo de Giambattista Vico sobre un actualísimo pensador español del siglo XIX." Ph.D. disertation, Faculty of Philosophy of the Angelicum, Rome, 1949.

———. "Donoso Cortés, en su tiempo y en el nuestro." *Arbor*, 17 (September–October, 1950), 50–64.

Kennedy, John J. "Donoso Cortés as a Servant of the State." *Review of Politics*, 14 (October, 1952), 520–55.

———. *Donoso Cortés as a Servant of the State*. Ph.D. dissertation, Columbia University, New York, 1954.

Larraz, José. *Balmes y Donoso Cortés*. "Crece o Muere" pamphlet. Madrid, 1964.

Letruria, P. "Previsión y refutación del ateísmo comunista en los últimos escritos de Juan Donoso Cortés, 1848–1853." *Gregorianum*, 18 (1937), 481–517.

McMahon, H. G. "Story of the conversation of Donoso Cortés." *Commonweal*, 14 (1931), 509–35.

Maier, Albert. "Donoso Cortés im Schriftum der Deutschen." *Hochland* (November, 1940).

Maeso, D. Gonzalo. "Donoso Cortés y la biblia." *Miscelánea de estudios árabes y hebráicos*. Granada, 1953.

Maetzu, Ramiro de. *Acción Española*, 1 (December 16, 1931).

Marías, Julián. "Una tradición olvidada." *Obras*, VII. Madrid, 1966.

Mayer, J. P. "Donoso Cortés' De Civitate Dei," *Dublin Review*, 225:451 (Spring, 1951), 76–88.

Mazade, Charles de. "Chronique de la quinzaine," *La Revue des Deux Mondes*, 10 (May 1853), 844–55.

———. "Un Penseur catholique espagnol: Donoso Cortès." In *L'Espagne moderne*. Paris, 1855.

Menczer, Bela. "Donoso Cortés." In *Catholic Political Thought, 1789–1848*, pp. 157–76. London, 1952. "Speech on Dictatorship," with introduction.

———. "A Prophet of Europe's Disasters." *The Month*, 183 (May, 1947), 269–77.

———. "Metternich and Donoso Cortés; Christian and Conservative Thought in the European Revolution." *Dublin Review*, 201 (last quarter, 1948), 19–51.

———. "Donoso Cortés, 1809–1853." *The Tablet* (May, 1953), 365–66. Menéndez y Pelayo, Marcelino. "Principales apologistas." *Historia de los heterodoxos españoles,* of *Obras Completas,* VII. 2d ed. Madrid, 1932.

Mesonero Romanos, Manuel. *Goya, Moratín, Meléndes Valdes, y Donoso Cortés. . . .* Madrid, 1900.

Minguijón, Salvador. "Donoso Cortés." In *Hombres e ideas.* Zaragoza, 1910.

———. "Donoso Cortés." In *Centenario del Fallecimiento de . . . Donoso Cortés.* Madrid, 1955.

Monsegú, Bernardo. *Clave teológica de la historia según Donoso Cortés.* Badajoz, 1958.

Montague, A. L. C. de (Marquis), *Études sociales d'après la révélation.* Réponse à M. Donoso Cortès. Paris, 1851.

Montalembert, Charles, Comte de. "Donoso Cortés. . . ." *Correspondant* (August, 1853); also in *Oeuvres de M. le Comte de Montalembert,* XV: *Oeuvres polémiques et diversés,* II. Paris, 1860.

Muñoz de San Pedro, Miguel (Conde de San Miguel). "La esposa de Donoso Cortés." *Revista de estudios extremeños,* 4 (1953), 375–439.

Neill, Thomas P. "Donoso Cortés." In *They Lived the Faith.* Milwaukee, 1951.

———. "Juan Donoso Cortés, Prophet of Our Time." *Catholic World,* 170 (November, 1949), 121–27.

———. "Juan Donoso Cortés: History and 'Prophecy.' " *The Catholic Historical Review,* 40 (January, 1955), 358–410. Presidential address to the American Catholic Historical Society.

Ors, Eugenio d'. "Fiel contraste de Donoso Cortés, político porque fué teólogo, y, por profeta, diplomático." *El Debate* (February, 1934), número extraordinario.

———. "Donoso y la emperatriz Eugenia." *El Debate* (January 20, 1934).

———. "Glosas. Otra vez Donoso Cortés." *A.B.C.* (January 1, 1931).

Ortí y Lara, Juan Manuel. "Prologue." *Obras de don Juan Donoso Cortés . . .,* I. Madrid, 1891–1894.

Ortiz y Estrada, Luis. "Donoso, Veuillot, y el 'Syllabus' de Pío IX." *Reconquista,* 1:1. São Pauplo, Brazil, 1950.

Palacios, L. E. "Donoso Cortés y el justo medio." In *A.B.C., El Artículo,* 1950–1955. Madrid, 1960[?].

Pardo Bazán, Emila. "Juan Donoso Cortés." *Heraldo de Madrid* (May 10, 1900).

Pascal, Georges de. "Donoso Cortès, un maître de la politique." *La revue critique des idées et des libres*, 19 (1912), 5–22, 310–23.

Pastor Díaz, Nicomedes. "Don Donoso Cortés." In *Galería de españoles célebres contemporáneos . . .*, Vol. VI. Madrid, 1845.

Penneta, E. "Donoso Cortés, el sue dottrine, e gli avvenimenti risorgimentali italiani." *Rassegna storica de risorgimento*, Rome, 41 (1954), fasc. 2–3, 542–49.

Pidal y Mon, Alejandro. "El Marqués de Valdegamas." *El Liberal* (May 11, 1900).

Przwara, P. Erich. *Heroisch*. Paderborn, 1936.

———. "Donoso Cortés und das Heroische." *Das Buch der Zeit*, Zurich (September 1936), 1–3.

Ríos, Fernando de los. "Donoso Cortés." *Encyclopedia of Social Sciences*, Vol. V. New York, 1931.

R., Dr. H. (Heinrich Rommen?). "Donoso Cortés, Eine Katholischer Verteidiger der absoluten Staatsgewalt." *Erste Beilage der Germania*, 3 (January 3, 1936).

Rossi, Giuseppe Carlo. *Estudios sobre las letras en el siglo XVIII*. Madrid, 1967.

Rubio Sáez, C. "Lo Social en Donoso Cortés." *Revista de trabajo*, 2 (February, 1950), 105–11.

Saiz Barberá, Juan. *Pensamiento histórico christiano*, Vols. I, II. Madrid, 1968.

Sappok, Gerhard. "Donoso Cortés, Politische Prophezeiungen und Einsichten vor 80 Jahren," *Rhein-Mainische Volkszeitung*. Frankfort a.M., 252 (October 27, 1933), 3.

Schmitt, Carl. *Donoso Cortés in gesamteuropaïsche Interpretation*. Cologne, 1950. (Includes the following older articles.)

———. "Donoso Cortés in Berlin." In *Wiederbegegnung von Kirche und Kultur in Deutschland*. Eine gabe für Karl Muth. Munich, 1927; also in *Positionen und Begriffe*. Hamburg, 1940.

———. "Der Unbekannte Donoso Cortés." *Hochland*, 27 (1929); also in *Positionen und Begriffe*.

Schneider, R. "Die Warnung des Donoso Cortés." *Weise Blätter* (January, 1935).

Schramm, Edmund. *Donoso Cortés. Leben und Werk eines spanischen Antiliberalen*. Hamburg, 1935.

———. *Donoso Cortés, su vida y su pensamiento.* Translated from German by Ramón de la Serna. Madrid, 1936.

———. "Der Junge Donoso Cortés (1809–1836)." In *Spanische Forschungen der Görresgesellschaft.* Münster, 1933.

———. *Donoso Cortés, ejemplo del pensamiento de la tradición.* Ateneo pamphlet. Madrid, 1952; 2d ed, 1961.

Schuettinger, Robert L., ed. "Donoso Cortés." In *The Conservative Tradition in European Thought.* New York, 1970.

Sevilla Andrés, Diego. "Donoso Cortés y la misión de España en Africa." In *Africa en el pensamiento de Donoso Cortés.* Instituto de Estudios Africanos. Madrid, 1955.

———. "Interpretación Marxista de Donoso Cortés." *Revista de estudios políticos,* 1954[?], 187–92.

———. "Donoso Cortés y la dictadura." *Arbor,* 24 (January, 1953), 58–72.

———. "Polémica española sobre el 'Ensayo' de Donoso Cortés." Pamphlet of the University of Valencia, 25:2.

Sprenger, Dr. Leopold. "Donoso Cortés und sein Shau in die Zukunft." *Schönere Zukunft,* 14–15 (January 4, 1933), 325.

Suárez Verdeguer, Federico. "La primera posición política de Donoso Cortés." *Arbor,* 16 (July–August 1946), 73–98.

———. *Donoso Cortés en el pensamiento europeo del siglo XIX.* Ateneo, "Crece o Muere" pamphlet. Madrid, 1954.

———. "Evolución política de Donoso Cortés," Discurso inaugural, University of Santiago de Compostela, Santiago, 1949.

———. *Introducción a Donoso Cortés.* Madrid, 1964.

Taparelli d'Azeglio, Luigi[?]. "Saggio sul cattolicismo, liberalismo e socialismo di Donoso Cortés. . . ." *Civiltà cattolica,* II an. quarto, 2ª ser. (April, 1853), 171–88.

Tejado, Gabino. "Introduction." *Obras de don Juan Donoso Cortés . . .,* Vol. I. Madrid, 1854–1856.

Tuebben, H. "Donoso Cortés." *Staatslexikon der Görresgesellschaft,* 5, I (1926).

Valverde, Carlos. "Presupuestos metafísicos en la filosofía social y política de Donoso Cortés." *Miscelánea comillesa.* Santander, 30 (1958), 5–81.

———. "Introducción." *Obras completas de Juan Donoso Cortés,* Vol. I. Madrid, 1970.

Valera, Juan. "*Ensayo sobre el catolicismo, el liberalismo y el socialismo. . . .*" In *Estudios críticos sobre filosofía y religión* (1856–1863) in *Obras completas.* Vol. XXXIV. Madrid, n.d.

Vázquez de Mella, J. "Donoso Cortés y el bolchevismo." In *Obras Completas*. Vol. XXIV. Madrid, 1934.

Vegas Latapié, Eugenio. "Autoridad y libertad, según Donoso Cortés." *Arbor*, 24 (1953), 53–57.

———. *Escritos políticos*. Madrid, 1940.

Veuillot, Louis. "Introduction." *Oeuvres de Donoso Cortès, . . . ancien ambassadeur d'Espagne*. Vol. I. Lyons, 3d ed., 1876.

Viereck, Peter. "Donoso Cortés." In *Conservatism: From John Adams to Churchill*. Princeton, N.J., 1956.

Villefranche, J. M. *Dix Grands Chrétiens du siècle*. Paris, 1892.

Westemeyer, P. Dietmar. *Donoso Cortés, Staatsmann und Theologe*. Münster, 1941.

———. *Donoso Cortés, hombre de Estado y theólogo*. Translation of the above by J. S. Mazpule, introduction by S. Galindo Herrero. Madrid, 1957.

Yanguas Messia, J. de. "Donoso Cortés, diplomático." In *A.B.C., El Artículo*, 1905–1955. Madrid, 1960 [?].

INDEX

Index